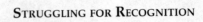

STRUGGLING FOR RECOGNITION

STRUGGLING FOR RECOGNITION

The Alevi Movement in Germany
and in Transnational Space

Martin Sökefeld

Berghahn Books
New York • Oxford

Published in 2008 by

Berghahn Books

www.berghahnbooks.com

©2008 Martin Sökefeld

Library of Congress Cataloging-in-Publication Data

Sökefeld, Martin.
    Struggling for recognition : the Alevi Movement in Germany and in
transnational space / Martin Sökefeld.
        p. cm.
    Includes bibliographical references.
    ISBN 978-1-84545-478-4 (hardback : alk. paper)
    1. Nosairians—Germany. 2. Turks—Germany. 3. Group identity—
Germany. 4. Group identity. 5. Immigrants—Germany. 6. Germany—
Emigration and immigration. 7. Emigration and immigration—History—
20th century. I. Title.

DD78.T87S65 2008
305.6'9783—dc22

2008008199

British Library Cataloguing in Publication Data

A catalogue record for this book is available from the British Library

Printed in the United States on acid-free paper

ISBN: 978-1-84545-478-4 hardback

Note

In order to preserve their anonymity, the names of most people quoted in this
study have been changed. This does not apply to the public persons of the Alevi
movement, like the functionaries of Alevi associations or well known dedes,
who are used to standing in the light of public debates and who even with
pseudonyms could easily be recognized.

⚜ Contents

❖ Illustrations

Figures

Tables

Pronunciation of Special Turkish Letters

ç   like *ch* in *chapter*

c   like *j* in *jar*

ğ   "soft" g that almost remains silent but prolongs the preceding vowel

ı   like *i* in *cousin*

j   like *s* in *measure*

ö   like the German *ö*

ş   like *sh* in *ship*

ü   like the German *ü* or French *u*

Acknowledgements

Ethnography is always a collective enterprise. I am very conscious of the fact that this book could not have been written without the engaged support of many people. First of all, I have to mention those who are quite ill-described by the technical term "informants," because what they contributed was much more than simply information. I refer to the many Alevis in Germany and elsewhere that allowed me to share their activities, that generously spend their time with me and that enabled me to share their concerns. They always made me feel welcome in their communities and took great interest in my work. Only a few of them can be mentioned here in person. Looking back to the beginning of my work I have to thank first of all Hüseyin Yavuz because he was the first Alevi I came to know. He aroused my interest that finally led to this study. Yet many others followed suit. Dede Hasan Kılavuz and Ibrahim Renkliçay accompanied my work over many years and, besides never being tired to answer my many questions, became close friends. Thanks have to be extended to Ibrahim's relatives that warmly welcomed me in their village of Çiğle. In Hamburg, I am also very grateful Halis Tosun, who explained me the early history of the Alevi movement; to the Kayaturan family that always opened their home to me, to Aşır Özek, not only for playing the *saz*; and to Gülten Uğur. I also would like to mention Oruç Yağbasan and Ahmet Yağbasan. There are too many people of the Hamburg Alevi Kültür Merkezi to mention them individually. I am very grateful to all of them because they enabled me to accompany their activities for many years. Further, I am highly indebted to the seven Alevi associations in and around Hamburg that allowed me to conduct a survey among their members. Beside the HAKM these were HAAK BIR, the Harburg Alevi Kültür Birliği, the Geesthacht Alevi Kültür Merkezi, the Wedel Alevi Kültür Birliği, Hak Evi, and Öğrenci Canlar Birliği. In this context especially Sultan Maden, Hüsniye Ergün, Ali Aksüt, Yusuf Çetin, Sevim Yüksek, and Ismet Çiçek have to be mentioned. I am grateful to everybody who answered my questionnaire.

This work would have been impossible without the cooperation of the umbrella association of Alevis in Germany, the Federation of Alevi Communities. I got the chance to participate in many of the Federation's conventions and activities, not only in many places in Germany but also in Turkey. I gratefully acknowledge the support of the Federation's managing committee, in particular of Turgut Öker, Hasan Öğütcü, and Seydi Koparan. Besides, there were especially Gülümser Keleş, who always made me feel welcome at the premises of the Federation in Cologne, and Ismail Kaplan, who worked incessantly for the right of Alevis to teach Alevism in German schools and who always kept me informed of the latest developments. In Turkey, Ali Yaman has to be mentioned, who facilitated access to Alevi associations in Istanbul. Further I thank Elise Massicard for inspiring discussions of Alevism over the roofs of Istanbul.

At the University of Hamburg, I have to thank in the first place Waltraud Kokot who had initiated a number of diaspora studies. When I started research on the Alevis, this was an invaluable forum for discussion. In this context, I am particularly indebted to Susanne Schwalgin. I could not have managed the survey among the members of the Alevi associations in Hamburg without the support of two student assistants. Özlem Vural assisted in preparing the survey and sent out the questionnaires. Yet when the questionnaires started to return, she tragically died from a terrible traffic accident. Rahel Wille took over and did a great job in deciphering the answers in the questionnaires and preparing the data analysis.

I thank Waltraud Kokot, David Shankland, Beatrice Hendrich, and Mijal Gandelsman-Trier for carefully reading the manuscript or parts of it and for their many thoughtful comments. I also gratefully acknowledge the generous financial support of the Deutsche Forschungsgemeinschaft, which in particular enabled extensive travel in Germany and in Turkey.

Finally, I have to mention my family, Mira, Carla, Nina, and Beate, who patiently bore my obsession with Alevis and Alevism. This book is dedicated to them.

❖ Introduction

Introducing Alevis

This book is an ethnography of the Alevi movement in Germany. In Germany, Alevis form a section of the larger migrant population of Turkish origin. The Alevi movement in Germany developed since the late 1980s, paralleling a similar movement in Turkey with which it is closely related. At the center of the Alevi movement is a complex quest for identity that includes questions of self-identification as well as the issue of identification by others. The debate on identity and recognition therefore provides the basic theoretical framework of this study. An axiom of this framework is that such a quest for identity cannot be separated from the political and historical context in which it takes place. Because in the case of Alevis this is a context of migration, transnationalism and diaspora provide a second theoretical frame.

Who are Alevis? What is Alevism? These are the guiding questions of a growing body of scientific and popular literature that has been published since the late 1980s. The answers given are manifold: Alevis have been defined as a religious community, specified as either simply Islamic, as "heterodox" or even as a non-Islamic community. Other perspectives see Alevis as a cultural community or as an ethnic group. In order to define the "character" of that community, reference has been made to moral values, political orientations, or religious practices. To ask: Who are Alevis? is to ask for an identification. And indeed identity has been the central focus of the debate. Alevi authors have published books bearing titles like *Living with Alevi Identity*[1] or *Alevism Crying Out its Identity.*[2] What strikes me about this debate is not that there are so many different answers and definitions of what Alevism is. I rather continue to be surprised by the verve and intensity with which the question for Alevi identity is posed.

Asking what Alevis are in the manner as it is done among Alevis, but also in much academic writing, indicates several things. First, it points toward a fundamental insecurity about what Alevism is. Second, it indicates that an Alevi community is presupposed that *could* be defined one way or another. And third, to ask for a definition is to look for a particular kind of answer, an answer that establishes both the boundaries and the contents of the phenomenon in question. To ask for a definition is to ask for a rather fixed, essentialist kind of identity.

---

[1] 'Alevi kimliğiyle yaşamak', Tosun 2002.
[2] 'Kimliğini haykıran Alevilik', Kaleli 1997.

This brings the ongoing debate on concepts of identity, which almost unanimously rejects essentialized identities, into focus. Agents of social movements that are preoccupied with issues of identity, however, continue to claim precisely such essentialized identities. Accordingly, an argument on Alevi identity has to deal with this duality of essentialist and antiessentialist concepts of identity. In order to tackle this problem I frame Alevi claims for identity, that is, Alevi *politics of identity*, within the debate on *recognition*. Because Alevi claims for recognition are diverse and relate to different contexts, this enables me to bring identity claims on local, national, and transnational levels into perspective. In doing so I will take a diasporic perspective, rooted in field research in Germany.

At this point I have already entered, unintentionally, the arena of identity claims and ascriptions: Saying that I assume a *diasporic* perspective on Alevis may be taken as implying an assertion of origin and belonging. It could be understood as saying that Alevis are not *from* Germany but from elsewhere and, again by implication, that they do not really belong *to* Germany. This echoes Floya Anthias' description of diasporic experience as "being *from* one place but *of* another" (1998:565, original emphasis). I certainly reject this implication, making thereby another claim of belonging. This very brief reflection on possible implications of the adjective "diasporic" sheds light on a very crucial condition of research in culture and society. Such research is almost unavoidably entangled in social, cultural—and thereby political—contexts. The concepts we employ are not politically irrelevant or innocent. Referring to the dual hermeneutics of the social sciences Anthony Giddens (1976) points out that the words we use as scientists are not our own, but are directly related to the discourses of the people we study. The meaning of scientific concepts is not ultimately controlled by academics, but concepts are appropriated by the people we study into their own discourses and struggles, being sometimes employed in ways that we would reject. The boundaries between scientific and nonscientific discourses are porous.

While these conditions of dual hermeneutics apply to all kinds of social and cultural sciences, they are especially significant for research on identity. Here our concepts are frequently taken from political discourse and reflect certain political conditions that are silently taken for granted. Liisa Malkki (1997), for instance, has convincingly pointed out how concepts used in the study of refugees are rooted in a discursive universe that is firmly nationalized, reflecting the modern condition of a world divided into separate nations. By its methodological nationalism (Wimmer and Glick Schiller 2002) such work tacitly confirms the "national order of things." Also the term "diaspora" that has recently become a key concept bears certain assumptions about a "normal," and this is again a national state of affairs. Hence, the study of migration and diaspora in Germany cannot avoid becoming implicated in political debates. In a context in which terms like "immigrant" or "foreigner" are highly controversial, the designation of a congregation of people as "diaspora" may have specific political consequences. In the case of anthropology at home, in which the researcher deals with the society in which he is deeply involved with his actions, attitudes and relations, political implications may more easily acquire a personal dimension than in field research abroad. Accordingly, the research has to be accompanied by heightened awareness and reflexivity. Again research on identities deserves special attention because in this context the researcher becomes an immediate projection surface for the actors' identity claims. For them, the researcher is not only a person to be informed but also a person to be *persuaded* of something, as Maranhao (1985) warns.

So far I have desisted from saying anything definite about the Alevis—except that they are "from Turkey" and that some of them are living in Germany. Most probably the reader by now expects a sentence that identifies Alevis more substantially, a sentence like "Alevis are a religious/cultural minority that originated in Anatolia since the thirteenth century." Such a proposition places Alevis into particular interpretative frames. To speak of a minority presupposes a majority in relation to which the minority is defined. To locate this minority in Anatolia is to place it within the historical conditions of successive political regimes, of which the Ottoman Empire was the most lasting one, being replaced by the Republic of Turkey only in 1923. To fix the origin of Alevis temporally in the thirteenth century CE is to locate it in a time of extreme instability and upheaval. Many Alevis would dispute this temporal placement. They would give instead the seventh century CE as the time of the origin of Alevism. By this they refer to the time of the Prophet Mohammed and his cousin and son-in-law Ali. Ali is considered the first of twelve Imams, the first leader of the community and the legitimate successor of the Prophet. He had to struggle against the first three caliphs who, according to Alevi perspective, usurped leadership after Mohammed's death and thereby created Sunni Islam. Thus, a number of Alevis would regard Alevism as the repository of the true teaching of the Prophet. A dominant perspective from the history of religions would rather locate the origin of the Shia in the schism after the Prophet's death and consider Alevism a later offshoot of Shia Islam. Here, a series of popular uprisings led by mystics against the changing powers in Anatolia since the thirteenth century are considered decisive—as well as the followers of the Safawid order in the fifteenth century that were called *Kızılbaş* ("red heads"). In this perspective, the victory of the Ottomans over the Safawids in 1516 is most important because it severed the relationships between the *Kızılbaş* of Anatolia and the Sawafids of Persia and enabled the development of a distinctive Anatolian *Kızılbaş* tradition. One of the most influential scholars of the history of Alevism,

Iréne Mélikoff, however, points to the importance of non-Islamic elements in Alevism and speaks about an "Islamized shamanism" (1998). Likewise, some Alevi scholars prefer to downplay the Islamic heritage of Alevism and to emphasize the role of shamanism (Birdoğan 1990).

Hence, the attempt to say something substantial about Alevis invariably leads to the consideration of a number of different and partly contradictory perspectives. Therefore, this introduction is not an attempt to define what Alevis are. It is rather the refusal to do so. My purpose is to expose the multiplicity of perspectives that are relevant to the topic and to argue that a reduction of this multiplicity by way of singling out a particular strand does not befit the subject. History is significant because it is a major dimension in the construction of present identities. Thus the diverse perspectives on Alevism in the present are related to particular perspectives on its past. The relevant question is: Where and when do Alevis turn to the past, and to which past? Here, especially one narrative is shared by most perspectives and can be considered a master narrative of Alevism. It is the narrative of Alevis in opposition against—and time and again as victims of—dominant powers, be they the caliphs in the heyday of Islam, the Ottomans or, much later, reactionary or Islamist forces in the Turkish Republic. It is the master narrative of Alevis as standing in opposition to Sunnis. In all realms like ritual, politics, history, values, and life-ways Sunni Islam is employed as a negative template in order to define what Alevism is.

Getting Involved with Alevis

In contrast with much ethnographic research, my academic interest in the subject did not precede my contact with Alevis. I first came to know a number of Alevis and then developed an ethnographic interest in their case. The story began in spring 1993 when, returned from fieldwork in northern Pakistan, I moved to Hamburg-Altona, just beside a couple of old buildings that had been transformed into cultural projects. One of these buildings, called "Haus 7" housed a number of migrant associations. Among them was the Hamburg Alevi Kültür Merkezi (Alevi Culture Center Hamburg, HAKM). I read the word "Alevi" for the first time on the large board above the entrance to the building. A few months later, in the beginning of July 1993, newspapers reported a violent incident in the Anatolian town Sivas. An Alevi cultural festival held in the name of the sixteenth century poet Pir Sultan Abdal had been attacked by fundamentalists, who set a hotel ablaze in which the participants of the festival were accommodated. Thirty-seven persons died. It was said that the reason for the attack was a speech held at the festival by the writer Aziz Nesin, who was known for his critical stance towards Islam. The report mentioned Alevis only passingly, saying that Pir Sultan

Abdal was revered by Alevis and that already at the end of the 1970s Alevis had been attacked by Sunni extremists in Sivas.[3] In 1995 I came for the first time into personal contact with Alevis while I worked in an intercultural center called Wir-Zentrum ("we-center"), which was situated in one of the other old buildings. One of my colleagues was Alevi, and the center was used by Alevis as meeting place because their own place in the other building was very small. In the afternoons the corridors were flocked by young Alevis sipping tea, talking and playing *saz*, the Turkish lute. Several times a week there were courses for playing *saz* and dancing *semah*, the Alevi ritual dance, organized by the HAKM. In this context I learned the full meaning of the "Sivas massacre" of 1993 for the Alevis—unfortunately because another violent event occurred. On 12 March 1995, assassins shot at the "Doğu Kıraathanesi," an Alevi teahouse in Gazi Mahallesi, a district in the outskirts of Istanbul. Three persons were killed. Huge, spontaneous demonstrations in the city followed during the next days in which Alevis protested against the role of the police. According to the Alevi protestors, the police had frequently harassed them and refused to protect them. More persons were killed by policemen shooting at the crowds. These events were hotly debated among the young Alevis in the Wir-Zentrum. I was told that the events in Gazi Mahallesi were just another example of the oppression that Alevis suffered in Turkey. The young people emphasized that also the festival in Sivas had been attacked because it was an Alevi festival and not because of Aziz Nesin. They told me that for fear of repression Alevis in Turkey could not dare to identify openly as Alevis, and that also in Germany it was a recent development that more Alevis got the courage to have their "coming out." I learned that only a few years ago Alevis in Hamburg had formed for the first time an explicitly Alevi organization and that both the Wir-Zentrum and my Alevi colleague had played a significant role in this move. I also learned that the little golden sword that all young Alevis at the center wore as a necklace was an Alevi symbol, signifying *Zülfikar*, the sword of the Imam Ali. They wore it as a token of open identification. On the other hand, the young Alevis told me that most of them knew virtually nothing about Alevism because their parents had not taught them anything about it— in many cases the parents had even concealed that they were Alevis. Being Alevi was a new experience for these young people, and especially their determination to be Alevis now aroused my interest. Slowly I developed the idea of studying this movement. Coming closer into contact with some of the leaders of the Alevi Culture Center, I got the opportunity to work for one year for this association, having thus the chance for intimate participant observation. During that year in 1998/99 I did a lot of quite tedious office work like applying for public funds and mail-

---

[3] *Die tageszeitung*, 5 July 1993.

ing information to the HAMK's membership. But I also made a first journey to Turkey together with young Alevis. We visited a number of Alevi places in the country, including the shrine of Hacı Bektaş Veli, who is considered the most important saint by many Alevis. I further did public relations work and organized some public events. I finally got the opportunity to start research formally when I became assistant professor at the Institute of Social and Cultural Anthropology at the University of Hamburg in late 1999.

Hence, I have been involved with Alevis to varying degrees since 1995. The decision to locate field research mainly in Hamburg was due to the fact that Hamburg had been an important place in the development of the new Alevi movement. Meanwhile, a quite differentiated landscape of Alevi organizations with different orientations had developed in the city. But research was not limited to Hamburg. The second important place of research in Germany was Cologne, where the Alevi umbrella organization, the Federation of Alevi Communities in Germany (Almanya Alevi Birlikleri Federasyonu, AABF) is located. Almost every few weeks I went to Cologne in order to do interviews or to participate in some activity of the AABF. Besides, I took part in events organized by or relevant to Alevi organizations in other German cities like Berlin, Augsburg, Lübeck, or Böblingen. To obtain a certain comparative perspective I also spent two weeks with the Alevi Culture Center in London in spring 2001. And I undertook several short trips to Turkey where I visited a number of Alevi organizations and places of pilgrimage.

Research among Alevis was a kind of part-time affair. I did research while I was working as assistant professor. Research had to be done beside all my other tasks, as there was no time completely set free for fieldwork. This type of "part-time anthropology at home" has both advantages and disadvantages. The disadvantage is obvious: I lacked a time in which I could simply be immersed in research and concentrate all my attention on this task. Yet my arrangement also meant that I spent a much longer period of time on the topic than the usual year of full-time research. Considering just the time of formal research, I had three and a half years in order to observe developments, to meet actors time and again, and to participate repeatedly in events. This was especially advantageous for strengthening the diachronic dimension of fieldwork. Otherwise I would have missed a number of important events and developments.

Questions of Research

Before starting fieldwork formally I had learned especially two things about Alevis in Germany: First, that the public identification of Alevis as Alevis and public activities of Alevism were a quite recent development, and second, that the establishment of formal Alevi voluntary organizations had played a decisive role in this development. Thus, my research centered on these two issues: on the transition from a private, concealed issue to a public affair and on the role of Alevi associations. On one hand, my interest was more historical and descriptive. I wanted to know how all that had happened, how the organizations got established, which actors and conditions were relevant for this innovation, and what trajectory the organizations took. On the other hand my interest was directed by several theoretical issues. First, there was the question of identity to which I referred already above: the contradictions between theoretical antiessentialism and practical essentialism, and the question of how identities get constructed and enacted in diverse politics of identity. I take "politics of identity" in a rather broad meaning. Given the multitude of identifications we are offered and subjected to in our lives, I consider identifications as "essentially" unstable so that particular politics of discourse and practice are necessary to stabilize a specific identity. This interest in identities met with my interest in the question of transnationalism. Transnationalism (which I take here provisionally to include "diaspora") has become a focal issue of the social sciences in the recent years. According to some voices, national boundaries have seemingly lost importance and a new space of freedom beyond and across such boundaries has developed, which cosmopolitan migrants are ready to exploit. Yet, as some doubts are in order in this respect, I wanted to explore which light the case of Alevis as a community of migrants could shed on concepts of transnationalism. The conjunction of both research interests is almost self-suggesting, as the formation of identities is a significant issue in transnationalism and as the concept trans*nationalism* seems to be dominated by the concept of the nation—national identity being arguably one of the most powerful and pervasive kinds of identity. Thus I wanted to know what kind of transnational relationships are constructed in the context of the Alevi movement, and whether or in which way Alevis could be considered a transnational community. I was especially interested in transnational politics of identity. Accordingly, the central topic of my research was the question of Alevi politics of identity in both local, translocal, and transnational context.

Methods

In order to pursue this question I employed mostly the methods of participant observation and interviews. Following the paradigm set by Malinowski, participant observation is the sine qua non of anthropological fieldwork. By getting immersed in the life-world of those whom we are studying, by simply sharing their activities and conversations, participant observation enables an intimate knowledge of concerns and practices. In contrast with interviews, participant observation facilitates knowledge of what people actually do. This may be quite different from what they say they do, and discrepancies between telling and doing may provide important insights. Hence, although the range of participant observation is quite limited because a fieldworker can be only at one place at a time, it adds an indispensable dimension to research. In this study, participant observation was mainly restricted to the context of Alevi organizations, their meetings and conventions, rituals, and other activities. However, I also made a trip with an Alevi friend in his holidays to his home village and stayed with his relatives there.

Due to my being employed for one year by the HAKM, the element of participation was rather strongly developed. Also, after employment had ended and research formally started I continued to assist this association in its correspondence or administrative tasks. Sometimes I was asked to represent Alevis at particular occasions. I generally refused to do this, arguing that Alevis can represent themselves. As a consequence of my close relationships with the HAKM and its members, my knowledge of this association is much more intimate than my knowledge of the other Alevi associations in Hamburg. Sometimes I was identified as a member of the HAKM by members of the other associations, although I strictly refused to become a member of any association.[4] My involvement with the HAKM was also an asset for research at the translocal level. As many members of the HAKM played an important role in the largest Alevi umbrella association in Germany, it was very easy to get access there. Hence much participant observation took also place in Cologne, where the umbrella association has its office, or at other places in Germany where activities took place.

Beside participant observation, interviews were equally important in research. The interviews were open-ended and only loosely structured. They dealt with the history and commitments of Alevi organizations and with the personal involvements of individual actors. This second type of interview had a loose biographical thread. I generally started with inquiring when and how the interviewee became conscious of being Alevi, and then explored the experiences of living as Alevi in different contexts of life. Interviewees were largely found through the Alevi associations. They comprised "simple" members of the associations as well as high-level functionaries. Yet only few people were interviewed that were located completely outside of the Alevi movement. Thus, this work relates specifically to the Alevi movement with its agents and associations, and not to Alevis in general. Because interlocutors were

---

[4] Membership is not restricted to Alevis and many associations are particularly eager to get non-Alevi members.

spread all over Germany, research included a lot of conversation on the telephone as well as e-mail communication.

I thought it useful to complement these qualitative data by a quantitative survey. The need for some quantification was felt especially when I dealt with citizenship as a significant category of belonging and identity. I had got the impression that many Alevis had naturalized in Germany—more than the average of migrants from Turkey. Yet as exact figures were missing, I decided to conduct a survey myself. Because it was impossible to identify all Alevis living in Hamburg and to determine a random sample among them, I took the membership of the Alevi associations in Hamburg and the immediate surroundings of the city as frame. In order to keep the research within a manageable time (and cost) frame, survey interviews were not conducted personally by interviewers but questionnaires were mailed out. All seven Alevi associations that were active at that time allowed me to use the addresses from their member directories. More than six hundred questionnaires reached their destination.[5] The return quota was relatively high (37 percent). Because interviewees were not selected at random but, by completing the questionnaire, rather selected themselves the results are not strictly representative for the membership of Alevi associations in Hamburg. Still, they provide a useful quantitative background for a number of questions. Only a small part of the resultant data is used in the present work.[6]

Data generated by interviews, questionnaires, and participant observation are complemented by the collection of documents comprising on one hand documents authored by Alevis like journals and other publications including websites and video tapes, flyers, or press releases. On the other hand there are documents, most importantly newspaper clippings, by non-Alevi authors. The documents by Alevis provide significant insights into Alevi discourses and self-representations, while the other documents exemplify the discourse about Alevis in the greater, non-Alevi public. The language of research was both German and Turkish. The majority of interviews in Germany were conducted in German because most Alevis in Germany are more fluent in German than I am in Turkish, so that after a few sentences in Turkish the conversation usually slipped to German. Participant observation, however, had to rely on Turkish because Turkish is the language of most Alevi events in Germany. Questionnaires were sent out in both Turkish and German, giving the respondents the option to choose either language.

The multilocality of research reflected the movement of Alevi actors and can be considered as inspired by the strategy of "following

---

[5] I had sent out more than seven hundred questionnaires, but many addresses proved to be invalid.

[6] A condensed report of the results has been published as Sökefeld 2003b.

the people" in multisited ethnography (Marcus 1995). I accompanied Hamburg Alevis to reunions, festivals, and seminars organized by the Federation of Alevi Communities in Cologne, taking place in that city or in some other German towns. I also joined them on their way to Turkey for attending a transnational Alevi culture festival in Istanbul, the annual celebrations in Hacıbektaş, or simply for their holidays. Due to time constraints the period spent for fieldwork in Turkey was rather limited and amounts to little more than three months in four trips.

The bulk of my data stems from the local Alevi context of Hamburg. Next come data on the translocal level, collected mostly in Cologne, while data from Turkey form the smallest portion. However, all three levels of research, the local, the translocal and the transnational, were discussed on all the levels of localities in which the research took place. My sources of data do not allow to speak simply about "the Alevis" in general. In fact, I have to admit that I cannot add much to knowledge about Alevis in Turkey. Yet I am of the opinion that the strong basis of my research in Hamburg allows some generalization about the Alevi movement in Germany, including its transnational perspective, because with its diversity of partially competing Alevi associations, the Alevi landscape in the city resembles the conditions of other German cities. Differences emerge, however, from the diversity resulting from local political contexts of municipal institutions as well as from the German federal system. Where such differences are significant for my work, as for instance in the debate about Alevi religious classes in schools, they will be addressed in the subsequent chapters.

Survey of Literature: Research on Alevis

The rise of the new Alevi movement since the late 1980s and the new interest in Alevi identity resulted in an "explosion" of writings on Alevism. A great number of books written by Turkish Alevi authors flooded the market, creating among Alevis a new profession called *araştırmacı-yazar* (researcher-writer). These *araştırmacı-yazar* were and are among the most significant agents of the new movement as they create the discourse on Alevi identity and set its topics. Some of their writings have become very popular. I call this body of texts "Alevi literature" and distinguish it thereby from "literature on Alevis," which is written in most cases by non-Alevi academics like social or cultural scientists, historians of religion, or turcologists. This distinction is to a certain extent arbitrary and does not intend to generally deny academic value of the first body of literature. Still I regard the distinction important because "Alevi literature" is clearly part of the game and characterized by varying degrees of commitment to the Alevi movement.

In this section I survey literature on Alevis, which too experienced a certain boom. Until the late 1980s academic publications that were devoted to Alevis or that at least mentioned them were quite rare.[7] A turning point was set by Krisztina Kehl-Bodrogi's (1988a) book *Die Kızılbaş/Aleviten* (The Kızılbaş/Alevis), a doctoral dissertation that for the first time provided a panoramic view on Alevis, dealing with the historical development from the time of the Safawids up to the Republic of Turkey, portraying a number of distinctive Alevi groups in Turkey, and giving an overview over social organization as well as religious beliefs and practices. In this book Kehl-Bodrogi struggles with a serious difficulty to collect data, because to a large extent Alevi practices were still kept secret. This difficulty to get information was almost completely abolished by the new Alevi movement and its transformation of Alevism into a public affair. In a subsequent study, Kehl-Bodrogi (1992, cf. Kehl-Bodrogi 1993) deals with the political context of Alevis in Turkey after the military coup of September 1980 and with the beginning of the Alevi movement. These are the central topics of another landmark study, by Karin Vorhoff (1995, cf. Vorhoff 1998). Within a framework of ethnicity and collective identity, Vorhoff analyses the Alevi self-image as outlined in Turkish Alevi literature published since the late 1980s and points to the importance of intellectuals for the formation of a new Alevi collective consciousness (cf. Engin 1996). Aspects of the new Alevi movement are discussed in a number of works that situate the Alevi movement within the context of contemporary politics in Turkey. Especially significant is the rise of political Islam, embodied most importantly in the *Refah Partisi* (Welfare Party) and its diverse successors. Alevis are portrayed as a secularist, non-Islamist community that comes under pressure of Islamist tendencies in the Turkish republic and is considered an important counterweight for the preservation of the Republic's Kemalist-secularist outlook. Çamuroğlu (1997) identifies opposition against Islamism as one of the most important motives for Alevis to develop a new public stance, and Vorhoff (1999) discusses attempts to define Alevism as a secular version of Islam. In his book *Islam and Society in Turkey* David Shankland (1999) similarly portrays Alevis as supporters of secularism and the separation of religion and the state. His study of an Alevi village (2003) is set in the same frame. This study is quite outstanding because most writings on Alevis refer to the new, urban Alevism. A direct confrontation between Alevis and Islamists is explored by Massicard (2001), who analyses discourses that

---

[7] Earlier works on Alevis include Bumke's paper on Dersim (Bumke 1979), articles by Mélikoff on Bektaşism that were later republished in a collection (Mélikoff 1992), Gökalp's study of Alevi Çepnis in western Anatolia (Gökalp 1980) and an article by Yalman (1969).

sprang from the demolishing of the building of an Alevi association by Istanbul's Refah municipality in 1994. The position and commitment of Alevis within the political system of Turkey is the topic several works. Dreßler (1999) discusses the veneration of Atatürk among Alevis and Schüler (1998, 2000) analyses Alevi support for social democrat and Kemalist parties. Other works discuss the changes of Alevi tradition triggered by the new Alevi movement, like the folklorization of Alevi ritual (Stokes 1996) and pilgrimage (Sinclair-Webb 1999). In contrast with Sunni Islam, music plays an important role in Alevi ritual and has become a significant reference point for Alevi self-identification. Reinhard and Oliveira Pinto (1989) discuss the role of *ozans*, the *saz*-playing Alevi poets and singers, and their music. Markoff's study focuses on professional performers (not only Alevis) of the *saz* and their styles of interpretation (1986a, cf. Markoff 1986b). Yavuz (1999) describes the emergence of an Alevi mediascape in Turkey.

History is doubtlessly one of the most important topics in the literature on Alevis. After Kehl-Bodrogi (1988a), Dreßler (2002) has attempted another complete history of Alevis. His approach is centered upon the concept of *longue durée*. Dreßler identifies the charisma of (religious) leaders as a constant core of Alevism that has found its expression in the last century in the Alevis' reverence for Atatürk. He contrasts Alevism with Sunni Islam, which is bound not to charismatic personalities but to the text of the Quran. Another attempt of a complete view on the history of Alevism is presented by Gümüs (2001), who interprets Alevi history within a theory of power and domination as the history of a minority marginalized and stigmatized by a powerful elite. Besides, there are especially works on the history of Bektaşism and the Bektaşi order of dervishes, the Sufi order derived from the teachings of Hacı Bektaş Veli, the probably most important of Alevi saints. A groundbreaking work was published by Birge in 1937, in which he discusses the history of the Bektaşi order, its teachings and ritual practices. A number of papers by Irène Mélikoff dealing with diverse aspects of Bektaşism like the history of Hacı Bektaş and Bektaşi literature have been jointly published in two collections (1992, 1998). A study of the social history of Bektaşi *tekke*s (convents) in Anatolia until the abolition of the Bektaşi order by Sultan Mahmut II in 1826 is offered by Suraya Farooqhi (1981). Hülya Küçük has recently analyzed the role of Bektaşis in the Turkish national struggle up to the second abolition of the order in 1925 by the government of Atatürk (Küçük 2002).

Alevis do not form a unified, homogeneous community, unmarked by difference. Several works deal therefore with particular Alevi groups like Tahtacı (Groenhaug 1974, Kehl-Bodrogi 1989), Çepni (Gökalp 1980) and, most importantly, Alevi Kurds (van Bruinessen 1997, Seufert 1997a). Here, most publications discuss the Zaza Alevis of Tunceli, the erstwhile Dersim (Bumke 1979; Fırat 1997; Kieser 1993, 1994; Kehl 1999).

Migration of Alevis has also been a topic of research. Turkish society has been deeply affected by both internal and external migration. Alevis left their villages in often mountainous areas of settlement for the rapidly expanding cities of Turkey, especially Istanbul and Ankara. In his pathbreaking study of *gecekondus* (illegal settlements) in Istanbul, Karpat (1976) devotes attention to the social and political organization of Alevis. Seufert (1997a) discusses the chain migration of Alevi Koçkiri Kurds to Istanbul and the subsequent transformation of their identity from a religious to an ethnopolitical frame of reference in the city. Wedel (1999) studies within a framework of gender and empowerment the local political commitment of Alevi women in two *gecekondu* settlements of Istanbul.

Also Alevi migrants in Europe have been studied. A paper on Alevis in Norway and the relations with their village of origin in Western Turkey (Naess 1988) apart, these studies deal with Alevis in Germany. Since the late 1970s there is a growing body of literature on Turkish migrants in Germany, especially in the field of educational studies. These studies emphasized elements that were understood as characterizing Turks in general and distinguishing them from Germans, like Islam, headscarves, patriarchal family structures and the discrimination of women. Such studies "orientalized" Turks and portrayed them as a homogeneous, undifferentiated community. Only when in the late 1980s differences *within* the "Turkish community" were "discovered," Kurds and later Alevis were put on the agenda of research. A number of papers represent this "discovery" of Alevis among the Turks in Germany and explore differences between Alevi and Sunni Turkish migrants. The location of such research was almost invariably Berlin, and in particular the city's district of Kreuzberg. Wilpert (1988) explores differences in the attitudes of Sunnis and Alevis. In a similar vein, Ruth Mandel has published a number of papers based on her unpublished Ph.D. dissertation (1988, cf. Mandel 1989, 1990, 1992, 1996). She analyses the history of labor migration to Germany and the shift from "guest workers" to "foreigners" (*Ausländer*), focusing on the construction of identity in the encounter between migrants and Germans, but especially among migrants. As an example of the shifting grounds of identity, affected by subjective experience, Mandel discusses Alevis and their identity in contrast with Sunni Turkish Migrants. This distinction is also analyzed by Karakaşoğlu-Aydın (2001) in a paper focusing on Alevi and Sunni female students.

In a further paper, Kaya analyses the Alevi resurgence as a response to the ethnicizing effects of the institutional layout of migration policy in Berlin. Equally significant for my topic is, finally, Şahin's (2001) unpublished study of the Alevi movement as a transnational movement. However, although her work extends into transnational social spaces, considers transnational relations, and emphasizes the importance of events and developments in the Alevi diaspora, Turkey firmly remains its main focus. Understanding social movements as complex outcomes of networks, opportunity structures, and communicative practice, she sees the Turkish state as a significant actor that responds to the global discourse on identity and shapes the Alevi movement.

Layout of the Book

Recent reservations notwithstanding (Thornton 1988), anthropology still proposes a largely holistic approach towards its subjects of research. A basic difficulty of writing ethnography is to bring a complex, inter-related matter into the linear sequence of a text. Spoken metaphorically, this requires to disentangle a multiplicity of knotted threads and to reduce them to basically *one* thread. This reduction rather violates the complexity and interrelatedness of the social reality that we encounter in research. While writing this book I have strongly felt the problem of reducing interrelatedness, because aspects with which I deal in one chapter often presuppose or are related with others that—in the linear sequence of the text—come only later. A form of hypertext consisting of multiple interlinks that allow to step back and forth between different aspects without necessarily implying a particular sequence would have been more appropriate for my subject matter. As a certain remedy I have inserted many cross-references to earlier or subsequent chapters into my text.

Taking off from the diagnosis that the question of identity lies at the core of the recent Alevi movement, the next chapter deals with concepts and theories of identity, departing from the recent antiessentialist critique of identity. I argue that the Alevi quest for identity has to be conceptualized as an instance of politics of recognition. Framing the Alevi movement as a *social movement*, chapter two presents the prehistory of this movement. I discuss early forms of migrant political organizations in which Alevis participated, and an institutional context of multiculturalism in the city that significantly contributed to making "identity" a pressing question among Alevis. This led to the formation of the "Alevi Culture Group" and to the "Alevi Culture Week" by which Alevism was turned into a public issue.

The topic of chapter three is the development of a differentiated landscape of Alevi associations in Hamburg and at the translocal level in Germany. Chapter four probes into conflicts within the Alevi movement, discussing contested perspectives on Alevism that strongly affect concepts of Alevi identity. Competing concepts of Alevism have provoked the split of Alevi associations or opposition within associations. Chapter five deals with discourses and practices related to the memory of the Sivas massacre of 1993 that stand at the focus of many activities of the Alevi associations. I analyze how the Alevi movement frames the commemoration of this event and turns it into a memory of community. Chapter six turns to the ritual sphere and takes up *cem*, the most important ritual of Alevism, and the *dedes*, its religious specialists. I analyze the transformation of *cem* from a secret to a public ritual, as well as the ritual as a site of conflict. In chapter seven the Alevi politics of recognition is put into the context of German politics of migration. I argue that under the condition of a paradigm of cultural difference that governs German perspectives towards migrants, Alevis represent themselves as the nonforeign migrants who share the essential values and orientations of German society. The issue of citizenship also clearly indicates the limits of recognition in Germany, because also as German citizens Alevis continue to be categorized as *foreigners* in public discourse and in quotidian interaction. The eighth chapter traces the transnational connections of the Alevi movement. I analyze transnational relationships as they have evolved within the Alevi movement. A focus on transnational politics of recognition, that is, on the commitment of German Alevi associations to efforts towards recognition of Alevism in Turkey and especially on the attempt to involve EU institutions in this issue, follows. Further, I analyze the response of the Turkish national discourse to this commitment of the German Alevi movement and its endeavor to achieve the firm and continuous inclusion of the Alevi diaspora within the Turkish nation. The conclusion, finally, sums up the arguments of the book and offers a comparative perspective on the role of institutions in diasporic movements.

1

Identity and Recognition

It has to be recognized Alevis are oppressed

In present day Turkey there is heavy pressure on twenty million Alevis in the form of a social, cultural and psychological burden that continues from the times of the Ottoman Empire. The time has come to bravely disclose this oppression.

Alevis have to be able to say without restraint "I am Alevi."

Even today Alevis experience fear because they are Alevis. This is not necessary. These people must be able to say openly "I am Alevi." It is one of their natural human rights. We appeal to those who conceal their being Alevi due to political or material anxiety to give up that attitude and to claim their culture. It is a human right that every human being should be able to express his or her identity freely. To stigmatize this identity as "sectarianism" or "chauvinism" is a lack of respect for a basic human right.[1]

These sentences are taken from the "Alevi declaration" (*Alevi Bildirgesi*) which was published in the daily *Cumhuriyet* on 6 May 1990, signed by a number well-known Alevi and non-Alevi writers, artists, and journalists, including Yaşar Kemal and Aziz Nesin.[2] The declaration was based on an earlier statement drafted by the founders of the "Alevi Culture Group" Hamburg that had been published in spring 1989 and promulgated especially on the event of the "Alevi Culture Week" in October that year. The two versions of the declaration mark the birth of the new Alevi movement and the transformation of Alevism from a secluded belief and practice into a public affair. The Alevi Culture Week in Hamburg was the first ever public event held in the explicit name of Alevis and Alevism. The publication of the declaration in *Cumhuriyet* was part of a series of articles on Alevism in this and other papers that marked the beginning of a public debate on Alevism of unprecedented scale (Kehl-Bodrogi 1992).

---

[1] Translation of this and all other quotations from Turkish (or German) by the author.

[2] Zelyut 1990, 295ff; Kaleli 1997,182ff.

In the next chapters I will analyze the development of the movement. Here I quote from the declaration in order to point out that the question of identity stands at the commencement and at the core of the Alevi movement. The quotation makes clear that the Alevi question of identity is not simply a "quest for identity" in the sense searching for "what Alevis really are." Significantly, the Alevi question of identity is the demand for the *recognition* of that identity. The declaration demands being recognized as a distinct community in a particular, nonstigmatizing way. The declaration even frames the recognition of identity as a basic human right.

The Alevi declaration exemplifies that questions of identity are inextricably entangled with questions of politics, of rights and power, and that the concept of identity entails a dialogic relationship because identity calls for recognition. In the present chapter I will analyze these questions of identity in a systematic way. In particular, I point out that identity is an inherently *political* idea. It is political not only in the sense that particular struggles for identity, like the Alevi example, are always struggles situated in specific political contexts, striving for particular political aims, but in the sense that the idea of identity was originally a political idea and has a specific political history. Only subsequently was it appropriated by the various sciences, most importantly psychology, and turned into a presumed universal, scientific concept. I argue that an examination of the political roots of the idea of identity enables a more appropriate understanding of what identity is and what it does than approaches that treat it as a "purely academic" concept.

Identity Discourse and the Politics of Identity

Undoubtedly, identity counts currently among the most influential concepts. This applies equally to academic and the nonacademic world. The rise of identity discourse, as I would like to call the phenomenon, in both realms is clearly interlinked. It is a fine example for the dual hermeneutics in social and cultural sciences (Giddens 1976, cf. Sökefeld 2001). The term "identity" in its present range of meaning is quite recent and can be dated to the writings of Erik H. Erikson since the 1950s (Gleason 1983). Before, the idea was expressed by other terms like "self," as in the work of George Herbert Mead.[3] In a famous passage Erikson gives

---

[3] I contend neither that "self" in the writings of Mead expresses exactly the same as like "identity" in Eriksons work, nor that the two are generally exchangeable (rather, I like to keep them separate, cf. Sökefeld 1999). However both terms point to the same realm of ideas. In the German translation of Mead's *Mind, Self and Society* (1967) "self" has consistently been rendered as *Identität* (identity). Within the tradition of symbolic interactionism Erving Goffman was the first to employ "identity" instead of "self" (1963).

a definition of identity that has remained quite uncontroversial until two decades ago. It is significant because it points to personal and to collective identity simultaneously: "The term identity expresses such a mutual relation in that it connotes both a persistent sameness within oneself (selfsameness) and a persistent sharing of some kind of essential characteristics with others" (Erikson 1980: 109).

The development of a strong individual identity, of individuality, is among the most highly esteemed values of our times, at least in the Western world. Identity is what ultimately makes the person. Yet, Erikson's definition refers not only to personal identity but also to collective identity. Not only personal identity has become a value, but equally various kinds of collective, social identities like national and ethnic identity, race and gender identity, or identity derived from sexual orientation. Identity-based collectivities have become the subjects of political struggles striving for rights and power. This is most notorious in the case of collectivities that claim national identity and that struggle for territory and statehood. We are in the realm of *identity politics*, which can be defined as politics based on a particular identity and at the same time struggling for a range of purposes for this identity. Frequently, identity politics is regarded (and criticized) as a new political paradigm that has replaced politics based on and struggling against particular material conditions. In this view, identity politics has largely replaced class politics (Aronowitz 1992, Fraser 1997, cf. Pratt 2003). The 1980s are mostly identified as the time in which politics of identity became a dominant paradigm. Socialist ideologies lost much of their persuasiveness, and the power of most of the political systems based on this ideology vanished. At the same time many movements and, frequently militant, struggles based on ethnic, national, and religious identities developed or gained new currency. But also feminist and gay or lesbian movements are regarded as prime examples of identity politics (cf. Fuss 1990).

Such politics of identity have served as point of departure for a critique of the conventional concept of identity as based on sameness. Identity as sameness as in the quotation from Erikson, points to stability and constancy. Erikson did not consider identity a "given" but as something that develops in adolescence. Once developed, however, identity remains more or less the same and should be stable—otherwise there would be a problem. A more or less stable self-identity is considered a necessary condition for successfully coping with later life-crises. Yet this privileging of sameness and stability of identity has been radically questioned by recent post-structuralist and postmodernist perspectives. Here, identities and the self are conceptualized as unstable, shifting, and volatile. In this view, identity politics is based on a kind of false consciousness. Identity is essentialized, that is, it is *presented* as fixed and stable in such political movements in order to mask the "real" aims, which may be privileged access to power or other resources. According to postmodernist perspectives, there is no essence behind the appearances of identity; there is no "real" core of identity that remains the same but "only" a range of shifting subject positions that are evocated by and subject to the power of societal discourse.

Difference, Multiplicity, Intersectionality

This questioning of essences erased sameness in the conceptualization of identity and almost replaced identity by difference. Central for this shift was a series of critiques emerging from political and personal experiences of discrimination, raised from peripheral positions against central, dominant theory. The moment of critique emerged first in the field of feminism, where the identity category "woman" was unmasked as a Western, white, middle-class construct. According to nonwhite feminists like bell hooks, the category "woman" is far from being identical. It is subject to all kinds of difference derived from other identities like class, "race," or ethnicity (Barrett 1987, 30; Crosby 1992). There is no common identity as woman, but only a multiplicity of subject positions marked by difference. This critique of essentialized identities, which are fixed and homogenized by disregarding and attempting to erase differences, is at the core of the postmodernist perspective. Yet, homogenization breeds difference, writes James Clifford (2000, 101) and difference subverts identity. Identity then becomes a question of power and representation in its dual sense (cf. Brunt 1989). It has to be asked: Who has the power to represent a particular identity in particular way, in order to ascribe it a particular meaning and achieve a specific inclusiveness, excluding thereby other meanings and positions? And: Who has the power to represent particular people on the basis of claims to a particular identity?

Identity politics, which almost invariably resort to the essentialization of particular identities, bears the danger of new repression even in movements for emancipation. There is the danger of silencing the voices of black women in white women's struggle for women's liberation, or of subduing minorities in the struggle for nationhood. Framing collective identity as a process of signification, Brah writes: "A given collective identity partially erases, but also carries traces of other identities. That is to say that a heightened awareness of one *construction* of identity in a given moment always entails a partial erasure of the *memory or subjective sense* of internal heterogeneity of a group" (1996, 124, original italics). The postmodern critique of essentialization has taken pains to analyze what difference and heterogeneity is silenced and erased in the construction of identities (Hall 1991). It points to the conscious or unconscious omissions in the construction of identity, rigorously taking up the insight of Ernest Renan (1990, 11), arrived at much earlier in a quite different context, that *forgetting* is as important for the construction of (national) identity as is remembering.

Under the attack of difference, identity is never fixed but always "under construction." However, difference is significant in another sense too. If identity is never really identical because it is saturated with internal differences, difference as contrast with other identities becomes the constitutive element of identity. What ultimately characterizes and delimits women's identity is not some positive essence of womanhood supposedly shared by all women, but simply the fact that women are not men. Difference is what *makes* identity. In a way, this recent conceptual shift from identity to difference was prefigured by the Barthian concept of ethnicity in social anthropology, which emphasized the boundaries and thus the symbolically marked differences as being constitutive of identity (Barth 1969).

Both the acknowledgement of what has been omitted from constructions and accounts of identity and the idea of difference as constituting identity by contrast result in a multiplication of identity. We cannot speak of a general identity of "the woman" but of women's identities that draw on diverse and perhaps contradicting sources of identification. Yet, in the first place identity makes sense only because there are other identities. We can speak about identities of women because there are men. Further, it makes sense to emphasize the multiplicity of identities because—in contrast with the Eriksonian idea of basically *one* individual identity—individual agents assume and are ascribed a number of different identities related to different times and contexts. Therefore we can never speak of identity in the singular; there is always a field of multiple identifications. The multiplicity of identities within a field poses the question of relationships between these identities. It is perhaps tempting to imagine identities as atomlike units that can be split or combined in innumerous ways. This would, however, emphasize identities as *units*, as bounded and in the final instance again fixed elements (Fuss 1990, 103). In contrast, I suggest to imagine identities in the field as constantly intersecting. Identities are related by constantly having effects upon one another; they form relations of mutual transformation and intrusion. Identities may be mutually reinforcing but also competing and subverting, threatening each other with erasure. The idea of a female identity is subverted by racial identities and ultimately, as we have seen, the identity of "the woman" is on the verge of being erased by intervening and competing identifications. Of course, the multiplicity of identities also intersects in individual agents and may create tension and conflict for the individual. It is easy to imagine conflicts over loyalty and priority: What is more important for a black woman vis-à-vis a white woman, to be black or to be a woman? Of course, priorities need not be set once and for all but may shift according to context and evaluation. However, there is a choice entailed—perhaps a compulsion to choose.

Consequentially, I suggest to conceptualize identity in terms of the three aspects or dimensions outlined so far: difference, multiplicity, and intersectionality. These dimensions serve as a bulwark against slipping into essentialist concepts of analysis. They underline that identities are never fixed, never clearly bounded and never single, that they are temporal, always subject to change and tension. This scheme can be easily used to analyze the Alevi case. Alevis assume and are ascribed a multiplicity of identities. By calling them "Alevis" I privilege a particular identification—just as Alevis themselves most of the time do. However, this privileging of one identification cannot escape the fact that there are others who raise their competing and subverting claims, identifying Alevis as citizens of the Turkish Republic, as Kurds, or as foreigners in Germany, to mention just a few possibilities. All these identifications threaten to cover up or even to erase the identification as Alevi. Thus, the nationalist identification as Turks does not acknowledge any difference according to religion within the Turkish nation. The existence of Alevis is largely silenced in official accounts. The identification of Alevis as Kurds in the context of the militant Kurdish movement separates Kurdish Alevis from Turkish Alevis, creates a difference within the Alevi community, and ultimately destroys the possibility to speak of a single Alevi community. The identification of Alevis in Germany as foreigners, lastly, again negates a specific Alevi identity, because in a discourse that frequently identifies foreigners sweepingly as "Turks" there is no place for distinction and difference within the undifferentiated mass of immigrants. On the other hand, it can be shown quite easily that Alevi constructions of a single and unified Alevi community are also flawed, because they conceal a number of important differences within that supposed community. Accordingly, a postmodernist critique of identity and politics of identity certainly makes sense in the Alevi case, because it uncovers a complex and contradictory configuration of identifications that is hidden in essentialist accounts of Alevi identity.

Beyond Antiessentialist Critique

Yet, analysis cannot stop here. One important effect of the antiessentialist critique of identity is that identity is generally regarded with deep suspicion today. It has resulted in the strange situation that everybody, including antiessentialists, talks about identity but that at the same time the idea of identity "is under erasure" (Hall 1996, 129). Essentialist conceptions of identity have become deeply delegitimized in the theoretical debate. "To espouse identity politics in the academy today risks being viewed as a member of the Flat-Earth Society", writes Alcoff (2000, 313). At close scrutiny, however, the postmodernist position bears, potentially, a number of flaws. It could be regarded as self-contradictory because the critique certainly "essentializes" identity as antiessentialist. One difficulty here is the implicit ontology of antiessentialism. First, the anti-essentialist, constructivist critique denies "reality" to essentialist constructions. It attempts to show that a given essential identity is not really what it intends to appear. Essentialized identities are *only* inventions, imaginations, constructions. The problem in this phrase is not that identities are inventions etc. — this has become trivial knowledge by now — but that they are said to be *only* inventions. This betrays a strangely naive "realist" conception of social life. Identities that are inventions are considered not real, implicating that nonessentialist conceptions are "more real." But for radical constructionism it is certainly a difficult idea to regard some constructions as more real than others. The problem springs from the surprisingly naturalist ontology hidden in the critique of essentialism, implying something is not real because it is an invention. Our social world is almost totally made of inventions, some of material and others of ideational kind. In fact, the boundary between both categories of invention is quite porous, as ideas are turned into more material things. Both kinds of inventions become tangibly real. Against Gellner (1964, 164), Anderson (1983) has insisted that the fact that the nation is an invention does not mean that it is unreal and false and that it could be disregarded. This applies to all kinds of essentialist identities that are "only" imagined and constructed and that are "only" representations, but which nevertheless have very real effects in our social world. Representations are social facts (Rabinow 1986), even if they are apparently wrong. Considering the primordialist/situationalist debate on ethnicity in anthropology, which in many respects prefigured the current argument between essentialism and antiessentialism, Wilmsen concludes: "The premise [of primordialism] is faulty, but if the phenomena are real in their effects, they are real; this is the power of primordial arguments" (1996, 2).

Eschewing the deadlock between naive (essentialist) realism and equally naive (antiessentialist) antirealism Satya Mohanty proposes to conceptualize identities as schemes that enable experience and the interpretation the world:

> Identities are theoretical constructions that enable us to read the world in specific ways. It is in this sense that they are valuable, and their epistemic status should be taken very seriously. In them, and through them, we learn to define and reshape our values and commitments; we give texture and form to our collective futures. Both the essentialism of identity politics and the skepticism of the postmodernist position seriously underread the real epistemic and political complexities of our social and cultural identities (Mohanty 1997, 216).

Similarly, I have proposed to understand identities as frameworks of interpretation that serve to (temporarily) make sense of the world, to (tentatively) order experiences, and to (provisionally) give orientation in order to act (Sökefeld 1998). Identities are real because they are part of the terms in which experience is made. This proposition neither presupposes an unquestionable authenticity of experience nor a belief in genuine identities. It recognizes, however, that it hardly makes sense to respond to the perception of Alevis, for instance, that they are stigmatized and sometimes persecuted because they are Alevis with the interjection that the category "Alevi" is "only" a construct. It is a construct, but it is real because some people employ this construct in order to stigmatize or discriminate against other people, and because these other people experience such stigmatization because they are identified (and identify themselves) as Alevis. Some critiques have pointed out that antiessentialist concepts of identity are completely at odds with the everyday usage of the term. Brubaker and Cooper (2000) have concluded that antiessentialist concepts are not actually about identity, that essentialist every-day ideas refer to the "real" meaning of identity and that identity should therefore be given up as a analytical category. Although I do not agree with the authors' final conclusion, I endorse their emphasis on actors' concepts of identity. As a social anthropologist I feel compelled, following Malinowski, to respect the "natives' point of view" and regard it as highly problematic and unsatisfactory to simply dismiss an emic category because it is analytically flawed.

The critique of essentialism originated as a critique of categories that are used as instruments of domination. Antiessentialism holds that all identities exert power and subject. If, following Foucault's conceptualization of power as dispersed in social relations, we assume that power is everywhere because it is simply an aspect of the social, power cannot be taken to be an unequivocally negative category. Jonathan Friedman (1996) unmasks the radical critique and dismissal of all kinds of essentialized identities in the service of a hidden agenda for the "true liberation" of the oppressed as just another kind of patronizing authoritarianism. Cynthia Mahmood has devoted considerable analytical effort to this problem in her study of Sikh militants in exile (1996). She discusses the heated response of Sikhs against a historical work by a Sikh scholar, Harjot Oberoi, who deconstructs Sikh identity as a reification created in particular colonial circumstances (Oberoi 1994). Referring to past efforts of anthropologists to categorize and classify the people they are studying, Mahmood argues that the (de)constructivist position has to be understood as a reaction against the discipline's earlier practice of constructing and reifying cultures and identities. The constructivist critique results "from a belated recognition of the discipline's partnership with the colonial enterprise, which used imposed identities to control and ultimately exclude others" (Mahmood 1996, 243). The constructivist, antiessentialist position then poses as an approach which apparently resists the compromising disciplinary complicity in identity politics. Accordingly, Richard Handler (1985) explicitly demands "destructive analysis" of identities. However, Mahmood emphasizes that antiessentialist deconstruction is neither necessarily liberating nor generally apolitical. Instead, she discovers a new "congruence of postmodern ethnography with the kind of power that asserts itself not by imposing but by *denying* group identities" (1996, 244, italics added). Talal Asad adds: "It is a notorious tactic of political power to deny a distinct unity to populations it seeks to govern, to treat them as contingent and indeterminate... It is precisely the viewpoint of interventionist power that insists on the permeability of social groups, and unboundedness of cultural unities, and the instability of individual selves" (1990, 239–269). Neither the reifying assertion of identities nor their antiessentialist deconstruction denial escapes political entanglement.

In the contemporary world, identity is clearly also an *emic* category that is used in much political and everyday discourse. As an emic category identity is obviously an essentialist idea. The analytical task is to make sense of the Janus-faced character of identity as both antiessentialist analytical concept and essentialist emic category. The first problem to be tackled in this regard is the question why identity has become a so successfully globalized, ubiquitous idea. The antiessentialist critique has no convincing answer to this question. To regard identity as a false consciousness that has to be overcome does not explain why so many people subscribe to this false consciousness. And to view identity as an ideology employed by elites for the purpose of mobilization in order to pursue certain interests begs the question why the ideology of identity has such a great appeal.

An Archaeology of Identity

In order to explain the appeal of essentialist ideas of identity, I suggest to undertake a kind of archaeology that unearths subsequent horizons in the development of the concept that today is labeled "identity." In this section I refer only to essentialist conceptions of identity, the "essence" of which is well expressed in the quotation from Erikson referred to above. Identity in this sense supposes a constant core of the self that is clearly distinguished from other selves in the case of individual identity, and a constant core of shared characteristics of the members of a group that create a clear distinction from other groups in the case of collective identity. Although the term identity was not employed in, say, the eighteenth century, we can clearly find aspects and ideas that prefigure the later use of the word.

The first consequence of such an archaeological endeavor is the acknowledgment that identity is a historical concept that has developed in specific historical circumstances. Identity is not in itself a psychological universal that could be employed for all times and places. Richard Handler (1994) has warned not to use identity as a cross-cultural category, because as a concept that developed in the West identity is culture-bound. Although I subscribe to Handler's diagnosis, I do not agree with him about the proper consequences of this diagnosis (Sökefeld 2001). I do not think that the application of the category should be restricted to the context of "Western" culture. My position results from the recognition that in consequence of historical processes, the idea of identity has spilled over the boundaries of Western culture. Actors of most diverse cultural backgrounds have appropriated the idea and adopted it to their specific circumstances. Thus, although identity is not a psychological universal in the sense that "it has always been there," it is obviously a globalized concept and has become an almost universal political idea. In the horizon of the present, to employ the archaeological metaphor, identity is ubiquitous. But what about the past?

I first turn to the development of the idea of individual identity, of a distinct core of every individual, but I will show also that this idea became closely related to a new understanding of collectivity: a collectivity made up of a plurality of such individuals who share a common, collective identity. In his work *Sources of the Self,* Charles Taylor (1989) traces the development of the idea that every human being has a unique self—which he largely equates with "identity".[4] Taylor emphasizes that present understandings of identity would not have been comprehensible for Europeans two hundred years ago. He points out that this idea is tied to a particular kind of introspection and inwardness that makes the self in its peculiarity an object of inquiry. Since the sixteenth century we find hints that point towards a new ethic of the self that regards the self as both unique and equal to other selves. One significant moment developed in consequence of the Protestant Reformation, which engendered what Taylor calls the "affirmation of common life": an ethic of rational work that valued all ways of life—in contrast with earlier ethics that valued only those life-ways which, like nobility and monasticism, were restricted to few human beings (ibid., 221). With the introduction of individual confession and the emphasis on the conscience of the individual, the Catholic Church also had its share in the development of the self (van Dülmen 1997, 39ff). Taylor (1989, 178ff) finds a decisive moment for the new idea of self also in Montaigne (1533–1592), who not only calls for considering the self, but also discovers at the same time that the self is not simply given but must be sought. It is volatile. The turn

---

[4] According to Taylor (1989, 34), identity is "what I am as a self," i.e., one's particular, personal form of self.

towards the self implies immediately a consciousness of the insecurity of the self.[5] The self cannot simply be relied on, it has to be cared for.

Interestingly, a short time after Montaigne, political theories developed that considered also human communities not as something simply given. Human communities are precarious too and have to be created by the consent of "lonely individuals." In contract theories since the seventeenth century, Taylor (ibid., 193f) discovers two aspects of a new individualism. First, human agents are set free from a cosmic order. Second, the human individual is "free" and sovereign by nature; he (I deliberately use the male form here) is not bound to any authority. The subjection to an authority is the consequence of a voluntary act of consent. The idea of the original equality and autonomy of all human beings is implicated here. Thus, the new political theories relied on the new notion of the individual as not predestined and fixed within a given social order, but as originally autonomous and free. We can say in turn that the idea of the distinct but equal individual necessitated a revised conception of the political. One such new foundation of the political community was suggested by Herder. He extended the idea of originality and uniqueness onto human communities. According to Herder, every people or nation possesses an originality that has to be sought and developed. What the self (or identity) is for the individual human being, *culture* becomes for a people. Every people has its specific character or *Volksgeist* (Berlin 1976, 181f.). The idea of culture was thereby radically transformed. Earlier, culture, understood in the sense of "being cultured," was attributed only to some few human beings and not to everybody (cf. Markus 1993). The nobility or the clergy possessed "culture" as a result of education and formation, but not the common people. However, after Herder, culture in the sense of shared attributes characterized a community, a people as a whole. Before, culture engendered a horizontal division, setting different strata apart. After Herder, it draws vertical boundaries, distinguishing one people from another. Culture is pluralized and at the same time particularized. The boundary drawn by culture does not separate higher and lower strata within a society, but separates the inside from the outside. In analogy with individual identity, we find a dialectic of equality and difference here: All peoples and nations are the same because they all have a culture, but they are all different because their cultures differ. Nations have, we could add, a distinctive collective identity. Accordingly, the historian Conze calls the nation in Herder's writing "the individuation of humanity" (1985, 30). Just like the Enlightenment emphasized the original autonomy of the individual human being, Herder demanded autonomy for the nations: due to the differences between the nations one nation should not be dominated by another one (Pagden 1995).

---

[5] On Montaigne's search for the self see also Coleman (1987, 114).

Although both Enlightenment and Romanticism emphasized the autonomy of the individual and the community, identity—individual as well as collective—was not only a liberating idea. Within a given political order the emphasis on individuality was regarded with deep suspicion. Hence, a short time after the individual self was discovered, techniques and institutions meant to control and discipline the self were devised. Michel Foucault shows in his work *Discipline and Punish* how since the seventeenth century individuals became the objects and products of new disciplining practices in schools, armies, and prisons. In contrast with earlier times not only privileged members of society were recognized as individuals now, and the newly "individualized" ordinary human beings were subjected to normalizing and disciplining powers:

> For a long time ordinary individuality—the everyday individuality of everybody—remained below the threshold of description. To be looked at, observed, described in detail, and followed from day to day by an un-interrupted writing was a privilege. The chronicle of a man, the account of his life, his historiography, written as he lived out his life formed part of the rituals of his power. The disciplinary methods reversed this rela-tion, lowered the threshold of describable individuality and made of this description a means of control and a method of domination. (Foucault 1991, 191).[6]

Systems of registration like censuses or identity documents were devised by which the individual human beings were recorded and seized (in the dual sense of the German verb *erfassen*) by the state and by which especially their movements were controlled (Torpey 2000). Thus, the new identification of human beings as equal individuals had ambivalent consequences. In the realm of philosophy and the arts in-dividuality became highly valued, but in the realm of public order and the state it was considered a potential danger that had to be controlled. While the arts cultivated individual identity, the state tried to contain it by subjecting the individual to a collective identity. The most important instrument for this subjection was a new concept of the nation, although here too the idea of emancipation was prevalent first. The model of the nation in the French Revolution was the political implementation of the idea of individual equality. Difference *within* the population had been constitutive for the absolutist state: The king and nobility were not part of the people; they did not belong to the nation (cf. Sieyes 1970). There was no shared identity. But the French Revolution turned against the rulers and created the nation as community of equal citizens. Na-tionalism became a new theory of political legitimacy. The nation was sovereign as the collective political body of its citizens. Originally, the identity of the nation was a political identity, created by the Revolution.

---

[6] See Ransom (1997) on Foucault's theory of discipline and the individual.

In the first days after the Revolution all those who subscribed to the revolutionary ideals could become members of the French nation. Yet Brubaker (1992) shows that within a short time after 1789 the revolutionary, cosmopolitan nation experienced a strict closure. In the radical phase of the Revolution after 1792 a xenophobos nationalism developed that turned against foreigners. Brubaker asks why foreigners now became a sort of culprits for the nation and concludes:

> The answer has to do with the logic of the nation-state. A nation-state is a nation's state, the state of and for a particular, bounded, sovereign nation, to which foreigners, by definition, do not belong. Legally homogeneous internally, it is by virtue of this very fact more sharply bounded externally than an internally heterogeneous state such as pre-Revolutionary France (Brubaker 1992, 46).

The logic of the nation-state is a logic of exclusion (cf. Wimmer 2002). After the old adversaries of the nation that served as the defining other, the king and the nobility, had been lost, opponents against which the nation had to be delimited were found on the outside, in other nations. Simultaneously, equality within the nation was no longer defined only in terms of political equality and equal rights of participation, but also in terms of homogeneity. A shared identity of the nation—much more in Herder's sense of a shared character than in the political understanding of the early Revolution—became positively valued. However, this homogeneity was not given, but had to be established in a long and arduous process by subjecting the population to a policy of assimilation and homogenization in institutions like the school or the military (Weber 1976).

The meaning of the nation changed dramatically after the French Revolution. By Napoleon's ascent to power the idea of equal rights was partly laid to rest, but the idea of the nation as a sovereign body that due to a shared identity is distinct from other such bodies persisted and gained unprecedented prominence. The legitimizing force of the nation was now directed towards the ruler: his rule was in the interest of the nation. Further, the idea of the nation became a powerful mobilizing force. Far from remaining a revolutionary force, nationalist ideology was turned into an instrument at the hands of established powers so that, only a few years after the French Revolution, it became a national imperative not to depose the king but to fight and to die for him.[7]

This short and incomplete history of the idea of individual and collective identity as sedimented in ideas about the self, culture, and the nation shows one important fact: these ideas are intimately intertwined with questions of agency and power. The release of the self from the grip of pregiven order invests it with the heightened necessity to make

---

[7] For these processes in the history of Europe see Schulze (1999).

decisions. The self is furnished with individual conscience and consequentially bears a new responsibility. The idea of the individual self
creates a new kind of agency. In political theory, this agency of the individual requires acts (like concluding a contract) that establish community because also the community is no longer conceptualized as
preordained. The relationship between power and identity is most obvious in the new concept of the nation: the nation, first as a community
of equal individual citizens and then as a community founded upon a
shared culture, becomes the legitimate locus of power. Although after
the French Revolution the original idea of the legitimacy of the nation
was turned upside down, the connection between national identity and
power became even more intimate. Since the time of Napoleon up to
the present, even a despotic ruler has to legitimate himself in relation
to the nation—by claiming to act in the interest of the nation. To put
it pointedly: just as the individual human being becomes an agent by
being endowed with an individual self/an identity, a collection of individuals becomes a collective agent, a community indeed, by assuming
a collective identity.

Power and Identity

The idiom of identity is an idiom of power. Claims for power and for
the legitimacy of power are expressed in a language of identity. Strategically, identity not only legitimizes power but provides also an effective instrument for mobilization. As an idiom of power, identity
became a globalized concept. This is again most obvious in the case of
national identity. The nation became a highly successful export of European thought not as a descriptive category that fitted the social and
political structure of societies in all corners of the globe but as a project
of power. Anticolonial struggles for liberation projected national identities of the colonized against the colonizing nations, and derived the
demand for rights, power and finally independence and sovereignty
from the idiom of the nation. The colonizers were attacked and in the
last instance beaten with their own weapons.[8]

Power requires actors, be they individual or collective agents. Agents
are founded upon unity. An agent that dissolves into diverging and conflicting parts and pieces is destroyed. The agency of an individual that

---

[8] The case of the Ottoman Empire and, later, Turkey is special in this respect.
Here, nationalist thought and strategy was raised against the Ottomans by
Greeks and others, although the Ottoman empire had a multinational, or, better, prenational, structure. Turks as the "core" population of the Ottoman empire developed their own nationalist thought only in response to those resistive
nationalisms, and later in response to dominant European powers.

"suffers" disunity as a consequence of psychological "disorder" like schizophrenia syndrome is destroyed, as is expressed by the fact that such an individual is legally not held accountable and may be stripped of personal rights.[9] Similarly, a collective body like a nation lacks agency if it lacks unity. This unity is embodied and institutionalized in the state. A nation without a state is not an agent in international politics, or a member of the "international community." Accordingly, the purpose of power is best served by an essentialist idiom of identity, which emphasizes unity, clear boundedness, and shared essence. No wonder then that identity as an instrumental emic concept, employed by individual or collective agents for the purpose of claiming rights and asserting power, is clearly essentialist.

The aporia of the dual conceptualization of identity as an essentialist emic and an antiessentialist analytical category can be solved in analogy with attempts to reconcile primordialism and situationalism in the debate on ethnicity. Here, primordialism is considered a code or idiom of ethnicity although ethnicity is not itself regarded as pregiven and stable. Thus, Wilmsen (1996, 2) considers primordialism an inevitable "subtext" also of nonprimordialist conceptualizations of ethnicity: "Indeed, primordialism cannot help but be a subtext—for ethnicity as an existential premise is founded on just one premise: The conviction of the reality of endemic cultural and social, often racial, difference." Similarly, essentialism is the subtext and (instrumental) idiom of emic identity discourse, because the reach towards power via identity requires clear-cut identities. A nationalist movement that does not assert the "essential" character of the proclaimed nation but deconstructs it and expounds how it is shot through with difference, multiplicity, and intersectionality is clearly doomed to failure. Therefore, essentialism is "strategic" (Spivak 1988, 13f) even if it does not appear as such but rather tries to cover its strategic character and to "dissimulate" (van Beek 2000) the inevitable multiplicity and intersectionality of identifications.

As an emic concept, employed by the agents of a society for particular purposes, identity is therefore not a descriptive category. Identity is a project. *Belief* in the significance of the projected identity is required in order that people can be motivated to enter a struggle for identity (Benhabib 1999, 24). As a project, identity presupposes what it seeks to achieve. In the case of a nationalist movement, the unity and reality of the nation, expressed for instance in a long and detailed history, is considered a fact even if political reality denies its factuality. It is real in a higher kind of reality. The particulars of political life have to be brought into line with that essential reality—not the other way round.

---

[9] The doxic character of the conjunction of identity and agency becomes most apparent by the fact that nonidentity is automatically expressed in terms of suffering and disorder. Cf. Lambeck and Antze (1996, xxii f).

Identity implies self-consciousness of identity. George Herbert Mead (1967, 136) has shown for the individual that in order to develop a self it has to make the self an object of itself, an object of reflection and self-consciousness. The self has to be made an object of its own narrative. The same applies to collective identity. In order to assume a collective identity a group has to become an object for itself. Most frequently, this is done with an idiom of culture: the culture of a group is not simply a descriptive category then, but an object of value and reflection, of research, proclamation, representation, and performance. An important means for the objectification of culture is a shift of location: culture is being taken out of everyday life context and transferred into pamphlets and books, enshrined in museum showcases and put on stage.

The identification of power as a core element—or even an "essence"—of identity requires a discussion of the concept of power. Power is one of the most complex concepts in the social sciences. The debate on power has been strongly influenced by Michel Foucault, who has emphasized that power is not simply a matter of political institutions or actors that in themselves either possess power or not. Power is not located in institutions or actors but in *relationships between actors.* Power is dispersed in social networks (Foucault 1979, 55). Touraine (1981, 33) has argued similarly that power is an element of all social relations—not only of relations of domination—and that there is no social action without power. Foucault (1982, 219f) describes power as a "more or coordinated (in the event, no doubt, ill-coordinated) cluster of relations." Significant in this conceptualization is the distinction between power on one hand and force or violence on the other. Violence does not recognize the agency or even the subjectivity of those who are subjected to violence. Violence and force create an almost causal, mechanical relationship between the one who exerts force and the other who is subjected to it. Power, in contrast, depends on agency. It does not have an immediate and direct effect upon another individual but upon his or her actions. Power requires that the individual who is subjected to power remains recognized and preserved as a subject that is able to act and that has a range of choices, including resistance, as response to the exertion of power (Foucault 1982, 220). In order to be effective, relations of power presuppose a certain consent, on the part of the actors who are expected to move in a desired way. If that limited consent is destroyed and if the agent who exerts power is met with total resistance, power vanishes because either its aims remain unaccomplished or it has to be replaced by violence. Power therefore requires a certain legitimacy. As an aspect of social relations, power has "two ends": one in the agent that exerts power and the other one in the agent that responds to the exertion of power. The disciplinary power exerted in the institutions studied by Foucault both normalizes and disciplines (that is, subjects) individuals, but this subjection becomes necessary only because individuals are *recognized* as individuals.

Power, Identity, Recognition

From the argument that, first, power is a core element of identity because identity reaches for power and that, second, power has "two ends"
because it requires the recognition of those whose actions are expected
to be influenced in specific ways, follows that identity also has "two
ends" and requires recognition if it is to achieve its claims. A concept
of recognition is an important supplement to concepts of identity, because it emphasizes the two-sided, dialogic character of identity. Frequently, the expression "politics of recognition" has been employed as
a synonym for "politics of identity," and it has been subject to a similar
critique. There has been an intense discussion in moral as well as political philosophy and the social sciences on the question whether or to
what extent and under which conditions "recognition" has replaced
"redistribution" as political goal and paradigm. The parallel with the
replacement of class politics by politics of identity is obvious.[10] I want
to argue here that a perspective on identity via recognition enables a
clear understanding of the situatedness of identity and its aspects of
multiplicity, difference, and intersectionality.

Charles Taylor (1992) is among the most influential authors that have
discussed the politics of recognition. However, his analytic discussion
of the category of recognition is surprisingly thin. In the beginning of
his essay he writes:

> A number of strands in contemporary politics turn on the need, some-
> times the demand, for *recognition*. The need, it can be argued, is one of the
> driving forces behind nationalist movements in politics. And the demand
> comes to the fore in a number of ways in today's politics, on behalf of
> minority or "subaltern" groups, in some forms of feminism and in what
> is today called the politics of "multiculturalism."
>
> The demand for recognition in these latter cases is given urgency by
> the supposed links between recognition and identity, where this latter
> term designates something like a person's understanding of who they
> are, of their fundamental defining characteristics as a human being. The
> thesis is that our identity is partly shaped by recognition or its absence,
> often by the *mis*recognition of others, and so a person of group of people
> can suffer real damage, real distortion, if the people or society around
> them mirror back to them a confining or demeaning or contemptible pic-
> ture of themselves. (Taylor 1992, 25).

In this passage Taylor points to the dialogic character of identity that
is expressed in a "need" for recognition, and to the idea that identity
is "partly" influenced by recognition or nonrecognition. Later I will argue that the cautious qualification laid down in the adverb "partly" is
probably too cautious. Here I would like to maintain, however, that by

---

[10] Cf. Fraser (1997, 2001); Honneth (2001).

proposing a "need for recognition," which he derives from concepts of "human dignity" and "authenticity" (ibid., 16) Taylor resorts to an essentialist concept of identity that sheds almost all the analytic power that the idea of recognition offers. The focus of his essay is the political question whether the recognition of cultural difference within a society could legitimate legal instruments that treat sections of the population differentially (i.e. that discriminate, if positively, in certain respects) and that thereby aim at the preservation of this difference. Taylor projects individual identity/difference onto collectivities and argues that if individual identity has become a positive value, also collective identity should be valued and guarded. His argument, taking most importantly the example of Quebecois culture, is quite complex, but in the end he legitimizes a politics of discrimination that is intended to ensure the "survival" of a culture considered to be endangered. Taylor's political conclusion can be—and has been—criticized from a number of perspectives.[11] Yet at this point I am less interested in Taylor's conclusion than in the suppositions assumed in order to arrive at this conclusion. Here, the most significant issue is what Taylor has omitted in his argument: he has completely left out the question how, by whom, and in what (respectively against which other) interests a collective identity is *constructed*. In fact, in his essay Quebecois culture is not presented as a construction that has been made in particular historical circumstances by, for instance, an interested elite and which is thereby indissolubly connected with particular politics of powers. In Taylor's discussion, Quebecois culture is simply there.[12]

In contrast with Taylor's idea that there is something—cultures, identities—simply given to be recognized I would like to argue that structures, relations, contexts, and agents of recognition (or nonrecognition and misrecognition) play an important role in constituting what is recognized (or not recognized) and in shaping the claim for recognition. In order to explain this we need to go back to the idea of power in identity. I have argued that to claim an identity is also to claim power. The claim for self-identity implies a claim for individual agency, and a claim for nationhood implies a demand of sovereignty or at least autonomy. Due to the structure of power and identity such a claim can only be achieved if it is recognized by others. This relationship of identity and recognition reflects the Hegelian concept of self-consciousness. Hegel (1981,

---

[11] Habermas (1997) argues against Taylor that "endangered" cultures are not in need of a kind of "cultural protection of the species" but rather of procedural provisions that ensure the articulation of disadvantaged positions on the basis of equal individual participation.

[12] For a in-depth analysis of the construction of Quebecois culture see Handler (1988). A detailed critique of Taylor's cultural essentialism and its political conclusions is provided by Baumann (1999).

145) wrote: "Self-consciousness exists in itself and for itself, in that, and by the fact that it exists for an Other [i.e., another self-consciousness], that is to say, it is only by being recognized." The same relationship can be applied to collective identities: In order to achieve sovereignty or autonomy as a nation the projected nation has to be recognized by other nations. In the struggle for recognition the agents of the nationalist struggle anticipate recognition because the nation is already represented as a nation, although it could be argued (as is done by some theoreticians of the nation) that as long as the projected nation lacks recognition it also lacks reality as a nation. The form of the identity to be recognized is constituted by the context and the model of the intended recognition. In order to achieve a particular kind of recognition, an identity has to be represented in a specific way — and this is generally an essentialist way of representation. The nation has to be represented as already possessing most of the elements necessary for claiming the status of a nation, like a long history, a homogeneous culture, a shared language, and a unified population on a clearly delimited territory. Those who prefer to deny recognition, in contrast, may argue either in antiessentialist, constructionist terms, maintaining that the nation is but a recent "invention," that it lacks unity and homogeneity, or in essentialist terms, that the projected nation "really" belongs to another nation, or in a mixture of both.

To frame the question of identity in terms of recognition makes clear that identity is not simply a matter of an individual or a group, but rather an issue *between* individuals or groups. It is not sufficient that a group claims a particular identity. This claim is voiced in particular contexts of other groups and agents that put forward their own ideas of identity. Very often, a group's claim of identity is made *against* the versions of identity that this group is ascribed by others. The identity of the group then aims at changing this ascription, at making it congruent with its self-ascription. Or a group is denied a particular identity and then struggles for being perceived in its self-proclaimed particularity. Ultimately, the struggle for recognition seeks to achieve congruence of self-ascription and ascription by others.

To analyze identity in terms of recognition prevents to speak simply about "the identity" of a group. Instead, it forces us to ask specific questions like: Who struggles for recognition? Who claims recognition for whom? Who is demanded to recognize? What kinds of representations of identities are there? What kind of recognition is intended and sought? What other ways of (mis-)recognition that are valued negatively are intended to be erased thereby? We are forced to identify particular agents in this struggle for recognition, agents that may seek recognition for diverse, competing versions of identity and, in turn, a range of agents that are expected to recognize particular claims of identity. We also need to identify terms and conditions of recognition. This also enables us to

understand why claims of identity put forward in different contexts—
for instance those put forward by a diaspora group and those voiced
in the "homeland"—may differ considerably, why in specific contexts
particular aspects may be emphasized or played down.

Alevis and the Struggle for Recognition

Within the framework of identity, power and recognition as outlined
here Alevi struggles for recognition will be analyzed in a transnational
context. I will employ the concept of identity in its duality: as a analytic
anti-essentialist concept that is able to disclose essentialist constructions of identity, but that nevertheless does not deny the reality of these
essentialism as both strategy and framework of experiences. Here, I provide a very brief outline that is intended to show the usefulness of my
framework. In this outline I assume an Alevi perspective.

The efforts of Alevis are directed first of all against nonrecognition or
misrecognition. Throughout the history of the Ottoman empire Alevis
have been stigmatized as a heterodox group. By being ascribed all kinds
of negative stereotypes they have been misrecognized by the state, by
religious institutions, and by the dominant section of the population.
In order to escape this misrecognition, which time and again entailed
violence and persecution, Alevis took to a strategy of nonrecognition,
i.e., they tried not to be recognized as "others" but to pass as Sunni
Muslims in the non-Alevi public. The new Alevi movement since the
late 1980s turned against both non- and misrecognition. Alevis entered
public spaces and raised their voices to assert both "we are here," i.e.,
that there is a distinct community within the population of Turkey, and
"we are different," i.e., that the negative stereotypes about Alevis are
wrong. Claims for recognition are made within specific discourses in
Turkish society in which different Alevi agents assume different positions and perspectives. But central for all is the claim for recognition
made in the Alevi declaration quoted at the beginning of this chapter:
the recognition as *victims* that suffered violence and stigma by state and
society.

In the German context of Alevi migrants, there is at the beginning
a similar claim against non- and misrecognition but with different ad-
dressees: a claim against nonrecognition is voiced towards the German
public which subsumed Alevis simply under the undifferentiated mass
of "Turks," not recognizing any difference, while the claim against
misrecognition is directed (sometimes via the German public) at Sunni
immigrants from Turkey that held the same stigmatizing stereotypes
about Alevis that also circulated in Turkey. But I will show that the basic claim for being recognized as Alevis in Germany was supplemented
by a range of more differentiated claims: claims for being recognized

as citizens with equal rights in Germany, and for being recognized as a religious community at par with other such communities. The most significant context for claims for recognition in Germany is the broad field of discourse and politics of migration. This discourse is largely about another question of recognition that has become central for German self-identity: the question of recognizing Germany as a country of immigration or not. Besides these two national fields in which claims for recognition are made, there is also a transnational politics of recognition in which German Alevis take efforts to support the struggle of Alevis in Turkey. These politics are significantly framed within the context of supranational integration, that is, Turkey's intended accession to the European Union.

Within these fields of claims for recognition, essentialist conceptions of Alevi identity are ubiquitous. For instance, Alevis are portrayed as the perennial victims, from Kerbela to Gazi Mahallesi, glossing over extended periods of complicity between the Ottoman state and the Bektaşi order of dervishes. Cultural elements like *musahiplik* (a form of ritual kinship) are represented as essential elements of Alevis although they are hardly practised today. Alevis are represented as a unified "community," but the urge for unity frequently only covers up intense conflict and contradiction. Alevis are certainly also subjected to essentialized identities imposed by others. I will start to disentangle these crosscutting identifications, essentializations, and claims for recognition by telling the story of the development of the new Alevi movement by which Alevis self-consciously entered the public and voiced their claims.

2

Going Public

Alevism as Social Movement

In this chapter I will narrate the passage of Alevism from a hidden to a public issue in Germany. In the course of this transition, Alevism was created anew in a number of aspects. Alevism was reconstituted in public space in the form of a social movement. I have to spell out why I conceptualize reconstituted Alevism as a social movement and not simply as a religious (or cultural) community. "Community" has recently been critiqued as a concept that accommodates too many different readings and interpretations, yet still signals a rhetoric of "interpersonal warmth, shared interests, and loyalty" (Baumann 1996, 15; cf. Amit and Rapport 2002). The notion of community implies the idea of largely unproblematic affiliation and membership. The concept of a movement, however, emphasizes that people have to be mobilized for a common cause. The activists of a movement do not belong "naturally," e.g., by inheritance, tradition, and birth to the movement. Instead, their commitment has to be achieved. The concept of social movement introduces a strong moment of reflexivity and self-instituted change into the social; it emphasizes the individual as social actor who takes initiative and moves not only him- or herself, but also something in society. The notion of movement thereby contradicts a conventional notion of society as integrated (and largely closed) by rules and norms (Fuchs 1999: 84f). Further, a movement implies different degrees of engagement: some people are leading activists, others are passive members, and many may remain completely aloof. This differential commitment characterizes the Alevi movement. The activists of the movement try to mobilize those who remain passive. This endeavor for mobilization is not always and not completely successful, to say the least. Thus, the Alevi movement can be distinguished from the Alevi community: the movement targets at mobilizing the community. It is the movement with its agents and organizations that becomes visible in public through activities and politics, not the community that is, however, discursively invoked and constructed by the movement.

Empirical research as well as theorizing about social movements has flourished recently, resulting in a broad range of conceptualizations of the matter. A common denominator of approaches is that social movements are not institutionalized collectivities that lack formal representation and that are engaged in contentious issues and interaction with opponents of various kinds (Tarrow 1996a). Yet beside contending, Tarrow emphasizes elsewhere, social movements do other things as well: "[T]hey build organizations, elaborate ideologies, and socialize and mobilize constituencies, and their members engage in self-development and the construction of collective identities" (Tarrow 1998, 3). While Touraine employs a concept of social movement that is based upon a concept of class (Touraine 1985, 1988, 66f.)—which is difficult to apply to the Alevi case because Alevis cannot be conceptualized as a separate class—Tarrow's understanding is broader and more easily applicable. He defines social movements as "collective challenges, based on common purposes and social solidarities, in sustained interaction with elites, opponents, and authorities" Tarrow (1998, 4). The four elements of Tarrow's definition can be identified in the case of the Alevi movement: The common purpose of the movement is formal and public recognition of Alevism in Germany and Turkey; practices of challenge include demonstrations and other forms of assembly in which the common purpose is expressed, but also formal practices like litigation and, on the individual level, the exhibition of particular symbols. Solidarity is invoked through the appeal to a common identity that includes the experience of victimization, and the continuity of contentious politics is achieved through the establishment of associations.

Recent interest in social movements has been sparked by the so-called new social movements that are said to have supplanted previous paradigmatic cases like the workers movement. New social movements focus on issues of culture and identity instead of centering on questions of class. Touraine therefore suggests to refer to these new movements as cultural movements and to reserve the concept of social movements specifically for social action that challenges a specific (dominant) adversary. Cultural movements "are centered on the assertion of cultural rights, rather than on a conflict with an adversary, who may be defined only in vague terms" (Touraine 2000, 102). The transition from class politics to politics of identity that has been discussed in the previous chapter is paralleled here. Although the periodization of "old" and "new" movements remains vague and questionable as economics continue to be an issue in "new" social movements and identity has been a concern in "old" ones (Calhoun 1995, 215; Melucci 1996, 5), it makes sense in the Alevi case because most of its pioneer activists had been engaged in the leftist movement before they committed themselves to Alevism. The Alevi movement exhibits characteristics of a cultural as well as social movement: it struggles for the recognition of Alevi culture and identity, but it also has a clear adversary that continues to deny this recognition: the Turkish government.

Reference to actors is important in social movements, because although movements are theorized in terms of collective action, the decisive questions remain how individual actors are mobilized for the movement, what specific actions they take, and how they participate in the constitution of the movement. New collective actors are created, but also individual actors that participate in a movement are transformed. This is especially important in movements related to identity because of the mutual relationship between collective and individual identity that is involved. The reconstitution of Alevism as a social movement also constitutes individuals as Alevis in a novel way.

The theory of social movements generally emphasizes that such movements constitute something new. They raise new ideas, voice new demands, or invent new kinds of action. Melucci, accordingly, considers social movements as "prophets" that speak out unsaid issues and point into initially unclear directions (Melucci 1996, 1). Yet movements do not appear out of nowhere but rise in certain contexts, are frequently based on previous networks, and have specific (pre)histories. Such histories also imply that social movements change their form. Social movements are mostly defined in contradistinction to institutionalized forms of organization (e.g., della Porta and Diani 1999), but empirically this distinction is difficult to maintain because social movements rarely remain totally uninstitutionalized for a long time. Practically, more institutionalized forms of organization, with associations, membership, elected leadership, and the like, develop sooner or later within all social movements. This institutionalization may even be a purpose of the movement. However, institutionalization may also be counterproductive because it inhibits further mobilization. In any case, I regard "movement" and "institution" not as mutually exclusive, dichotomous forms of the social, but rather as poles on a continuum. The Alevi movement certainly strove for institutionalization, and successful institutionalization—which includes being recognized in institutionalized form by other institutions—is clearly understood as an indicator of achievement and recognition, of success of the movement.

On 24 December 1988, a group of Alevis met together in a flat in Hamburg and discussed the situation of Alevis and Alevism. They came to the conclusion that Alevis should stop the dissimulation that had been practiced in Germany and in Turkey, and have their coming out as Alevis. They formed the Alevi Kültür Gurubu (Alevi Culture Group) that grew rapidly during the following months. In October 1989, the Alevi Culture Group organized the Alevi Culture Week (*Alevi Kültür Haftası*), which was the first time ever, event announced explicitly in the name of Alevism. In the perception of Alevi activists not only in Hamburg, this event was the starting point of the Alevi movement. Indeed, it had effects far beyond the limits of Hamburg. The purpose of the current chapter is to discuss the development and conditions that led to the Alevi Culture Week. The topic is a kind of prehistory of the Alevi movement in Germany. I will discuss the circumstances of Alevi migration to

Germany, the Alevis' experience of *takiya* and defamation in Germany, their involvement in Turkish migrants' political organizations, and finally the role of an institutional framework in Hamburg that provided an environment for making "identity" an issue.

Alevi Migration to Germany

Alevi migration to Germany started with the beginning of labor migration from Turkey to Germany. This migration was enabled by an agreement concluded between the Turkish and German governments in 1961. Like other such agreements for recruiting foreign labor it was intended to overcome the then labor shortage that threatened to seriously hamper economic growth in Germany. There was no special provision for Alevis in the agreement with Turkey, as "Alevi" was (and is) a legal category neither in Turkey nor in Germany. Alevis constituted an undistinguished and unrecognized part in the growing movement of laborers from Turkey to Germany. As the general conditions of migration from Turkey provided the framework of Alevi migration too, it is necessary to dwell a little on this general migration. Labor migration was not the only way in which Turks came to Germany. Family reunion, which allows under certain conditions that a migrant is joined by her or his spouse and minor children, political exile, and the seeking of university education constituted further avenues of migration. Indeed, labor migration was stopped due to a ban of recruitment issued by the German government in November 1973. This ban was motivated by economic crisis and a growing rate of unemployment in Germany. To that date, the number of Turkish citizens living in Germany had risen to more than 900,000. The ban of recruitment did not stop the influx from Turkey but reduced the numbers of people entering into Germany. In 1974 still 161,430 Turks migrated to Germany. Family reunion had now become the major avenue for immigration. In its original version, the German-Turkish agreement for recruiting laborers had explicitly ruled out family reunion because the German government intended to prevent immigration of Turks—in contrast with temporal sojourn for the purpose of employment. For the same reason, periods of employment in Germany were initially strictly limited to two years without any possibility for extension. These restrictions applied solely to workers from Turkey and distinguished them from others like Italians or Portuguese. However, in a renegotiation of the agreement both restrictions were lifted. Family reunion was enabled and became significant especially after the ban of recruitment of 1973.

In the late 1970s, Turks started to enter Germany as political refugees. This was due to the growing polarization between left and right in Turkey and increasing political violence that affected especially schools and universities. Polarization culminated in the military coup of 1980, which led to the persecution of leftist activists. That year saw a doubling of the number of asylum seekers from Turkey in Germany. In the following time, immigration from Turkey declined due to the restrictive policy of the German government, which also sponsored remigration. However, with the exception of the years 1983–1985 total numbers of Turks in Germany continued to grow. The increase accelerated again after 1987, parallel to the intensification of the war between the Turkish army and Kurdish separatists, which again engendered a movement into exile. In 1995 the line of two million Turks living in Germany was crossed.

Considering numbers of immigrants, three major movements can be detected: the first from the start of labor migration to the ban of recruitment 1973, the second during the late 1970s and early 1980s, and the third from the late 1980s to the mid 1990s. The first movement was mainly constituted by labor migration, the second and third movements by seeking exile and asylum, with family reunion providing additional immigration in all periods. Legal avenues of immigration, however, are not a precise reflection of motivations for migration. For instance, political refugees came by way of family reunion if that was possible for them and did not apply for asylum, or seekers of employment came as political refugees because the avenue of labor migration was closed. Besides immigration, the number of Turkish citizens in Germany also increased by Turkish children born in Germany, who until the adoption of a new citizenship law in 2000 automatically retained the Turkish citizenship of their parents.

Because "Alevi" is not a legal category, no official statistics of Alevi immigration are available. My survey of members of Alevi associations in Hamburg revealed, however, that the pattern of Alevi migration largely conforms to the general image of migration from Turkey. Figure 2.1 shows the same three phases of movement. The absolute peak of immigration was reached in 1980, the year of the military coup in

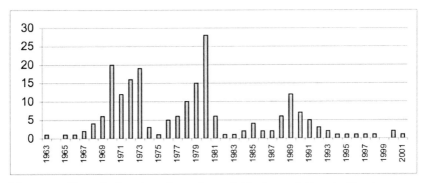

Figure 2.1 Year of migration of members of Alevi associations in Hamburg

Turkey. Alevis were engaged exclusively on the left side of the political spectrum, and only the leftists were persecuted by the military after taking over the government. Due to the lack of official statistics, there are no reliable figures of the total number of Alevis in Germany. Estimates of Alevi associations assume that between 600,000 and 700,000 Alevis live in the country (Kaplan 2004, 25).

Takiya as Strategy and by Default

Alevis remained unrecognized in Germany not only because "Alevi" did not constitute a legal category but also because they themselves did not identify openly as Alevis. Thus, by default, they continued *takiya*, the strategy of dissimulation and nonidentification in public that characterized the life of Alevis in Turkey. *Takiya* is a strategy legitimized also in Shia Islam, which allows to hide one's religious belonging in order to avert danger (Strothmann 2002). It is a strategy to cope with potential or manifest religious persecution. Alevis, called *Kızılbaş* ("red heads") in earlier times due to their red headgear that marked them as followers of the Safawid Şah Ismail, were subjected to persecution in various phases of Anatolian history. For instance, after the final victory of the Ottoman Sultan Selim Yavuz over the Safawid Şah Ismail in 1513, large numbers of Şah Ismail's followers in Anatolia were either killed or deported. Sunni *ulema* issued *fetwas* (religious judgments) that declared the persecution and killing of *Kızılbaş* as lawful because Alevis were considered apostates and nonbelievers. As a consequence, Alevis settled especially in not easily accessible, mostly mountainous regions of Anatolia in order to escape the danger of persecution. It was particularly important not to be recognized as Alevi in a non-Alevi environment, most importantly in the cities. Cases of violent persecution are deeply inscribed in the collective memory of Alevis. They continued to serve as an explanation for *takiya* also after the foundation of the Turkish republic. Memory of violence was refueled by recent "massacres." Yet not only open persecution but also fears of more subtle kinds of discrimination, like being denied a job or simply suffering the contempt of neighbors based on a number of libelous prejudices, were important motivations for continuing dissimulation. The most significant of such prejudices referred to the Alevi ritual *cem*, in which women and men participate jointly and in which music and dance play important roles. *Cem* constitutes almost an antithesis of Sunni prayer and invoked all kinds of imaginations about what men and women actually do in the ritual. The rumor emerged that at a certain point the candles are extinguished and that in the darkness men and women indulge in sexual, even incestuous, orgies. The expressions *mum söndürmek* ("to extinguish candles") and *Aleviler ana bacı tanımaz* ("Alevis do not know

their mothers and sisters," i.e., they even do not refrain from incestuous sexual relations) are well known elements of this libelous discourse
about Alevis. Through the centuries, the term *Kızılbaş* continued to be
used for Alevis by non-Alevis. *Kızılbaş* was a swearword that implied
all negative stereotypes attributed to Alevis like having no morals, no
honor, and no belief. Such ideas even made their way into the diction-
aries, where it was later fought by Alevis (see below). The eleventh
imprint of 1990 of the New Turkish-English Redhouse Dictionary explains the term "*Kızılbaş*" among other things as "person of loose morals." The Turkish-German dictionary by Karl Steuerwald of 1972 gives
the meaning of *Kızılbaş* among other things "a person who commits
incest". Accordingly, "Alevi" instead of "*Kızılbaş*" is strongly preferred
as self-designation today.

Alevis brought vivid experiences of *takiya* and the fear of discrimination to Germany. Zeynep Yılmaz, a Kurdish Alevi woman that had
moved from the province of Tunceli to Istanbul before migrating to
Germany, told about *takiya* in the city:

> In Istanbul, where my parents lived, in Bakırköy, there were neighbors
> (…) who did not know that we were Alevis. We could not tell them that
> we were Alevis. Because one never knows when and how people would
> act. (…) They know that we did not keep fast in Ramadan, but there are
> many Turks who do the same. Who do not keep fast in Ramadan. That is
> not the problem. But to be Alevi and additionally Kurd, that is danger-
> ous. For reasons of security my parents said, no, nobody should know it.

Takiya marked the difference of life in Alevi villages and life in the
cities. In villages of either purely Alevi or mixed population where nevertheless everybody knew who was Alevi and who was not, *takiya* was
unnecessary. But it was regarded as unavoidable in the cities, which
were considered a much more insecure environment. Many young Alevis had their first experience with Sunnis and, consequentially, with
takiya when they went to provincial towns for the purpose of middle-
school education, and many tell that they have been called names or
were even beaten when it somehow leaked out that they were Alevis.
Referring to his youth in the 1960s in the province of Erzincan, another
migrant in Hamburg, Ali Çelik told:

> I am fifty-one by now, and I know since forty-eight years that I am Alevi.
> But we were Alevis only when we lived in the village. When Alevis went
> to the town or somewhere else in order to work, then they said nothing.
> They did not tell their colleagues or their boss, and during the military
> service nobody said, "I am Alevi." We never said this. And when we re-
> turned in our village (…) we knew when we were all together, then we
> knew that we were Alevis.

Of course, not every Alevi living in a city practised *takiya* and not everybody who was known to be Alevi suffered a kind of social rejection.

But in the discourse about *takiya,* dissimulation is represented as the general rule and nondissimulation as exception that relates always to particular individual circumstances and experiences.

For the greater part, Alevi migrants continued *takiya* in Germany. It was simply a part of their life. Also in Germany Alevis were subject to the prejudices of Sunni fellow migrants with whom they lived and worked together. *Takiya* had the consequence that also Alevis themselves frequently did not know for sure who was a fellow Alevi and who was not. In order to find out, various strategies were employed. For instance one's place of origin provided important clues. When Turks who do not know each other meet and start to talk one of the first questions usually is: *Memleketin neresi?* Where do you come from? The province of origin allows a certain assessment of whether the interlocutor could be Alevi or not: If he or she comes from Sivas there is a high probability of being Alevi, because the province has a large Alevi population. If somebody is from Tunceli it is almost certain that he is Alevi, and if he comes from Konya it is quite obvious that he is not, because the population of Tunceli, the erstwhile Dersim, is almost completely Alevi whereas in Konya there are nearly no Alevis at all. One may also talk about musical predilections and conclude from certain genres mentioned whether the other is Alevi or not, and one may observe attentively how the other talks about religious belief and practice. The meeting of an Alevi with a stranger can be imagined as a cautious and careful sounding out. A name of a favorite musician might be dropped as a clue in order to test how the other reacts to this name, and a conversation may come to a quick end if it becomes obvious that the other is not Alevi. At least this was the case in the time before the Alevi movement, which attempted, in many respects successfully, to break *takiya.* But still today it is quite uncommon to ask a stranger directly whether he is Alevi or not.

Hasan Kılavuz, a *dede* (Alevi religious specialist) who as a consequence of his strong religious family background did not practise strict *takiya* even in Turkey, came first to Hamburg as student for a period of practical training. He told how he found out in the mid-1970s who of his fellow students were Alevis:

> Within one or two months I found out that there were three Alevis among us. I sang songs, and I always sang Alevi songs. The other Turks had their music, Turkish music. But I sang Alevi songs. When I sang the other Alevis said to me: [H.K. imitates a cautious voice] "Yes, this is a nice song, where did you learn it?" I told that I knew it because my father always sang like that and played saz. "Do you play saz" [the others asked]? "No, but my father plays," and so on. "Your father plays?" "Yes, my father is a *dede.*" [H.K imitates the low voice of his interlocutor:] "You are Alevis?" "Yes," I said! "Yes," he said [now H.K speaks with a barely audible voice], "I am Alevi too!" [H.K laughs] This is funny. I was completely open and said I am Alevi, but they did not tell it to others.

Sometimes Alevi parents in Germany preferred not to tell their children that they were Alevis, because they feared that their children might suffer discrimination if their being Alevi became known to others. However, this did not always have the desired effect. Due to elements of behavior, attitudes, and opinions or simply because of their ignorance of Sunni belief and practice, such children were sometimes identified as Alevis by Sunnis although they themselves did not know anything about being Alevi. I recorded a number of stories by young Alevis who were called names by Sunni class fellows in school and who only thereby learned that they were Alevis. I started many interviews with questions about how my interlocutors came to know that they were Alevis, because for many of them this was a conscious affair that marked the beginning of a conscious involvement with questions of identity. Ercan, the second son of Ali Çelik whom I have quoted above, answered my question how he came to know that he was Alevi:

> It was when I was called names for the first time. That was when I was thirteen or fourteen or twelve. About that time. Then, a class fellow of mine looked at me during class and said: "Tell me, you are *Kızılbaş*, aren't you?" I said: "What do you mean? I do not know that word." I did not know what to answer. And when I came home I asked my parents: "Can anybody tell me what a *Kızılbaş* is?" And then my parents took me and [my father] said, "Son, I think it is time now." You are this and that, you are coming from this and that is your past, and thereby I learned it.

Similarly, Ergin, who is now in his late twenties, told that he came to know about being Alevi only when he was sixteen years old. He had been born in Germany but went to Turkey for the purpose of schooling, and lived there for eight years because his parents intended to leave Germany after a few years of work. Ergin returned to Germany at the age of sixteen when it had become obvious that his parents would not return to Turkey. Neither in his early years in Germany nor during his time in Turkey did anybody tell him about being Alevi. He was confronted as Alevi by his neighbors in Hamburg, and he too asked his parents about being Alevi only after this incident.

Prejudice and Defamation

The stories of Ercan and Ergin are significant because their parents were deeply committed to the newly founded Alevi organization in Hamburg. Thus, it was not due to simple disinterest or neglect that they did not tell their children about being Alevi. Many of those children or young people who were told by their parents that they were Alevis were asked at the same time not to speak publicly about it in order to avoid conflicts and difficulties. The parents' fear that their children might be discriminated or confronted with prejudices was certainly justified. Just like Alevis carried *takiya* to Germany, many Sunnis brought defamation and preconceptions against Alevis.

Murat, a young man who teaches *saz* in an Alevi association in Hamburg, told that he never had personally encountered prejudices in Turkey because he had kept strict *takiya* after he had migrated from his village to Istanbul. But he was confronted with defamation in Hamburg:

> When I was in Germany, in school, for example, there somebody … this is a very blatant prejudice. "Yes, Alevis, you are Alevi? I have heard that Alevis sleep with their brothers and sisters. Is that true?" You think that this cannot be true, but when you are asked such a question it is … as if you hit a wall. I have experienced this in Germany. "You are Alevi too, do you do that too or did you do that? Why do you do this?" And so on. I have experienced this in Germany because in Germany I had the freedom to express myself as Alevi. I could do that and everybody in school knew, he is Alevi. And then they have said: "Alevis, we have heard this and that about Alevis, you are this and that, you are doing this, you are…" and they said time and again, Alevis sleep with their sisters. (…) Of course, this is not human. Once we have watched soccer on TV, in a Turkish café. There was a man who was drinking, he was drunk. He said, "Here are *Kızılbaş*, I know that!" And he said really bad words: "I will do to their mothers this and that." And then we really fought.

The episode in the café had happened in 1993. Similarly Hüsniye, a girl who had just completed school, told about her experiences after she had moved with her family from a mixed part of Hamburg to a neighborhood in which strict Sunnis and Turkish nationalists dominated:

> It was terrible. There we had no neighbors whom we knew, who greeted us. They are all *bozkurt*. At once they looked at us. One could not go out there without wearing a headscarf. When we moved into a ground floor flat, somebody wrote "*Kızılbaş*" on the wall. And once I came home there were an old man and children on the street. The man told the children: "She is one of those!" And then the children started to throw stones at me. They did not stop. I was totally enraged.

In a story narrated by Ayfer Karaköy, a woman of forty-five, the idea entertained by many orthodox Sunnis that Alevis have no belief plays a focal role. Ayfer had recently separated from her husband and was living in a women's shelter. There she met a young woman whom she identified as Sunni because she strictly wore a headscarf. Ayfer told that in order prevent conflict she tried not to get involved with this woman. However, as the other woman was newly arrived and lacked a number of things Ayfer helped her out. After a few days they watched a news report from Turkey about a heavy earthquake at Erzincan. Several thousand people had died in the quake. Erzincan has a large Alevi and Kurdish population. Ayfer narrated the reaction of the Sunni woman:

She did not know that I was Alevi but I knew that she was Sunni. And she said, "They [those who have died in the earthquake] are not Muslims, aren't they?" I asked: "Why that?" And she said: "Yes, they are Alevis and Kurds." I said that Alevis and Kurds are Muslims too! "No!" [she said.] What are they then? I said to myself, Ayfer, be patient, don't explode at once. She said: "They have no belief, no God and no prophet." — "How do you know that?" — "I have studied the Quran." She was a *hoca* [religious teacher]. She said, they aren't Muslims, they are Kurds and Alevis. I asked her: "Did you come to know these people more intimately?" — "No." — "Then, how do you know?" — "I heard it like that." — Then I have asked her: "Are you Muslim?" — "*Elhamdüllilâh* [thank God], I am Muslim!"

Ayfer told her interlocutor that a Muslim should not give importance to hearsay but should rely on knowledge and experience. She continued her narrative:

Then I asked her what a kind of human being she thought I was. She said, "You are a good woman." I said: "You know me since three days, you know me just a little." (…) And she said: "For me, you are a good woman. You are a good Muslim. You are only lacking the headscarf. You are very open." I said to her: "Do we have to cover our heads in order to be good Muslims, or do we have believe with our hearts?" — "Of course with our hearts, but God also demands that we cover our heads." Then I said to her: "I am Kurdish and I am Alevi." She said: "No, that cannot be true!" — "Why?" — "Because you know to much, you know God and the Prophet." I had quoted a few sentences from the Quran. (…) Our conversation lasted for hours. We talked every day. And now she says that Alevis are very good people. But that took a long time!

In a fourth episode Arzu, a young woman, told about her confrontation with Sunni women:

Several times I sat in a park between other women. Some women talked about Alevis. They said: "I have never seen Alevis, I have only heard about them." And one of them said, Alevis are like this and that. I asked her then: "Since how long do you know me?" She said: "Since two years." And I said: "I am Alevi, I come from Sivas, I am a real Alevi." And she said: "No, I thought Alevis are not really human beings." "No," I said, "I am Alevi, I am a human being, I am a woman, I do not keep fast in Ramadan, we have our own time of fasting." We talked like that. They are all ignorant" [she laughed].

I (MS) said: "After that she knew that Alevis are human beings too."

Arzu continued: "She turned crimson. She did not know that. It is strange, that was the first time that I heard that Alevis are not human beings. But after that our friendship became closer. I have talked about Alevis and she listened."

These four episodes contain a number of elements of confrontation between Sunnis and Alevis. Murat's story focuses on the allegation of illicit sexual relations, Hüsniye was even confronted with violence in her new neighborhood, Ayfer was denied Muslimhood, and Arzu learned that Alevis were simply not human beings. The experience of prejudice, defamation, and rejection are important points of reference in Alevi discourse. Two kinds of relations between *takiya* and prejudice emerge from these accounts: According to Murat, he was confronted with prejudice because he did not deny being Alevi. In the stories of Ayfer and Arzu, in contrast, the experience of prejudice served as motivation to break *takiya* and to reveal that they belong to the very group that was defamed as not believing and not human. They practised a strategy of countering prejudice by confronting it with "reality," presenting themselves as a counter example that belied the defamation. All these episodes happened after the Alevi movement started, that is, in a time in which self-confidence and courage to directly confront anti-Alevi discourse had grown. However, the stories show that strategies of dissimulation were not completely erased by the movement. After all, Arzu had not told her later friend for two years that she was Alevi and also Ayfer first intended to keep herself distant from her new acquaintance.

Significantly, Sunnis emerge through such stories as essentialized others of Alevis. In Alevi discourse it is not individual Sunnis, like Sunnis holding particularly strict and narrow views that are represented as rejecting Alevis but Sunnis in general. To the contrary, "tolerant" Sunnis that do not hold prejudice about Alevis are considered the exception. It is said about such "exceptional" Sunnis: He is a Sunni, but he is a democrat. That is, he has other qualities that more or less erase his being Sunni. I will return to the issue of essentializing Sunnis later (see chapter four). In anticipation of the later discussion I want to point out, however, that stories about prejudice and defamation show that in Germany Alevis still define themselves in the first place in contrast with Sunnis and not with those who form the dominant majority in society. This stands in sharp contrast with many other cases of migrant groups who, almost naturally, contrast themselves with the dominant population of the host country. Yet the focal difference for Alevi self-identification is difference from Sunnis, not from Germans.

Political Organizations of Alevis in Germany: The 1970s and 1980s

By discussing migration to Germany, the practice of *takiya* and the experience of defamation in Germany, I have set significant elements of the stage on which the Alevi movement started. In the introductory paragraphs of this chapter I have argued that social movements are built on certain preexisting relations, networks, and experiences that can be utilized as resources and in which the guiding ideas of the movement (pre-)developed. The actors of a new movement have often been committed to other issues before. Tarrow (1998) points out that a movement is not an amorphous collective but is rather constituted by many (and often small) intersecting networks and groups. Such networks do not necessarily develop simply with the movement, but may already provide a fundament upon which a new movement comes into being, bringing preexisting relations, networks, and actors into a new context. The genesis and development of the Alevi movement cannot be understood without reference to preceding networks of the movements' actors. Most of the central actors were committed to various organizations of the left political spectrum. This section presents a short outline of the prehistory of the Alevi movement. Because Hamburg was an important location for the development of the movement and because my fieldwork was predominately located there, the following outline refers to Hamburg, if not stated otherwise.

Alevis did continue *takiya* in Germany also in the sense that they did not organize explicitly as Alevis. In Turkey, all forms of organizations bearing the word "Alevi" in their name or referring to Alevism in their statues were prohibited by associational law. There were no special legal provisions against Alevis in Turkey, but a general prohibition of all kinds of activities that could be understood as promoting particular identities at the expense of the idea of a homogeneous nation embodied in a unitary state. Hence, there were organizations by Alevis in Turkey since the 1960s that however did not pose as Alevi organizations. In Germany, Alevis did not have their first organizational experience in such "organizations by Alevis" but in general political organizations of the left. Two political orientations prevail here. On the one hand there were more moderate, social democrat organizations, and on the other hand more radical leftist groups committed to fundamental opposition against the Turkish state. The most important organization of the first category was the HDF (*Halkçı Devrimci Federasyonu*, Popular Revolutionary Federation), founded in October 1977 in West Berlin as an all-German umbrella organization of a number of Turkish workers associations in cities like Berlin, Hamburg, Stuttgart, and Munich (Özcan 1992, 275–312). The local organization of the HDF in Hamburg was called HDB (*Halkçı Devrimci Birliği*, Populist Revolutionary Union). The HDF was closely related with the CHP (*Cumhuriyet Halk Partisi*, Republican People's Party) in Turkey, the party that had been founded by Mustafa Kemal Atatürk in 1923. Therefore, the HDF supported the government of Bülent Ecevit, who had been the leader of the CHP's left of center reorientation and who served in three terms during the 1970s as prime minister. Generally, the CHP was supported by a strong Alevi faction and Alevis also participated in the HDF. The HDF entertained close relations with the

German SPD (*Sozialdemokratische Partei Deutschlands,* Social Democrat Party of Germany), and a number of HDF members, including Alevis, were at the same time members of the SPD (1992, 281–288).

Because of ideological struggles the radical leftist scene was very much split up. The most important left-extreme organization on the local scene in Hamburg was *Dev Yol* (Revolutionary Path), the organizational history of which is quite complex: It was a follow-up organization of the THKP-C (*Türkiye Halk Kurtuluş Partisi-Cephesi,* Turkey People's Liberation Party-Front), which in turn was a successor of *Dev Genç* (Revolutionary Youth). The THKP-C and Dev Genç were involved in militant actions in Turkey, particularly in militant conflicts with organizations of the extreme right. Dev Yol was founded in the late 1970s. Its sympathizers living in Germany had formed organizations in various cities. These organizations were not formally called "Dev Yol" in Germany but had changing names. The association in Hamburg was originally called "*Gençlik Dernegi*" (Youth Association), then "*Türk-Alman Dostluk Derneği*" (Turkish-German Friendship Association), and lastly "*Türk-Kürt-Alman Dostluk Derneği*" (Turkish-Kurdish-German Friendship Association). However, also the names "Devrimci İşçi" (Revolutionary Worker) and, in German, "*Türkei-Komitee*" (Turkey Committee) were used. For the purpose of convenience, and because the former activists use "Dev Yol" generically in order to refer to these organizations, I also employ the name Dev Yol. Dev Yol was more a network of organizations and activists than a tight, cadre-like structure. Dev Yol in Hamburg and in other German cities grew rapidly after the end of the 1970s due to the large number of Turkish leftists that sought asylum in Germany. In Hamburg, Dev Yol became a kind of first-aid and contact organization for newly arrived refugees, arranging also for shelter and employment. Dev Yol entered into alliances with German political parties like the *Kommunistischer Bund* (Communist Alliance). Although there was no formal structure like an umbrella organization, the local association in Hamburg was for several years a kind of head office of Dev Yol in Germany. Like in most of the leftist organizations of that time, the commitment of activists was extremely strong. Activists tell that after their normal work they met at the premises of the association, discussed for hours politics and strategies, did their publishing work until late in the night, or went through the bars and cafés of the city in order to sell their bulletins. Activities became especially significant after the military coup. There was a short-time occupation of the Turkish Consulate General in Hamburg and a hunger strike that lasted for several weeks. According to members, the proportion of Alevis among the activists of Dev Yol was very high, and Alevis also held important positions in the leadership of the organization.

Originally, Alevism was neither a topic in HDF nor in Dev Yol. There were many Alevi members in both organizations, but they neither positioned as Alevis, nor did they form a kind of Alevi faction. Especially in radical left organizations like Dev Yol, religion in general was anathema and, in the past in Turkey, Alevi activists of the radical left had been on the forefront of erasing Alevi religious practice in the villages. *Dedes*, the religious specialists of Alevism, were denounced as exploiters who lived at the expense of the people. Selected Alevi symbols were used as symbols of leftist resistance, most importantly Pir Sultan Abdal, the seventeenth century Alevi poet-saint of Sivas who defied the orders of the Ottoman governor and was therefore executed. But the appropriation of such symbols did not mean that Alevism as religious tradition or practice was of any importance for the left. However, Alevi members of both HDF and Dev Yol in Hamburg started later to give importance to being Alevi. In the case of HDF, this was a sudden move in consequence of a conflict, whereas in the case of Dev Yol there was a slow, gradual change of attitudes.

The decisive event in the case of the HDF was the "Maraş massacre." In late 1978 the conflict between right and left factions escalated in the southeastern Anatolian city of Maraş, which had a sizeable Alevi population. From 22 through 25 December of that year activists of the ultra-right and nationalist MHP attacked houses and shops of Alevis in Maraş, killing more than one hundred persons and leaving many more wounded. Police and other security forces, which are generally said to lean strongly towards the right, did not intervene (Sinclair-Webb 2003). At that time, Bülent Ecevit was prime minister in Turkey, heading a coalition government of his CHP. The Maraş massacre shocked Alevis. Halis Tosun, one of the Alevi activists of the HDF in Hamburg, called the then chairman of the HDF, Ertekin Özcan, in order to discuss how the HDF should react. Tosun proposed to organize a large demonstration against the massacre in Germany, but he was stopped by the chairman who argued that the HDF could not protest against its own party and government. As a consequence, the HDF remained silent about the massacre. Halis Tosun and like-minded members, however, called for a meeting to discuss the issue. As a consequence of the discussion, forty Alevi members of the HDB, the local association of the HDF in Hamburg, declared their resignation from membership and, together with other sympathizers, formed the *Türk İşçileri Barış Birliği* (Turkish Workers Peace Union) in May 1979, which was practically an organization of Alevis. Halis Tosun became its chairman. Shortly after, the name of the organization was changed to *Yurtseverler Barış Birliği* (Patriots Peace Union, in short *Yurtseverler Birliği*, YB). Although the newly formed organization did not position explicitly as Alevi organization, it was clearly recognized as an organization of Alevis by other leftist associations in Hamburg and caused considerable consternation. Tosun (2002, 34) writes: "These organizations tried to bar our way with the cry 'the Alevis organize themselves!'" They were branded by some groups as "reactionary" and "chauvinist" because they gave up class solidarity for the sake of a particularist stance. The YB of Hamburg contacted like-minded people in other German cities. In Munich there was a similar group of social democrat Alevis called *Amele Birligi* (Workers Union), which had close contacts with the *Türkiye Birlik Partisi* (TBP, Turkey Unity Party), a party founded by Alevis in Turkey in 1966. The chairman of the TBP, Mustafa Timisi, joined a meeting of the various organizations that took place in Frankfurt in June 1979. In this meeting an umbrella organization was established, which was given the name *Yurtseverler Birligi Federasyonu* (YBF, Federation of Patriots Unions) in early 1980. Thirty associations became members of the Federation, with a combined membership of around 4,000 persons (Tosun 2002: 62). Among other things the YBF organized the tour of a theater company called *Kerbela Tiyatrosu* (Kerbela Theater), which presented a drama dealing with the recent massacres of Maraş and Çorum. Further, the YBF raised protest, supported by a German member of parliament, against defamation against Alevis in the German-Turkish dictionary published by Langenscheidt. Here, the German word *Blutschande* (incest) was translated as "fornication with close relatives, *kızılbaşlık.*" The publishing company complied with the demands of the YBF and dropped *kızılbaşlık* as explanation of incest from the future editions of the dictionary.

The local YB association in Hamburg organized cultural events like a "Pir Sultan Night." However, the military coup of 12 September 1980, had its effects also on Turkish associations in Germany. In Turkey, all political organizations were banned and leftist activists were imprisoned. Many migrants in Germany feared that their activities in Germany would be closely monitored from Turkey. As a consequence, membership of the YB rapidly eroded. The association in Hamburg was finally closed in 1984. The Federation was disbanded too.

In Hamburg, the *Yurtseverler Birligi* was a quite short-lived affair. It was, however, an important step in the prehistory of the Alevi movement as it was the first time that Alevis organized themselves and raised their issues. The organization resulted from the protest against a massacre against Alevis in Turkey—and from the demand to recognize Alevis as victims of violence. Other activities like the cultural events or the protest against the dictionary publishers pointed into the same direction. However, although the word "Alevi" was by no means banned in the discourse of the YB, they did not position themselves explicitly and openly as an Alevi organization but preferred to employ a harmless name. Similar activities continued after the dissolution of the association. Especially Halis Tosun remained an important actor, working in a number of different organizational contexts. Together with others he organized the first public Alevi *cem* ritual that took place in 1984. He was also active in the Turkish Parents Union (*Türk Veliler Birligi*), and demanded in a discussion with the Turkish consular general that not only Sunni teachers should be sent for the purpose of teaching Turkish to the migrants' children, because the language lessons also included religious classes that were limited to Sunni teachings only. In 1986 he was among the founders, both Alevis and Sunnis, of the *Türk Sosyal Demokrat Dernegi* (TSDD, Turkish Social Democrat Association). The association organized a guest performance of a theater company from Turkey that performed a play about Pir Sultan Abdal. From 1987 until 1989 Halis Tosun was chairman of the TSDD. In 1988 he organized another *cem*. Although he did not do this in his position as chairman, Sunni members of the organization's managing committee accused him of turning the TSDD into an Alevi organization. Halis Tosun was also a member of the committee of the *Haus für Alle* (House For All), an intercultural meeting place that was part of a network of multicultural centers in Hamburg that formed an important frame for the development of the Alevi movement in the city. Before I turn to this topic, however, I have to return to Dev Yol.

From Politics of Exile to Politics of Migration

Dev Yol never experienced a kind of rupture like the HDF, in which a number of Alevi members resigned and formed their own association. The importance of Dev Yol for the history of the Alevi movement consists in having created a network of (Alevi) activists that later became important actors in the movement, and in having provided training in organizational techniques and strategies of mobilization to these activists.

Dev Yol eroded slowly after the mid-1980s because leftist ideology lost much of its purchase and prospects for revolution in Turkey had become rather bleak. Most of its activists in Turkey had been either imprisoned or gone underground, if they had not taken refuge in other countries. In Hamburg, conflicts with other leftist groups developed. In 1985, a leading member of Dev Yol was shot by an activist of the Kurdish PKK. After some quarrels about the future Dev Yol in Germany, the central office was shifted from Hamburg to Hanover. Dev Yol vanished in Hamburg. There was no direct step from Dev Yol to the Alevi movement. Instead, some of its members who had given up the utopia of revolution turned towards the issue of migration in Germany.

The 1980s were the decade in which the "foreigners problem" gained much currency in Germany. Foreign workers were especially hit by a growing rate of unemployment, but popular slogans were raised that the foreigners were taking the jobs of Germans. The government of Chancellor Helmut Kohl of the Christian Democratic Union (CDU) came to power in 1982, promoted an antiforeigner rhetoric, and started a remigration program that was intended to provide incentives especially for returning Turks. Already in 1981 the "Heidelberg Manifesto" had been published in which fifteen university professors voiced racist ideas. The *Überfremdung* ("foreign infiltration") of Germany was lamented and the right of the German people to preserve its cultural identity demanded (von Dirke 1994). The first cases of racist violence against migrants occurred. In 1985 two young Turks, Mehmet Kaynakçı and Ramzan Avcı, were killed by skinheads in Hamburg. However, one reaction to the growing currency of racism was also the dissemination of multiculturalist and antiracist ideas. Identity and culture became focal ideas on both sides of the political spectrum.

In this context a number of Dev Yol activists abandoned the politics of exile that had been directed at producing political change in Turkey and committed themselves to antiracist and multiculturalist politics in Germany. Former members of Dev Yol, both Sunnis and Alevis, started to publish *Göçmen* (Migrant), a short-lived journal in which issues of migration, multiculturalism, and identity were discussed. Among the members of this group was Turgut Öker, who had earlier been chairman of Dev Yol in Hamburg and who is presently chairman of the Federation of Alevi Communities in Germany (*Almanya Alevi Birlikleri Federasyonu*, AABF), the largest Alevi umbrella association in Germany.

In Hamburg, as in other cities that were mostly governed by the SPD, antiracist and multiculturalist discourse and activities became institutionalized either in municipal institutions, in non-governmental organizations, or a mixture of both. In Hamburg, socalled *Deutsch-Ausländische Begegnungsstätten* (meeting places for Germans and foreigners) were established in districts with high proportions of migrant population. These multicultural centers were run by nongovernmental organizations but financed by the city government. The centers offered consultation for migrants and organized German language courses, but they were also engaged in antiracist activities and in activities intended to preserve the cultural identity of migrants. Among these were various folklore groups, but also campaigns for dual citizenship and for school instruction in the migrants' native languages. The centers also provided a place in which different migrants' groups could meet and carry out their own activities. They offered an institutionalized environment for the discourse on multiculturalism and cultural identity. This discourse touched not only upon identities of migrants in Germany, but also upon questions of identity within the migrants' countries of origin like the Kurdish-Turkish issue in Turkey.

Institutions like these centers were the embodiment of the shift from leftist class politics to politics of culture identity that I discussed in chapter one. They and the people that worked within their context conceptualized Germany as a multicultural country. In many cases, they had earlier been active in leftist organizations. Most of them continued to consider themselves leftists. Also some Alevis now took up commitment in the multicultural centers, and they became the prime actors in starting the Alevi movement in Hamburg. I have mentioned already Halis Tosun, who was engaged in the managing committee of the Haus für Alle, one of the centers, but there were also Turgut Öker, social consultant in the same center; Hüseyin Yavuz, social consultant in another center; and Ismail Kaplan, who worked as coordinator in the department of the city authorities that was responsible for the centers.

In retrospect, Öker criticized that there had been no consciousness for questions of culture in the radical left. He disapproved of Dev Yol for always having accepted a kind of "cultural Sunnism" (in contrast with "religious Sunnism") but not a "cultural Alevism." He told that in the place of Dev Yol sweets were distributed on the occasion of *şeker bayramı*, the holiday marking the end of Ramadan, as it is custom among (Sunni) Turks: "Although in the organization everybody identified himself as atheist and Marxist this was just normal! As a leftist organization we prepared sweets for Ramadan! But it never occurred to us that we could do this also in *Muharrem*, for Alevis." According to him, the discourse on multiculturalism produced a decisive change: "This debate opened my eyes. When we started to talk about multicultural society. I said: We demand that in Germany all religions, languages, nationalities should enjoy equal rights. Alevism is a culture too! That time, this discussion made me think that we too should organize something [as Alevis]."

The Alevi Culture Group

The process of organizing explicitly as Alevis started when Halis Tosun invited some of his friends, listed in table 2.1, to his home on 26 December 1988. He told about this event:

> After we had eaten Ismail Kaplan rose and said: "We thank you very much for the meal but you have invited us, could you tell us the purpose of this invitation?" I said: "Dear friends, we all are Alevis. We have worked in different [political] associations, like me, for example with the social democrats. But what matters now is multicultural society. Now I ask you, what should we say, to which culture do we belong? I tell you, we are in different organizations but we are all Alevis. Our children are here in Germany, in school, the teachers come here from Turkey and again our children learn about Sunni belief. Many Alevis cannot eat at their workplace in Ramadan because there are Sunnis. Many have dissimulated, they could not tell their neighbors: We are Alevis."

The diagnosis was that in a multicultural society Alevis should stop dissimulation, organize openly, and work for the preservation of Alevi identity. Besides multiculturalist discourse in Germany, two contexts of events in Turkey were significant for this shift towards Alevi identity. These were the renewed importance of Sunni Islam in Turkish politics and society, and the escalation of the Kurdish struggle. After the coup, the governing military had sought for a new kind of Turkish national identity that could possibly overcome the rifts of political polarization experienced in the 1970s. The military turned towards religion as a means to enforce national unity and propagated the *Türk Islam Sintezi* (Turkish-Islamic synthesis) (Poulton 1997, 181–6). Islam in this context again meant Sunni Islam only. For Alevis the Turkish-Islamic synthesis implied just another policy of assimilation. One means to enforce the "synthesis" that was especially resented by Alevis was the introduction of mandatory religious (i.e., Sunni) instruction in school. Another one was the state-sponsored construction of Sunni mosques in Alevi villages. In a way, the policy of the military paved the way for later Islamist politics in Turkey. In Germany, Alevis resented that teachers sent by the Turkish state for the purpose of teaching the migrants' children the Turkish language taught religion too—again exclusively Sunni Islam. The policy of Turkish-Islamic synthesis was regarded a way of marginalizing Alevis. The Kurds were a further example of a marginalized group in Turkey. The Kurdish struggle brought this marginalization to the light of day and although none of the early Alevi activists was a sympathizer of the PKK nor opted for a similar militant struggle of Alevis in Turkey, parallels between the situation of Alevis and of Kurds were drawn. Further, a considerable number of Alevis who were Kurds themselves felt directly affected by the Kurdish struggle and its violent repression by the Turkish military. If Kurds struggled for their identity, it was concluded, Alevis should do the same, if by different means. The men who met at Halis Tosun's place decided that Alevis should organize on a nonparty base, and formed the Alevi Kültür Gurubu (Alevi Culture Group). Table 2.1 shows that all men who attended the first meeting of the group had come from a political commitment (with the exception of Ismail Kaplan who only a short time before had moved to Hamburg) and that most of them later occupied significant positions in Alevi organizations, either in the Hamburg Alevi Kültür Merkezi (HAKM, Alevi Culture Center Hamburg) which evolved as a formal organization out of the Alevi Culture Group, or in the AABF. Therefore, the table can also be read as representing the transition of actors from general (non-Alevi) political commitments, mediated by the multicultural centers, to a commitment in the Alevi movement. Especially four of these actors contributed significantly to the rising of the movement by offering links and resources for a growing network: Halis Tosun knew many Alevis in Hamburg and other cities due to his long involvement with the Alevi issue and thus could make many contacts. Ismail Kaplan established contacts with educational institutions like the University of Hamburg. Turgut Öker contributed his skills in motivating and organizing people as well as his remarkable oratorical talent. Hüseyin Yavuz, finally, embodied a continuing link with the

Table 2.1 Founding members of the Alevi Culture Group in Hamburg

Name	Former political alignment	Commitment in the context of the multicultural centres	Subsequent positions in the Alevi movement
Ali Altundağ	TSSD		
Halis Tosun	HDF/HDB, YB, TSSD	Member of managing committee	Chairman, HAKM
Hüseyin Dörtyol	TSDD		
Hüseyin Yavuz	HDB, TSDD	Social consultant	Member of committee, both HAKM and AABF
Ismail Kaplan		Coordinator for multicultural centres at city authorities	Chairman, HAKM, Consultant of AABF for press and education
Musa Şen	YB, TSDD		
Oruç Yağbasan	Dev Yol		Member of committee, both HAKM and AABF
Rıza Cömert	HDB, YB, TSDD		Chairman, HAKM
Turgut Öker	Dev Yol	Social consultant	Chairman, HAKM, chairman and member of committee, AABF

Wir–Zentrum ("We-Center"), one of the multicultural centers, which provided important resources for the Alevis.

The founders of the Alevi Culture Group called for a second, this time public, meeting and invited other Alevis. Thirty to forty people are said to have participated in this second meeting. It took place in the Wir-Zentrum, which to date has remained an important meeting place for Alevis in Hamburg. The group continued to meet there regularly and attracted more and more people. In order to publicize the idea of organizing Alevis, the group invited representatives of Turkish and Kurdish migrants' political organizations to a meeting. The reaction of many of the other organizations was quite reserved due to what was perceived as a particularistic or, in terms of the traditional left, even reactionary position of the Alevis. Further, the group organized a public lecture on Alevism by Fuat Bozkurt, a professor of Turkish studies who at that time taught at the University of Hamburg. Activists of the PKK tried to disturb this lecture because they feared that an organized movement of Alevis might weaken the Kurdish movement.

The group also made contacts with Alevis in Turkey. Arif Sağ, the famous Alevi singer and musician, played an important role in this respect. In 1989 he was a member of parliament for the CHP. Together with Ibrahim Aksoy, another member of parliament, he came to Hamburg in January that year in order to speak and to play *saz* at a function commemorating the victims of Saddam Hussein's poison gas attack on the Kurdish village of Halabja in Iraq. Some members of the Alevi Culture Group met both members of parliament there and invited them to a meeting. After initial reservations Arif Sağ agreed to cooperate with the group and to arrange for contacts with Alevi authors and intellectuals in Turkey.

In May 1989 the group published the statement that subsequently became known as the *Alevi Bildirgesi* (Alevi Declaration). The declaration stated that there were about twenty million Alevis among Turkey's population of (at that time) fifty-five million, i.e., that Alevis did not form a small minority. The declaration referred to the Universal Declaration of Human Rights and to the Turkish constitution of 1982, both of which guarantee the freedom of conscience, opinion and religion. The declaration pointed out that Alevis did not enjoy freedom of religion in Turkey. It demanded the official recognition of Alevism in Turkey as an important step towards democratization of the country. The declaration also dealt with the situation of Alevis in Germany, stating that because of ignorance also in Germany only Sunnis are taken into account, and that Alevis should enlighten both Sunni fellow migrants and the German public about Alevism. It was added that Alevi culture signified a source of (cultural) wealth in the multicultural society of Germany.

The Alevi Culture Week

Most important, however, was the group's plan to hold a weeklong event with concerts, lectures, discussions, and a *cem*. This *Alevi Kültür Haftası* (Alevi Culture Week) was organized together with the department of education of the University of Hamburg and took place in October 1989. In his opening speech for the Alevi Culture Week Ismail Kaplan explained that many Alevis in Turkey dissimulate their belief in order to escape discrimination and defamation. He referred to the mandatory Sunni religious classes in Turkish schools, to the Sunni mosques that were erected in Alevi villages, and to the fact that through the Directorate for Religious Affairs the state funded exclusively Sunni Islam. He called all this "a grave attack on the freedom of religion and conscience of twenty million Alevis." Concerning the situation of Alevis in Germany, he said that Quran courses in mosques and Sunni Imams sent by the Turkish state exert psychological pressure on the Alevi minority:

This pressure has the consequence that many of our Alevi compatriots feel compelled to conceal that they are Alevis because they fear that their relations with [Sunni-Turkish] neighbors would break and that they would be discriminated. We realize that Alevi culture is today endangered in a particular way. This new situation had motivated some of our compatriots that live in Hamburg to form the Alevi Culture Group.

Ismail Kaplan went on to explain that the Alevi Culture Group was open also to non–Alevis and that it is the task of all people to defend the human rights of a minority:

It is our task, irrespective of ethnic or religious affiliation, skin color, or gender, to work for freedom and tolerance and against discrimination and oppression. In this sense the [Alevi] Culture Group does not aim at spreading Alevism; the group simply wants to attain the right that all who want to do that may say, "I am Alevi."

The Alevi Culture Week was a great success. According to the organizers, every discussion was attended by more than five hundred people and many more witnessed the concerts of the week's last day. Not only Alevis from Hamburg came but Alevis from all over Germany. The Alevi Declaration was prominently reprinted in the program and was thus disseminated to a larger public. The Alevi Culture Group had already started to break *takiya*, but with the Alevi Culture Week this move had reached a new dimension: Alevis had gone public. For many of the participants this meant a deeply liberating experience. One of the participants told me that during the week he was visited by a cousin coming from Turkey. He took his cousin directly from the airport to one of the discussions where they sat among hundreds Alevis, discussing Alevism. After the event the cousin told his host: "This was the first time ever that really felt to be an Alevi among Alevis!" A similar experience was told by Murat who, as a youth, had migrated to Hamburg only a few months before the week. In an interview that took place twelve years later he told me what the week had meant to him:

I was new in Germany, only three months. Oh, I have seen "Alevi Culture Week" [on a poster]. It was the first time that I had seen the word [Alevi] written on a piece of paper. *Alevi Kültür Haftası.* I had never before read it! This is no exaggeration, I was shocked! I saw Arif Sag and others who were to come, that was a dream! I had always dreamt to see these people. And then, as Alevis! You go there and you look around and everybody is Alevi, our people! In Istanbul I could not say, "You are Alevi, I am Alevi too." That was a secret matter. It was very strict. And then this, it lasted for five days. I went to every event, also to the concert. I had been in my school for three weeks and I met people who too had tickets [for the concert]. And then I met there many students from my school. I realized, oh, they are Alevis too! That time it started, it really started. (…) We felt very well. I felt like being newborn. (…) I felt free. It was something I cannot

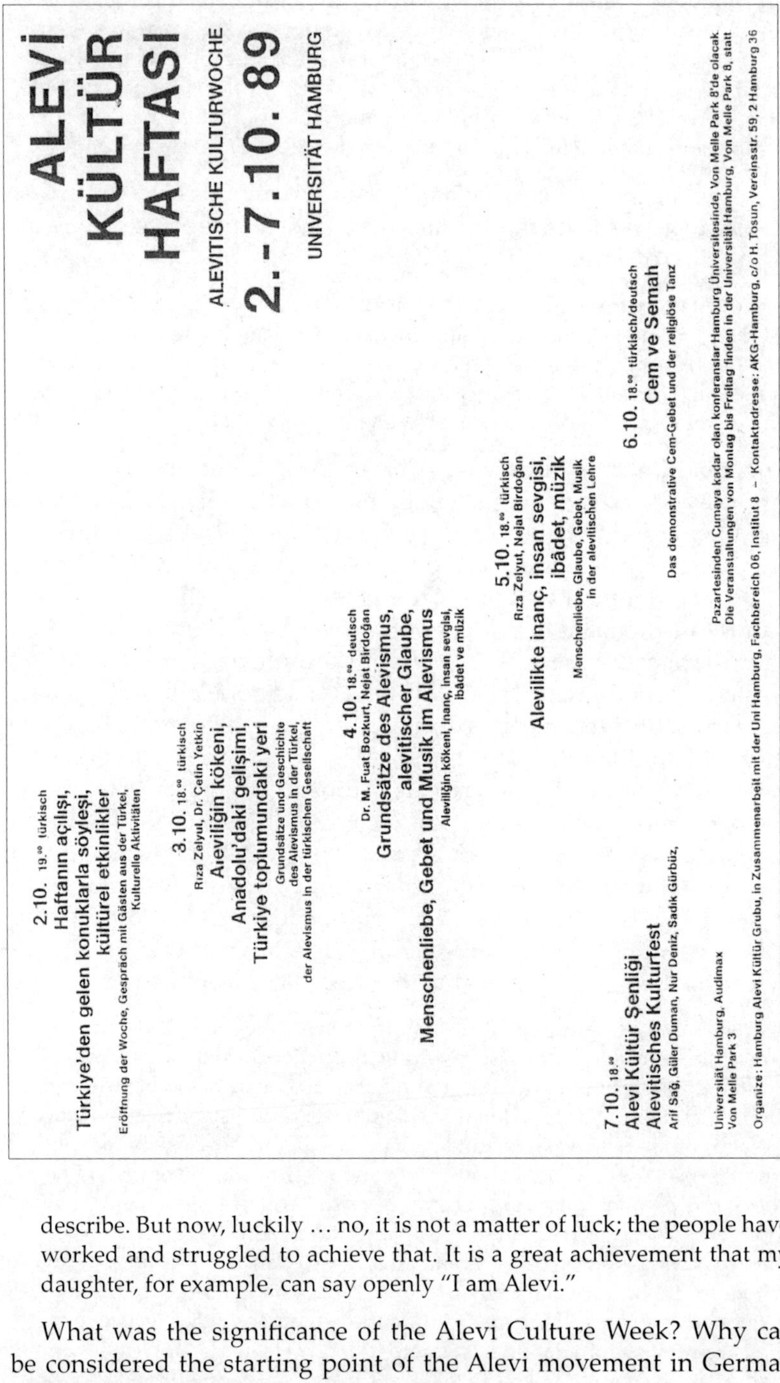

ALEVİ KÜLTÜR HAFTASI

ALEVITISCHE KULTURWOCHE

2. - 7.10. 89

UNIVERSITÄT HAMBURG

2.10. 19.⁰⁰ türkisch
**Haftanın açılışı,
Türkiye'den gelen konuklarla söyleşi,
kültürel etkinlikler**
Eröffnung der Woche, Gespräch mit Gästen aus der Türkei,
Kulturelle Aktivitäten

3.10. 18.⁰⁰ türkisch
Rıza Zelyut, Dr. Çetin Yetkin
**Aeviliğin kökeni,
Anadolu'daki gelişimi,
Türkiye toplumundaki yeri**
Grundsätze und Geschichte
des Alevismus in der Türkei,
der Alevismus in der türkischen Gesellschaft

4.10. 18.⁰⁰ deutsch
Dr. M. Fuat Bozkurt, Nejat Birdoğan
**Grundsätze des Alevismus,
alevitischer Glaube,
Menschenliebe, Gebet und Musik im Alevismus**
Aleviliğin kökeni, İnanç, insan sevgisi,
ibâdet ve müzik

5.10. 18.⁰⁰ türkisch
Rıza Zelyut, Nejat Birdoğan
**Alevilikte inanç, insan sevgisi,
ibâdet, müzik**
Menschenliebe, Glaube, Gebet, Musik
in der alevitischen Lehre

6.10. 18.⁰⁰ türkisch/deutsch
Cem ve Semah
Das demonstrative Cem-Gebet und der religiöse Tanz

7.10. 18.⁰⁰
**Alevi Kültür Şenliği
Alevitisches Kulturfest**
Arif Sağ, Güler Duman, Nur Deniz, Sadık Gürbüz,

Universität Hamburg, Audimax
Von Melle Park 3

Pazartesinden Cumaya kadar olan konferanslar Hamburg Üniversitesinde, Von Melle Park 8'de olacak.
Die Veranstaltungen von Montag bis Freitag finden in der Universität Hamburg, Von Melle Park 8, statt

Organize: Hamburg Alevi Kültür Grubu, in Zusammenarbeit mit der Uni Hamburg, Fachbereich 06, Institut 8 – Kontaktadresse: AKG-Hamburg, c/o H. Tosun, Vereinsstr. 59, 2 Hamburg 36

Figure 2.2 Program of the Alevi Culture Week

describe. But now, luckily … no, it is not a matter of luck; the people have worked and struggled to achieve that. It is a great achievement that my daughter, for example, can say openly "I am Alevi."

What was the significance of the Alevi Culture Week? Why can it be considered the starting point of the Alevi movement in Germany? Neither was the Alevi Culture Group the first instance of efforts to organize Alevis, nor was the Alevi Culture Week the first public event organized by Alevis in Germany. Besides the Yurtseverler Birliği, Alevis had founded a number of Hacı Bektaş Veli associations (Hacı Bektaş Veli Dernekleri) in various cities, named after the important Alevi saint. Also demands for the recognition of Alevis had been voiced before by the Yurtseverler Birliği. The demand of the Yurtseverler—to recognize Alevis as the victims of the Maraş massacre—was however much more parochial and did not imply a violation of the terms of debate (or nondebate) on Alevism. After all, in spite of all Alevism-related activities that were undertaken, the Yurtseverler organized and positioned themselves as patriots and not as Alevis. The Alevi Culture Week, however, radically redefined the terms of the debate. The Alevi activists in Hamburg assumed a position to speak in the name of Alevis in general, in the name of an Alevi community that they said numbered twenty million individuals in Turkey and between 350,000 and 400,000 in Germany. They thereby discontinued *takiya* and created the Alevi movement as a public, visible, and collective actor. They demanded recognition and equal rights for this community on par with the Sunni community. We can consider the Alevi Culture Week as a critical event in the sense of Veena Das, that is, as an event after which new modes of action came into being and traditional categories were redefined (Das 1995, 5f). These new modes of action and newly defined categories were taken up by a rapidly growing number of Alevis. Therefore I speak of a social movement that resulted from this critical event. The discourse of community and the demand for recognition were extremely appealing, almost contagious, among Alevis. The consequence of the Alevi Culture Week was that Alevis started to form new local associations all over Germany and also in other European countries, which later formed a large umbrella organization. Also associations that had been founded earlier in the name of Hacı Bektaş Veli and not in the name of the Alevi community were now renamed as Alevi associations and joined in the demand for recognition. I will discuss this spread of organization in more detail in the next chapter. Here I want to ask why all that happened in the late 1980s—why, for example, a similarly strong movement was not created by the Yurtseverler Birliği.

Sidney Tarrow (1996) emphasizes the importance of political opportunity structures in the birth of social movements, opportunities that enable the articulation, mobilization, and organization of contention. Şahin's study of the Alevi movement uses the concept of opportunity structures as a fundamental organizing concept (2001). Yet under the rubric of social and political opportunity structures, she simply summarizes a history of preconditions of the Alevi movement in Turkey from early Kemalism via political polarization in the 1970s to the growth of Islamism. The issues she refers to are significant. The growth of political Islam in the years following the military coup made issues of religion more contentious in Turkey and provoked reaction. This, however, does not explain why Alevis responded as Alevis to the debate. We could well envision a contention of Islamism from a strict secularist perspective that demands the exclusion of religion in general from the public political sphere without relating to alternative religious traditions. Şahin (2001, 177) emphasizes the role of Alevi organizations in Germany as precursors and models for the Alevi movement in Turkey. In order to understand the history of the Alevi movement in general, not only in Germany, it has to be asked why an event like the Alevi Culture Week could happen in Hamburg in the late 1980s. Most conditions like discrimination and occasional violence against Alevis or the need to dissimulate had existed for many decades or even centuries, and also the breakup of tradition was not a recent affair. New, however, were the ideas of identity and culture, here emerging in the German debate on immigration and multiculturalism, that enabled a new articulation of concerns about Alevism. In this new discursive context reference to Alevism and Alevi identity was not "reactionary" — as it would have been in the context of the left before — but simply up to date. My argument is that the discursive environment of multiculturalism, embodied in institutions like the multicultural centers in Hamburg, was the decisive new element in the ensemble of opportunity structures that enabled the rise of the Alevi movement.

In social movement theory, interpretive schemes and ideas that are employed to motivate collective action, are called "frames." The concept relates back to Erving Goffman's idea that social situations have to be framed within particular interpretive schemes that give specific meaning to the situations and enable appropriate action (Goffman 1974). Relating to social movements, McAdam et al. (1996, 6) define framing as "the conscious strategic efforts by groups of people to fashion shared understandings of the world and of themselves that legitimate and motivate collective action." The idea of Alevi identity can be regarded as the principal frame of the Alevi movement. For the movement, identity was the focal idea through which claims could be conceived and articulated in novel ways. Yet the specific idea of Alevi identity should be distinguished from the general idea of identity because the latter enabled conceiving the former. The general idea of identity can be conceptualized as a "master frame" (Snow and Benford 1992) that does not relate specifically to one movement, but which is a more fundamental interpretive paradigm that enables the emergence of many different movements. Such a general master frame can be understood as being part of the cognitive and discursive opportunity structure of a particular movement.

From the beginning, identity was understood by the Alevi actors as a political idea — identity as a right — which implied the claim for public recognition. Therefore, the movement was not content with attempts to renew the Alevi traditions and to cater for spiritual needs of Alevis themselves by organizing ritual life but, as was prominently expressed in the Alevi Declaration, demanded recognition of Alevis and Alevism, in Germany as well as in Turkey.

Movements are generally framed in terms of collective action. Considering the history of the Alevi movement, however, it has to be emphasized that collective action depended on the initiative of identifiable individual actors who contributed their respective skills, experiences, and, most importantly, networks. They, in the first place, recognized new opportunities, were able to make use of them, and started to mobilize others.

❖ 3

Organizing Alevis

Movement, Organizations, Actors

I have introduced social movements as relatively uninstitutionalized collectivities engaged in contentious issues. I also emphasized, however, that social movements strive for one form of institutionalization or another in order to sustain themselves and to create a reliable and durable basis for their struggle. The efforts towards institutionalization in the Alevi movement resulted in the creation of new collective actors, the Alevi associations. These associations became the principal protagonists of the Alevi politics of recognition. Yet to speak about collective actors and collective action is potentially misleading. The emphasis on collective action must not result in obscuring individual action and individual actors. Alberto Melucci (1989) warns against treating collective phenomena as "unified empirical data," as reified "things" or "subjects." The relationship between individual and collective action has to be explicated. Melucci emphasizes the plurality of perspectives, meanings, and relationships in collective action (ibid., 25) and calls for investigating how collective action is produced by individual actors. The crucial feature for him is the construction of a shared *collective identity* that serves to orient individual action and helps to obtain solidarity within a social movement. Yet what if a collective identity is not only a vehicle for the constitution of a social movement, but its very purpose? Will a collective identity that constitutes the purpose of a movement provide at the same time an identity that is able to establish shared orientation and solidarity?

The Alevi example shows that this is not necessarily the case. In chapter one we have seen that identities are constituted through difference and the intersection of multiple identifications. Identities are never finally fixed but always fluid and changing. Making an identity the purpose of a social movement that struggles for the recognition of this identity inevitably results in essentializing this identity. The movement has to say what this identity is and how it should be recognized. The movement needs to develop a shared understanding of identity. But it may be that this process of negotiating a common understanding, in which the different members of the movement participate from their various positions, reveals only the plurality of perspectives and meanings of this identity. As a consequence, instead of producing a shared understanding, the process of negotiating an identity may result in dragging differences out into the open. If this is the case, the identity in question is quite unsuited as a vehicle for providing a shared orientation within the movement. It may rather result in a tendency for fission. In the Alevi case the negotiation of understandings of Alevism has brought to light many differences, which have resulted in endless debates about the question whether Alevism is part of Islam or not, or whether it has to be understood in a broad sense as "culture" or in a more narrow sense as "religion," to mention only two contentious issues. Together with other intersecting identities, in the first place ethnic and political identities, this has resulted in a strong tendency towards fission. As a consequence, the purportedly common purpose of the movement constitutes at the same time the most important threat to its unity.

Further, individual actors' purposes, orientations, and interests are not exhausted by collective ones. Collective purposes and forms of action are negotiated by individuals. The institutionalization of a movement in the form of particular organizations implies the adoption of certain structures, procedures, and visions and thereby inevitably results in an unequal distribution of power among the individual members of the movement. Conflicts about visions, structures, and the distribution of power and resources is almost unavoidable even if all ostensibly subordinate their own purposes to a presumed common aim. Collective actors like associations, once established, do not act themselves but through individuals that act within them. Accordingly, collective actors—like the Alevi associations—can be conceptualized as environments and frameworks for individual action. The concept of opportunity structures that Sidney Tarrow (1988, 1998) emphasizes for the analysis of social movements can also be extended onto individual action within collective actors. Collective actors provide certain opportunities for individuals who strive for particular positions or for putting through their personal vision of Alevism. In view of such opportunities, individuals pursue their own purposes *within* collective actors. The structure of collective actors can enable or obstruct certain avenues for individual actors and may provide specific arenas of conflict and competition.

Part of the actions of individuals within collective actors is structured by practices that are collectively and explicitly agreed upon. In the case of democratic associations, such practices are most importantly the formal procedures laid down in the by-laws like rules for conventions and for electing individuals to positions of leadership within the association. Practices that take place within the environment of collective actors are, however, never exhausted by such formal and agreed practices. Formal practices provide a kind of structure with considerable interstitial spaces, which are filled by other kinds of practices like gossiping or building networks of alliances within and across the movement. Although such "interstitial practices" are neither agreed upon nor openly negotiated like formal procedures, they may become very significant for a particular movement and its form of organization, especially in relation with conflicts. Interstitial practices may even subvert formal practices. Accordingly, the ethnography of "collective actors" like associations cannot be content with simply detailing the formal structure of an association because the association is not exhausted by its formal structure.

In the present chapter I analyze the efforts towards organizing and institutionalizing the Alevi movement in conjunction with the conflicts that accompanied that endeavor. The emphasis in this chapter will be on the evolution of the formal structure of the new collective actors, resulting in a differentiated "landscape of Alevism" in Germany, because they set the stage for the many conflicts within the movement and its politics of recognition. A case from Hamburg will exemplify the interstitial practices that take place within this formal structure.

Organizing the Alevi movement in Germany took place at two levels. At the local level the movement became embodied in local Alevi associations. Presently, there are more than a hundred such associations. At the trans-local, federal level Alevis are represented by umbrella organizations, most importantly the Federation of Alevi Communities in Germany (AABF). Alevi organizations exist today in many German cities and towns, with the exception of eastern Germany. Besides the local organizations that are combined in the AABF, there are also independent organizations as well as others that combined to a much smaller federation of Kurdish Alevis. Further, there are about eighty Alevi local organizations in other European countries[1] that have their own national federations. All these national Alevi umbrella organizations together have recently formed the European Confederation of Alevi Communities (Avrupa Alevi Birlikleri Konfederasyonu, AABK). Both the local and the translocal level will be detailed in this chapter. For the local level, the focus will be Hamburg again. In a certain respect both levels of organization sprang from the Alevi Culture Week in Hamburg, because this event was not only an incentive to form similar initiatives in other cities but also provided initial contacts between Alevis of different places.

Before I turn towards the development of Alevi organizations in Germany on the local and federal levels, however, I have to deal with two violent events that occurred in Turkey in the 1990s. Both events are categorized by Alevis as "massacres" (*katliam*) and had a decisive impact

---

[1] These countries are The Netherlands, Belgium, France, Switzerland, Austria, and Denmark, with a number of local Alevi communities and a federation each. In addition, there is one Alevi organization each in England, Sweden, and Norway. Outside of Europe Alevis have also organized in Australia.

on the further course of the Alevi movement. It is safe to assume that without the events at Sivas and Gazi the Alevi movement would have acquired much less strength. Especially Sivas has become a constant point of reference for Alevis. In order to emphasize the importance of Sivas and Gazi I interrupt the temporal order of the development of the Alevi movement and narrate these events before resuming the chronology of the movement.

Sivas and Gazi Mahallesi: New Massacres

In the first days of July 1993 the Pir Sultan Abdal Culture Association (*Pir Sultan Abdal Kültür Derneği*, PSAKD, founded in 1988) celebrated its fourth "Pir Sultan Abdal Festival" in the city of Sivas. Sivas is situated close to the village of Banaz where Pir Sultan Abdal, a famous Alevi poet and rebel, had lived in the sixteenth century, a time of social and religious upheaval. Pir Sultan belonged to an *ocak*, a holy lineage of Alevis. His original name was Haydar. Pir, Sultan, and Abdal are honorific titles that were given to dervishes. The story goes that Pir Sultan sent one of his students, Hızır, to the Sultan's court, saying: "Go and study further, you will become a *paşa* and even a *vezir*. But then you will return here in order to hang me!" Hızır indeed became a *paşa* and was ordered by the Sultan to subdue revolts in the area of Sivas. In the course of events Hızır Paşa also captured Pir Sultan Abdal, who was a leader of the insurgent people. In his fortress, Hızır Paşa said to Pir Sultan Abdal: "I will spare your life if you compose three poems that do not contain the word '*şah*' ('king,' meaning Ali)." Yet Pir Sultan composed three poems, each of which contained the word *şah*. As a consequence, Pir Sultan Abdal was hanged. A legend says that there is no tomb of the Pir because his dead body disappeared from the gallows. Pir Sultan is highly revered by Alevis.[2]

The first two days of the festival of 1993 took place in the city of Sivas, while the second two days were planned to take place in Banaz. Beside Alevi intellectuals and musicians also writer Aziz Nesin had been invited to deliver a speech. Nesin was not only a well-known author but also a critical intellectual committed to the struggle for civic freedom in Turkey. Although he was not an Alevi himself he was closely related with the Alevi movement. In 1999 he had signed the Alevi Declaration that was published in Turkey. On the invitation of the Culture Group, Aziz Nesin had also come to Hamburg. As a commitment to the freedom of expression he had published the translation of a section of Salman Rushdie's controversial *Satanic Verses* in the paper *Aydınlık* in May 1993. In two Islamist pamphlets distributed in Sivas before the festival,

---

[2] On Pir Sultan Abdal see Jansky (1964); Mélikoff et al. (1998).

Nesin was heavily attacked and a war against the "friends of Satan" was called for.[3] Nesin spoke on the first day of the festival, i.e., on 1 July. On the next day, Friday, 2 July, a crowd of radical Sunnis gathered after the Friday prayer in front of the Sivas culture center where the festival took place, shouting Islamist slogans. A statue of Pir Sultan Abdal was torn down by the demonstrators. After that the crowd moved to the Hotel Madımak, in which the writers and musicians participating in the festival were accommodated. The Islamist demonstrators shouted aggressive slogans and hurled stones at the building. Those who stayed in the hotel barricaded themselves. The situation escalated and the hotel was set on fire. The crowd blocked the way for the fire brigade as well as for the people inside the hotel to escape. The fire brigades reached the hotel only by 8:30 P.M. At that time, many people inside had died. Others, including Aziz Nesin and Lütfi Kaleli, an important Alevi writer, suffered injuries but could be saved. As some persons had been injured critically, the death toll reached thirty-six by the next day.

This Sivas massacre was a shock for the whole secularist section of Turkish society. The demonstrators had also shouted slogans against the secular republic and destroyed a bust of Atatürk. In 1993, the Sivas municipality was headed by a mayor of the Islamist Refah Partisi. The mayor spoke to the crowd, but instead of dispersing the demonstrators he encouraged them by saying "*gazanız mübarek olsun*" (Eral 1995, 238), an expression meaning "well done" but saying literally "your holy war may be blessed." Security forces on the spot were few and contended themselves with watching the events. The intervention of police and gendarmerie was also blocked by a dispute of competence between the mayor and the governor of the province Sivas. Whereas the governor urged that additional forces be called, the mayor asserted that everything was under control (Gölbaşı 1997, 30). As a result, the demonstrators were able to rage for hours in front of the hotel. Only after it had been set ablaze did security forces seriously start to disperse the crowd.

According to the opinion of many Alevis, the Sivas massacre showed that Islamism had become a real danger for Alevis and for the Turkish republic, and that for their protection Alevis could not trust in the state. The need for self-organization was seen as the most important lesson of the incident at Sivas. Indeed, a multiplication of Alevi organizations and a renewed impetus that Alevis should struggle for recognition were significant consequences of the massacre. An important element of that struggle was directed at the public perception of the Sivas massacre itself. In public discourse and in the press the event was framed in terms

---

[3] The two pamphlets have subsequently been published in Kaleli, n.d., 16–18 and Gölbaşi (1997, 14–16). My account of the incidents relies mainly on these two books in which also the text of Nesin's speech can be found.

of a struggle between Islamism and secularism, with Aziz Nesin being the person who inflamed the rage of Islamists. Alevis hardly played a role in this representation. Alevi organizations have spent much effort in the subsequent years to spread the message that an *Alevi* festival had been attacked, that almost all victims were Alevis, and that Alevis were targeted as secularists by Islamists.

Almost two years after Sivas, Alevis suffered another violent incident, this time in the Gazi district of Istanbul where mainly eastern Anatolian Alevi migrants live. On the evening of 12 March 1995, unidentified gunmen captured a taxi by killing the driver, drove past a number of coffee houses and fired into the crowds sitting there, killing another person and wounding about fifteen people. Although a police station was situated only a few hundred meters from the coffee house, the police did not take any immediate action. The news of the assassinations spread rapidly and hundreds of people immediately took to the streets. Many people in Gazi suspected that the assailants had been helped by the police in one way or another. A few days earlier people had protested in front of the Gazi police station because a young man had died in police custody after having been tortured. The atmosphere in the district was explosive. When the crowd learned that the assailants had escaped, people started to riot. Stones were hurled at shops, cars were overturned and burned, and makeshift barricades erected. Now police forces gathered rapidly and blocked the street. For several hours the demonstrators faced the police, throwing stones and shouting slogans. Neither side moved until, in the first hours of 13 March, events quickly escalated: Demonstrators climbed up an armored carrier and, after a scuffle, policemen shot into the crowd. Two more people were killed and others wounded. Turmoil ensued. Police forces hunted demonstrators through the streets. The district was blocked, the army took control, and a curfew was issued. In spite of the curfew the burial of the victims on 15 March resulted in another demonstration of several thousand people. Alevis also started to demonstrate in Ümraniye, a district in the Anatolian part of Istanbul. There too police forces shot into the crowd and killed four people. Unrest continued for days. According to official reports fifteen Alevi demonstrators were killed by police bullets (Dural 1995 and Marcus 1996).

For Alevis the events in Gazi signified that they had become the victims of a massacre again. According to this perception, the state and its forces again had sided with those who attacked Alevis. The sentiment of alienation of Alevis within the Turkish republic was reinforced. The impact of the events on the Alevi movement was equally strong in Turkey and in Germany. Sivas provided the motivation for many young Alevis to declare themselves openly as Alevis. They did so especially by wearing a necklace with a small double-tipped golden sword, signifying *Zülfikar*, the sword of the Imam Ali. Some even had a *Zülfikar* tattooed on their arms. Among young people, this ornament became the most popular and visible symbol of Alevism.

In Germany, Sivas was especially important for the Alevi Federation, because the Federation was reorganized as a direct consequence of the massacre and was joined by many more associations. In Hamburg, many more Alevis became members of the associations. Sivas and Gazi had a decisive effect on the mobilization of Alevis. Sivas became a focus for the construction of a collective Alevi memory, as I will detail in chapter five. However, the story of organized Alevism in Hamburg had started already before Sivas.

Alevi Local Associations in Hamburg

The Alevi Culture Group was not registered under German associational law and had no formal organs. The group continued to meet after the Alevi Culture Week and the idea to establish a formal organization emerged. For that purpose another, smaller festival was organized which lasted three days in June 1990. The festival's first day saw a panel discussion with writer Aziz Nesin and Alevi intellectuals. The second day had a concert and on the third day the public inaugural meeting of the Alevi Culture Center Hamburg (*Hamburg Alevi Kültür Merkezi*, HAKM) took place. Because the meeting was held publicly, not only sympathizers of the idea of Alevi associations came but also Kurdish activists of the PKK who perceived the establishment of an Alevi organization as a threat to the Kurdish movement. The organizers of the meeting were accused of acting according to orders of the Turkish state that wanted split Kurds by attracting Kurdish Alevis to the issue of Alevism instead of the Kurdish struggle. The PKK activists demanded that a commitment to the Kurdish struggle was to be included in the by-laws of the HAKM. Their demand was rejected, but many Alevis who attended the meeting, both Kurds and non-Kurds, were afraid of getting involved in Kurdish politics. As a consequence, more than half of the people present left the meeting and instead of more than two hundred, the HAKM had only ninety-three founding members. The Kurdish issue remained a contentious point throughout the following years.

Ismail Kaplan was elected the first chairman of the HAKM. No one else from the core section of the Alevi Culture Group became a member of the managing committee because, as they explained, they wanted to involve more and new people. This strategy engendered the next grave conflict, because the original core group and the new committee—except Ismail Kaplan—did not agree on the purposes of the HAKM. Ismail Kaplan was the one who had made contacts with various German institutions, most importantly the University of Hamburg. Already the Alevi Culture Week had formally been a cooperation of the Alevi Culture

Group with the university's faculty of education. Together with his early companions Kaplan was interested in enlightening the German public about Alevism. He therefore organized a series of lectures about Alevism together with the Department of Education that took place at the university in spring 1991. The other members of the managing committee, however, did not give the same importance to such efforts. They saw the first purpose of the organization as serving the religious needs of Alevis. They also disagreed with some of the speakers that had been invited for the lectures. For instance, writer Nejat Birdoğan had been invited, who had written a book on Alevism at the request of the Alevi Culture Group (1990). In this work Birdoğan advanced the thesis that Alevism has close historical relations with central Asian shamanism.[4] This view was emphatically rejected by Ismail Aslandoğan, a *dede* who was member of the HAKM's committee. He, among others, was not ready to organize a lecture in the name of the HAKM with Birdoğan as speaker. Further, he did not accept another *dede,* Ahmet Kömürcü, who was invited to speak about *cem.* Aslandoğan would have preferred to speak himself on this topic. He espoused a version of Alevism as a form of Islam, accepting the Quran as holy scripture, that was rejected by other members. They preferred to see Alevism as a tradition entirely separate from Islam. As a consequence of such differences the committee accused the chairman Ismail Kaplan of having acted high-handedly without the consent of the committee, and expelled him from membership not only in the managing board but also in the HAKM. Because this action of the committee violated the procedures prescribed in the by-laws, the exclusion was not valid. An extraordinary general meeting was held in May 1991 in which the old members of the Alevi Culture Group succeeded in forming a new managing committee. Now, Halis Tosun became chairman and Turgut Öker secretary. Except Ismail Kaplan who became a member of the committee, none of the members of the first committee was elected to a position. A few weeks later thirty-three persons under the leadership of the first committee left the HAKM and founded their own association called "Hamburg Union of Anatolian Alevis" (*Hamburg Anadolu Alevi Kültür Birliği,* HAAK BIR).

Thus, within a year after the foundation of the HAKM the organization split and only sixty-five members were left with the HAKM. The splitting of the HAKM was quite paradigmatic for the efforts to organize Alevis in Germany. In Hamburg competition between the HAKM and HAAK BIR determined the development of the local Alevi movement in the subsequent years. The strict rivalry hampered mobilization. Compared with the initial excitement that had become visible in the Alevi Culture Week, both associations grew quite slowly in membership and experienced a boost only after the Sivas and Gazi events.

---

[4] On the idea of shamanistic roots of Alevism see also Mélikoff 1998.

Originally, both associations resided in rented locations. The HAKM had a small place in a building shared with other migrant organizations, and continued to utilize premises of the *Wir-Zentrum*, which was situated just next door. Because this situation was considered as quite inconvenient, the HAKM undertook efforts in 1996 to acquire a large building where not only the ongoing activities of the association could find a place but also economic enterprises like a shop, a hairdresser, a travel agency, and social services like a kindergarten. In spite of intense efforts, which also comprised the organization of a second "Alevi Culture Week" for the purpose of winning more support, the plans could not be carried out. The building that the HAKM had intended to buy turned out to be much too expensive. Yet, this effort to get a more suitable place again sparked competition with HAAK BIR. Quickly HAAK BIR developed similar if smaller plans and, in contrast with the HAKM, succeeded in acquiring a former company building in an industrial area. Formally, this building was not bought by HAAK BIR but by a cooperative society formed by some members of the association. The acquisition engendered great financial strain and brought the cooperative society and the association several times to the brink of bankruptcy. HAAK BIR and also the cooperative society were dominated for almost a decade by a single person: Mehmet Zülküf Kılıç. He had been the secretary of the first committee of the HAKM, he led the split-away faction to the establishment of HAAK BIR, and he remained the chairman of this organization from 1991 through 1999. He was frequently criticized for dominating the association in a quite possessive manner, and as a consequence some members left HAAK BIR in order to join the HAKM. Under his leadership a rapprochement between HAAK BIR and HAKM was impossible.

The separation of HAKM and HAAK BIR was not the only splitting of Alevi organizations in Hamburg. HAAK BIR itself suffered the splitting of a faction under the leadership of the *dede* Ismail Aslandoğan, who had been among the original members of the association. According to Aslandoğan himself, he had been promised a more religiously oriented policy in HAAK BIR, but he was not satisfied. He left together with some adherents and, in 1995, formed a third Alevi association in Hamburg, called Hamburg Alevi Community (*Hamburg Alevi Cemaatı*, HAC). Except for several times organizing *cem*, this association undertook no further activities and was practically defunct after a few years.

In order to complete the picture of organized Alevism in Hamburg, five more associations have to be mentioned. The first of these is the *Hamburg ve Çevresi Alevi Kültür Evi* (Alevi Culture House in Hamburg and surroundings, HAK EVI), founded in 1995. HAK EVI differs from all other associations in being an exclusively *Kurdish* Alevi association. It was accused by others of sympathizing with the PKK. The next is a students' organization called Students' Canlar Union (*Öğrenci Can-*

lar Birliği, ÖCB), which was established in 1996 as a consequence of Sivas and Gazi. After Gazi, an Alevi medical student wrote an article in a students' journal about both massacres. In this article he accused functionaries of the Refah party, the Turkish Islamist party that in 1993 controlled the municipality of Sivas, of being responsible for the massacre. This article roused the protest of some Turkish Sunni students. They issued flyers in which the author of the article was attacked and defamed. These flyers and some additional anonymous letters motivated Alevi students to establish their own organization. As a token that they did not intend to exclude non-Alevi students, they did not call themselves explicitly "Alevi." The word *can* (plural: *canlar*) in the name of the association means "soul," "life," but also "beloved friend." The word is very often used among Alevis to refer to themselves. In a way, *canlar* can be understood as just a synonym for Alevis, but for outsiders this understanding is not immediately obvious. ÖCB was thus the only Alevi association in Hamburg that preferred to use an equivocal name instead of presenting itself as unequivocally Alevi.

The other two associations were founded by members or sympathizers of the HAKM living in smaller towns with a considerable Alevi population, Geesthacht and Wedel. Both towns immediately adjoin the city of Hamburg.[5] The rationale in establishing these associations was to offer Alevis in these areas a more convenient place to meet. A second reason for founding the association in Wedel was a new Sunni mosque belonging to the Süleymancılar movement. Members of the mosque tried to get also Alevi children into their Quran courses. Yet no conflict with other Alevi associations was involved in the establishment of associations in the two towns. Both cooperate closely with the HAKM and a number of members of Wedel and Geesthacht continued also their membership in the HAKM. Because of these close relationships I count the two associations among the Alevi associations in Hamburg, although strictly speaking they do not belong to the city.

Also the last Alevi association in the city, the Harburg Alevi Culture Union (*Harburg Alevi Kültür Birliği,* HAKB), was established in 1997 with the intention to create a place for Alevis in a particular district of Hamburg. Yet in contrast with the associations in Wedel and Geesthacht, a different vision of Alevism was also significant. The association in Harburg entertained a certain sympathy for CEM Vakfı, an Alevi foundation in Turkey that is considered as being too close to the Turkish state by the other Alevi associations. The association was joined by

---

[5] The full names of these associations are *Geesthacht ve Çevresi Alevi Kültür Derneği* (Alevi Culture Association in Geesthacht and surroundings, GAKD) and *Wedel ve Çevresi Alevi Kültür Birliği* (Alevi Culture Union in Wedel and surroundings, WAKB). Wedel borders on Hamburg in the west and Geesthacht in the east. Both towns are situated in Schleswig-Holstein.

some former members of the HAKM who considered this organization as "too Kurdish."

Altogether, then, eight Alevi associations were established in Hamburg. For various reasons three of these, ÖCB, HAK EVI, and HAC, have hardly been active in recent years. ÖCB suffered from a lack of committed students, HAK EVI was affected by a loss of a place where its activities could be held as well as by the de-escalation of the Kurdish issue, and the HAC depended exclusively on the activities of Ismail Aslandoğan, who became aged and ill and therefore stopped to commit himself to the association. The other five associations continue their activities. Since the year 2000 there have been efforts to establish a closer relationship among the Alevi associations in Hamburg, for instance by holding more or less regular coordination meetings.

Contested Chairmanship in the HAKM

After the establishment of the HAKM, its chairman changed every year. The very first managing committee of the association had produced the conflict that resulted in the split and the establishment of HAAK BIR. Contention within the HAKM did not stop after the establishment of HAAK BIR. A serious conflict occurred on the occasion of the election of a new committee in 1995. I learned about it only years later through a number of different, at times contradicting shreds of memory that conveyed less events or "facts" than rumors and accusations.

The basic story is quickly told: In February 1995 a new committee of the HAKM had to be elected. Two persons stood for the position of the chairman: Necati Turan and Hasan Kılavuz. Necati Turan scored eighty-one votes, Hasan Kılavuz only sixty-nine. Accordingly, Necati Turan became chairman. The supporters of Hasan Kılavuz, however, did not accept the result but started to campaign for a new election and collected signatures among the members in order to convene an extraordinary general meeting. Why was the election so contested that the subsequent campaign was started? My purpose in discussing this incident is not to sort out what "really" had happened then, but to show what kind of arguments and allegations were significant in the course of events.

A number of facts about the candidates are undisputed: Necati Turan came from Pülümür in the province of Tunceli (Dersim). He was ethnically a Zaza-speaking Kurd, had studied in Turkey and Switzerland and came to Hamburg only a few months before the election. Necati Turan was affiliated with the *İşçi Partisi* (Worker's Party), a leftist party in Turkey. Hasan Kılavuz was a son of a *dede*-family, again from Tunceli, but from a different district. He was ethnically a Kurmanci-speaking Kurd. He had been living in Hamburg for almost two decades. For many years he had been a member and also chairman of KOMKAR, a nonmilitant Kurdish exile association. He had also been committed to the Alevi Culture Group and was among the original members of the HAKM. When I first heard about the elections and the ensuing conflict in an interview with Halis Tosun, I asked my interlocutor what the point of the conflict was. He answered: "I can't tell that. There was no real point, just as in the case with Ismail Kaplan [i.e., the conflict in the first committee of the HAKM]. One could say Necati Turan belonged to the İşçi Partisi. The others supported another party. But that had nothing to do with the HAKM. They made a mistake."

Necati Turan was proposed as candidate by other members of Pülümür origin, like Rıza Cömert and Halis Tosun. Rıza Cömert had been chairman in the year before. He told that he suggested Necati because due to insufficient knowledge of German, he himself had experienced problems in managing the affairs of the associations "We needed a well–educated person, and Necati had studied, he was a teacher. But the young people did not want to have a teacher as chairman!"

Zeynep Yılmaz, a relative of Necati Turan, told that he was well known among the people from Pülümür in Hamburg because his father had held an important office in the administration of schools. Zeynep knew that Hasan Kılavuz was to run for chairmanship too, and warned Turan against standing for this office because Hasan Kılavuz had many supporters. Initially, Turan accepted this advice but then, she told, some of Hasan Kılavuz's supporters started to spread all kinds of accusations against Necati Turan. After that he was no longer ready to abandon his candidature but decided to run for the office. According to Zeynep, Turan got his votes especially from the "Turkish block" of the HAKM, that is, from the non-Kurdish members. She told that a member of the previous committee had told the ethnically Turkish members of the HAKM that Turan was going to commit the association to Kurdish politics and the Kurdish members that he was against the matter of the Kurds. Yet, it was well known that Turan was related with the İşçi Partisi, she added, and that this party was of leftist and strict Kemalist orientation and therefore had no business with the Kurdish issue.

Halil Akdemir, another member of the HAKM, told about the election:

> Necati was favored by the Dersimli [i.e., the people from Dersim/Tunceli] because he was educated. Both candidates were asked to introduce themselves in the general assembly. Necati let Hasan go first because he was older. Hasan introduced himself just speaking normally, as is his nature. At that time he was not considered a *dede*. Then Necati got his turn. He boasted about his academic achievements. I did not like that but many people were impressed. Furthermore, some of his supporters had told before the assembly that Hasan was a Kurd and a sympathizer of the PKK.

Turan was Kurd too, but that was of no importance, because, Halil said, the dissemination of rumors was not a matter of logics. Also the charge that Hasan Kılavuz was a sympathizer of the PKK was quite implausible, because his commitment with KOMKAR was well known and because there had been severe conflicts between KOMKAR and the PKK in Germany. "But," Halil continued, "many people are influenced by such rumors, they do not think! After the elections another man explained me that he had been told that Hasan was Kurd. So what, I replied, aren't you Kurdish too?"

According to several members, the first action that Necati Turan took after having become chairman was to subscribe to *Aydınlık*, the journal of the İşçi Partisi, in the name of the HAKM. He also wanted to organize a discussion with Doğu Perinçek, the chairman of the party, but that plan could not be realized. These members were of the opinion that Necati Turan wanted to become chairman in order to turn the association into a group of supporters of the İşçi Partisi. This party is criticized by many of the former leftists who allege that the party collaborated with the Turkish police and intelligence agencies. Names and whereabouts of activists of other leftist parties had been published in the 1970s in *Aydınlık* and as a consequence of this denunciation many leftists of competing parties were imprisoned.

Halil Akdemir told that after the election of Necati Turan the supporters of Hasan Kılavuz began to address Hasan as *dede*: "Ahmet started this in order to annoy Necati. The others followed. And Necati indeed became very angry whenever somebody referred to 'Hasan *dede*.' He always insisted: 'Hasan is not a *dede*!' In the beginning also Hasan Kılavuz himself rejected being addressed as *dede* but after a time this form of address became common usage."[6]

Deniz Demir, who held an office in the committee together with Necati Turan, explained that the committee was accused of doing nothing for the association: "Already one and a half month after the election we were asked to step down although everybody knew that in such a short time nothing can be done. We were threatened, I was called a fascist and supporter of the PKK!"According to Deniz, the problem was not the İşçi Partisi but the upcoming elections of the managing committee of the Alevi Federation: "Turgut Öker wanted to run for the committee and needed the votes of the HAKM. He was afraid that he was not getting sufficient support if the HAKM was headed by Necati Turan!" Zeynep added that after the election the supporters of Hasan Kılavuz continued their campaign against Turan and collected signatures for an extraordinary general assembly and new elections. She also told that another member of the committee had been threatened and therefore wanted to resign.

---

[6] On *dede*s and Hasan Kılavuz as *dede* see chapter seven.

As a consequence of the dispute, the activities of the HAKM came to a standstill. Looking back, several of the opponents of Necati Turan told that they succeeded in holding an extraordinary assembly after a few months and in voting him out of office. But this is not true: the next elections were held exactly a year after the previous elections in February 1997, as was prescribed by the by-laws. Necati Turan did not run again but Hasan Kılavuz did. His rival candidate was one of Necati Turan's supporters. This time Hasan Kılavuz scored 117 votes, whereas his rival got only twenty. Hasan Kılavuz became chairman and the HAKM resumed its normal activities.

In this conflict about the person of a chairman a multitude of identifications of the involved actors were referred to: Actors were identified as Kurds or as non-Kurds, also specifically as Zaza-Kurds or as people originating from a particular part of a province, as *dede,* as supporters of the PKK or the İşçi Partisi, or as fascists. Most significant were political identifications as supporters of the PKK (or simply as Kurds because a Kurd was considered a potential PKK sympathizer) and of the İşçi Partisi. No matter whether the involved accusations were correct or not and whether the dispute was indeed about party affiliation, the conflict reveals two things: First, political affiliation did matter in an Alevi association. Political orientation was an important component of a person's identity and it apparently structured relations of alliance and contention. Second, what I have called "interstitial practices" play an important role in conflicts. Although the conflict was about a formal issue, namely the question who should be the chairman of the association, which was to be decided by formal elections, it was attempted to influence the result of the formal procedure (both before and after) through other practices: the spreading of rumors, allegations, accusations, and threats. Apparently, the plausibility of such rumors and accusations was of little importance, because for both of the antagonists the accusation of supporting the PKK obviously made no sense. What mattered was simply to spin a web of rumors and allegations for the purpose of trapping the targeted persons. Issues about Alevism did not play a role in the conflict, apart from the (in this context) minor question of who should be called *dede.* Similar conflicts of competition between persons aspiring for an office were quite frequent in the Alevi associations, not only at the local level. In the context of such contention rumors and allegations invariably played an important role.

My short history of Alevi associations in Hamburg shows that conflicts are a characteristic feature of the development of organized Alevism in the city. Different lines of contention have been mentioned that resulted in conflicts between associations as well as within them: a divergence of visions of Alevism in general and of ideas about the purpose of the associations in particular, the Kurdish issue, and support of particular political parties. As a consequence of these conflicts the Alevi movement in Hamburg was not institutionalized in the form of one singular organization but differentiated into a multiplicity of bodies. This condition also holds for other cities like Berlin, Cologne, or Duisburg. In Hamburg the events of the inaugural congress of the HAKM and the subsequent splitting of HAKM and HAAK BIR meant a severe blow to the mobilization of Alevis in formal organizations. Following the dispute with the PKK sympathizers, much fewer Alevis joined the HAKM than had been expected after the euphoria of the Alevi Culture Week. The splitting of HAKM and HAAK BIR did not make the mobilization of new members for both associations easier. Mostly young Alevis flocked to the associations because they wanted to learn to play *saz* and dance *semah*, whereas many older persons preferred to stay away. After Sivas and Gazi, however, the associations became much more popular. Towards the end of the decade mobilization was on the decline again, and especially the HAKM suffered a considerable loss in membership and a decline in activities. This decline was also a consequence of internal conflicts like the one about chairmanship in the association.

Activities of Alevi Organizations

With certain variations, all the associations have similar activities. Most important are the courses offered to young people. They also constitute the most important avenue for recruiting new members. All associations offer courses for playing *saz*, the Turkish longneck lute. The *saz* has become one of the most central symbols of Alevism. The instrument, which is also called *bağlama*, is associated with poet-saints like Pir Sultan Abdal and *ozans* (minstrels, folk singers) in general (Reinhard and Oliveira Pinto 1989). In the oral tradition of Alevism, songs accompanied by the *saz* have been a very important medium in order to spread the teachings of Alevism. The instrument is also called *telli kuran*, Quran with strings, among Alevis. The instrument and particular sacred hymns play an important role in Alevi ritual. The revival of Alevism was also a revival of Alevi music in which musicians like Arif Sağ, Mahzuni Şerif, or Musa Eroğlu, all of which play the *bağlama*, emerged as the heroes especially of young Alevis. In many cases, young people identify Alevi culture with Alevi music. In addition, there are also courses for folk dance and *semah*, the ritual dance that like music is central to Alevi ritual. *Semah* courses are much less frequent than folk dance courses because teachers for *semah* are lacking. In the last years most of the associations in Hamburg could not offer *semah* classes. These courses are the most regular activities of the associations. They take place on a weekly basis, mostly on the weekends.

Other activities are less frequent, because they require greater organizational efforts. Among these are culture festivals, commemorative ceremonies, *muhabbet* nights, and ritual events like *cem*. Cultural festivals are essentially concerts in which a number of musicians of both general and local fame play consecutively, interspersed with speeches by Alevi functionaries or intellectuals. Also performances of *semah* and recitals of poetry are frequently included. Commemorative ceremonies, which will be discussed later, take place in early summer, around the anniversary of the Sivas massacre. *Muhabbet* nights again involve music and speeches but also a meal. *Muhabbet* means "love," "affection," or "friendship." Among Alevis it refers to a meeting of friends in which they drink *rakı*, dine and sing together, and entertain themselves with edifying discourses. In Alevi village settings in Turkey *muhabbet* is a quite ritualized event (Shankland 2003, 142). *Muhabbet* as organized by associations in Germany is not formalized. It is intended as an occasion to socialize and express friendly relations. *Cem* is the central communal ritual of Alevism and will be discussed in depth in chapter six. Another ritual event is *aşure,* the day in *Muharrem,* the month of mourning, on which the Imam Hüseyin was murdered in the year 680 near Kerbela by the followers of the Caliph Yezit. Alevis prepare a sweet soup of twelve different ingredients that is distributed on this day. The number twelve refers to the twelve Imams, all of whom suffered martyrdom except the last Imam Mahdi who disappeared in order to return at the end of times. Therefore, *aşure* commemorates not only Hüseyin and his suffering in the desert, but all Imams. In the Alevi tradition the preparation and distribution of *aşure* soup is a family event, and many families continue to prepare *aşure* also in diaspora. Besides, however, the associations have taken over this custom and organize events in which *aşure* is distributed. *Aşure* at an Alevi association again includes singing songs accompanied by the *saz*, one or two speeches, and a prayer offered by a *dede*. The events described so far are organized once a year by most of the associations. *Aşure* and the ceremony for remembering Sivas are fixed in the calendar. As it is bound to the Islamic lunar calendar, *aşure* moves slowly through the Gregorian solar calendar, being held approximately ten days earlier each year. *Cem* is organized most frequently either during *Muharrem* or on the occasion of *Hızır,* a three-day period of fasting commemorating the mythical saint Hızır who is revered as the one who helps human beings in their hardships. But *cem* may also be organized independent of such calendrical points of reference. Culture festivals and *muhabbet* nights are not fixed to certain dates.

A final type of event brings in the gender aspect: The associations also organize events that target women specifically. Such events are held on international Women's Day (8 March) and/or on Mother's Day (first Sunday in May). These events normally comprise music and speeches, and are considered as significant because they are seen as exemplifying that women have equal rights in Alevism. More specifically, however, such events reveal that the structure and practice of Alevi associations is clearly gendered. There are special events for women because in general the associations have a strong male bias. Although two associations in Hamburg (HAAK BIR and HAK EVI) have been led for some time by women and although it is generally attempted to have at least one woman on the managing board of an association, the vast majority of chairmen are simply that, men, and also most seats in the managing committees are occupied by men. Female members of the committees are regarded as representatives of women while male members simply represent Alevis. Men dominate the membership of the associations. Further, the artists that perform at the culture festivals are predominately male and the leaders of ritual, the *dedes*, are exclusively men.

My short description of events shows that all these events employ common elements that make up their syntax. None of these events can be held without music, i.e., songs sung to the saz, and speeches. The different types of events can be distinguished by the characteristic shaping of these elements and by specific additional elements as presented in table 3.1. In addition, there are meetings of the membership of the association. A general assembly is held at least once a year. Every year or every other year, the managing committee of the association is elected in a general assembly. There may be further meetings to discuss specific problems of the association. None of the elements of the other events play a role in such membership meetings, except speeches. But speeches here are generally shorter, specifically focused on issues of the respective association, and they are followed by a discussion. Another type of events is panel discussions on topics related to Alevism. Topics may be formulated quite broadly, such as "Alevism yesterday, today and tomorrow."[7] Different speakers are invited to share their views in quite lengthy discourses, which are followed by questions and comments of members of the audience.

The activities discussed so far are organized for an Alevi target group but not only for an association's own members. Most events, even the membership meetings, are attended not only by the formal members of the respective association. Some events, especially the cultural festivals, draw large crowds of sometimes up to 1,500 or even 2,000 people. Among these are also non-Alevis. Such an audience is, however, composed almost entirely of people of Turkish origin. The language of the events is generally Turkish. Native Germans or other migrants hardly attend these events. Further, among the Turkish migrants the audience is limited to people of secularist or even leftist orientation. Among the audience of a culture festival there are almost never Turkish women who wear headscarves and who can thereby be identified as "orthodox" Sunnis. The large crowds that are attracted by a culture festival cannot be hosted in the premises of any of the Alevi associations. At

---

[7] This was the title of a panel discussion organized by the HAKM in 2001.

Table 3.1 Types of events organised by Alevi associations

Type of event	music/saz	speeches	meal	other elements
culture festival	yes	yes, on general issues	no	*semah*, poetry (optional)
commemoration	yes	yes, focusing on Sivas	no	exhibition of portraits of victims
muhabbet	yes	yes, on general issues	yes	
aşure	yes	yes, on religious topics	yes, *aşure*	
cem	yes, religious hymns (*deyiş*)	yes, religious discourses of *dede*	yes, *lokma*	liturgical elements, including *semah*
Women's day, Mother's day	yes	yes, speeches by women on gender-issues	optional (snack)	

present two of the associations, HAAK BIR and HAKB, are able to accommodate one hundred fifty to two hundred persons and can therefore organize events of a certain size in their own places. In all other cases, halls have to be rented for the respective events.

Besides organizing such events, the Alevi associations are also committed to activities that address the German public. The aim of these activities is to achieve recognition by the German public, in the sense that Germans shall learn that there are Alevis among the migrants from Turkey and what the specific characteristics of Alevism are. Such activities are, however, much less frequent and, generally, of a more limited scale. We have seen already that right after its establishment the HAKM had organized public seminars on Alevism in the German language. The HAKM continued to be the most active association in this respect. However, instead of holding seminars for a general public, it has concentrated on activities within the framework of interdenominational dialogue. The association participates in two interdenominational roundtables, one specifically dedicated to the issue of religious classes in public schools, the other to religious issues in general. Other associations take part in occasional multicultural activities. A remnant of the old days of leftist commitments is that many Alevi associations participate annually in the Labor Day demonstrations.

In all their activities, the Alevi associations maintained a strict distance from the Turkish state and its institutions. The associations were never involved in events organized by the Turkish Consular General. The Consular General or other representatives were never invited to a panel discussion. This distance and opposition towards the Turkish state is explained by the state's discriminatory policy towards Alevis. It stems, however, also from the experiences of the former leftists with the Turkish state especially after the military coup.

The Federation of Alevi Communities

In the late 1980s Alevis had started to organize in other German cities. In places like Cologne, Dortmund, and Mainz associations were established in the name of the Alevi saint Hacı Bektaş Veli. Some representatives of these associations, for instance Derviş Tur of the association in Mainz, contacted the Alevi Culture Group in Hamburg and attended the Alevi Culture Week. It became obvious, however, that these associations had an orientation that differed considerably from the purposes of the activists in Hamburg. The founders of these associations did not have a background in the leftist movement and they did not assume a position of opposition towards the Turkish state. Their purpose was less to struggle for public recognition of Alevism—accordingly they did not call their associations explicitly *Alevi*—but they were more interested in catering for the spiritual needs of their local Alevi community. As a consequence of such differences no regular working relationship with the Alevi Culture Group and its successor, the HAKM, ensued. On the other hand, associations that shared the orientation of the group in Hamburg were established in cities like Hanover, Lübeck, Mannheim and again in Cologne. In Berlin, the Yurtseverler Birliği was reactivated and renamed as the Culture Center of Anatolian Alevis (*Anadolu Alevileri Kültür Merkezi*, AAKM) in December 1990. These associations called themselves "Alevi Culture Centers." Thus two factions of Alevi associations were established. Close contacts developed among the associations belonging to either of the factions, but not between them. From the perspective of the Hacı Bektaş Veli associations the Alevi Culture Centers were strongholds of Marxism and atheism, whereas the Alevi Culture Centers tended to regard the others as almost fanatic Alevis that isolated themselves instead of opening up. The Alevi Culture Centers saw themselves as entertaining a broader vision of Alevism as "culture" (hence the name, Alevi *Culture* Centers) whereas the Hacı Bektaş Veli associations viewed Alevism more narrowly as "religion."

In October 1990 eleven associations of the Hacı Bektaş Veli faction, among them also a group from Austria, met near Frankfurt in order to form an umbrella organization that was called *Alevi Cemaatları Federasyonu* (ACF, Federation of Alevi Communities), but was quickly renamed as *Alevi Birlikleri Federasyonu* (ABF, again Federation of Alevi Communities). Derviş Tur, a *dede* who had also been among the founders of the association in Mainz, was elected as the first chairman of the federation. The Alevi Culture Centers had not been invited to the inaugural meeting and did not become members of the Federation. Activities of the ABF were quite limited. However, nine of the Alevi Culture Centers too discussed the option of forming a federation. In spring 1992 there was a meeting of the ABF with representatives of the Alevi Culture Centers for the purpose of discussing a joint form of organization. The Alevi Culture Centers were invited to become members of the ABF but rejected this option. According to Turgut Öker who participated as representative of the HAKM, the Alevi Culture Centers were not ready to simply subordinate themselves to the existing umbrella organization. They insisted on establishing a new organization with a new name. Another meeting of the Alevi Culture Centers and the ABF was called for to take place in Mainz on 3 July 1993—which happened to be just the day after the massacre in Sivas. Turgut Öker told about that meeting:

> We did not know anything about Sivas. I was driving by car towards Mainz together with a friend. When we arrived we saw that all the people were crying. We asked what had happened and the people told us about the massacre that had happened on the evening before. All the Culture Centers and the ABF were present. We have discussed a lot but nobody wanted to do anything. I criticized this attitude strongly and said: "This is impossible, how can we remain quietly on our chairs in this place and cry simply?"

Turgut Öker and his companions suggested to organize a public demonstration against the Sivas massacre. The committee of the ABF agreed. Because the members of the committee, in contrast with the former leftists activists, had no experience in organizing demonstrations, the representatives of the Alevi Culture Centers were asked to carry out this task. They decided to hold the demonstration in Cologne. Turgut Öker took a week off from his job—he was still employed in one of the multicultural centers in Hamburg—and started to organize the demonstration that was to take place on 7 July 1993. Announcements were published and sent to all associations. According to the organizers, 3,000 people were expected to join in the demonstration. But this expectation was proved wrong: about 60,000 came. The demonstration became a completely unexpected success and proved that the Sivas massacre was another critical event in the development of the Alevi movement. The demonstration was joined by Alevis from all over Germany and neighboring countries. Many of those who were roused by Sivas became members of the existing associations or formed new ones. Within a year after Sivas, more than a hundred Alevi associations were established anew in Germany and also in the Netherlands, Austria, Belgium, France, and Switzerland.

Although neither Turgut Öker nor the HAKM that he represented were members of the ABF, the success of the Sivas demonstration turned him into a leading person in the Alevi Federation. The Alevi Culture Centers decided to join the ABF and the committee of the federation decided to entrust the organization to the "young people" of the Culture Centers. In October 1993 a general meeting elected a new committee with Ali Rıza Gülçiçek, an Alevi social democrat who had been among the founders of the Alevi Culture Center in Cologne, as chairman and Turgut Öker as secretary. The task of organizing Alevis at the federal level was again supported by the multicultural *Wir-Zentrum* in Hamburg, which secured public funds in order to employ Turgut Öker for this purpose for one year. The ABF moved its seat from Mainz to Cologne. In the end of 1993 forty-one local Alevi associations were members of the Federation. The number rose towards one hundred until the end of 1994. Because there were now also associations from Austria, France, Switzerland, and England among the members of the ABF, its name was changed into *Avrupa Alevi Birlikleri Federasyonu* (European Federation of Alevi Communities, AABF) in October 1994. In 1998 again the name was changed to *Almanya Alevi Birlikleri Federasyonu* (German Federation of Alevi Communities): the non–German Alevi local associations left the AABF to form their own national federations. Later, in 2002, all the Alevi federations of European countries formed together the *Avrupa Alevi Birlikleri Konfederasyonu* (European Confederation of Alevi Communities, AABK).

Being an umbrella organization, only local Alevi associations can join the AABF. Every local association that has joined the federation is represented in the general meeting of the AABF. The number of representatives a local association is allowed to send to the meetings depends on the size of its membership: For every fifty members an association sends one delegate. The federation is financed by fees paid by the local association, the amount of which again depends on the number of members. The general meeting elects the members of the managing committee of the federation. The members of the committee then elect certain positions like the chairman, secretary, and treasurer among themselves. In the beginning, the committee was elected anew every year, but a recent modification of the by-laws extended the period of office to three years. Beside the general meeting and the committee, there are other organs and sections: a women's branch, a youth branch, a *dede*'s council and regional representatives who form a link between the committee and the local associations. In the beginning, the women's and the youth branches were legally sections of the AABF, but became separate organizations under German associational law in recent years. This step was undertaken because the youth wing could benefit from certain youth schemes in Germany only as an independent organization.

Activities and Conflicts

After Sivas, the Alevi federation became a political organization whose politics in the first instance opposed the discriminating policy of the Turkish state towards Alevis. Two points were regarded as most important in this respect. The first was the mandatory religious instruction in Turkish schools, which was limited to the Sunni version of Islam. The second was the fact that the Directorate for Religious Affairs (*Diyanet İşleri Başkanlığı*, DİB) is engaged in the institutionalization and promotion of exclusively Sunni Islam by establishing mosques and religious schools, although its considerable funds are derived from the taxes paid by all Turkish citizens, including the Alevis. The critique against the policy of the Turkish state was regularly expressed in all events organized by the AABF. In order to establish and disseminate a new discourse on Alevism, the Federation established its own journal, called *Alevilerin Sesi* (Voice of Alevis). *Alevilerin Sesi* has been published in Turkish since February 1994. Because Alevi issues were not represented impartially in the Turkish media, the AABF and its local organizations collected funds to establish a radio network called *Radyo Mozaik* in Istanbul. Due to financial problems, however, this enterprise had to be abandoned after a short time.

The AABF made contacts with Alevi associations in Turkey. Also in Turkey, Alevi associations have multiplied since the beginning of the 1990s. In a meeting held in Istanbul in November 1994, the *Alevi-Bektaşi Temsilciler Meclisi* (ABTM, Council of Alevi-Bektashi Representatives) was founded as a transnational umbrella association. Besides Ali Rıza Gülçiçek and Turgut Öker of the AABF, also representatives of a Dutch Alevi association participated. Ali Rıza Gülçiçek was elected chairman of the ABTM. This organization was a short-lived affair. Among other things it broke apart because some members of its committee who represented the Alevi journal *Cem* sided with İzzettin Doğan, an Alevi professor of international law who espoused a nonoppositional Alevism in Turkey (Kaleli 2000, 90). İzzettin Doğan founded another organization, *CEM Vakfı*, in 1995. The journal *Cem* became the official journal of this foundation. CEM Vakfı and İzzettin Doğan were criticized by almost all other associations for having entered into too close relations with the Turkish state.[8] But without a formal transnational umbrella organization the AABF continued its relationships with the other Alevi associations in Turkey and later new attempts for a transnational umbrella organizations were made.

In Germany, the AABF, like the local associations, organized Alevi culture festivals that attracted large crowds of people. Three such festivals took place as open–air events in soccer stadiums, beginning in

---

[8] On İzzettin Doğan see Engin 1998.

Heilbronn in 1995. The second and third festivals were held in the stadium of Cologne. These two festivals were each attended by about thirty thousand people, but produced a huge financial loss for the Federation. In 1995 the AABF acquired a large building in an industrial area of Cologne. Besides an office building of considerable size, this place contained an even larger hall. It was intended to rebuild the place into a multipurpose center for Alevis. The Federation considered the acquisition of the building an important step, which symbolized that it had become an established body. However, the process of rebuilding turned out to be much more expensive than had been foreseen, and again produced huge financial liabilities that very much impeded the Federation's work in the following years.

In order to meet the liabilities, the Federation required its member associations time and again to contribute large sums. Because this constituted a heavy burden for the local associations, relations between the AABF and some of its member organizations became strained. The Federation's policy of spending much money on big projects was criticized and in some instances even charges of corruption were voiced. Some associations left the AABF because they could not bear the required contributions. There were also other conflicts: In October 1995 the general meeting of the AABF excluded the Hacı Bektaş Veli Association in Cologne and three other associations from membership, because they had organized a discussion with İzzettin Doğan without inviting the chairman of the Federation for the same occasion.

Ali Rıza Gülçiçek remained chairman of the AABF until January 1997. After that he was replaced by Ali Kılıç, a journalist who had served as general secretary of the AABF after replacing Turgut Öker in this office in 1996. Turgut Öker became again general secretary in 1997 in the committee headed by Ali Kılıç. In January 1999, Kılıç resigned as chairman because he ran for a seat in Parliament in the general elections in Turkey in April of that year. Turgut Öker took over as chairman.

These changes in office and generally the work of the committees AABF were by no means free of conflicts. There was a lot of personal rivalry, and political ambitions also played an important role. Because it was felt that the Alevi case was not properly represented by the political parties in the Turkish parliament, members of the ABTM together with the Alevi businessman Ali Haydar Veziroğlu took efforts in 1995 to establish an Alevi party. The AABF was involved in this endeavor and Ali Rıza Gülçiçek was elected in autumn 1995 to the committee of the *Demokratik Barış Hareketi* (DBH, Democratic Peace Movement), which was established as precursor of a full-fledged Alevi party. The expenses of these efforts were born completely by Ali Haydar Veziroğlu, who accordingly dominated the process of forming a party. In spring 1996 the DBH was turned into the *Barış Partisi* (Peace Party). Ali Rıza Gülçiçek was not able to obtain the position he had hoped for in that party and left in order to side with the CHP, with which he had established close relations already before.[9] Instead, Ali Kılıç became involved with the Barış Partisi and ran the April 1999 elections on a ticket of this party. However, the elections turned out to be disastrous for the Barış Partisi as it was not able to score more than 80,000 votes in the whole of Turkey (Kaleli 2000, 95). The party was quickly closed down.

The failure of the Barış Partisi contributed to a reorientation of the AABF's activities. Although a commitment for Alevis in Germany and Europe had always been among the aims of the organization, there had been few practical efforts in this respect. Already in late 1998, after the election of a new committee of the AABF, the slogan was raised that the Alevis living in Europe should turn their face towards Europe instead of looking back to Turkey. In a contribution to *Alevilerin Sesi* Necati Şahin, who had been elected a member of the committee, criticized that Alevis, although living in Europe, had their hearts and minds still in the villages of Anatolia. He demanded: "We should put our faces, hearts, minds and bodies together. Our bodies, our presence is in Europe" (Şahin 1998, 10). An important step towards this reorientation was the establishment of a new position at the AABF that was responsible for all kinds of projects in Germany. In 1999, this position was filled by Ismail Kaplan. Among the projects started since the was an information campaign about the new German citizenship law, a project for the professional training of migrant youths, a project for interdenominational dialogue, and efforts towards Alevi religious instruction in German schools. Quite successfully, the AABF established close contacts with German authorities at all levels, including the federal government in Berlin. In this context a relief project for the victims of the disastrous earthquake that shook western Turkey in August 1999 was significant. This project was started by the AABF together with Turkish Alevi associations in the city of Izmit. The AABF was able to secure funds from the German Ministry of Foreign Affairs for this project. Another indication of the new orientation of the AABF is the fact that the *Alevilerin Sesi* has been published bilingually with sections in Turkish and German since 2001.[10]

In November 2000 a new committee of the AABF was elected and the new orientation towards Germany and Europe was expressed by the lineup of this committee. Turgut Öker became chairman again, but besides him there were some younger professionals who were well versed in dealing with German authorities. Although they were by no means indifferent about the situation of Alevis in Turkey and continued

---

[9] Ali Rıza Gülçiçek ran the elections of October 2002 successfully on a CHP ticket and became member of Parliament.

[10] The Turkish section, however, still outweighs the German section in quantitative terms.

to lobby for recognition in Turkey, they saw their commitment as being firmly based in Germany. Especially two persons have to be mentioned here: Seydi Koparan, a young lawyer who became vice chairman, and Hasan Öğütcü, a consultant who was elected general secretary.

The reorientation of the AABF did not mean that conflicts subsided. To the contrary, one of the most serious conflicts surfaced on the occasion of the elections of the new committee in late 2000 (see chapter four). A faction of "oppositional" local associations attempted to get another committee elected. One bone of contention was the question how to handle the federation's large debts. Subsequently all kinds of accusations against the committee and especially the chairman Turgut Öker were leveled in the pages of *Hürriyet*, the largest–selling Turkish language daily in Germany. This press campaign will be analyzed in chapter eight. A split of the Federation seemed imminent, yet did not materialize. All internal conflicts and debates notwithstanding, the AABF is the largest and most important Alevi umbrella organization in Germany.

Other Associations at the Federal Level in Germany

Besides the AABF, other Alevi bodies were active for some time at the federal level in Germany, but none of them achieved a similar importance. These were the Kurdish Alevi Federation, a German representation of CEM Vakfı, and the Alevi Academy. The work of the academy was mainly restricted to publishing bulletins and booklets. In February 2003, however, the academy has started courses for the education of Alevi *dedes*. The Kurdish Alevi Federation has been closely related with the position of the PKK. Since the mid–1990s, a number of explicitly Kurdish-Alevi associations were founded in different German towns. In 1996 the *Federasyona Elewiyen Kurdistanî* (FEK, Federation of Kurdistan Alevis)[11] was established as an umbrella organization. Also the Kurdish Federation has its seat in Cologne. The Kurdish Alevi Federation assumes that about fifty percent of Alevis are Kurds and that therefore the Kurdish and the Alevi issues are inextricably intertwined. It was felt, however, that other Alevi associations, notably the AABF, were not sufficiently committed to the Kurdish case and that Kurdish Alevis were not represented by the AABF. Some associations that left the AABF joined the Kurdish Alevi Federation instead. The Kurdish Alevi Federation organized about twenty local associations, including HAK EVI in Hamburg. The establishment of Kurdish Alevi associations did not mean that other Alevi associations were devoid of Kurdish members. Those Kurds who are members of the other associations,

---

[11] In Turkish the association is most frequently referred to as *Kurdistan Aleviler Birliği* (Kurdistan Alevi Union).

however, generally reject the politics of the PKK. The Kurdish Alevi Federation also issued a journal called *Zülfikar*.[12] There were some un-successful endeavors since end of the 1990s to establish working rela-tionships between the AABF and the Kurdish Alevi Federation. Like the PKK, the Kurdish Alevi Federation also underwent a considerable weakening and a subsequent reorganization after Abdullah Öcalan was captured. In February 2002 the Kurdish Alevi Federation was renamed *Demokratik Alevi Federasyonu* (Democratic Alevi Federation) and the name of its journal was changed from *Zülfikar* to *Semah*.

CEM Vakfı is the only Turkish Alevi organization that has a direct representation in Germany. In 1997, CEM Vakfı opened an office in Es-sen. CEM Vakfı was represented there by Halis Özkan, who belonged to a *dede* family and was a relative of Izzettin Doğan. CEM Vakfı in Germany is not an umbrella organization, yet a number of local Alevi associations are closely related with the office in Essen. There is almost no cooperation between AABF and CEM Vakfı in Germany, just as co-operation between CEM Vakfı and other Alevi associations in Turkey is almost nonexistent. It is alleged that CEM Vakfı received considerable financial aid from the Turkish government. One of the most significant differences is that CEM Vakfı accepts the Directorate of Religious Af-fairs (DİB) as the body of the state that organizes religion in Turkey, and seeks either a representation of Alevis within the DİB or the establish-ment of a separate but similar state authority for Alevis.

In order to complete the image of Alevi organizations in Germany, splinter groups of the extreme left have to be added. A subsection of Dev Sol formed *Al-Genç* (Al[evi]-Youth). In the context of this group a jour-nal called *Kerbela* has been issued in irregular intervals since 1996. Ru-mors tell that members of the group have unsuccessfully tried to subvert several local Alevi associations. Another such group was *Alevi Cephesi* (Alevi Front) which operated a now defunct website and unsuccessfully attempted to mobilize young Alevis for a radically left cause. These endeavors are quite insignificant within the overall context of the Alevi movement, but they show that some Alevis continued a radical leftist commitment and tried to mobilize for the left through an Alevi avenue.

Local and Translocal Commitments

In this chapter I have detailed the emergence of local and translocal associations within the Alevi movement. In a way almost all Alevi asso-ciations claim to represent Alevis and Alevism at a particular level.

---

[12] In fact, the journal *Zülfikar* predated the Kurdish Alevi Federation as its first issue was published already in 1994 by an "office" of the Kurdish movement that was later turned into the Kurdish Alevi Federation.

Closely connected with the claim to represent Alevis is the idea of a basic, almost primordial unity of the Alevis. According to this idea, the Alevi community is in itself undivided. If it appears to be actually divided into various branches and perspectives, this is the result of the efforts of all kinds of agents, like a divide-and-rule policy of the Turkish state or competing and particularistic claims of other Alevi bodies. Among the translocal associations, the AABF embodies this claim to represent Alevis most powerfully. The claim to represent is translated into political commitments and relations with the authorities and other kinds of institutions like religious bodies. Because the Kurdish Alevi Federation and CEM Vakfı are much smaller they cannot express their claims to represent Alevis on the same scale. Rather, their claims are mediated by the idea that the AABF does *not really* represent Alevis — either because it downplays the religious aspect of Alevism, as is maintained from the perspective of CEM Vakfı, or because it does not represent properly the connection between the Alevi and the Kurdish issue, as is the view of the Kurdish Alevi Federation.

The claim to represent is also made by local associations at the level of their respective city or town. Thus, the HAKM was established as the body that represents Alevis in Hamburg. Fission notwithstanding, the HAKM never definitely relinquished this claim. Until the end of the 1990s HAAK BIR was always regarded as a kind of illegitimate body by the HAKM. The claim of a single and unified representation at the local level was made explicit in the by-laws of the AABF, which prohibited that more than one local association of a particular city could join the federation. However, because both the HAKM and HAAK BIR were already present when the AABF was established, both local associations became members of the AABF.[13] Yet, the local competition for representation was also transferred to the arena of the translocal organization: because the AABF was dominated to a certain extent by personnel emerging from the HAKM, HAAK BIR frequently assumed an attitude of opposition towards the federation's managing committee. Further, HAAK BIR's membership in the AABF was for some years suspended, because after the acquisition of its premises HAAK BIR could not afford to pay the membership fees.

Membership in an umbrella organization is the most obvious relation between local and translocal Alevi associations. Besides the HAKM and HAAK BIR the associations in Hamburg's neighboring towns of Wedel and Geesthacht are members of the AABF. HAK EVI, the Kurdish Alevi association in Hamburg, is a member of the Kurdish Alevi Federation. Finally, the association in Harburg (HAKB) as well as Dede Ismail Aslandoğan, who founded the Alevi Cemaatı, show a strong

---

[13] Recently the rules of the AABF have been relaxed so that now also several local associations from one place can to join the federation.

inclination towards CEM Vakfı. Thus, the various claims of translocal representation of Alevis are reproduced at the local level.

Membership in an umbrella organization is not only a formal relationship, but entails a considerable movement of people that participate in activities at the different levels. The chairmen of the local associations that have joined the AABF regularly meet in Cologne to discuss current affairs and to make decisions. Alevis travel across Germany to participate in large cultural events that the AABF organizes. Sometimes local events are specially promoted by the AABF and turned into translocal events. One such occasion was the opening of the *cem* house in Augsburg (Bavaria) in October 2000, which was the first *cem* house outside of Turkey that was built from the ground. Delegates of Alevi associations from all over Germany attended this event. But there is also movement in the other direction, from the translocal to the local level, as the members of the committee regularly visit local associations on the occasion of assemblies, panel discussions, or cultural events. The central members of the AABF's committee, like the chairman, the vice chairman, or the general secretary, are constantly on the move.

A Landscape of Alevism in Germany

In the course the years since the birth of the Alevi movement, a highly differentiated landscape of organized Alevism has evolved in Germany. As we have seen, different perspectives have become embodied in different associations at the local and at the translocal level. Besides the associations, media and events are significant elements of this landscape. The media, not only the journal *Alevilerin Sesi* but also the smaller journals and an exploding number of websites on the Net,[14] sustain a discourse on Alevism in which both shared perspectives and contested issues are articulated. Events create opportunities for individual Alevis—including those who are not members of associations—to participate in the movement, to express themselves as Alevi, and to have the experience of being part of a community. In such events, especially in the large cultural festivals, the Alevi community ceases to be a discursive construct, an idea that may be affirmed or disputed, and becomes a tangible, experiential social reality.

The Alevi movement is significant also for those Alevis who are not directly and personally committed to it. In order to assess the transformation engendered by the movement, we have to recall Alevism in Germany as it existed before the rise of the movement: it was virtually absent. There was no public discourse about Alevism and, after the late 1970s, only very limited efforts to form associations or to organ-

---

[14] On the role of the Internet for the Alevi movement see Sökefeld 2002.

ize events. These activities were not explicitly carried out in the name
of Alevism. Alevis mostly practiced *takiya*. For those committed to the
left, being Alevi was irrelevant or even anathema. Publicly, Alevism
was a nonissue. Yet the movement turned Alevism into a public affair.
First of all, it became public among Alevis themselves who met in the
context of associations and in the events organized by these associations. Second, it became public in the greater Turkish-language public
in Germany, because Alevism became an issue in the Turkish media
that reported on Alevi events and affairs. Third, Alevism became also
an issue in the German-language public, although here it was mostly
limited to discourses of specialists related with questions of immigration and interdenominational dialogue. As a consequence of Alevism
having become a public issue, the practice of *takiya* has been greatly
reduced in Germany. The landscape created by the Alevi movement in
Germany radically transformed the horizon of experience of the Alevis
who live in the country. Of course, many Alevis are simply not interested in Alevism. Others explicitly keep a strict distance from the Alevi
movement because they regard it as "only political." But they all have
the choice to relate to the issue of Alevism, if they want to. In terms of
associations and events the Alevi movement is present almost everywhere in the urban areas of Western Germany. The movement has created new opportunities of experiencing Alevism as a collective issue.
After the "old" generations of Alevis, who hid their affiliation, and the
intermediate generation that personally experienced the break of *takiya*,
the first generation of Alevis is currently growing up in Germany for
whom *takiya* is simply out of question.

In this chapter I have detailed the development of the Alevi movement. Collective action of the Alevi movement comprised the establishment of new collective actors, the Alevi associations. We have seen that,
after a brief initial phase, the common purpose of the movement indeed
did not result in overall solidarity and the maintenance of unity within
the movement. To the contrary, the negotiation of that common purpose,
Alevi identity, revealed differences in the approach towards this purpose,
which resulted in competing claims of representation and in the fission
of associations. Although the idea of identity served as a frame that motivated collective action and enabled the articulation of claims, it did not
constitute a common denominator of the movement, but worked rather
as a divisor producing disagreement. We have also seen that the collective actors of the movement, the associations, are not amorphous bodies
but "live" through the actions and decisions taken by individuals that
have assumed certain, at times bitterly contested, positions within the collective bodies and that exploit also the interstices within the formal structure and practices of these associations. In the following chapter I will
further probe into issues of dispute within the Alevi movement and discuss important differences that intersect with the idea of Alevi identity.

4

CROSSCURRENTS OF IDENTIFICATION

Crosscutting Differences and the Alevi Movement

The Alevi movement diversified into a number of different associations at the local and the translocal level. This diversification related to a number of contentious issues like Kurdish politics or specific ideas about what Alevism is. Alevis are subject to the play of intersecting differences (cf. chapter one): to identify as Alevi does not preclude the possibility—and necessity—to relate in specific ways to other identifications, to embrace or to reject them. Rather than answering all questions concerning one's identity, the identification as Alevi opens up a broad discursive field of contesting claims of ethnic, regional, political, or religious identifications, to mention just a few. Such contested issues are not limited to discourse, but are partly translated into social relations. A visible result of crosscutting differences is the differentiation of the Alevi movement into competing associations that are centered upon specific differences like the Kurdish issue. However, the issue does not stop here. To separate into Kurdish and non-Kurdish Alevis, for instance, does not solve the question whether Alevis should identify with Islam or not. One could imagine that Kurdish as well as non-Kurdish Alevis divide into an Islamic and a non-Islamic faction, and so on, until we have reached infinitesimal but clear-cut units of subidentity associations. Yet, this idea is obviously absurd. A strict hierarchy of identifications is only a theoretical option (Sökefeld 1997, 1998). Social practice does not operate in this way. Instead, intersecting differences work within the Alevi community and within the associations. They are endowed with changing salience and may become more or less important, according to circumstances. They can temporarily acquire such a degree of significance that they indeed may result in the split of an organization, but this is not a necessary outcome. And even where such a split occurs this does not mean that "pure" subsections emerge. The existence of Kurdish Alevi associations does by no means imply that there are no Kurdish members in the other associations.

Accordingly, this chapter is not meant to provide a kind of catalogue of Alevi subidentities. Instead, I intend to probe into the discursive field of differences that operate between and within the Alevi associations. Before I can turn to these differences, however, the "master difference" needs to be explored, which, as a consequence of unequal power relations that lasted for centuries, forms the point of reference for most aspects of the debate on Alevi identity. This is the difference between Alevis and Sunnis. Although opinions differ about what Alevism is and what Alevis are, it is undisputed what Alevis are *not:* they are not Sunnis. Yet, this negative definition of Alevism leaves open an extensive realm of frequently contradicting possibilities for determining positively what Alevism is or should be.

Alevis Are Not Sunnis

As more and more people in Germany learn that there are people called "Alevis," Alevis are increasingly required to explain what Alevism is. Until now I never came across a single statement of Alevi self-identification that does not refer to the difference between Alevis and Sunnis. Accordingly, I call this difference a *master difference.* On its Internet homepage the AABF has published a short introduction to Alevism titled "A Summary: Alevilik—Alevism." After a sentence about the number of Alevis, the text turns to the difference:

> Alevism was formed in Anatolia between the thirteenth and sixteenth centuries. Because Alevis in Anatolia maintained a strong relationship with pre-Islamic culture (…) they differ from orthodox Islamic Sunnis as well as from Iranian Shias. A difference from Sunni as well as Shia orthodoxy is that Anatolian Alevis do not accept the *sharia*, the Islamic legal system, as the word of God.[1]

This paragraph locates the origin of the difference between Alevism and Sunni/Shia Islam in history and emphasizes that Alevism right from its origin was different from Sunni and Shia Islam. The text continues to describe Alevis by referring to Sunni Islam. It mentions the exclusively Sunni orientation of DİB, the construction of Sunni mosques in Alevi villages, and compulsory Sunni religious classes also for Alevi children in Turkish schools. Frequently, explanations of Alevism are purely negative and content themselves with saying that Alevis neither pray in mosques, nor fast in Ramadan and travel to Mecca. Very significantly, it is emphasized that Alevi women do not wear the headscarf. Alevism is defined in contrast with Sunni Islam. A central point of contrast is the *rules* of Sunni Islam. Sunni Islam is defined as a religion of a fixed set of rules that prescribe prayer, pilgrimage, etc. A shorthand for these rules is the *sharia* (Turkish: *şeriat*), the Islamic system of rules that, ideally, is meant to govern all aspects of human life. Yet the sharia does not apply to Alevis. Alevism as a mystic teaching sees the Alevi path (*Alevi yolu*) as divided into four "gateways" (*kapı*) that have to be passed until the

---

[1] <http://www.alevi.com/sites/lehre/Alevitentum%20/aleviten> (2/9/04).

human being finally encounters God. The first *kapı* is *şeriat*, and it is said that all Alevis have already passed this gate.[2] The rules of Sunni Islam therefore do not apply to Alevis. Sunnis, however, still stick to this rather preliminary step on the way to God.

Alevism is defined as a religion that does not center upon rules but upon the human being. This is expressed in a frequently quoted saying of Hacı Bektaş Veli: *Benim Kaabem insandır.* (My Kaaba is the human being). While the Sunnis have to direct their prayer towards the Kaaba in Mecca, the practice of Alevis has to be directed towards the fellow human being. While Sunnis have to abide by myriad rules—there is for instance not only the rule to pray five times a day but also specific and detailed rules saying how to clean the body before prayer and how to perform the prayer—Alevis have to keep one commandment only, which again is attributed to Hacı Bektaş Veli: *Eline beline diline sahip ol!* (Be the master of your hands, your loins and your tongue!) That is, Alevis are called to control their actions, their sexuality and their words. Its intention is to enable a social life free of conflicts. An increasing number of Alevis in Germany, although still a minority, identifies Alevism simply as the other of Islam. The question whether Alevism is part of Islam or not is one of the most significant lines of contention in present day Alevism in Germany. Yet, before this issue can be discussed, another question has to be tackled first. This is the question whether Alevism is a kind of religion at all.

Religion or Culture?

Many Alevis oppose religion to culture and emphasize that Alevism is not religion but culture, or that religion is only one aspect of Alevism that is outweighed by its cultural dimension. The significance of this opposition of culture and religion for Alevis is derived from two issues. The first relates to the question of atheism, the second to a specific understanding of religion (*din*) that is derived from the Alevi vision of (Sunni) Islam.

When I started to discuss with Alevis during my fieldwork I took Alevism rather by default as a religion. I was surprised to learn that many ex-Marxists were committed to the Alevi movement, that even most of its first and foremost activists were ex-Marxists and that many of them continued to declare themselves atheists. Why do atheists engage with a religion? I asked this question to Ahmet Şahin, one of these ex-Marxists. He explained:

---

[2] The other three gateways are *tarikat* (mysticism), *maarifet* (knowledge) and *hakkikat* (truth). Each *kapı* is governed by ten rules (*makam*) (Bozkurt 1988, 92ff).

At the core of Alevism there is nothing like religiousness. The essence of Alevism is also the essence of socialism. Because in socialism there is comradeship [*yoldaşlık*], in Alevism there is *musahiplik*. In socialism there is people's justice [*halk mahkemesi*], in Alevism, in *cem*, there is people's justice too. Many things are shared by Alevism and socialism. We took to Alevism in order to defend its social aspects: we do not want the religious aspect of Alevism, but its social and political aspects. [...] According to my philosophy Alevism is a way of life. Alevism is democracy, Alevism is human rights, Alevism is laicism, Alevism is freedom, Alevism is human love, Alevism is to be a friend of goodness, beauty, and truth, therefore I am Alevi. The essence of Alevism is to regard all human beings as equals. Therefore I love Alevism.

For Ahmet, there is no contradiction between Alevism and socialism. Many values and practices he endorses are shared by these two systems of thought. He equates socialist comradeship with Alevi *musahiplik*. *Musahiplik* is a specific, lifelong bond that is concluded between two married couples. It entails total responsibility of each *musahip* for his or her companions in moral and material regard. Originally, *musahiplik* entailed also the final initiation to Alevism: only *musahips* were considered full members of the community and only they were allowed to join in *cem*. *Musahiplik* is always referred to as one of the core institutions of Alevism, yet it is hardly practiced today. All of the few *musahips* that I know in Hamburg entered into their relationship three decades ago in Turkey. Yet *musahiplik* continues to be referred to as an important symbol of close interpersonal relationships and responsibility in Alevism. Ahmet equates this symbolic meaning with comradeship. Similarly, *halk mahkemesi* (literally "people's court") refers to a particular element of the initial phase of *cem* in which all participants are called to disclose conflicts and strained relationships among them. Before the ritual can proceed such conflicts have to be solved and mutual consent (*rızalık*) has to be established within the congregation.

The appropriation of ritual elements like *musahiplik* and *halk mahkemesi* for the purpose of likening Alevism with socialism disregards the religious dimension of these elements. This approach continues the previous appropriation of elements of Alevism by socialist groups that occurred in the political struggles of the 1970s in Turkey. Here, especially the poet-saint Pir Sultan Abdal became a symbol of resistance. He was represented as raising his *saz* over his head. Looked at with a quick glance this image is easily mistaken for a militant revolutionary who shows off his Kalashnikov. This representation became an icon of leftist struggle in Turkey, like the portraits of Che Guevara or Deniz Gezmiş, a student activist who was executed in 1972.[3] The very term

---

[3] Such icons continue to be traded at large Alevi events like the annual festival of Hacıbektaş. Here, portraits of Che Guevara and Deniz Gezmiş are sold

halk mahkemesi exemplifies this socialist appropriation and reinterpretation of Alevi elements but also their reappropriation by the Alevi movement. *Halk mahkemesi* is not the original Alevi term. Originally, this phase of the ritual was referred to as *görgü* or *dara çekmek*.[4]

Ahmet saw Alevism as a "way of life," others define Alevism simply as "culture." Cem, an Alevi student, said: "The Alevi culture is a way of life. … It is a way of life that is more humanist, it is based upon the human being, not upon a book like the Quran or the Bible." Religion may be an aspect or part of this culture, but it is not the most significant part as Halis Tosun explained: "In Sunni faith you only go to the mosque five times a day and then you leave. But it is not like this for Alevis. They have their *cem* only once or twice a year; otherwise they do everything through their culture. Or through politics. Our culture is also political."

Implicit in such statements is a specific concept of religion. Religion is based on a book, not upon the human being, and therefore it makes many prescriptions. Further, religion constitutes a sphere of life that is separate from ordinary, everyday life. A secularist concept of religion is expressed here that clearly restricts the applicability of religion to certain areas of life. Alevism, as culture, not as religion, does not implicate such a separation, it pervades the whole of life. I spoke about this point with Cem and Canan. Canan, a sixteen year old Alevi girl, reported a dispute with a Sunni friend in order to give an example for this contrast between Alevism and religion:

> I once quarreled with my friend. I said: "I think everything you do is in vain! OK, you go to the mosque, I know you, I have seen you going to the mosque in order to pray. I do not mind that, to the contrary. I respect your attitude. But I cannot accept that you do exactly the opposite, you get out [of the mosque] and you smoke, drink alcohol. Alcohol is forbidden by the Quran. You must not do that. You have to decide."

Cem continued:

> We [Alevis] are even allowed to eat pork. I eat pork too; I have no problem with this. We are not so narrow minded, with so many prohibitions. We have only one rule: you have to control your hands, your loins, and your tongue. That means, you must not steal nor beat, lie or say evil words.

Religion, as exemplified by Sunni Islam, is limited to some extra realm like the mosque. Sunnis do one thing in the mosque and another outside of the mosque. But Alevism as a culture that pervades all areas of life

---

together with other devotional objects like pictures of the Imam Ali or Hacı Bektaş Veli.

[4] The general meaning of *görgü* is "good manners," but in Alevism the term refers specifically to the element of *cem. Dar* refers to the position in front of the *dede* in *cem, dara çekmek* means "to go to the *dar.*"

does not allow such a limitation and separation. Alevis have only one "commandment," which is a social norm that has to be kept in all areas of life. Culture is seen as more inclusive and pervasive than religion.

A further aspect is that religion is understood in the first place in terms of faith, not in terms of specific religious practices. A practice is religious only if it is done with faith. Accordingly, also *cem* is not in itself a religious ritual, it can also be regarded as a cultural event or practice. The essence of religion is *inanç*, belief. When Alevis talk about Alevism as religion, they mostly use the phrase *Alevi inancı*, Alevi belief. The Turkish word that is generally translated as "religion," *din*, is employed by very few Alevis only. *Din* is a concept too closely associated with (Sunni) Islam. It is employed only by those Alevis who identify Alevism with Islam. Many prefer even more neutral terms to refer to Alevism and speak about *Alevi öğreti* (Alevi teaching or doctrine) or *Alevi felsefesi* (Alevi philosophy). These terms can be used for Alevism without coming too close to the idea that Alevism is a religion. They are fully compatible with the concept of Alevism as culture.

Yet, not all Alevis share this concept. There are also Alevis who insist on Alevism as a religion. Sedat Köyoğlu, a man in his early forties, told that he disputed continually with his father about the question whether Alevism is religion or culture. For his father, Alevism was essentially religion. Sedat denied this and even rejected the idea of a specific Alevi teaching. He told that he explained nothing about Alevism his children. According to his understanding, they do not need to know anything about the twelve Imams or some tenets, for instance. What his children need to know is a specific "way of life," which they learn without being taught Alevism. Yet especially many older persons are concerned about the fact that many Alevi children or youth know very little about specific Alevi doctrines. They emphasize Alevism as religion that should be passed on to the children. This point of view is expressed especially by many Alevi *dedes*, the Alevi religious specialists.

I discussed Alevis as religion with *dede* Ismail Aslandoğan and *dede* Remzi Örer. Both *dedes* emphatically reject the idea that an atheist can be Alevi. According to their view there can be no nonreligious, "cultural" Alevism. Alevis need to have the right faith. Both explained the move towards Alevism as culture with a lack of Alevi religious instruction that was a consequence of its prohibition in Turkey. As a result, the Alevi youth became disoriented and looked towards Marxism as a kind of substitute. But Alevism needs to be understood as a religion. "Culture is nothing," Ismail *dede* said, "could you say that the bible is a *cultural* book? Not at all!" Within the HAKM, Ismail *dede* met with strong resistance against his idea of Alevism as religion. As a consequence he left the association and cofounded HAAK BIR, where he was promised the opportunity to teach his understanding of Alevism. Yet, according to Ismail *dede,* even the members of HAAK BIR were not much interested in his religious teachings of Alevism. Therefore he left again and established his own, short-lived association, the HAC. In most Alevi associations there are discussions about the question whether Alevism is religion or culture. There are some associations that decidedly follow the view of Alevism as religion. Such associations are mostly not members of the AABF, but have remained independent or established ties with CEM Vakfı. In many of them *dede*s have an important position. Yet, the position that Alevism is religion is also expressed within the AABF. For Derviş Tur *dede,* the long-time chairman of the federation's *dede*s' council (*dedeler kurulu*), the idea that Alevism is culture and not religion is simply ridiculous. I discussed the matter with him and his son, Kennan Tur:

> Derviş Tur: "Well, what is Alevism, is it religion or a sports club? What is it?"
>
> I: "Many say that Alevism is not religion but culture."
>
> Derviş Tur: "Wait a moment, no, culture, just look, also an animal has culture. An animal eats too!"
>
> Kennan Tur: "It has eating habits."
>
> Derviş Tur: "Culture is what the people do in their lives. Cuisine is a part of culture, eating is a part of culture, language is a part of culture, look, my son is more than thirty–five years old. When he came into the room he kissed my hand. This is culture. But religion is something very different! These people do not know what is religion and what is culture. They are ignorant! Also chickens have culture!"

According to Derviş Tur and other *dede*s, it is in the first place the responsibility of *dede*s as religious specialists to ensure the continuity of Alevism as religion and to teach its tenets to the younger generation. In their view, to regard Alevism as culture is to miss the core of Alevism. Also the intermediate idea, professed by most people, that Alevism is both culture and religion is a much too weak statement in their view. Religion has to come first. Religion, belief, faith is the essence of Alevism. The question whether Alevism is religion or culture continues to be discussed and sometimes results in bitter disputes. Alevis who vote for culture sometimes describe themselves as "modern" and "enlightened" Alevis who have overcome religion. They call those who speak for Alevism as religion "conservative," sometimes even "fundamentalist." Conversely, religious Alevis speak about "cultural Alevis" as ignorant —according to them they are not really Alevis. The question whether Alevism is religion or culture is closely related to another issue: Given that Alevism is religion, what kind of religion is it? Is Alevism Islam?

Is Alevism Islam?

"There are five conditions[5] for Islam. We do not comply with them. We do not pray in the mosque, we do not fast in *Ramadan*, we do not go to Mecca. Why then should Alevism be a part of Islam?" (Hasan Kılavuz)

"In *cem* we invoke *Allah Mohammed Ali*. How could we assert that Alevism is not a part of Islam?" (Halis Tosun)

The question whether Alevism is part of Islam or not is the most bitterly disputed issue among Alevis. This question is even more intricate than the dispute about Alevism as religion or culture, because the debate is not limited to Alevis themselves but touches also the question whether Alevis are (and should be) recognized and accepted as Muslims by other Muslims. The issue overlaps with the question whether Alevism is religion or not: generally those who emphasize that Alevism is religion also take Alevism as a part of Islam. Yet among those who regard Alevism as culture (including also religious dimensions) are proponents of Alevism as Islam as well as those who consider Alevism as outside of Islam.

The basic arguments for both positions do not require theological expertise. They are neatly summarized in the quotations at the beginning of this section. They form an aporia that cannot easily be solved. The question is mainly a diasporic issue. In Turkey the overwhelming majority of Alevis simply takes for granted that Alevis are Muslims. Among the Alevi associations in Turkey only the PSAKD expresses a more equivocal position and emphasizes Alevism as a syncretistic culture and religion that has absorbed elements of many different religions. In Turkey the idea that Alevis are Muslims is strictly enforced by the state. Turkish passports state the religious affiliation of their bearers and identify Alevis as Muslims. The identification of Alevis as Muslims is also the main argument for the policy of the DİB: the DİB caters to the needs of Muslims, Alevis are Muslims, and therefore there is no need that the DİB specifically gives attention to the demands of Alevis. This inclusive policy of the Turkish Republic reverses the previous exclusive policy of the Ottoman state in which Alevis were mostly regarded as heretics. But in the Kemalist endeavor to weld a unified Turkish nation Alevis were taken by default as Muslims. Kemalist "laicism" notwithstanding, a "controlled" Islam is an important dimension of the dominant national self-understanding in Turkey: "to be Islamic has become as important as to be Turkish" (Shankland 1999, 25).[6] Yet, the reli-

---

[5] In Turkish, the "five pillars" of Islam are referred to as the *beş şart*, "five conditions."

[6] Cf. Seufert 1997b, 204ff and Cetinsaya 1999.

giously inclusive policy of the Turkish Republic implies that Alevis are subjected to the Sunni version of Islam: being Muslims, Alevi pupils are required to attend the Sunni religious classes in schools. In no realm of official policy are there special provisions for Alevis. As a consequence, although Alevis in Turkey regard themselves as Muslims, they insist on being a particular kind of Muslims, that differs fundamentally from the version of Islam that is endorsed by the state. In the German diaspora, the parameters of religious and national identity have changed. Some Alevis do not continue to regard themselves as members of the Turkish nation in the first place, and even for many of those who do so the connection of Turkish national identity with Islam has become highly questionable. Thus, all theological considerations apart, the necessity to identify as Muslim has become considerably weakened. As a result more than one third of respondents in my survey among the members of Alevi associations in Hamburg expressed the opinion that Alevism is not a part of Islam today (figure 4.1).

Although this view is still outweighed by the opinion that Alevism is part of Islam, I was rather surprised by the number of Alevis who negate the close relationship between Alevism and Islam. As a second question on this topic I asked whether historically Alevism originated from Islam. More than a quarter of the respondents even denied this historical relationship between Alevism and Islam (figure 4.2).

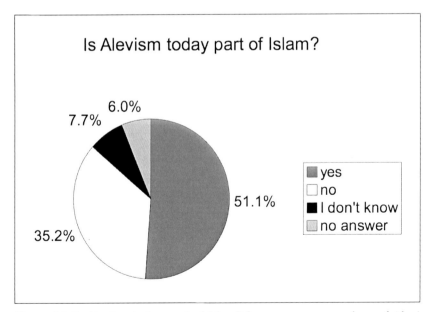

Figure 4.1 Is Alevism today part of Islam? Survey among members of Alevi associations in Hamburg.

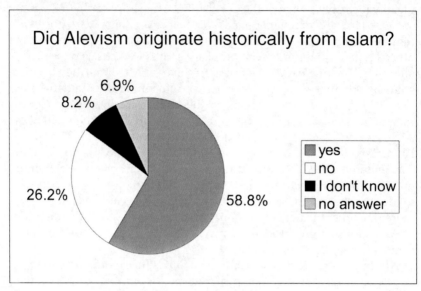

Did Alevism originate historically from Islam?

- yes
- no
- I don't know
- no answer

6.9%
8.2%
26.2%
58.8%

Figure 4.2 Did Alevism historically originate from Islam? Survey among members of Alevi associations in Hamburg.

Whereas the majority of those Alevis who regard Alevism as part of Islam hold this opinion rather by default, others, especially some *dedes*, endorse a quite different identification of Islam and Alevism. For them, Alevism is *true Islam* while Sunni Islam is only a distorted version of the original revelation. One proponent of this idea was *dede* Şinasi Koç, a *dede* who frequently toured Germany in the 1980s and who also presided over the first *cem* that took place in Hamburg in 1984. In a book that is aptly titled *Gerçek Islam Dini* (True Islam Religion) he argued that in consequence of the struggle about successorship after the death of the prophet Mohammad, the Muslim community was led astray by the Umayyads and that for 1,400 years Muslim scholars hid the truth and spread hypocrisy in order to please those in power (Koç 1989, 10–14). In this work, *emeviler* (Umayyads) is almost a synonym for Sunnis. Koç takes all efforts to prove Sunni Islam wrong: Sunni Islam is not true Islam. Significantly his arguments are based on the Quran. He argues, for instance, that the Quran (and thus true Islam) neither prescribes *namaz* (ibid., 105) nor prohibits alcohol (144). The word Alevism does not appear in the book, it is simply *true Islam*.

This line of argument that defends Alevism on the basis of the Quran is also supported by other *dedes*. Scriptural knowledge is regarded by them as a sine qua non of Alevi religious authority. *Dede* Ismail Aslandoğan too has studied Arabic and the Quran. Also Derviş Tur argues from the Quran that Alevism is the mystic path of Islam, which is opposed to the "external" Islam of *şeriat*. Present-day Sunni Islam, however, is not based on *şeriat* as it had been established by the Prophet Mohammed; this original *şeriat* was distorted and turned upside down by the Umayyads (Tur 2002, 279ff.). Derviş Tur defines Alevism as "a faith that interprets Islam differently from Sunni *şeriat*, that does not accept what has been added to Islam by *icma*[7] and that is not bound by the backward and fanatical rules of *şeriat*" (ibid., 285). Alevism is again presented as true Islam that is free from the distortions of Sunni religion.

The concept of Alevism as true Islam strictly opposes not only the idea that Alevism is culture, but also the position that it is a syncretistic religion. Together with other *dedes*, Ismail Aslandoğan was a strong critic of the book written by Necat Birdoğan and published by the HAKM because it proposed a close relationship between Alevism and Shamanism (Birdoğan 1990). Among other things this book convinced Aslandoğan that the HAKM propagated a false version of Alevism.[8] The idea of Alevism as a positively valued syncretism is especially popular among Alevi activists and intellectuals of leftist leanings. According to this view, Islam is only one source of Alevism besides many others like Buddhism, Shamanism, Zoroastrism, and early Christianity. Alevism is compared with a mosaic in which many stones of different colors produce an image. The preeminence of Islam is thus rejected. Can, a young Alevi, explained:

> I have nothing to do with Islam. It may be that population movements from Arabia or from Iran brought something [i.e., some elements of Islam] and that something remained. But true Alevism originated in Anatolia where all religions formed a mosaic. Therefore it is called Anatolian Alevism. This is what I call Alevism. That is, it comprises elements of Judaism, of Christians that came over from Greece. The mosaic was formed [with elements] from every culture, from every nation.

A different version of the relationship between Alevis and Islam is expressed by Halis Tosun. Referring to Sunnis he said:

> "They have the Quran, the book. They honor Abu Bekir, Ömer, and Osman.[9] But from the beginning they opposed Mohammed. They have

---

[7] *Icma* (Arabic: *ijma*) is the knowledgeable consent of the *ulema* that beside the Quran and the *sunna* is accepted as a source of law in Sunni Islam.

[8] When Ismail Aslandoğan later established the HAC, the affiliation of Alevism with Islam was even written into the by-laws of this association.

[9] These are the Turkish names of the first three caliphs Abu Bakr, Omar, and Uthman who, according to Alevi (and Shia) conviction usurped the successorship of the prophet and violated the right of Ali who became only the fourth caliph. Ali was killed in the fifth year of his caliphate by a follower of Muawiyya, a relative of Uthman, who became the next caliph and the founder of the Umayyad dynasty. The assassination of Ali and later the battle of Kerbela sealed the schism of Islam into a Sunni branch (i.e., the adherents of the first three caliphs and the Umayyads) and the Shia/Alevi branch of the followers of Ali.

killed Ali! *They* have written the Quran, Mohammed did not write the Quran himself. Are they [really] Muslims? (...)

In the lifetime of Mohammed there was no Quran. It was written later by other people. Therefore the Quran does not simply contain what Mohammad has said. The Quran is not above discussion and interpretation. (...)

For us the heart is important. One needs to carry the faith in one's heart. This is what Ali said. And faith has to be renewed, reformed. One has to learn, to acquire knowledge. Ali said: Go to China if you can learn something thereby. This is the most important thing. Religion cannot be today the same thing that it was thousand years ago. We have to decide ourselves what is correct and what is not correct. We do not have a book in which everything is written. We have to learn ourselves.

Although Halis Tosun considers Alevism as Islam (and Alevis better Muslims than Sunnis), he does not reject syncretism but agrees that Alevism has been influenced by other religious tradition. As a consequence, his understanding of Alevism is not based exclusively on Islamic sources. In contrast with the *dede*s that have been quoted above, he does not consider the Quran the preeminent source of Alevism but rather rejects it because it has been written—and thus distorted—by Sunnis.

The debate on the relationship between Islam and Alevism continues within the Alevi community. Consonant with the idea that any form of dogma is alien to Alevism, there has never been a formal statement of the AABF on this issue. Rather, the range of positions on this issue that are expressed within the association mirrors the whole range of views that can be found among Alevis. Yet, although the idea of Alevism as true Islam is strongly endorsed by Derviş Tur, who for many years was the chairman of the federation's *dede*s' council, it rather remained a minority opinion. The position of the chairman of the *dede*s' council does not carry the authority to issue binding doctrinal statements. Derviş Tur's ideas were rather considered as extreme and were opposed by committees of the AABF. Most of the time the relationship between the committee of the AABF and the *dede*s' council was difficult and full of conflicts. In spring 2003, after a reorganization of the *dede*s' council, a new *dede* became its chairman. This was Hasan Kılavuz from Hamburg, who decidedly holds the view that Alevism is *not* Islam and that the Quran, due to its distortions, is not a source of Alevism. He emphatically endorsed the idea that Alevism is a separate religion in its own right. Hasan Kılavuz repeated the argument that Alevism does not accept the principles of Islamic religion and that the rules of Islam reject central elements of Alevism like music and dance in ritual, the lawfulness of images, and the equality of the sexes (Kılavuz 2003). He said: "The people think, we have Allah, Mohammed, Ali, they belong to Islam and therefore we belong to Islam too. But Islam is not only Allah, Mohammad, Ali, Islam is much more! And all that has nothing to do with us!" Hasan Kılavuz was severely attacked for his views by other *dede*s, including Derviş Tur. He countered these attacks by reproaching his critics for having become assimilated by Sunnis, arguing that in calling Alevism Islam they have succumbed to centuries of pressure exerted by the Sunni powers. He said about the *dede*s who include Alevism within Islam:

> Their [Alevi] faith is rejected by Islam but they do not have the courage to say that Alevis have nothing to do with Islam. They are blind Alevis! They look into the mirror but are unable to recognize themselves. Islam has fought against Alevism and tried to annihilate it. Now the Muslims say: You have Ali, Mohammed, Hüseyin, therefore you belong to Islam. But Islam murdered Ali and Hüseyin! We have preserved their memory *against* Islam! (…) If we are Muslims too and if the Quran is also our book, then why were we never accepted by Islam, why then all these massacres in history?

This objection emphasizes that the question whether Alevis are Muslims or not is not only an intra-Alevi issue, but concerns also the question whether Alevis are recognized as Muslims by other Muslims. During the greater part of their history Alevis have been rejected as heretics, but recently in Turkey they have been accepted as Muslims. The question of being recognized as Muslims by Muslims complicates the issue of Alevi self-identification: It is one thing to insist within Alevi circles that Alevis do not belong to Islam, but it is something else to be rejected by Islam and to accept this rejection. If Alevis insist today that they are not Muslims, would that not be a belated legitimation of the centuries of rejection and nonrecognition by Islam? How should Alevis identify in interaction with Muslims?

The intricacy of this question was brought to my attention by several debates of the interfaith round table in Hamburg that develops interfaith religious instruction in the schools of the city (see chapter seven). Besides other religious communities, Alevis as well as Sunni and Shia Muslims participate in this body. At one meeting the question of Islamic instruction in other German *Bundesländer* was discussed. In Hesse, the Islamic Conference, a union of several Muslim associations, had submitted an application for Islamic religious classes in schools. The Islamic Conference had issued criteria to decide who is Muslim and who is not, and also, which organization could be accepted as a member of the conference. According to these criteria Muslims have to accept the Quran, the sunna, and the hadith as guidelines for their lives. By these criteria Alevis are not Muslims. These particular criteria were not openly discussed or disputed in the roundtable meeting. Yet, during informal talk after the meeting a representative of the Shia community said to the Alevis who were present that for him the only criterion for Muslimhood is whether this person himself identifies as Muslim.

On the way home the issue was discussed by the two Alevi delegates to the round table. One of them was Hasan Kılavuz. Although at that time, a few years before he became chairman of the *dede*s council, he was of the opinion that Alevism did not belong to Islam, he expressed strong discontent with the criteria of the Islamic Conference. It makes a difference whether Muslims exclude Alevis from Islam or whether Alevis themselves decide to be something different. The first issue is a question of recognition. In the context of the interfaith round table, Alevis were rather tacitly accepted as Muslims by Sunnis and Shias. To my knowledge, the issue was never openly discussed. Yet Hasan Kılavuz also expressed doubts about the attitude of the Muslim representatives towards the Alevis. According to his opinion, the acceptance of Alevis as Muslims was at best the private point of view of the Muslim representatives that was not shared by the communities of their mosques.

At another meeting the question emerged again. The members of the round table had come together for the purpose of writing a press statement to explain that they favored interfaith religious classes instead of separate Islamic, Christian, Buddhist, etc. classes in schools. The intention of the declaration was to emphasize that religious instruction should be an endeavor for dialogue and for highlighting the contribution of the different religious tradition to the development of European culture. As all religious communities participating in the round table should be mentioned in the text, the question arose how to refer to the Alevis: should they be mentioned as Muslims? Hasan Kılavuz was not present at this occasion. Müslüm Aslan, one of the Alevi delegates said: "We see ourselves as Muslims, we have no problem with being included within 'Islam.' But," he added with a smile, "there are Muslims who are of the opinion that Alevis are not Muslims!" A Muslim delegate responded that for the members of the round table the Alevis were Muslims. Yet when it came to word a concrete sentence, Müslüm said: "Alevis should also be mentioned separately, because otherwise our people complain that they are identified with Sunnis. We do not want this." Therefore, Alevis were mentioned separately. But then a Muslim objected: "Now you are mentioned in contrast with Muslims, as if Alevis were not Muslims!" Müslüm accepted this objection and the sentence was reworded. The formulation became: "Muslims, including Alevis." Then the question surged whether Alevism should be mentioned specifically as a religion. Now Ercan Çelik, another Alevi delegate, objected because he considered "Alevi *religion*" as too religious a phrase. He suggested "Alevi teachings" instead, but finally the expression "Alevi religion" remained in the text.

In summer 1999 the different mosque communities that were represented in the round table formed their own umbrella association, called

Council of Islamic Communities in Hamburg—Schura[10] (*Rat der Isla-mischen Gemeinden in Hamburg—Schura*). At a subsequent meeting of the round table the then chairman of the HAKM was addressed by a German Muslim who asked whether the Alevis wanted to join in the *Schura*. She said that she knew that many Muslims did not consider Alevis as part of Islam, but that she was ready to convince them if the Alevis were interested in becoming a member. The chairman told me about this encounter rather as a joke. He personally took Alevism nei-ther as Islam nor as religion, yet it was clear that also Alevis who con-sider Alevism as "true Islam" would never be ready to join an umbrella association of mosque communities.

Identity and Opposition

Besides the unresolved issues of religious identification there are other crosscutting identifications that contribute to disputes and to the devel-opment of factions and fission among Alevis in Germany. Most signifi-cant in this respect are regional and ethnic, but also political identifica-tions. We have seen already that the Kurdish question impressed its mark upon the Alevi movement. In the present section I will analyze how different, and changing, identifications are employed as a resource for mobilization or as a framework of interpretation of politics within Alevi associations. I will discuss the role of crosscutting identifications in the power struggles in Alevi associations.

The last chapter showed that in many Alevi associations leadership was almost continually disputed. A very serious conflict concerned the AABF from 1999 to 2001. In the beginning of 1999 the managing com-mittee of the federation was reorganized. The chairman Ali Kılıç relin-quished his position because he wanted to run parliamentary elections in Turkey on a ticket of the Barış Partisi. Turgut Öker became the new chairman of the AABF. In late 1999, five members, lead by the general secretary Hıdır Ali Bingöl, resigned from the managing committee. They explained their move in an open letter to all membership associations of the AABF. They accused the remaining committee, and in particular the chairman Turgut Öker, of having acted without the required demo-cratic decision-making within the committee. These accusations were also published in the daily *Hürriyet*. I cannot discuss these accusations here but want to explore the ensuing formation of opposition within the AABF. All persons who stepped down from their positions in the man-aging committee happened to be ethnically Zazas from Tunceli, the erst-

---

[10] *Schura* is the Germanised version of the Arabic word for council.

while Dersim, and adjacent areas. Several of them come from the district of Pülümür in the northern part of Tunceli.

Tunceli stands out from the other provinces in Turkey as the only province that is inhabited by a majority of Alevis. The population of Tunceli is divided into speakers of the languages Zaza[11] and Kurmanci. The Zaza speakers form the majority and all of them are Alevis while among the minority of Kurmanci speakers there are also Sunnis. The area—originally called Dersim—was only marginally integrated into the Ottoman Empire. In the Koçkiri uprising of 1920–21, Zaza–speaking Alevis of Dersim and adjacent regions resisted the Turkish national movement. They feared that they might suffer the same fate as Armenians, with whom they had had close contacts: erasure from the Anatolian landscape in the effort to create a homogenized Turkish nation (Kieser 1993, 2003). Also after the establishment of the Turkish Republic the population of Dersim resisted integration into the new state. People refused to do military service and to pay taxes (Kaya 1999, 1). In 1935 the Turkish national assembly adopted a special *Tunceli Kanunu* (Tunceli law), which renamed Dersim as Tunceli and took a number of repressive measures. The area was virtually besieged. Many people were required to do forced labor and the local languages were prohibited. As a consequence of such repression, an insurgence rose in 1937 that was defeated by the Turkish military in 1938. The leader of the movement, Seyit Rıza, was executed and, with the intention to assimilate them to the Turkish nation, many people from Dersim, especially children, were deported to other areas of Turkey.[12] In the Kurdish struggle of the 1980s and 1990s Tunceli again became a hotspot. Originally it was less a stronghold of PKK than of TİKKO, the militant wing of the TKP/ML.[13] Yet, when the PKK tried to extend its basis there and attacked positions of the Turkish army, an embargo was placed on the area in order to cut off supplies for the militants. Hundreds of villages were destroyed and their inhabitants deported (Leezenberg 2003). Until recently, Tunceli remained under martial law. As a consequence of the long history of resistance against state forces in Tunceli/Dersim, especially people from the province itself, the Dersimli, regard Dersim as a symbol of resistance and of an Alevism untainted by assimilation.[14]

The resignation of the five members from the managing committee of the AABF produced considerable unrest among the Alevi associa-

---

[11] Besides Tunceli, Zaza speakers live also in adjacent provinces like Bingöl and Muş. On the formation of Zaza and Zaza/Alevi identity see Kehl 1999, 2000.

[12] On this uprising see Kieser 2003, 191ff and van Bruinessen 1994.

[13] TİKKO is the abbreviation of *Türk İşçi Köylü Kurtuluş Ordusu* (Turkish Workers and Peasants Liberation Army), TKP/ML is *Türk Komünist Parti/Marksist-Leninist* (Turkish Communist Party/Marxist-Leninist), a party of Maoist orientation.

[14] On Alevism in Tunceli/Dersim see Bumke 1979, and Fırat 1997.

tions. Some of the associations supported them against the remaining committee. Hıdır Ali Bingöl and his fellows joined hands with Mustafa Düzgün, the chairman of the *Alevi Akademisi* and with Ali Kılıç, the previous chairman of the AABF. Both of them are also Zaza from Tunceli. Subsequently, this group came to be known as "the opposition" (*muhalefet*). Elections for a new managing committee of the AABF were scheduled for November 2000. Rumors leaked out that on this occasion the opposition would attempt to take over the committee and to make Mustafa Düzgün the new chairman. On the first day of the general meeting of the AABF accusations against the committee were again published in *Hürriyet*. During the meeting the opposition distributed a new program for the AABF in which the accusations were presented in detail (Yıldız et al., no date). The booklet was signed by the representatives of twenty-one local associations, including HAAK BIR in Hamburg. A heated debate developed at the meeting, in the course of which it turned out that the majority of the delegates would not support the opposition. Rather, the opposition was accused of siding with an "enemy of Alevism," i.e., the newspaper *Hürriyet* that had attacked the AABF many times. Because their chances for a victorious election were gone, none of the members of the opposition stood for the elections of a new committee. Instead, Turgut Öker presented a list of candidates that were elected unopposed.

In the subsequent weeks and months, the campaign of the opposition within the AABF was completely taken over by *Hürriyet*. Every day, new accusations against the AABF were raised by the paper, ranging from allegations of financial irregularities to the support of Armenians or Kurdish separatists or, simply, betrayal of the unity of the Turkish nation. This campaign by *Hürriyet* is another story that will be analyzed later in this work (see chapter eight). Yet, as a consequence of the campaign, a great unrest surged in the Alevi associations. The new committee was almost continually on the move to visit the various associations, including those of the opposition, in order to defend against the accusations.

In the HAKM, some repercussions of the opposition in the AABF were already felt before the general meeting of the federation. A considerable number of the association's members (15.1 percent) stem from Tunceli.[15] Among the members of the association's managing committee was Rıza Cömert from Pülümür/Tunceli, who previously had also served as chairman of the association. He was considered as belonging to the opposition, and because the majority of the association supported the AABF he was not selected as a delegate for the general meeting.

---

[15] The number of persons from Dersim equals the number of people from Maraş, another Kurdish province. Only people from Sivas form a larger section among the membership of the HAKM (21.9 percent).

Therefore he resigned from the committee of the HAKM. Subsequently, many rumors could be heard that he was conspiring with other people from Tunceli against the managing committee of the HAKM. Yet it was never clear whether such rumors and allegations had any basis or whether they just sprang from the imaginations of the people from other regions. When several weeks later Turgut Öker attended a meeting of the HAKM, he and the committee of the HAKM were severely attacked by Rıza Cömert, in accordance with the critique of the opposition. On the following day, Cömert was extensively quoted by *Hürriyet*. The paper revealed that Cömert had not been selected as delegate for the general meeting and accused Öker of picking his favorite delegates himself.[16] A few weeks later the elections for the general committee of the HAKM were held. Rıza Cömert unsuccessfully stood for the position of the chairman.

During all these developments, Kurdish or Zaza identities were not explicitly made a topic by the opposition, neither in the AABF nor in the HAKM. The issues of contention raised by the opposition were always allegations relating to the policy of the AABF that were totally unrelated with Kurdish issues. Yet, Zaza or Dersim identity became a kind of subtext of the disputes. After the resignation of the five members of the managing committee of the AABF some Kurdish Alevis alleged that the federation was being purged of Kurdish members. This accusation was especially voiced by members of the Kurdish Alevi Federation, although it was obviously wrong because other Kurds remained with the committee of the AABF. On the other side, the AABF and its supporters alleged that there was a "Dersim faction" conspiring against the federation. The Dersimli were accused of *bölgecilik* (regionalism) and *feodalizm* (feudalism). Feudalism here meant the favoring of one's own tribe and kin. It was pointed out that several of the Dersimli involved belonged not only to the same area but also to the same *aşiret* (tribe) or shared *kivrelik*.[17] A member of the committee of the AABF told me:

> These people think only in categories of "my village," "my family," "my *aşiret*." When there is nobody from Pülümür in the committee of the AABF, they think, we are no longer represented in and by the AABF. And then they become opposition and turn themselves against the federation. Mustafa Düzgün attempts to exploit this kind of thinking.

A rather unofficial, backstage discourse about the pretensions of the Dersimli for their special tradition of resistance and original Alevism became popular among non–Dersimli. The Dersimli were criticized for

---

[16] *Hürriyet*, 6 February 2001.

[17] *Kivrelik* is a kind of godparenthood that is concluded on the occasion of a boy's circumcision. In several respects relations of *kivrelik* resemble consanguineal relations (Kehl 1996).

their exaggerated regional pride. Once I witnessed a *sofra* (a kind of dinner party) where the *saz* was played and songs were sung. After a while, a joking debate ensued whether a famous song about the mountains of Dersim should be sung. After an exchange of arguments it was decided that the song could be sung because nobody from Dersim was present. In the presence of Dersimli the song only had further increased the "nationalism" of the Dersimli. Somebody said that Dersimli suffered from the "disease" that either they had to take a leading position in an organization or to split off. There was no intermediate option. Jokes about their tendency to occupy opposition stances were told: When two Dersimli meet they establish three parties: One by each of them against the other, and the third they form together against the rest of the world!

At the time of the subsequent elections in the HAKM, rumors about "the Dersimli" became a constant phenomenon—at least among the non-Dersimli members. Also people that were not of Dersim origin were counted among the "opposition" in the HAKM, but the discourse against the opposition referred explicitly only to the Dersimli. Rumors appeared to be rather self-supporting. Some individuals from Dersim were counted as siding with the opposition, although I knew for certain that this was not true.

In 2001 Necati Turan, the former disputed chairman of the HAKM (see chapter three) who hails from Pülümür in Dersim, was proposed as chairman of HAAK BIR by Mehmet Zülküf Kılıç, the former longtime chairman of the association who still dominated its politics. Necati Turan was indeed elected. A member of the HAKM explained to me that this move was again the result of the conspiracies of "the Dersimli." I argued that this could hardly be the case because Mehmet Zülküf Kılıç, a Turkish Alevi from a region with a majority with Kurdish Sunnis, was decidedly suspicious about everything Kurdish. Why should he side with "the Dersimli"? I was told that a brother of Kılıç was a good friend of a Dersimli member of the HAKM, who again was related with Necati Turan. It was supposed that the move had been set up along these lines. Yet, the identifications that were referred to as an explanation of the election intersected. I attended the general meeting of HAAK BIR, and Bülent Ceylan, another man from the HAKM who was present too said to me:

"Did you see, all the Dersimli are coming here, Necati Turan and Rıza Cömert [who was also present as a visitor]."

I questioned the alleged "Dersimli connection" and said: "I thought that there are less Kurds with HAAK BIR and more people from areas like Çorum, Tokat, or Yozgat."[18]

---

[18] Indeed, membership from Kurdish provinces is negligible in HAAK BIR. Only 1.9 percent of members come from Tunceli and 3.7 percent from Maraş.

Bülent: "Yes, but Necati Turan belongs to the İşçi Partisi and Zülküf Kılıç is İşçi Partisi too."

I: "But Rıza Cömert is not İşçi Partisi, I suppose."

Bülent: "No, he is a social democrat."

Here, my interlocutor quickly and unconsciously moved from an "ethnic" explanation of relationships to a political explanation. For him, the political explanation did not contradict the ethnic explanation, but rather supplemented it. To me, the political explanation of Necati Turan's candidature made much more sense than the alleged "Dersimli connection," because shared political affiliation continued to be an important resource for networking within the Alevi movement. Many of the leading persons of the AABF, the HAKM, and other associations are connected by their former relationship with Dev Yol (and they are therefore decidedly against all sympathizers of the İşçi Partisi). Accordingly, also the fact that Mehmet Zülküf Kılıç of HAAK BIR supported the opposition within the AABF can be explained much more convincingly by political ramifications than by reference to some alleged Dersim connection.

In my interpretation, the story of the opposition within the AABF and the HAKM showed that regional affiliations and identities indeed play a certain role within the Alevi movement. The shared affiliation with Dersim served as one resource to recruit support for the opposition. Yet other kinds of identifications are also important, most significantly shared political affiliation. The formation of an opposition cannot be explained by a single factor only. Rather, different aspects overlapped and intersected. While one person was co–opted onto the opposition because of kinship, another one joined because of shared ethnic, regional, or political identification. The common ground for opposition was not a particular kind of identity, but rather the shared critique against the majority faction of the AABF or, at the local level in Hamburg, the HAKM. Some of these points of critique were also shared by others in the AABF, who nonetheless did not side with the opposition but continued to support the managing committee. The opposition rose at a time of widespread discontent with the activities of the association and a considerable decline of mobilization especially in the HAKM. Yet the dominant factions of the associations employed regional and ethnic identity as a framework to explain the movement of the opposition. Identity served to interpret the action of *others*. As a consequence, specific elements of a "Dersim identity" were discussed not by Dersimli themselves but by their opponents. To a certain extent this "ethnicization" of discontent by the dominant faction enabled the specific issues of critique to be left out of consideration, because according to their particular representation these points of critique were only a political instrument of the opposition.

It is necessary to discuss the particular concept of "opposition" that became visible in the disputes. The idea of opposition (*muhalefet*) in the Alevi associations differs considerably from the idea of a parliamentary opposition in which despite all rhetoric of difference, a certain will to reach compromise prevails. In the context of Alevi organizations, opposition is in most cases a fundamental opposition. From the point of view of the dominant faction opposition, is regarded as a threat to unity. Seeds for opposition are frequently laid when the leadership of an organization changes. Close cooperation between a former and a newly elected chairman of an Alevi organization is very rare, even if the former chairman gave up the office voluntarily. The former chairman almost invariably starts to criticize the new one, although in most cases the particular activities undertaken by both persons do not differ much. Opposition precludes cooperation between the opposition and the dominant faction and almost any attempt to come to terms between them. Although the opposition may demand or reject certain purposes and activities in the program of the respective committee, it is mostly directed against particular persons. Accordingly, Turgut Öker was the main target of the opposition in the AABF. It is almost unthinkable that the leaders of the dominant section and the opposition come to terms and cooperate for the sake of specific aims. The opposition also does not pose as representing a certain section of Alevis, as for instance a parliamentary opposition may represent the working–class section of a population. In contrast, the Alevi opposition claims to represent the whole of the Alevi community, just like the dominant faction does.

This particular concept of opposition is mirrored by a specific idea of unity (*birlik*) in the Alevi associations. The necessity of unity of the Alevi community is almost constantly emphasized in Alevi discourse. Slogans like "*Aleviler tek yürek, tek ses*"[19] ("Alevis single heart, single voice") abound. This unity is represented as being required in order to build up strength against the "opponents" or "enemies" of Alevis, like Islamists, the daily *Hürriyet*, or the Turkish government. On the other hand, enemies are dangerous precisely because they threaten *birlik*. Although Alevism is frequently likened to a mosaic, whenever it comes to a dispute *birlik* is imagined as homogeneity and as absence of dispute and difference, not as a "unity in diversity."

Alevis operate on a model of unity and dispute which is widespread in Turkey among many different groups, and which produces a strong tendency towards factionalism and fission. In her study of a village in central Anatolia, Carol Delaney links the split of the village into two antagonistic factions that sprang from the establishment of two, opposed, political associations with cosmological ideas of duality, but also with

---

[19] This is the title of a bulletin issued on the event of the foundation of the AABK in June 2002.

national politics in Turkey. Referring to Dodd (1983) she writes: "differences of opinion became polarized; instead of trying to work out a compromise, each party did its best to delegitimize the other" (Delaney 1991, 219). Writing on elite politics, Frey (1975,66) emphasizes the operation of a strong "ingroup-outgroup orientation" in Turkish politics: "The involvement, warmth, commitment, and sharing displayed in ingroup interactions are, however, balanced against almost antipodal tendencies displayed in outgroup interactions. Any ordinary opponent easily becomes regarded as *düşman*, the enemy. Political competition becomes polarized, almost automatically." Şerif Mardin (1966) already earlier pointed towards a strategy of delegitimizing opposition that pervades the political approach of dominant groups. Seufert (1998,380) advances the thesis that democracy, tolerance, human rights, and other values are in the Turkish political context not understood as general values of which the values of a particular party, faction, or group present but one example. Instead, each group sees its own norms and morality as the best—and sometimes even the only—possible embodiment of these values and thereby radically delegitimizes the claims and approaches of others. Harris (1970, 1) similarly emphasizes the "profound intolerance of each political faction for its rivals." Some observers link this kind of radical factionalism with a political culture of distrust that has been inherited from Ottoman times (Tachau 1984, 67). For Paul Stirling the lack of mutual trust among the villagers of the place where he did field research was so remarkable that he wondered how villagers were at all able to establish a workable voluntary association (Stirling 1960, 69f). Also the dialectic of unity and separatism in the discourse of the Turkish nation has to be added to this quite diverse evidence of a strictly polarizing factionalism that delegitimizes the respective other, as well as the development of almost infinitesimal factions within the Turkish left since the 1970s. We have seen that especially this latter example provided the framework for the political socialization of many present Alevi activists.

In Alevi discourse, Alevi identity is literally considered as a function of unity. In the discourse of the dominant faction, then, *muhalefet* is a threat to *birlik* and endangers the whole community. Crosscutting identities, like in the current example a regional or ethnic identity of Zaza and Dersimli, are considered as a danger to (unified) Alevi identity. Thus, to explain an opposition as a movement based on particular ethnic ties as has been done by the dominant section of the AABF is also a means to challenge its legitimacy. In order to prevent such a challenge, the Dersimli members of the opposition strategically never referred to a specific Dersim identity. Although recently there have been efforts to organize a specific Zaza/Dersim identity in Germany (Kehl 1998; 1999, 447f), the Dersimli of the opposition within the AABF never related to such efforts but remained strictly within the framework of Alevi identity and community.

The Alevi Movement and the Intersection of Difference

Beyond the limits set by the master difference of Alevis versus Sunnis, Alevi identity is open to the intervention of a number of intersecting identifications. These refer to ideas about what Alevism essentially is (religion? culture? Islam?), but also to other identifications like ethnic and regional identifications that are not in the first place emphasized discursively but remain rather tacit—and perhaps only alleged. The latter identifications can be employed as a resource and as a framework for interpreting interaction in the formation of alliances in order to achieve certain political ends. Identifications here link up with interstitial practices of competition for power. They also operate as structuring relations of loyalty. This could be seen also after a personal conflict between a middle–aged leader of the HAKM and a young man of different regional affiliation in Turkey. When this conflict could not be resolved within the association, almost all members of the HAKM that stemmed from the same region as the young man left the association. Another very significant identification that intersects with Alevi identity is the nation: should Alevis identify in the first place as members of the Turkish nation? This issue will be discussed in detail in chapter eight.

In the current chapter we have seen that the common baseline of identification as Alevi is the emphasis on difference from Sunnis. In the next chapter I will turn again towards this master difference and show how a historical experience that culminated in the Sivas massacre and discourses and practices of commemoration related to this experience of violence establish a common ground for the construction of Alevi community beyond the divisive encroachment of intersecting differences.

5

THE POLITICS OF MEMORY: SIVAS

Social Memory

"Sivas'ı unutmadık, unutturmayacağız, anılarını yaşatacağız!" —"We did not forget Sivas, we will not allow it to fall into oblivion, we will keep its memory alive!" This call has been the motto of many commemorative ceremonies that were organized by Alevi associations after the Sivas massacre. Memory and its social relationships have become a prime object of interest in the social and cultural sciences after the writings of Maurice Halbwachs were rediscovered in the 1980s. Strongly influenced by Émile Durkheim and his idea of social representations, Halbwachs proposed that like ideas also memory was a social issue. Halbwachs (1985) coined the notion of a "collective memory" and emphasized that individual memory always takes place in a social context. In the communicative context of our social environment we remember certain things and forget others. In Halbwachs's view, individual memory is secondary to collective memory. Like Durkheim, Halbwachs has been criticized for unduly privileging the social over the individual. Gedi and Elam argue, accordingly, that memory is never collective in the sense of being the recollection of a collective subject, because there is no actually *collective* subject but only a collection of individual subjects. They insist that the only legitimate use of the concept "collective memory" is a metaphorical one (Gedi and Elam 1996, 43). Yet, if we concede that the memory and remembering is never *collective* in a literal sense, it does not cease to be *social* because the individual memory is developed in discursive social context (Fentress and Wickham 1992, 7).

In the recent debate on memory, however, another idea has become significant that turns the relationship between memory and collectivities upside down: not only is memory based on a particular community, but community is constituted by shared memory. Individuals become members of a community by sharing particular strands of memory. A community is therefore always a "community of remembering" (*Erinnerungsgemeinschaft*, Assmann 2002, 40). Images of the past, events that are remembered, stories that are narrated and reenacted time and again constitute the continuity of a community. Particular ways of relating to past events also delimit the boundaries of a particular community: others remember differently. Identities are constituted by relating in specific ways to the past. In chapter one I have emphasized the nation as a model of concepts of identity. This model resonates here strongly as the imagination of nations goes hand in hand with the creation of particular images of the past: a nation without particular historical narratives is unimaginable. The new interest in memory has also sparked a new debate on the relationship between history and memory. Is all history just a specific kind of social memory? Or is (academic) history opposed to memory because it endeavors to bring to the light also those aspects of the past that are omitted by memory? Burke (1989) emphasized that both history and memory have to be historicized. History as well as memory is told from particular vantage points in the respective present. Both are selective: they create meaning by highlighting certain aspects of the past and omitting others. Following again Halbwachs, Assmann (2002, 40) emphasizes therefore that memory works through reconstruction. Because memories work from specific perspectives in the present, they are subjected to the social and political conditions of the present. Accordingly, memory is *social* not only because it may be *shared* by a number of actors who thereby form a community, but also because it may be *contested* by different actors and communities.

The memory of Sivas, of the attack on the Alevi cultural festival in July 1993 that caused the death of thirty-seven people, has become a central aspect of the construction of Alevi identity. The memory of Sivas highlights the master opposition of Alevis and Sunnis: Sunnis are remembered as the perpetrators of violence, Alevis as its victims. This difference is given additional meaning by a series of parallel oppositions that are related to the event: the opposition of backwardness and modernity, of intolerance and tolerance, of fundamentalism and enlightened secularism. Because identity is not only a matter of construction but also of recognition, the story of Sivas is not only told among Alevis but efforts are taken to disseminate the Alevi reading of the event among others. The agents of memory are in the first place again Alevi organizations and their activists. This chapter describes and analyses the discourses and practices and the iconography of remembering Sivas within the Alevi movement.

Remembering Sivas

The arson in Sivas in July 1993 was no doubt a terrible event. Thirty-seven people died, most of them in consequence of fume poisoning. The majority of the victims, thirty-two people, were participants of the Pir Sultan Abdal culture festival. Not all of them were Alevis, as there was also a Dutch student who researched about Alevism. Sivas was not the first time that Alevis suffered deadly violence. Other events that Alevis categorize as "massacres" had occurred in Maraş in 1978 and in Çorum in 1980. The number of victims killed in these earlier massacres was much higher. However, the events in Çorum and Maraş did not have comparable effects. Some consequences like the separation of Alevis in Hamburg from the HDF after the Maraş massacre notwithstanding, these were not "critical events" that sparked a mass mobilization of Alevis. With a certain emphatic tone that is not unusual in Alevi discourse, this is expressed by a young Alevi writer in Germany with the following words:

> Although incursions on Alevi residential areas occurred already in the 1970s in Çorum and Maraş, the lethargy [of Alevis] could be broken only after the Sivas massacre. Like a phoenix that burns himself and that rises in rejuvenated form from his own ashes, a broad consciousness grew that it was necessary to organize the Alevi masses anew and to restore their institutions (Erbektaş 1998a, 87).

What is peculiar about Sivas, then? In order to explore this question I will turn to the personal memories of young Alevis.

The arson in Sivas on 2 July 1993 was also a media event. Due to the new satellite TV networks, news about Sivas spread immediately even outside of Turkey. The arson was partly broadcast live in the news of the day. With many of my interlocutors I discussed, therefore, how they received this news. In the following section Murat, a young man who since the Alevi Culture Week had been involved with the HAKM and who devoted much of his energy to learning how to play *saz*, tells about his own experience. He was twenty-two years old when Sivas happened.

I: "What happened when you got the news of Sivas in summer 1993?"

Murat: "Oh, that … it does not befit a normal human being to hear something like that. I was in Pinneberg [a town near Hamburg], at our friends' place. I was playing something [on the *saz*]. We were drinking something. Then somebody said, they had the new Turkish TV networks, they had got a new antenna. He said, Murat, please five minutes, I would like to watch the news. Suddenly I heard the first word, Muhlis Akarsu was dead. I saw fire and all that and I thought I had got it wrong. Then I saw the list [of victims], it was half an hour after the end of the massacre. Then I saw, Hasret Gültekin. I was thinking, what is this? I lost my voice; I could not talk any more. The next day when I got up I had red spots on my skin everywhere and I could not talk, my voice was still gone. Then I went to the association [the HAKM] immediately, we assembled there and discussed about what to do. Many came to visit us, from different associations. Also from communist organizations. They all came to our place [and discussed] what we should do together. They were shocked. I prepared posters, such things, I wrote. We had to organize something for Cologne, that is, centrally, and also for Hamburg, regionally. We organized that. But, somehow, we were gone. I had lost my voice. We all were, some even more than me, we all were shattered. I don't know, I mean, one does not have to be very sensitive, but, (…) I don't know, that was actually the worst thing that one can imagine."

Murat remembers having been deeply moved and shocked by learning what had happened in Sivas. He remembers Sivas as a bodily experience that caused him to lose his voice and to get red spots on his skin. The event in Sivas obviously had a deep, personal meaning for him. The memory of Özlem, a young woman who was twenty-four years old when the massacre happened, is quite different:

> Well, to be true, of course, I was sad. But I did not get it like this … that is, now I perhaps would see it different. I don't know, more intensely perhaps. OK, maybe, now I am a little older, perhaps I think differently. OK, also at that time I was not very young. Well, of course I was very sad, especially after I had heard that the people who had lit the fire were coming from the mosque. I could not understand this. I could not get this into my head. I say, how can a human being that claims to be a religious human being pray, pray in a mosque and then walk out of the mosque and simply kill people. I cannot understand something like that, no matter what kind of people there are, whether they are Alevis or others. How can a Muslim do that, how can they reconcile this with their conscience? These are the questions that I still cannot answer, to be true. And I was especially angry that the government did nothing against it (…) And then you saw again, yes, you are Alevi, you could well have been inside such a thing. It also can happen to me, in Turkey, in such a festival.

Özlem had no vivid memory about the circumstances of how she learned about Sivas. She just remembered that "of course" she had been sad. It seems that the news about Sivas did not have a specific message for herself. It was more like any news about a violent event or an accident in which many people lost their lives—news that roused human compassion but that did not have a personal meaning for herself. She said that she did not get it "like this." She did not get it *right,* she wanted to say. In our conversation, Özlem apparently tried to excuse herself for not having got the message of Sivas immediately right. Later, Özlem continued, she saw things differently. Later she understood that Sivas had a particular message for herself: "It also can happen to me."

We have two short stories of memory here. Murat remembered Sivas as a kind of personal experience that had specific effects upon himself as a person, as a bodily as well as a social being. Özlem, in contrast, originally lacked such a personal experience. For her Sivas was a distant event. In contrast with Murat, Özlem had not been involved with the Alevi movement at the time when Sivas happened. For Murat, the commitment to the Alevi movement had already had a great personal significance. He had taken part in the Alevi Culture Week shortly after he had come to Germany as an eighteen–years–old youth. Previously he had moved from his village to Istanbul, and there he had acquired a clear understanding that Alevis were considered negatively in Turk-ish society. He had experienced the Alevi Culture Week as a kind of personal liberation.[1] After the foundation of the HAKM, Murat became deeply committed to the activities of the associations. He joined the *saz* and *semah* courses and participated in the organization of all kinds of events. Özlem migrated to Hamburg together with her mother and her sisters in 1980 when she was eleven years old. Neither she nor her fam-ily was involved in the Alevi movement in Hamburg during its forma-tive phase. Only much later, in 2000, she joined the HAKM.

Murat learned about the Sivas massacre when he was already part of the Alevi movement. The people who died in Sivas were involved in the same movement to which he was committed. Further, among the victims were some *saz* players whom he strongly admired. Murat had a sense of community with the victims of Sivas. Özlem developed such a sense only in retrospect, after she had become involved in the move-ment. Thus "later," as she said, she started to see Sivas differently.

An experience comparable to Özlem's was made by Nermin. She was sixteen years old when the massacre happened. Her parents were pi-ous Alevis but they had no relations with the associations in Hamburg because they considered them "leftists". Nermin had not been told by her parents about Alevism, but she had perceived differences between herself and her friends. Not liking such differences that set her apart from her friends she even wanted to wear a headscarf at one time. Ner-min told:

> It was when I slowly, slowly started to ask myself who I was, why I was different from my schoolmates, why did my classmates behave differ-ently. Well, somehow they were different and I was different. (...) At that time we were on summer vacations [in Turkey]. They [her parents] sat in front of the TV in the evening and I saw only that something was burn-ing. (...) I did not take it to heart because I thought such fires happen time and again. I thought that it was just a normal building that was burning. (...) But my parents reacted very differently. My father was really out-raged, he was watching the news all the time, and also my mother was incensed and agitated, she even cried. But I did not know why this fire had agitated my parents so much. And later, in Germany, I understood that people had deliberately put fire to the hotel because they [the vic-tims] were people that belonged to my religious community.

Like Özlem, Nermin had perceived the burning hotel as just some "nor-mal" fire. She could not understand the quite extraordinary reactions of her parents. In Nermin's perception, the fire had nothing to do with herself. She had no idea of being part of a community to which also the victims of the fire belonged. This was not only due to her young age, but also to the fact that her parents had not told her about being Alevi.

---

[1] See chapter three.

Like Özlem, Nermin acquired a different understanding of the event, an understanding of community with the victims of Sivas, only later, after she had been told about being Alevi. Subsequently, she became engaged in HAAK BIR and later in the youth wing of the AABF.

The massacre of Sivas was conceived by the activists of the Alevi movement as an event that had targeted the entire community. In the mainstream media, the massacre was explained mainly as the result of an Islamist riot that had been provoked by Aziz Nesin's disrespectfulness with regard to Islam, expressed, among other things, in his translation of Salman Rushdie's *Satanic Verses*. In such a construal, Alevis figure only as victims by chance, as marginal to the event and not as the targets of the attack. Furthermore, part of the responsibility for the event is ascribed to the victims, because they were the ones who had invited Aziz Nesin and participated in such a "provocative" event. At issue was, therefore, the recognition of Alevis as the victims of Sivas. A simple and direct expression of this issue is the word that is used to designate what had happened in Sivas. In Germany, Alevis strictly employ the unequivocal word "massacre," that is, *katliam* in Turkish or *Massaker* in German, whereas non-Alevis that do not sympathize much with Alevi perspectives frequently use the neutral expressions *olaylar* (Turkish) or *Ereignisse* (German), i.e., "events."[2] In order to avoid a strict polarization also many Alevis in Turkey employ the expression *Sivas olayları* (events of Sivas).

In the Alevi movement, the Sivas massacre was not conceived as a unique incident, but as a paradigmatic event that revealed the precarious position of Alevis in general. It was conceived as an event that could have happened to any Alevi in Turkey. Commitment to the Alevi movement engendered a particular reading of the Sivas massacre, which in turn confirmed the necessity of the movement. On the other hand, the massacre helped to extend this understanding to other Alevis who had not yet committed themselves to the movement. After Sivas it was argued again and again that Alevis needed to organize themselves, that they required strong associations in order to protect themselves. This means on one hand that the Alevi community was imagined and defined essentially in opposition to others who were seen as potential or actual attackers and perpetrators of violence against Alevis, and on the other that the commitment to the Alevi movement, membership in the associations, and participation in their activities was predicated to a considerable extent on a sense of living under a constant threat. The immediate

---

[2] This distinction of vocabulary raises the question of which term should be used by the anthropological observer. In this chapter I have employed both expressions. I am of the opinion, however, that the death of thirty-seven people in consequence of a violent attack certainly justifies the employment of the term "massacre."

signs for the mobilization sparked by the Sivas massacre were the demonstrations that followed. There were large protest marches in Ankara and Istanbul on the following day. The majority of the victims were laid to rest at a cemetery in Ankara because many of them had been the members of a *semah* group from the city. The burial too was turned into a powerful demonstration. Almost a week later, the large demonstration in Cologne took place and there were also smaller expressions of discontent in other German cities and elsewhere in Europe, like in London where 10,000 people are said to have joined in a protest march.

Commemorative Events

In subsequent years, this protest against what had happened in Sivas was turned into efforts to remember the massacre and its victims. Sivas became a constant topic of discourse in the Alevi movement in Turkey and in Germany. Already in July 1994, the *Alevilerin Sesi* published a special issue under the headline "*Sivas katliamını unutmayacağız!*" ("We will not forget the Sivas massacre!") and associations of the AABF held commemorative conventions. Commemorative conventions have become regular annual events since then. Such events are organized by local Alevi associations as well as on a larger scale by the AABF or by its regional branches.

On 6 and 7 July 2001, such a commemorative event was held by the HAKM in Hamburg. The event took place in a large auditorium of the university. It comprised a panel discussion on the first day and a cultural event on the second day. I will go with some detail into the flyer that was distributed for this event because it presents a good example for the discourse and the iconography of commemoration. The A5–sized folded flyer (figure 5.1) bore on its first page in capital letters the headline "We did not forget Sivas, we will not forget it." Below that the word "YANIYORUZ…" ("We are burning") was printed in capital letters of the same size. In the program printed below, only the second day was headed as "*Sivas Şehitlerinin Anma Günü*" ("Memorial Day for the Victims of Sivas"). The first day was simply announced as a panel discussion under the title "The yesterday, today and tomorrow of Alevism." The background of the first page was formed by a blurred photo of the burning hotel. The whole page of the flyer was framed by little portrait photos of thirty-three of the victims. Inside, the flyer had a poemlike declaration of the HAKM on its left side and verses by Ataol Behramoğlu, a Turkish poet, on the right. The left and right margins were formed by the word "Sivas" written with one letter on top on the other. The individual letters were again composed from the portraits of the victims and the background of the margins was formed by a flame. The declaration was headed in capital letters by the sentence

Figure 5.1 Flyer for the commemoration of Sivas (front page), HAKM, 2001

"SIVAS'TA YAKILDIK IŞIK OLDUK!" (We were burned in Sivas and became a light!). The text continued as follows:

> They have set fire!
> They have set fire to our enlightenment.
> They have set fire to our young daughters and sons.

They have set fire to our *ozans*,[3] our writers, our friends, our companions that we have bred with a thousand and one labors.

They have burned them while they were dancing *semah* and chanting *deyiş*.[4]

They have set fire to the brothers of the Anatolian people.

They have set fire to thirty-seven *cans*.

They have set fire to the human being, to humanity.

Just like before, they have set fire in Sivas on 2 July 1993

They have set fire like the arson of Hazro, Şırnak, Lice, Kulp, and İdil.

In the brook of Kasaplar they have killed sixteen people and burnt them afterwards.[5]

Because they are afraid.

They fear the Anatolian people's future of brotherliness, humanity, equality and enlightenment. They fear the shoots of humanness, peace and friendship that grow from a soil soaked with the blood of brothers after centuries of provoked struggles.

They are afraid of those who think, who speak, and who ask questions.

They are afraid of the human being.

Therefore, burning and destroying, they kill.

Being those who have been based on oppression, cruelty, and blood, they fear the breakdown of their systems of interest.

They are afraid of those who make the people conscious and who say "It is enough!"

Their hands are full of blood, they smell of blood.

It is necessary to face them with disgust and to call them to account for our blood which they have shed and to throw them out.

In the eighth year we remember our thirty-seven companions once again with bowed heads because we could not hold them to account.

We should not forget the murderers.

We cry it out!

We did not forget Sivas and we will not forget it…

This text was written by Ibrahim Renkliçay, who was then chairman of the HAKM and at the same time representative of the AABF for northern Germany. A clear characterization of Alevis emerges from this text: Alevis are those who suffered violence, not only in Sivas, they are those who have been oppressed, but also those who are enlightened, who think and establish consciousness. However, this characterization is not linked with Alevis in a parochial way. Rather, Alevis appear as an example of a universal condition of peace, brotherliness, humanity—and as standing generally for those who are oppressed. The text refers explicitly to cases of violence in Kurdish villages. Thus, Alevis are

---

[3] An *ozan* is an Alevi folk singer.

[4] *Deyiş* are the spiritual hymns that are sung in the Alevi ritual *cem*.

[5] Hazro, Şırnak, Lice, Kulp, and İdil are Kurdish villages that have been set on fire by the Turkish army. Also Kasaplar is a place in Kurdistan that was affected by the Kurdish war.

not characterized as a particular category of mankind, as a community labeled with an identity of difference, but as a community embodying the universal values of humanism. In contrast with Alevis, those who have committed violence against Alevis and others, those who have put fire to the hotel in Sivas are parochial, fighting for their particular interests against the universal community of enlightened humanity. This poemlike declaration is a typical example for the Alevi discourse that connects Alevi identity with a universalist perspective and that, in the context of remembering Sivas, creates a bridge from the particular violent event to the general issue of a struggle of enlightenment against darkness, of peace against violence and of humanity against inhumaneness. The reverse of the flyer is covered with a picture: A woman and a man dancing *semah* on a line of flames. They carry a big *saz* on their raised hands. Above the *saz* a stylized white pigeon is flying in front of a yellow sun. The background of the picture is bright red. The image repeats the symbolism of the HAKM's logo, which is printed in the upper corners of the page and which also exhibits a pair dancing *semah* in front of a white pigeon. The symbolism of the picture is of course quite explicit: the *saz* and *semah* are general symbols of Alevis and Alevism, the flames and the red background represents the fire of Sivas, and the pigeon stands for the peacefulness of Alevis. The message is thus: we are continuing our efforts towards peace also in times of violence and oppression.

The panel discussion on the first day of the event negotiated Alevism and the Alevi movement in a very general way, referring also to Sivas. Participants in the panel were Attila Erdem, an academic from Ankara who was also chairman of the Hacı Bektaş Veli Culture Associations in Turkey; Arif Sağ, the singer and *saz* player who was among those who were trapped in the burning hotel in Sivas and survived; Turgut Öker as the chairman of the AABF, and Hıdır Temel, an Alevi intellectual who is also closely related with the AABF. In the discussion they addressed topics like the necessity for Alevis in Germany to be vigilant about and committed to the situation of Alevis in Turkey and the precarious relationship between Alevis and the state in Turkey, also criticizing CEM Vakfı for being too closely related with the state. Arif Sağ, who had himself been a member of parliament in Turkey, endorsed the necessity of Alevis taking up political commitments in order to improve their situation. He also argued that Alevis should not identify as Muslims. Attila Erdem also addressed less controversial topics like the place of *cem* in Alevism. Thus, in accordance with its inclusive title, the discussion that lasted for almost four hours was quite broad and unspecific but the diverse topics were united by the shared subtext of discrimination of Alevis in Turkey.

The following *Sivas Şehitlerini Anma Günü* (Day of Commemoration of the Victims of Sivas) was a cultural program that consisted for the

Figure 5.2 Children present images of Sivas victims at a commemorative convention of the HAKM, 2001 (photography by Martin Sökefeld).

greater part of musical performances of local and international Alevi artists. Many of the performers spoke a few sentences about Sivas and the musical performances were interspersed with more direct references to the massacre. Another survivor had been invited, the poet Zerrin Taşpınar. She narrated in full detail the occurrences in Sivas and recited a few of her poems. In a break between two musical performances, slides of the event were presented that showed the raging masses in front of the hotel, the fire, the people trapped inside, the victims' bodies at a hospital, and the protest marches of the following days. In another break thirty-three children stormed the stage, each of them carrying a portrait of one of the victims.[6] They lined up on the stage and presented the pictures to the audience, who rose from their chairs and applauded.

This commemorative event and its flyer acquaint us with a number of important elements of commemoration. First, there is a commemorative symbolism that connects images of fire with symbols of Alevis like the *saz* and *semah* and with the pigeon as a general symbol of peace. Images of people dancing *semah* in the flames abound in the iconography of commemoration. This symbolism is supplemented by the icons

---

[6] There is a certain variation in the numbers of victims that are commemorated. In total, thirty-seven persons died in the massacre, but only thirty-three were participants of the Pir Sultan Abdal festival. Sometimes all victims are mentioned, sometimes only thirty-three. But invariably only the thirty-three participant victims are named and represented by portraits.

of the victims that pervade the commemorative events in the form of exhibitions, portraits displayed by, for instance, little children in the course of the conventions, or graphic arts illustrating the flyers and brochures about Sivas. A second important element of commemoration is the narration of the events, most importantly by surviving witnesses like Zerrin Taşpınar, Arif Sağ, or Ali Balkız, the organizer of the Pir Sultan Abdal festival at Sivas and later chairman of the PSAKD. This narrative aspect is frequently supported by the display of documentary photographs. The documentary element of commemoration does not only refer to the massacre itself but sometimes also to the juridical consequences of the event. Therefore also lawyers who were engaged in or who observed the court procedures are frequently invited to the commemorative conventions. The third element of commemoration is the insertion of the Sivas massacre into a general discourse about Alevis that relates Alevism to universal humanist values and puts them in opposition to all those who disrespect these values. This third element, then, establishes a particular meaning of Sivas. With a certain variation, these elements of symbolism and iconography, of documentation and of meaning characterize the practices and events of commemorating Sivas.

Commemorative events take place at different scales that reflect different levels of organization. The convention of 2001 that I have described was organized and financed by the HAKM, also in the name of the secretariat of the AABF for northern Germany, with the (largely moral) support of the other Alevi associations of the Hamburg region. I estimate that four to five hundred persons participated. Originally it had been intended that all local associations shared equally in the responsibility for the convention, but due to a dispute about financial contributions and about the question whether also the Kurdish-Alevi association HAK EVI should be included, this could not be realized. In the two previous years, commemorative conventions that took place in the hall of HAAK BIR had been jointly organized by the local Alevi associations of Hamburg, with the exception of HAK EVI and ÖCB. The convention of the year 2000 was fraught with conflicts about the representation of the associations and about financial liabilities. Because Mehmet Zülküf Kılıç had again been elected as chairman of HAAK BIR, the old rivalry between HAAK BIR and the HAKM rose again. There had been no such problems in the year before when the convention had been supplemented by a commemorative vigil in a pedestrian area in Hamburg-Altona. The convention of that year included a kind of symbolic commemorative ritual: thirty-three persons carried thirty-three red roses slowly through the hall and laid them down on a table that also held a condolences book. Subsequently, many of the participants entered their names into the book.

In 2003, that is ten years after Sivas, the commemorative events were organized on a European level. In the year before the AABF had formed

Figure 5.3 Commemorative vigil in a pedestrian zone, Hamburg-Altona, 1999 (photography by Martin Sokefield).

the European Confederation of Alevi Communities (Avrupa Alevi Bir-likleri Konfederasyonu, AABK) together with the Alevi federations of the other European countries. Being by far the largest of the Alevi feder-ation, the AABF took the lead in organizing the confederation and con-tributed most of the required resources. The German Alevi Federation organized a veritable commemorative caravan of Alevi artists, intellec-tuals, and representatives of associations that crossed Europe from the north to the south. It started in Sweden and continued through Den-mark, Switzerland, Austria, France, and Holland. Besides, there were more than ten commemorative conventions in different cities of Ger-many. The commemorative campaign of that year had a special tone, because in November 2002 the AK Partisi had won the parliamentary elections in Turkey and formed the government. The AK Partisi had emerged, after reorganizations and splits, from the Refah Partisi, which controlled the Sivas municipality in 1993 and which is therefore held responsible for the massacre by the Alevis. Accordingly, the announce-ments of the new Turkish government about Sivas were critically moni-tored. Alevi organizations demanded a formal word of apology by the government, but the government took no explicit stance and rather rec-ommended an attitude of forgiveness. A group of AK Partisi members of parliament favored a law of amnesty for those who had been accused or convicted of the crime in Sivas together with convicted members of the PKK and the Turkish Islamist organization Hizbollah.[7] Already before, the events of Sivas and Solingen, the German town near Cologne where on 29 May 1993, neo-Nazis had set fire to a house of Turkish immigrants and killed five people, had been compared in Alevi discourse. Now this comparison was extended to a comparison of attitudes of the Turkish and German governments as they were expressed on the tenth anniversary of these crimes. At the commemorative conventions speakers emphasized that whereas the German President Johannes Rau had visited the site of the arson in Solingen on the occasion of the anniversary, expressing sorrow and sympathy, nothing comparable could be expected from the representatives of the Turkish state.

Remembering Sivas is not limited to the particular time of year in which the commemorative ceremonies are held. In Ankara, two memorial sites have been established that are frequently visited by Alevi groups or individuals. The first such site is the graveyard where a number of Sivas victims have been buried. Besides the individual tombstones, each of which is accompanied by a bush of roses, a memorial has been erected. Two large slabs of granite face each other rough edges. The two slabs are connected with thirty-seven iron rods. Two brass plaques with the names of the victims are attached to the granite slabs. In autumn 1998 I visited this site together with a youth group of the HAKM. The young Alevis from Hamburg paused in silence in front of the graves and laid down flowers. Later in the day we visited a branch of the Pir Sultan Abdal Kültür Derneği in Ankara's Dikmen district. Nineteen members of this association who had participated as a *semah*-group in the Sivas festival died in 1993. The chairman of the association explained the meaning of the memorial to us: The two slabs of granite symbolize the danger that Turkish society may break apart. The iron rods between the slabs stand for efforts towards peace and reconciliation in order to keep the segments together. The number of the iron rods, which equals the total number of the victims of Sivas, is meant to express, then, that Alevis invest their lives to keep the society together. In this branch of the PSAKD as well as in another association, the Hacı Bektaş Veli Anadolu Kültür Vakfı, we were brought together with relatives of the victims. The next day we visited the central office of the PSAKD. Here, we were again told about the massacre and we visited the second memorial site: a room set aside as a kind of memorial shrine. Photos, personal belongings, and works of the victims are displayed in thirty-three showcases. In the showcase dedicated to the writer Behçet Aysan, for instance, some of his books are kept as well as pens and his broken glasses that were recovered from the ruins of the burnt hotel. Showcases for the younger victims of the *semah* group from Ankara exhibit things like toys, letters, paintings or favorite audiotapes. In this

---

[7] See *Cumhuriyet Hafta*, July 4, 2003.

exhibition the victims are deeply personalized, and this personaliza-
tion enabled a strong identification of the young members of our group
with the victims. They took much time to look at the showcases. Some
girls wept quietly and an almost sacral atmosphere prevailed in the
room. Like our group, many Alevi groups or delegations from Turkey or
abroad visit these sites in Ankara and pay their respect to the victims.

Practices of remembering Sivas are also part of the large Alevi festival in the central Anatolian town Hacıbektaş, which takes place every
year in mid-August. For many years, the PSAKD has had a stand in the
first courtyard of the old Bektaşi *tekke* at which photos of the victims are
displayed. Members of the association collect signatures in support of
an appeal to turn the site of the massacre in Sivas, the Hotel Madımak,
into a memorial site. The conversion of the hotel has been demanded
by Alevi associations for many years, but as of yet there is not even a
memorial plaque. The opening ceremony of the Hacı Bektaş Festival in
2003, ten years after Sivas, comprised a strong element of commemoration. In between the speeches of Alevi activists and politicians (which
included the Turkish president Ahmet Necdet Sezer) the names of the
Sivas victims were read aloud and every victim was briefly introduced.
The names of the victims were greeted with applause by the audience.
The chairman of the PSAKD was given a medal in commemoration of
the victims. Subsequently, a large banner with portraits of the victims
was displayed on the stage.

Posters with portraits of the victims are omnipresent in the premises
of Alevi associations in Turkey as well as in Germany, and an aspect of
commemoration pervades nearly all activities of the associations. Almost every Alevi convention starts with a *saygı duruşu*, a moment of
respect in which the participants rise from their seats and remain silent:
"Now we will have a moment of respect in memory of our victims from
Kerbela through Sivas." There is a certain variation in these calls for
saygı duruşu: Kerbela and Sivas are almost always mentioned, sometimes other events categorized as massacres like Maraş and Gazi are
added. But sometimes simply a moment of respect "for our victims"
is called for. Kerbela is the site where the Imam Hüseyin, the second
son of the Imam Ali, was defeated together with his companions by the
troops of his adversary, the Khalif Yezit in 680. Kerbela is remembered
as the first event of violence suffered by Alevis at the hands of Sunnis
and signifies the separation of Alevis from (Sunni) Islam. Irrespective
of the particular phrasing, the intention of a call for a moment of silence
at the beginning of Alevi conventions establishes a historical continuity
that links Kerbela and Sivas as two paradigmatic events that demonstrate and emphasize an identity of Alevis as victims of violence. The
saygı duruşu is a "micro ritual," which disseminates the memory of the
victimization of Alevis in all kinds of events and conventions.

Representing Sivas to the German Public

In Germany the Alevi associations also attempt to disseminate their interpretation of Sivas among the German public. For this purpose the booklets published about Sivas by the AABF or its associations always contain also one or two texts in German. In 1999, the AABF published an entire brochure on Sivas in German.[8] This booklet makes use of the same graphic elements that we have found in the flyer analyzed above. Also in the German brochure there is the element of fire and flames that form the background of the pages. The front page is framed by the same little portraits of the victims. The texts are for the greater part translations of articles from a special issue of the journal *Pir Sultan Abdal*, published by the PSAKD in 1993, immediately after the massacre. Ali Balkız narrates the event as witness and survivor, the victims are introduced with photos and short texts, and Lütfi Kaleli, as a second survivor, makes a short comment. Fifteen pages of the brochure are filled with photographs of the Islamist demonstrators in front of the Hotel Madımak, of people waiting for their rescue inside the hotel, of the victims' dead bodies in a hospital, and finally of the subsequent protest marches that took place in Ankara. The same photographs are frequently projected as a slide show about the massacre at commemorative events.

Besides these republished elements, there is also a text that has been written specifically for this publication. According to a short preface, this text is intended to convey the "current meaning of commemorating the victims of Sivas." This text is of particular significance because it attempts to establish a meaning of Sivas for society in Germany. The text opens with a paragraph that briefly describes the event of Sivas, emphasizing that the massacre was a planned action that was carried out with particular brutality and that was not prevented by the security forces. The text continues telling that Alevis still remember the victims of Sivas, and that Sivas has been a turning point in the history of Alevis because it motivated an unprecedented self-organization on which Alevis embarked "in order to unite their democratic potential in a community and to stop becoming victims of religious violence" (AABF 1999, 3). The third paragraph turns to the significance of the massacre for Germany and relates Sivas to the debate of immigration and Islam in Germany:

> Especially at a time when the debate about Islam in Germany has reached
> a peak, we perceive the necessity to cling to the heritage of the victims that

---

[8] AABF 1999. The text was reissued two years later in a brochure on Sivas published by the Baden-Württemberg regional section of the AABF.

is a declared belief in Western democracy and freedom. Due to considerations of the context of the politics of migration, the greater part of German society agrees to the integration of Islam in Germany. In the first instance, this attitude has to be appreciated. Yet the public overlooks a pertinent, potential danger for German and European society that emerges from certain Islamist circles, which have hitherto successfully disguised their true intentions. They pose as tolerant and signal their readiness to accept the Western way of life. In fact, however, they do not tolerate people of a different faith. This attitude stems from the archaic idea that their own religion is the better religion. In the service of their religion they intend to erect a theocracy according to the rules of the sharia. This and nothing else is their ultimate aim in Germany (ibid.).

The text refers further to the fact that hitherto no Turkish Islamic association in Germany has officially condemned the Sivas massacre. This is seen as a proof for the alleged intentions of these associations. It is deplored that Islamist associations intend to cooperate with the German state and plan to teach Islamic religion at public schools in Germany. Although no Islamic association is explicitly mentioned, these passages refer in the first place to *Milli Görüş* ("National Vision"), the (in terms of membership) largest Islamic association of Turkish migrants in Germany. Milli Görüş originated as the foreign support association of the Islamist Turkish Refah Partisi (RP, Welfare Party). Although representatives of Milli Görüş frequently denied close relations with the RP in Turkey, this denial has to be taken with a grain of salt. The leadership of Milli Görüş and RP even shared close family relationships: Mehmet Erbakan, the former chairman of Milli Görüş, is the nephew of Necmettin Erbakan, who was the chairman of the RP and for a short period even the prime minister of Turkey. In recent public statements, Milli Görüş has dissociated itself from Islamist political aims and declared itself to fully accept the constitutional principles of the German state. Yet, there is an ongoing discussion in Germany about the question whether this new public outlook is based on a true reorientation or whether it is just the public camouflage of a continuing Islamist commitment (cf. Ewing 2003). Alevis decidedly endorse the second opinion.

The subsequent paragraph of the text on Sivas represents Alevis as the victims of religiously motivated violence that has not only started with the recent cases. It explains that there has been no satisfying juridical procedure on the Sivas massacre in Turkey, yet Alevis, in spite of their dissatisfaction with the courts, never opted for taking the law into their own hands and taking revenge because they believe in the democratic state under the rule of law. After this the text returns to Germany:

> In this context it is perplexing why the German public falls short in recognizing the traditionally democratic ethos of the Alevis. As a consequence, it [the Alevi community] is not taken into account in the debate on Islam

in Germany. In this way the German public overlooks a religious community of about 600,000 people among the migrants from Turkey that does not come into conflict with the law and that introduces a great democratic potential to German society. Thereby an important opportunity for multicultural German society is missed. This has to be considered as a heavy loss on the way to successful religious integration (AABF 1999, 4).

Departing from the memory of the Sivas massacre, this text primarily achieves three things: First it establishes a clear opposition and contrast between Alevis and Islamists. Second, it transposes this opposition to Germany and the German debate on Islam and migration, emphasizing that Islamism is a danger to German society. Third, it highlights Alevis as an asset of multicultural society and integration in Germany because they are so different from Islamists. In the presupposed opposition of Islamism and democratic (Western) values, Alevis and Germans are situated on the same side of the divide. However, at the same time it is deplored that the democratic ethos of the Alevi community is not recognized in Germany. From remembering the Sivas massacre, the text derives a call for recognizing Alevis as a democratic community that shares the fundamental values of German society. Sivas confirmed the Alevi-Sunni master difference. Alevi discourse parallels to a great extent a widespread German discourse on Islam that identifies Islam as a potential or actual political menace, which has to be kept under strict surveillance and control. I will return to this point in chapter seven when I discuss the self-representation of Alevis vis-à-vis the German public with more detail.

Sivas and Alevi-Sunni Relations in Germany

Sivas has also had some effects on the social and political relations between Alevis and Sunnis in Germany. Alevi-Sunni relations were affected by the massacre at two levels. The first level refers to personal interaction of Alevis and Sunnis, in the context of mixed neighborhoods, for instance. The second level belongs to the political realm and refers to relations between Alevi and Muslim associations or to the activities of Alevis in associations with a mixed membership.

I discussed the effects of the Sivas massacre with Ali and Selda Çelik, a couple that has lived for two decades in Veddel, a poorer district of Hamburg with a large population of migrants from Turkey. Ali told me that Sivas has widened the gulf between Alevis and Sunnis:

> In the beginning, in Germany, there were no problems between Alevis and Sunnis. Alevis had nothing against Sunnis and Sunnis were not against Alevis. Until Sivas, when the Madımak hotel burned. Until this time Alevis and Sunnis in Hamburg, in Europe, had no problems among

themselves. Perhaps there were small problems but no big problems. But since Sivas we are separate. Automatically. For example, before we were together with three or four families, but after Sivas we separated.

Ali referred to Sunni families whom they had befriended, and explained that after Sivas they never came together again. When they met by chance on the street they greeted each other but there was no feeling of warmth and heartiness. He explained:

This is because … we do not say that all Sunnis are responsible [for the massacre]. (…) We do not say that the whole population of Sivas is responsible but only those who have set fire to the hotel. But still … the others, the Sunnis, not all Sunnis but many Sunnis say, look, the Alevis, they have a totally different faith. And [they say] for instance, they have burnt us only because of Aziz Nesin. But it was not against Aziz Nesin, it was against Alevis! Aziz Nesin was only present by coincidence. But then Sunnis say, well, Aziz Nesin has no faith, he has no God, and when Alevis are together with Aziz Nesin they can burn too…

The overwhelming majority of migrants from Turkey that live in Veddel are Sunnis. Ali and Selda explained that even before Sivas they had only a few closer relations with Sunni families in the district, and that even these relationships broke apart. As an example they said that only three or four families from Veddel had attended the marriage of their eldest son Hasan a few years ago. They asserted that the number of fundamentalists and right-wing radicals had risen in the last few years. Selda narrated that she stopped going to the local *bakkal* (grocer) because he was a fundamentalist and she felt discriminated against by him:

"I went to the grocer's, I wanted to shop. In the rear [of the shop] they were talking about Sivas. Sivas had been burning some time ago. They said: 'Well done!' They said that it was right to burn Alevis at Sivas."

Ali: "That the Alevis had deserved it!"

Selda: "You know, I went there a second and a third time, once again, and again they talked about it. I said: 'Osman, I want half a kilogram of beef.' It was almost half past seven. I repeated myself and then he replied: 'I have no time.' I said: 'Why don't you have time, Osman? I want to buy half a kilogram of beef!' I did it intentionally, I wanted to make a fuss. He said that he did not have time. I said: 'Osman, stop this. You must have time for me, I am shopping here!' 'Why [should I have time] especially for you?' he said. I said: 'Osman, this is already the third time that I have heard this [talk about Sivas]. I am fed up!' (…) Since two years I do not go to this shop. They openly abuse Alevis, openly! I have heard it! I have heard: 'It was right what they did to the Alevis. They do not recognize mother and sister, these Alevis.' (…) I don't go to this shop any more, I have no contacts in Veddel. I definitely cut them. I have heard many people. They all talk like this in this shop."

Since then, they go shopping at another place in the center of Hamburg, two stops of the city train away from Veddel. The owner of this shop is a Sunni too, but, according to the categorization of Selda and Ali, he is not a fundamentalist. After narrating this story about the shop in Veddel as an example for the deterioration of relationships between Sunnis and Alevis after Sivas, the couple virtually bursted into telling many little anecdotes that further instantiated their idea of Sunni Muslims and their perception of Alevi-Sunni relations. They told about a Sunni woman who dragged a crying child across the street to the Quran classes while the child obviously did not want to go there, they spoke about another woman that wanted to give Selda a headscarf as a gift in order that she could cover her hair, and about an bearded man for whom Selda had interpreted at the doctor's and who afterwards too asked her to cover herself: "He said: 'You should cover your head!' I answered: 'My husband doesn't care whether I wear a headscarf or not!' He continued: 'Yes, it is like this in Germany, it's not good! Everybody can see your hair! And they are all Christians here, the Germans, they aren't Muslims!'"

Selda was laughing when she told this episode but it was an angry laughter. In spite of what Ali and Selda told, I am not sure whether Sivas really changed relationships between Alevis and Sunnis to a large extent. From the conversations with this couple and from many other interviews emerged that even before the massacre the relations of Alevis and Sunnis were characterized mainly by avoidance. In everyday contexts Alevis avoided coming into contact with people that were categorized as "real Sunnis," i.e., as Muslims with a strong commitment to religion. Conversely, many of these Muslims also avoided close contact with Alevis because they considered them as impure infidels. The consequence of Sivas was then more probably an accentuation of avoidance and not a complete restructuring of Alevi-Sunni relationships. However, Sivas changed the Alevis' reasons for their avoidance: a decade or more ago, abhorrence of "fundamentalism" did not play the same role as today because at that time political Islam was only beginning its new inroads into the political landscape of Turkey, and fundamentalism was not a central figure of discourse. As a reason for the avoidance of close contact with Sunnis, the earlier fear of discrimination and slander was replaced by the rejection of fundamentalism.

To a large extent more intimate relationships are also avoided with "liberal Sunnis." This is proven by a very high degree of endogamy among Alevis. According to my survey, only 5.4 percent of the married members of Alevi associations in Hamburg had entered into marital bonds with non-Alevis. Among these few non-Alevi spouses are not only Sunnis but also Germans. Accordingly, the percentage of marriages with Sunnis is even lower. Again, Sunni-Alevi marriages are avoided from both sides. If a mixed relationship is started by young people, their families mostly attempt to convince or even force them to stop that relation. Difficulties with Alevi-Sunni marriages may begin already with the wedding celebration and details like whether alcoholic beverages should be served or not. Alevis reason that real problems start, however, after the birth of children: How should they be educated? Should they become Alevis or Sunnis? Many Alevis also suppose that even liberal Sunnis become more conservative—that is, more "Sunni-like"—when they grow older. What if a Sunni husband then forces his Alevi wife to wear the headscarf? Not only the Sunni spouse may become a problem, but even more so his or her family that cannot be reliably assessed from the outside, that is, before marriage. Many stories about difficult and aborted intermarriages circulate among Alevis and certainly also among Sunnis, although there are of course also contrary examples. Yet it seems that intermarriage involves a certain distancing of the couple from one of their families. I have been told about several Alevi-Sunni marriages in which only a few people from the Sunni side attended the celebration. Also with reference to endogamy I conclude that Sivas has not very much changed actual relations between Sunnis and Alevis, but the massacre has produced new arguments for the avoidance of inter-marriages. Ali and Selda have a daughter who was planning to marry a Sunni at the time of our conversation. They said to me: "Well, she has to decide this herself. We have told her everything. We have told her: 'Gül, you have seen all this, Maraş and Sivas, you know everything!'"

Relationships—or better the avoidance of relationships—with Milli Görüş stand at the center of the effects of the Sivas massacre on the political level. Due to the alleged involvement of Milli Görüş with the Islamist RP in Turkey that is held responsible for Sivas, the avoidance of cooperation with Milli Görüş is a continuing imperative for Alevis and their associations. However, as consequence of entangled relationships of cooperation with other bodies it is sometimes difficult to stick to this imperative. In this context I will consider two conflicts that occurred in Hamburg. The first of these conflicts concerned not an Alevi association but the Association of Turkish Social Democrats (TSDD) which had been founded in the mid–1980s and was dominated by Alevi members for many years. The TSDD was a member of the *Türk Göçmen Birliği* (TGB, Union of Turkish Migrants), an umbrella association of Turkish migrants' associations in Hamburg. The local branch of Milli Görüş was also a member of the TGB. In the beginning of the 1990s, after the establishment of the HAKM, many Alevi members of the TSDD reduced their interest in this association and concentrated their commitment on the HAKM. However many Alevis retained a dual membership in both associations. In early autumn of 1993, thirty-nine Alevi members of the TSDD demanded an extraordinary general meeting of their association with the intention of issuing a declaration on the Sivas massacre. In the same year a Sunni had become chairman of the association. The Alevi members called for a general meeting because the managing committee of the TSDD had so far not issued a public statement condemning the Sivas massacre. The Alevi members regarded such a statement necessary also in view of their membership in the TGB and the implied relationship with Milli Görüş. The Alevi members demanded that either Milli Görüş would be excluded from the TGB or that their own association would withdraw from the umbrella organization. With a number of formal tricks like denying the membership status of several people who had signed the petition for the extraordinary meeting, the committee of the TSDD took efforts to avoid the convention of the general assembly. The reason for this attitude was that the managing committee wanted to prevent renewed domination of Alevis in the association as well as an open conflict within the TGB. The Alevi members responded with legal action, and succeeded in forcing the committee to convene the meeting. However, invitations for this meeting were sent out late and some Alevi members never received an invitation. Therefore, the (mainly Sunni) supporters of the committee found themselves in a majority position and were able to reject the demands of the Alevis. Due to the late invitations, the meeting was successfully challenged again. As a consequence of litigation, the work of the association came to a standstill and an emergency committee was installed by the courts. At this point, the Alevi members gave up their commitment.[9]

The second case is more recent. The HAKM is a member of two interdenominational round tables in Hamburg. Among the other members are not only the Christian churches, Tibetan Buddhists, and the Jews but also the local Muslim umbrella association *Schura*, which combines a number of mosque associations. Among the members of the Schura is also the Central Mosque (*Merkez Camii*). Although the relation of this mosque with Milli Görüş is officially denied, the Hamburg branch of the association is housed in the mosque and, among Alevis, the relationship of the mosque with Milli Görüş is taken for granted. Although the Schura was frequently represented in the interdenominational round tables by a prominent member of the committee of the Central Mosque, this was never a bone of contention for the Alevis. Pragmatically, it was seen that there was no direct relationship or cooperation between the HAKM and Milli Görüş but rather a kind of coincidence mediated by the round tables. After all, the Central Mosque was only one Muslim community among the many that formed the Schura.

Yet things were assessed differently when in May 2000 representatives of the Schura expressed the desire to visit the HAKM. The two

---

[9] In summer 1994 the TGB itself decided to exclude Milli Görüş from membership. The reason for this move was not the Sivas massacre but a general concern about the growing influence of Islamism in Turkey, especially after the success of the RP in municipal elections of that year, and among the Turkish community in Germany.

members of the HAKM who represented the association in the round tables and who were approached with this desire did not reject the idea outright. However, they said that they had to discuss this idea first within their association. When they presented the idea of the visit of the Schura at a meeting of representatives of all Alevi associations in Hamburg, they encountered strict opposition. One representative said: "We could do that only under the condition that they officially condemn Sivas as an act of inhumaneness. But they would never do this." Also at a meeting of the managing committee of the HAKM the idea of the visit was ruled out. It was argued that there were Islamists among the Schura and that they had been among those who had killed Alevis in Sivas. One person pointed out that a visit was completely unimaginable in the current season, that is, in late spring and early summer, shortly before the annual commemorative programs. It was further argued that the visit was also not advisable because of the uncertainty what the Schura would make of it afterwards: "Maybe we read the next day in *Hürriyet* that Alevis and Sunnis have been reconciled!" Another member of the committee said: "It is safer not to meet them. After all, they are the culprits and we are the victims!"

The two examples show that on the political level the experience of and discourse on Sivas was translated into a strict avoidance of links with Islamists and especially with Milli Görüş. If Sunnis are the others of Alevis, this otherness is most visibly embodied in that association, which is considered closely linked with those who instigated and committed the Sivas massacre. This link was again confirmed, according to the Alevis' understanding, when in 2002 news spread that at least six of the men who had been convicted due to their involvement with the Sivas massacre had somehow escaped from Turkey to Germany. Two of them had been granted asylum in Germany, and one of them apparently had taken the position of Imam in a mosque linked with Milli Görüş.[10]

Discussing the Alevi-Sunni Boundary

Alevi discourse draws a strict boundary between Alevis and Sunni Muslims. This boundary is based on an image of Sunni Muslims as the com-

---

[10] *Frankfurter Allgemeine Zeitung*, 29 January 2002, *Hürriyet*, 9 May 2003. Cf. the press statement of the AABF, issued on 14 May 2003. After a German member of Parliament had spread this news in Germany, procedures were started to revoke the legal status of asylum of the men in question. The AABF demanded that the Turkish government apply for the extradition of the culprits. The fact that convicted persons could escape from Turkey was considered as a proof for the laxness of the Turkish political and judicial systems in dealing with the Sivas case.

plete other of Alevis. We have seen that a certain ambivalence inheres
in this boundary, because not all Sunnis conform to that image of total otherness. However, the boundary is finally reinforced by treating
"democratic Sunnis" as exceptions that confirm the rule. Most of the
time the discourse that draws the boundary, that identifies Sunnis with
violence and fundamentalism, takes place in a purely Alevi environment and no objection is raised. Sometimes, however, Sunnis "invade"
this discursive space. Frequently, Sunnis who are exposed to this discourse prefer not to respond, but sometimes Sunnis raise their voices
against the Alevi construction of otherness. Here I will discuss one
such case, an exchange between Mesut, an Alevi, and Emine, a ("democratic") Sunni girl. Both were in their early twenties. They belonged to
a circle of friends in which Emine was the only Sunni. Emine was the
girlfriend of Yüksel, another young Alevi.

I met them in the café area of the *Wir-Zentrum* where they were
waiting for their other friends. Mesut was working in the *Wir-Zentrum*
and therefore the center had become a meeting place for the group of
friends. Some time ago I had distributed some questionnaires among
the young Alevis. The discussion started when I asked Mesut about
the questionnaire and when Emine remarked to me: "You should also
study *my* people!" I was quite surprised by this injunction, because earlier I had witnessed that Emine endeavored to play down the difference between Sunnis and Alevis. "My people," however, here clearly
referred to Sunnis and thus confirmed the distinction. Yet Emine indeed tried to play the Alevi-Sunni difference down and complained
that Alevis were always emphasizing the boundary with the effect that
they isolated and separated themselves from the Sunnis. To this complaint Mesut responded: "Alevis never isolate themselves, we are tolerant and open, everybody can join us!" But Emine insisted that Alevis
fenced themselves off and that, for instance, she could not come to an
Alevi event and express her opinion openly. Mesut denied that. Then
Emine said: "I have an Alevi boyfriend and I suffer from that separation!" Mesut replied at once: "You do not suffer, those who suffer are
always the Alevis!" I asked Emine why she felt she was suffering and
she explained that she suffered because both her own family as well as
Yüksel's opposed their relationship. She then complained that in the
discourses of Alevis, Sunnis are always represented as fundamentalists
and perpetrators of violence, and argued that the present generation
was not responsible for what had happened in earlier times. She emphasized that there are many democrats among Sunnis who thought
like Alevis, and mentioned her parents as an example. She called for
differentiation and said that neither all Sunnis nor all Alevis were fundamentalists. At that point Mesut contradicted, emphasizing that there
were no fundamentalists at all among Alevis. But he conceded a certain
one-sidedness and said: "It is true, whenever I see a bearded Sunni I

think at once that he is a fundamentalist and that maybe he has something to do with Sivas. But of course one cannot see that. One gets a kind
of limited perspective." Still, Mesut insisted that in Turkey Alevis are
the victims: "When I have to show my passport in Turkey and a police
officer sees that I am born in Tunceli, he knows that I am Alevi. And he
will treat me as one! This is because there are so many fascists among
the police." Emine argued that there are also Alevi policemen, and that
it is not the Sunnis who discriminate against Alevis but that the Alevis
isolate themselves. She continued: "Alevis say that they cannot go to
the mosque because Ali was killed in a mosque. Is that a reason? If Ali
had been killed on a bridge, would Alevis avoid bridges then? Mosques
are open to everybody, also Alevis can go there, they are not excluded!"
Yet Mesut replied that Alevis simply do not want to go to the mosque
but have their own places, and that Alevis are never left in peace to do
their own business.

This dispute exemplifies very well the traps of Alevi-Sunni relations.
Mesut operated with the clear-cut image of Alevi discourse where Alevis are the victims and Sunnis the perpetrators of violence. Emine tried
to question this stereotypical representation, arguing that it is also an
artifact of Alevi discourse and self-separation. She felt hurt by being
excluded by the Alevi construction of a boundary and by being implicitly put on the side of those who committed violence against Alevis.
But she was even denied the feeling of suffering due to separation
and exclusion that she experienced through her relationship with Yüksel because, as Mesut emphasized, it is always the Alevis who suffer.
Yet by arguing that Sunnis do not generally exclude Alevis but welcome them, for instance in the mosques, she fell short of understanding Mesut's and the Alevis' position: they are not interested in being
welcomed as part of the Sunni community, they insist on being recognized in their difference. From this perspective, then, the difference
between Alevis and Sunnis is undeniable—although not all Sunnis are
fundamentalists or fascists. Sivas clearly emerges as the touchstone of
this difference: Mesut cannot deny his generalized suspicion that any
bearded, that is, "real" Sunni he meets could be linked with the Sivas
massacre.

Memory and Community

In this chapter I have analyzed the Sivas massacre as the critical event
that stands at the focus of a new construction of Alevi identity. Pandey
(2001, 4) has observed that "in the history of any society, narratives of
particular experiences of violence go towards making the 'community'."
The perpetration and experience of violence frequently marks identi-

ties and distinguishes aggressors from victims.[11] Violence then acquires an overall meaning that transcends the particular instance in which it was experienced. Similarly, many communities for whom experiences of violence and victimization have become important elements of identity have developed practices that are intended to keep the memory of victimization alive. Susanne Schwalgin shows, for instance, how Armenian diasporians in Greece observe rituals of commemorating the Armenian genocide. According to her, the work of remembering turns the experience of violence, including, in the case of Armenians, the trauma of genocide, into a meaningful event that serves as a point of reference for collective and individual identity (Schwalgin 2004, 129).

For Alevis Sivas is the event that, according to the commemorative discourses and practices, revealed the predicament of the Alevi community with unprecedented clarity: Alevis are under siege, they are essentially victims. The discourse of remembering Sivas is the clearest example of what Yavuz (1999a, 188) calls a "Manichean dualism of good and evil, justice and injustice, freedom and oppression," relating back to the time of Kerbela, that governs the historical imagination of Alevis. Yet Sivas was also the event that laid open a radical change and reconfiguration of the Alevi community: for the first time, Alevis did not simply suffer violence but subsequently asserted themselves. Due to the Alevi movement that organized the protest against the massacre and offered a communal space that prevented dispersal, Alevis emerged strengthened from the massacre. At any rate, this is the essential message of Alevi discourse on Sivas.

As a consequence, Sivas has the equivocal status of a terrible event that nonetheless had some highly positive effects on the community. Many Alevi activists point out that the mobilization that was achieved by the Alevi movement depended on that horrible event that brought forward both the predicament and its possible redress. Ongoing mobilization, then, depends on keeping the memory of Sivas alive. A weakening of mobilization, like a decrease in membership in some associations, is interpreted accordingly also as a consequence of an erosion of the memory of Sivas. It is not surprising, therefore, that discourses and practices dedicated to the commemoration of Sivas occupy such a focal position in the Alevi movement. Remembering Sivas is ritualized in commemorative practices. It has become a fixed point in the calendar of Alevi associational life, which prevents that the massacre falls into oblivion. On the other hand, through the "micro ritual" of *saygı duruşu,*

---

[11] This is not to say that those who suffer and those who commit violence can in all cases be neatly separated into two different communities. Yet memory discourses on violence frequently silence ambivalent experiences and turn violent events into stories of either victory or victimization.

commemoration is dispersed through all kinds of events and has become an almost omnipresent element.

The discourses and practices of commemorative events establish a
multilayered meaning of the massacre. Two meanings are immediately
forthcoming—one more parochial, the other universal in intent. First,
Alevis have been attacked by Sunnis; Sunnis are therefore the others of
Alevis. Those who perpetrated the violence in Sivas are portrayed in
a peculiar way in commemorative discourse: they were cruel fanatics
and fundamentalists, they were people completely unmarked by the
achievements of modernity, enlightenment, and reason. Alevis, however, are the exact opposite. The memory of Sivas therefore contributes
to drawing an unequivocal, clear-cut boundary between Alevis and Sunnis and confirms what I have called the master difference. Yet, while on
the one hand commemorative discourse draws a line of distinction that
fences the Alevi community off from its others, it also opens the community up towards a broad field of shared universal humanity. Thus,
in this second meaning, Alevis are portrayed not as a parochial community but as people who hold universal human values in common
with other people that are likewise committed to reason and modernity.
Solidarity with all those who are oppressed by violence and fanaticism
is invoked: "We are on the side of those who are oppressed and against
the tyrants" (Öker 1994, 7). The commemorative discourse contributes
to representing Alevis as a tolerant, modern, and open community.

A third meaning refers more directly to the massacre and its victims
themselves. Here, it is emphasized that the victims were members of the
community who died for the community. The word which is used for
the victims in Alevi Turkish language discourse of commemoration is
şehit. *Şehit* is a peculiar kind of victim—the word can also be translated
as "martyr."[12] The Arabic root of the word (*shahida*) means "to witness."
Şehit is a term with a deep religious connotation. In the original sense
a *şehit* is, like a martyr, a person who was killed for the sake of her or
his faith. Later, in the context of nationalism, the word was transferred
from the field of religion to the political, where "martyrs" who died
for their nation stood less for the secularization of a religious concept
than for the sacralization of the political. Islam has a strong tradition of
martyrdom, promising the martyr instant access to the abundance of
paradise. In an Islamic context the religious significance of martyrdom
easily reinforces its nationalist meaning (e.g., Lindholm Schulz 2003:
128f.). Alevis, however, do not relate to this Islamic significance of martyrdom. Their usage is rather derived from leftist discourse of the 1970s,
in which the leftist victims of the security forces or of rival rightist

---

[12] In my text I use the more equivocal term "victim" instead of "martyr" because
its equivalent German term *Opfer* is employed in Alevi German–language discourse on Sivas.

groups in Turkey were called *şehitler*, too. Yet in any case, to speak of a *şehit* establishes a strong bond between an individual and a community. A *şehit* is a person who is killed for his community, be that a religious or a political group. To speak of the victims of the Sivas massacre as *şehitler* (plural) includes them unequivocally in the Alevi community. Just like the death of a martyr affirms his faith, the death of the *şehitler* of Sivas affirmed the Alevi community. This sense is brought forward by an article published on the occasion of the third anniversary of Sivas: "It has to be established in everybody's head (…). Our martyrs did not lose their lives in a traffic accident. They died in the name of Alevism, which is a humanitarian, democratic, universal culture. Truthfulness begins with acknowledging this undisputable fact" (Eral 1996, 12).

The memory of Sivas is also selective: the significance of the presence of Aziz Nesin as translator of the *Satanic Verses* at the festival, which in the Turkish media has been given as the cause of the attack, is consistently omitted from the Alevi discourse of commemoration. This omission contributes to turning the memory of the massacre into a memory of community: Alevis have not been the accidental victims but the very targets of the attack. This omission mirrors the equally selective media discourse that played down the role of Alevis in the event. Referring to individual memory, Michael Lambek (1996, 243f.) writes:

> Memory of any kind implies a self or subject who perceives the memory or does the remembering. Today our understanding of the nature of this self is increasingly dependent upon the reference to memory—I am the product of who I was and what I experienced—just as the nature of memory is implied and constituted by the theory of the self or subject (…) I take memory to be an intrinsic part of selfhood (such that memory and identity serve to mutually validate each other).

These sentences can be equally applied to memory of community. Community as a collective subject that is established through shared memory is given a particular meaning by remembering past events in specific ways, by establishing a specific significance of the past that continues into the present. In order to enable this communal memory, individual memories have to be tuned accordingly. This is done through commemorative practices that ritualize commemoration. Memory thereby becomes a *moral practice* (Lambek, ibid.): Not only does memory establish a particular moral of the past, but it becomes equally a moral imperative to remember correctly.

Although many issues are vehemently disputed among Alevis, the meaning of Sivas for the Alevi community goes undisputed. Sometimes particular practices of commemoration are criticized, yet this critique never questions the meaning of Sivas but rather affirms it. It is argued, for instance, that commemorative conventions sometimes resemble culture festivals and concerts too closely. It is alleged that many people attend the ceremonies because they want to listen to the music played by Arif Sağ or others and not because they are moved by the memory of the massacre. Some people deplore that the character of the events detracts from the original message of memory. Frequently, the presenters remind the audience at the commemorative conventions that they do not attend simply a concert and that they should behave appropriately, i.e., that they should not dance or respond to the performances with expressions of joy and enthusiasm.

The victims of Sivas, the martyrs, are represented as a focus of identification. They are both represented as prototypical members of the community and, by means of the little iconlike portraits, as just normal people. Identification is thus made easy: "It could well have happened to me." The memory of Sivas creates a strong bond for the Alevi community and equally a strict difference between Alevis and Sunnis. The memory of the massacre is presented as a sine qua non of the Alevi community. Once I attended a meeting of the youth group of the HAKM. Yasemin, the leader of the group, presented the upcoming program of the association and also said that there will be a convention on 2 July. One of the young people asked about the cause of this convention. Yasemin responded with a strong emphasis: "The cause is the commemoration of the Sivas victims. You always must have this date in your heads, like New Year's Eve. Whenever you open the newspaper and see, oh, it's 2 July, you have to know immediately what happened on this date. You have to remember it. You always have to think about it, it has to be written in your heads!" None of the young people asked further questions.

6

RITUAL AND COMMUNITY
The Changing Meaning of *Cem* and *Dedes*

Ritual and the Social

This chapter focuses on two central elements of Alevism: *cem* and *dedes*.[1]
Cem is the central ritual of Alevism and *dedes* are its religious specialists
that, among other things, preside over *cem*. Both *cem* and *dedes* have
been subjected to significant transformations in the course of the reconstitution of Alevism by the Alevi movement. Ever since Durkheim's
Elementary Forms of Religious Life (1965 [1915]), ritual has been seen as
an instrument for establishing and maintaining community. According
to Durkheim, ritual creates a sphere in which the community is sacralized and turned into an object of worship, a sacred sphere in which the
individuals are "tuned" with community. The discussion of commemorative rituals in the previous chapter has shown that this function is not
limited to "religious" rituals. While not denying the social function of
ritual, later authors like Max Gluckman (1963) and Victor Turner (1957,
1974) have argued that rituals are not necessarily expressions of social
cohesion, but may well be social loci of tension and conflict. Subsequent
approaches based on ideas of symbols and performance emphasized
the multivocality of ritual and the creativity involved in ritual activity.
Ritual is not simply an instrument for establishing social cohesion, a
means of dramatizing conflict before returning to equilibrium, but "a
performative medium for social change … ritual does not mold people;
people fashion rituals that mold their world" (Bell 1997, 73). Instead
of simply offering a stage or framework in which conflict may be expressed and solved, ritual may become itself a matter of dispute concerning its meaning and practice. This is what has happened to *cem* in
the course of the Alevi movement. *Cem* is one of the most important
elements of Alevism that have been revitalized by the Alevi movement,
but this revitalization has deeply transformed the meaning and practice
of the ritual, both of which continue to be disputed in the Alevi communities. Closely connected with disputes about the ritual are debates
about the function and position of *dedes*. In many aspects, these con-

---

[1] This chapter is partly based on two previously published papers (Sökefeld
2002b, 2004a).

flicts mirror the disputes of identity that have been analyzed so far. *Cem* is also the ritual that unequivocally distinguishes Alevism from Sunni Islam. Alevis do not practice the prayer (*namaz*) that is prescribed for Muslims five times a day. When asked why they do not practice *namaz*, Alevis say: We have *cem* instead! *Alevilerin ibadeti cemdir*: The prayer of Alevism is *cem*. Yet *cem* is very different from Muslim prayer—it could indeed be read as a ritual antithesis of *namaz*—and therefore again illustrates the master difference of Alevis and Sunnis.

Before I turn to the conflicts and debates that concern the present-day practice of *cem*, however, I will give a kind of ideal description of the ritual and the religious specialists involved, synthesizing thereby Alevi representations of the ritual that generally do not refer to the actual practice but to some ideal model of *cem*.

Cem and *Dedes*—the Ideal Model

According to the Oxford Turkish Dictionary, *cem* means "crowd"; the derived verb *cem etmek* means "to bring together", "to collect."[2] When Alevis are asked about *cem*, they usually set out to describe what is supposed to have been the ritual practice in the Alevi villages in Turkey before the village communities have been exposed to emigration and the inroads of the state bureaucracy. They describe what is supposed to have been celebrated for centuries by the Alevi village communities. The use of the ethnographic present in the following outline of the ritual is not intended to express that *cem* is practised in this manner even today. Rather, it conveys that according to Alevis themselves this description portrays a kind of timeless essence of *cem*.

A *cem* cannot take place without a *dede* (literally: "grandfather"). *Dedes* belong to holy clans, called *ocak* ("hearth"), which are believed to be genealogically derived from the twelve Imams and, ultimately, from the Imam Ali and, via his wife Fatma (Fatima), the daughter of Mohammed, from the Prophet himself. That is, *dedes* are *sayyids* (*seyit* in Turkish). Within these holy clans, religious knowledge is orally transmitted. Traditional Alevism relied only to a very little extent on written sources. Many *dedes* were illiterates and they were praised for their great memnonic power. Their authority depended also on their ability to orally reproduce the sources of Alevism. *Dedes* are expected to have high moral standards. They are not allowed to divorce. Every Alevi family has a fixed relationship with a *dede* and his *ocak*. That is, every Alevi is supposed to be a *talip* (student, follower) of a *dede*. Also every *dede* is the *talip* of another *dede* who is his *pir* or *mürşit*, and who has to

---

[2] The word is derived from the Arabic root *jama'a*, to gather, to collect, to unite, to combine.

take care of his moral conduct. Yet, taken as a general category, the designation "*talip*" refers to persons who are not *ocakzade*, i.e., who are not members of an *ocak*. *Dede-talip* relationships involve whole families and are not a matter of individual choice. They are transmitted by heredity. A man is the *talip* of the same *dede* and *ocak* as his father has been, and when a *dede* passes on his duties to his successor, usually one of his sons or nephews, the successor assumes the same responsibility towards this family. Intermarriages between members of an *ocak* and *talip*s are not permitted. Every *dede* serves a whole network of *talip*s that may be spread over a considerable area. The *dede* is responsible not only for the spiritual but also for the moral conduct of his *talip*s. Usually, all *talip*s of a village are related with the same *dede* if the village is not too large. Each community of *talip*s has to be visited at least once a year by the *dede*. On the occasion of his visit the *dede* receives contributions in cash or kind from his *talip*s called *hakullah* ("God's right"). During his visits the *dede* presides over *cem*. That is, the ritual is celebrated normally only once or a few times a year. As is implied by the meaning of the term, *cem* is a communal ceremony in which several families of *talip*s participate. In most places there are no particular buildings in which *cem* is held. Particular buildings called *cemevi* (*cem* house) exist only in special places such as centers of pilgrimage. Only in recent years have Alevi associations in Turkey started to erect specific *cem* houses. In ordinary villages the ritual simply takes place in a large room of a family house. *Cem* is held most frequently in Thursday evenings.[3] The sequence of the ritual may last for many hours or even the whole night. Both men and women participate. The following account of *cem* draws on Tur 2002 (352–420), Yaman (1998), Korkmaz (2003, 91–99) and on oral accounts.[4]

Entering the room, the participants have to remove their shoes as an acknowledgment of sacralized space that has to be saved from mundane impurity. The participants are seated in a circle or semicircle so that ideally all face each other. The place of the *dede* is a frequently slightly elevated place in the front of the room, usually opposite of the entrance. The place of the *dede* is marked by a sheepskin (*post*) that symbolizes the spiritual authority of the *silsile*, the genealogical chain of the holy clan.[5] The participants and the *dede* encircle the *dar* or *meydan* (place) in the center of the room where most of the ritual activity takes place.

---

[3] In Alevi as well as general Islamic tradition a day starts after sundown, so that a "western" Thursday evening is already Friday (*cuma*) according to Alevi ritual time reckoning.

[4] For an early description of *cem* see also Yalman 1969.

[5] Alevis share this symbolism of the sheepskin with Sufism. The highest authority of a Sufi brotherhood is called *post nişin:* the one who is sitting on the sheepskin.

Table 6.1 Twelve duties in *cem*

Oniki hizmet (twelve duties):

1. Dede	directs the ritual
2. Rehber	assistant of the *dede*
3. Gözcü	in charge of order and silence during *cem*
4. Çerağcı/delilci	in charge of the candles
5. Zakir	musician, player of the *saz*
6. Süpürgeci	in charge of cleanliness
7. Sakka/İbrikçi/Teszekar	in charge of water
8. Kapıcı	watchman at the door
9. Kurbancı/Lokmacı	in charge of the offerings
10. Semahcı	dancing semah
11. İznikci	guarding the shoes of the participants
12. Peyik	in charge of announcing *cem*

The performance of a *cem* requires "twelve duties" or "services" (*oniki hizmet*) to be carried out. The number of the duties echoes the number of Imams revered by Alevis. The first and most important of these duties is the *dede* who directs the course of the *cem*. He is assisted by the *rehber* (guide) who normally also belongs to an *ocak*. The other ten duties are carried out by *talips*. Both men and women may act as *hizmet*. Sometimes the duties are shared by several persons. Frequently, these duties are "owned" by and handed down within particular families of the village communities.

A communal meal is part of the *cem*. One or more families of a village slaughter an animal as sacrifice (*kurban*) for the *cem*, but all other participants also bring offerings that are later distributed among the congregation.

Before the *cem* actually starts, a number of preparations have to be made. First, the *peyik* announces the *cem* in the village. Slowly the people gather in the place of the *cem*, which thereby becomes the *cemevi*. Outsiders are not allowed in the ritual, therefore the *kapıcı* keeps watch at the door. The *iznikici* takes care that everybody removes the shoes before entering the *cemevi*.

Usually, the *rehber* and the *zakir* are already seated to the right and to the left of the *post* when the *dede* enters the room. A basic principle of *cem*—and, it is said, of Alevism in general—is *rızalık* (consent). Consent has to be established within the congregation, but the *dede* also has to ask the consent of the congregation that he is allowed to preside over the *cem*. When the *dede* enters the congregation he stops in front of the *post* and asks three times whether the people agree that he conducts the *cem*: *Rıza mısınız?* Do you agree? The congregation has to answer three times: *Rızayız!* We agree! Only then the *dede* is allowed to take seat on the *post*. Thereby he assumes the role of directing the *cem*. The *rehber* then offers a prayer in the name of the *dede*. The *dede* continues by giving an educating speech. Then a religious hymn (*deyiş*) follows that is played and sung by the *zakir*, but sometimes also by the *dede* himself. After that the *süpürgeci* enters the *meydan*, holding a besom under the arm. Whenever one of the *hizmet* or a *talip* in general steps onto the *meydan*, he or she first has to prostrate[6] in front of the *dede*. The person then has to stand with the upper part of the body slightly bowed towards the *dede* and with the big toe of the right foot over the big toe of the left.[7] Standing with this posture in front of the *dede* the *süpürgeci* offers a prayer and sweeps the floor three times, exclaiming: *Ya Allah! Ya Mohammed! Ya Ali!*

The next part of the ritual is the *halk mahkemesi* or *görgü* that has been discussed already in chapter four. This part of *cem* is also called *dara çekmek*, because those that are accused of some guilt have to step into the *dar* for inquiry. *Halk mahkemesi* is the part of the ritual that establishes *rızalık* within the congregation. The *dede* gives a speech about the necessity of unity and peace and then asks three times: *Dargın küskün var mı?* (Are there some that are angry and offended?) Those among the congregation who are involved in conflicts have to respond to this call by stepping forward into the *meydan*. Disputes are then dealt with one by one. The *dede* inquires about the problem, hearing both sides and also additional witnesses. After the relevant facts have been established, the *dede* discusses the appropriate punishment and compensation for the guilt together with the congregation. In a very severe case, the offender may be ostracized from the community for a certain period of time and thereby becomes *düşkün* (fallen). In other cases the offender may be ordered to offer a sacrifice for the community. Yet the punishment has to be agreed to by the offender as well as by the congregation, and therefore the *dede* again asks three times: *Rıza mısınız?* If there is no consent, the *cem* cannot continue. Those who are not ready to accept a punishment have to leave the congregation.

---

[6] The prostration is called *niyaz*.

[7] This position of the feet is called *mühür* (seal) and refers back to Fatma. The story goes that Fatma was once called by her father Mohammed to bring water. On the way to the well she bumped her toe against a stone and the toe started to bleed. She did not want to worry her father and therefore hid the wound with the other toe when stepping before Mohammed and offering him the water. *Mühür* is understood as a posture expressing respect and modesty. Symbolically the posture can be interpreted as expressing that the relation between the *talip*s and the *dede* equals the relationship between Fatma and Mohammed.

In the next stage of the ritual all the *oniki hizmet* come together on the *meydan*, offering *niyaz* towards the *dede*. A hymn of the twelve duties is sung. The prayer of *tevella* and *teberra* follows that calls to love the family of the prophet, the *ehlibeyt*, and to hate all those who are the enemies of the *ehlibeyt*.[8] Then the *hizmet* leave the *meydan*, and the *çerağçı* is called for his duty. After offering *niyaz* and prayer, he lights the candelabra while the *dede* says a prayer expressing that the candles burn as a token of love for the twelve Imams and the Alevi saints. Subsequently the *zakir* again sings a *deyiş*.

After that it is time for the service of the *teszekar*, which is carried out together by a man and a women. They bring a jar of water, a washbasin, and a towel to the *meydan*. First, the man washes and dries the hands of the woman and then the other way round. Then they go to the *post* and wash the hands of the *dede*. Next comes the duty of the *kurban* and *lokma* (morsel). Those who are in charge of this service bring plates with the meal that has been cooked in order to be distributed as *lokma* among the participants before the *dede*. The *dede* says a prayer and blesses the *lokma*. Again a hymn is sung. The next stage of the *cem* is the closure of the ritual. Now the *cem* is "sealed" and its inner part begins. It consists again of hymns and prayers. The congregation expresses repentance of its sins and asks for forgiveness (*tövbe istiğfar*), and hymns are sung in memory of the twelve imams (*düvazimam*). Then the unity of God is affirmed (*tevhit*) in another hymn and the *miraç*, the mystical ascension of the prophet Mohammed, is sung subsequently (*miraçlama*). The *miraç* is important because at the end of this mystical journey Mohammed enters the "assembly of the forty" (*kırklar meclisi*), which can be interpreted as the original assembly of Alevis and provides a kind of original myth of Alevism in general and *cem* in particular. Setting out for *miraç*, Mohammed was ordered to put his ring into the mouth of a lion that was standing by the way. On his return, he came to a house and knocked at its door, saying that he was the Prophet. Yet he was denied entry. This happened two times. Only the third time when he said "I am a servant of the poor" was he allowed to enter. Mohammed saw thirty-nine people in the house, men and women. Ali was among them, but Mohammed did not recognize him. Mohammed asked: "Who are you?" He got the answer: "We are the forty, we are all one heart and one body." Mohammed said: "But one of you is missing, you are only thirty-nine persons." They said: "This is Salman, he has gone out. Our one is forty, our forty is one. When one of us bleeds a drop of blood it is the blood of all of us." The prophet asked: "How can that be?" Ali

---

[8] The *ehlibeyt* (from Arabic: *ahl-e bayt*, "the people of the house") are Mohammed, Ali, Fatma, and their sons Hasan and Hüseyin. Those who are considered the enemies of the *ehlibeyt* are of course the Sunnis, in particular the first three caliphs and the Umayyads.

raised his arm, somebody cut it with a knife and the wound started to bleed. At the same time blood started to flow from the arms of all who were present, and another drop of blood came from outside. This was the blood of Salman who was not present. When Ali's arm was bound, the blood of the others stopped as well. Then Salman entered the assembly and placed one grape in front of Mohammed and said: "Oh servant of the poor, share this grape!" The angel Gabriel appeared, bringing a plate. But Mohammed did not know how to share a single grape with forty people. A hand appeared that wore the ring that Mohammed had put into the mouth of the lion. The hand turned the grape into *şerbet* (a sweet dish). Everybody took from the *şerbet* and all became intoxicated and started to dance *semah*, exclaiming "*Ya Allah hü!*" (Oh God exists!). Then Mohammed saw that Ali was wearing his ring.[9]

The story of the *kırklar cemi* establishes not only the precedence of Ali over Mohammed, but also the identity of Ali and God. Further, it affirms the spiritual union of the community and introduces specific ritual elements like the *semah*. In the *cem*, *miraçlama* is followed by *semah*. Those who perform *semah* enter the *meydan* and offer *niyaz*. The *zakir* plays and the *semahcı* start to rotate and to move in a circle through the *meydan*. There are many different kinds of *semah* with different movements. Normally, a slow *semah* is followed by a faster one. In some forms of *semah* men and women dance in pairs, yet without touching each other.

Semah is followed by the service of the *sakka*, which remembers the tragedy of Kerbela. A hymn called *mersiye* is sung about the suffering of the Imam Hüseyin and his followers, telling how they suffered thirst before the battle because the army of their adversaries blocked the way to water. Sometimes people are moved by the story to the extent that they start weeping. Following the *deyiş*, the *sakka* first offers the *dede* a glass of water and then distributes water among the congregation. Sometimes water is also sprinkled over the congregation. This is the last stage of the "inner" part of the *cem*.

After that the *cem* enters its final phase: the *çerağcı* is called again and extinguishes the lights of the candelabra, then the *süpürgeci* comes and symbolically sweeps the *meydan* again. Now it is time for *lokma*: the meal is brought into the room and distributed among the participants. The *dede* says a *sofra duası* (grace) and asks the congregation whether everybody is content with the share he or she has received. Only when the congregation replies "*razıyız*" (we are contended) everybody starts to eat.

Although the ritual focuses on the *dede* on the *post* and the *oniki hizmet* in the *meydan*, also those participants who do not carry out a special ser-

---

[9] This version of *miraçlama* is taken from Tur (2002, 396–397). Another version is given in Shankland (2002, 80–82). For the hymn of *miraçlama* see Yaman (1998, 61–65). For an ethnomusicological study of *miraçlama* see Yürür (1989).

vice are in manifold ways integrated into the performance of the ritual. They respond to the prayers of the *dede* with the affirmative call "*Allah Allah*," they perform gestures expressing respect whenever the name of a holy person is uttered,[10] beat their chests rhythmically during *tevhid*, and may join in the *semah*.

Change and the Decline of Ritual

Cem is a ritual that affirms community in a social as well as in a spiritual respect. *Cem* establishes a sacred time and space in which the community of the village is renewed and in which mundane conflicts and differences are eliminated. A kind of *communitas* is established, a "moment in and out of time" (Turner 1995, 96). Equality is emphasized and social differences, including difference of gender, are played down. Even the *dede* appears more as *primus inter pares* than as a person of an entirely different status, because he too needs the consent of the community. Yet, despite its liminal character *cem* is firmly bound to the extraritual social conditions. Historically, *cem* had to be performed under the threat of the persecution of Alevis as "heretics." The ritual was carried out in strict secrecy. No outsiders were allowed, and the *kapıcı* issued a warning whenever outsiders approached a *cemevi*. Stories can be heard about *cem* rituals that were quickly turned into fake wedding celebrations when some stranger approached. The disguise of *cem* was a central aspect of *takiya*.

The most important social fundament of *cem* was the relationships between the *dede* and his *talips*. Yet social change that affected Alevis in Turkey in consequence of economic development and migration affected in the first place also the relationships between *dedes* and *talips*. When since the 1950s people started to leave their villages for the Turkish cities in search of work or education, *dede-talip* relationships were stretched and most of them eventually broke. *Dedes* also went to the city, yet they did so not in order to fulfill their ritual duties but for some mundane professions. Of course, migrants in the cities continued to visit their villages, but they did so mainly in summer whereas the *dedes* visited the communities mostly in the leisurely time of winter. More and more people fell out of the ritual networks. Ritual practice slowly declined. The orientation of the Alevi youth towards the left in the 1970s meant a further blow for *cem* and the *dedes*: in many instances the revolutionary youth denounced *dedes* as exploiters that lived at the expense of the people and generally preached against the practice of "backward

---

[10] When for instance *şah* ("king," meaning Ali) is uttered in a prayer, the participants kiss their right hand, move the hand to their forehead, and finally place the hand on their heart.

religion." Sometimes the *dede*s were even driven out of the villages by fervent Marxists.[11] The consequence of these changes was that the practice of *cem* was given up in more and more villages. And even while those who stayed behind might have had the chance to participate in *cem* now and then, migrants, especially those who went out of Turkey, lacked all such opportunities. Before the start of the new Alevi movement, *cem* was for most Alevis in Germany only a distance reminiscence from the days of their village childhood. Many had even never witnessed a *cem* personally. Although there were also *dede*s among the migrants, no *cem* was performed, to the best of my knowledge, during the first fifteen or twenty years of Alevi presence in Germany.

In contrast with the Alevis, many Sunnis quickly transferred their ritual practice to their new country of residence. A *dede* who came to Germany as a laborer in the early 1970s recalled that already in the train to Germany some Sunni fellow workers spread their prayer mats and said *namaz*.[12] Sunni and Alevi migrants stayed together in a hostel. The *dede* recalled:

> After some months there was a meeting in our kitchen. One of the Sunni fellows said: "Friends, we are staying anyway in rooms with three or four beds. Let us empty one room. We can put these beds into the other rooms. Then we will have one room as prayer room." This is how they started. And today, whether it is right or wrong, there are mosques everywhere in Germany. In Hamburg alone there are forty mosques. We Alevis did nothing like that.

Sunnis need only a physical place, a mosque, for prayer, but Alevi ritual is based upon a particular social structure that is much more difficult to relocate.

Yet in the 1980s *dede* Şinasi Koç from Ankara started to tour Germany and to visit his *talip*s there. During his journeys he also held *cem*. The first *cem* that took place in Hamburg was organized in 1984 by former activists of the Yurtseverler Birliği. Şinasi Koç also presided over this *cem*. This *cem* and most of the other *cem* that were subsequently organized in Hamburg or in other places in Germany were very different from the ritual that I have described above. The most decisive difference was that this ritual did not take place in the house of a family, but in a large hall of a school in a suburb of the city. As a consequence, the *cem*

---

[11] Cf. Mandel 1992, 423.

[12] Telling this story, the *dede* made a joke about the Sunnis. He said that because the train was moving and kept on changing its direction the Sunnis had great difficulties to establish *kibla,* the correct orientation of *namaz* towards Mecca. They had to reorient themselves time and again and finally gave up, frustrated. The *dede* made fun about what he considered the exaggerated rule-boundedness of Sunni prayer.

was not a ritual in a small, intimate community. Instead it was a large public event in which several hundred people participated. Of course, not all of the participants were the *talip*s of the *dede*. Another *cem*, also with Şinasi Koç, was organized by the same people a few years later, and a third *cem* was held in October 1989 as part of the Alevi Culture week. After that the practice of *cem* in Hamburg multiplied together with the number of Alevi associations in the city, because every association (with the exception of ÖCB) had a *cem* at least once a year.

Cem as a Public Ritual in the Context of the Alevi Movement

Cem was revived by the Alevi movement and the ritual became itself a significant site of the movement. Because the central purpose of the Alevi movement was the public recognition of Alevism and the end of *takiya*, it was only natural that also *cem* entered the public sphere, becoming a public marker of difference and identity. Traditional, ideal *cem* had been a ritual that renewed the little village community. The new *cem* that was revitalized as a ritual of identity also constituted and renewed a community—but a community of a very different kind. The community that was established and reaffirmed by the new *cem* was the *imagined community* of Alevis as a whole. While the traditional *cem* was limited to a particular congregation of *talip*s served by a specific *dede*, there were no such restrictions in *cem* as public ritual. Now Alevis did not participate in *cem* because they belonged to a specific *dede-talip* network but simply because they were Alevis. To participate in *cem* equaled the public statement: "I am Alevi—I belong to the Alevi community." The intention of *cem* is not only directed towards the members of the community but also toward those outside. In the context of Alevi self-representations, *cem* again exemplifies the Alevi-Sunni master difference. Those aspects of *cem* that distinguish it from Sunni *namaz* are emphasized: the joint participation of men and women, the prominent role of music and dance, as well as the communal meal. In all these aspects *cem* is an antithesis of Sunni prayer. As a public ritual of identity, *cem* is a "ritual implicating others" in Gerd Baumann's sense. Baumann (1992, 113f.) emphasized that rituals are not only referring to the "ritual core community" but also to different kinds of others, be they visible participants or invisible, categorical referents. In the case of public *cem*, the ritual is directed also at the German public as a means to distinguish Alevis from Sunnis and refers, by implication, also to Sunni Muslims and their rituals. In the first years of the Alevi movement it was therefore considered important that *cem* draw a large number of people. The number of people attending the ritual was considered as a measure for the success of *cem*—and the Alevi association that organized it—just as the size of the audience measured the success of a culture festival.

Yet the revitalization of *cem* as a public ritual of identity had a number of consequences for the specific practice of *cem*. As a result of the decline of ritual practice since the 1960s, many Alevis lacked appropriate ritual knowledge and few attempts were made to re-educate Alevis in this respect. Therefore many people, especially the youth, had difficulties in following and understanding the ritual. In large celebrations of *cem*, it happened quite regularly that people moved in and out because they felt bored by the long ritual sequences, because they had to go to the toilet, or wanted to smoke a cigarette. Considerable unrest resulted from this comportment, which again made following and understanding the *cem* more difficult. Because of the spatial structures in which the ritual was held—frequently school halls or university auditoriums—the arrangements differed much from the "ideal" *cem*: people were seated in rows not facing each other. The *meydan* was frequently placed on a stage where also the *dede* and the *zakir* were seated, in considerable distance from the other participants. When the *oniki hizmet* had to perform their services they entered the stage. In such an arrangement only the stage was treated as a sacralized space, that is, only those who entered the stage had to remove their shoes. Most of the other people even did not respond to the prayers of the *dede* with the exclamation "*Allah Allah!*" and did not perform the appropriate gestures. As a consequence the large mass of people who participated in the *cem* were not really participants. They were rather spectators. Edmund Leach's (1976, 45) assertion that in ritual "there is no separate audience of listeners. The performers and the listeners are the same people" obviously does not fully apply to the new *cem*.

Yet also those who participated directly, the *oniki hizmet*, were very frequently ill-prepared for their duties. They did not know how to stand in front of the *post* and how to prostrate, so that the *dede*s had to instruct them in the course of the ritual. Mostly, they did not know the prayers they had to say. Most of the times, the prayers were written on a piece of paper and handed to the *oniki hizmet* shortly before the *cem* started. When a person performed a *hizmet*, he or she took the paper and started to read, often making mistakes due to excitement. Sometimes a duty had to be repeated because it had not been performed properly.

In ritual theory, the idea of ritual as performance has gained much currency. Whereas Victor Turner employed drama as a metaphor for transformative social processes in general and ritual in particular, later authors, most importantly Richard Schechner (2002), equate ritual much more literally with drama and theater.[13] Alevis too describe their

---

[13] Schieffelin (1998) criticized the concept of ritual as performance, because this frequently applies Western ideas of theater and drama to non-Western cultural contexts. According to his view, these "Western" ideas are characterized in the first place by the separation of actors and spectators. Yet we see that it is precisely this "Western" idea of drama that can be applied to the Alevi *cem*.

ritual, *cem*, as performance and drama and as a "symbolical act." Yet in doing so, they do not refer to the transformative or community-building power of symbols but oppose the "symbolical" to the "authentic," the "real." According to their view, the new kind of *cem* is *only* symbolical. *Cem* could in fact be likened with drama, but frequently with a drama characterized by deficient dramaturgy. The "only symbolical" character of the ritual does not only refer to the character of *cem* as a whole, but also to the specific significance of particular elements of the ritual. It is obvious that the question of the *dede* whether there are any conflicts and misgivings among the hundreds of participants of a *cem* is only a rhetorical question, which has to be asked because it is part of the ritual sequence and not because all disputes are actually expected to be solved in a *cem*. On the contrary, everybody knows for certain that not all people in the audience are reconciled with each other, but frequently nobody feels compelled by the *dede*'s question to step forward and to disclose conflicts and problems, and if somebody does so the *dede* lacks all appropriate means to find an acceptable solution.

A number of members of the Alevi associations criticized this state of the ritual. According to their judgments, this kind of *cem* lacks the spiritual qualities that the ritual should embody and convey. Many Alevis explain the "only symbolical" character of the revitalized *cem* with a loss of faith, and thereby link the discussion about *cem* with the debate whether Alevism is religion or culture (cf. chapter four). According to this diagnosis, the problem is that *cem* is regarded as a "cultural show only." *Cem* was folklorized. A *cem* without belief is desacralized, according to this view. The folklorization of *cem* became visible, for instance, in that people sometimes clapped hands after a speech of the *dede* or after the musical performance of a *zakir*. The response of the audience followed the model of panel discussions and culture festivals, where it would be inconceivable *not* to clap hands after a contribution. The debate related also to one particular element of *cem* that is very prone to folklorization, the *semah*. When the first *cem* were held in Germany in the 1980s and early 1990s, only a few elderly people were able to perform *semah*. Yet the Alevi associations established many *semah* courses in which the dance was taught to the youth. Quickly *semah* became a very popular symbol of Alevism among young Alevis, a practice of identity comparable with playing the *saz* or wearing the golden necklace with *Zülfikar*, the sword of the Imam Ali. Yet *Semah* was not necessarily taught as a spiritual practice that has to be performed in a special, ritual context, the *cem*. Accordingly, young Alevis began to dance *semah* at all kinds of celebrations, most importantly at weddings. Only towards the end of the 1990s was this practice criticized and *semah* was emphasized as a spiritual practice.[14]

---

[14] Cf. İlhan 1998.

In the HAKM the debate intensified after a *cem* that was part of a series of events commemorating the tenth anniversary of the association
in October 1999. This *cem* took place in one of the largest auditoriums
of the university and was attended by several hundred people. The *dede*
invited to conduct the ritual was Mehmet Ocak from Pazarcık, a district
in the province of Maraş in southeastern Anatolia. Many members of
the HAKM come from this area. Mehmet Ocak enjoys a considerable
reputation not only among these people but also among those from
adjacent regions because his mother, Elif Ana, is considered a saintly
woman with great spiritual powers. Her tomb has become a regional
center of pilgrimage that is managed by Mehmet Ocak. There was only
one problem with Mehmet Ocak *dede:* his surname notwithstanding,
he does not belong to an *ocak* and therefore, in the strict sense of Alevi
genealogical rationality, he is not a *dede*. He derives his ability to conduct *cem* not from descent from a holy lineage, but from the spiritual
charisma of his mother. The issue whether a *dede* who is not a "real"
dede could be invited to conduct a *cem* was discussed among the members of the HAKM. Few people expressed serious reservations. It was
argued that it was better to invite a *dede* who did not belong to an *ocak*
but who was widely known among Alevis in Hamburg and therefore
could draw more attention and more people to the *cem*, than to bring a
"real" *dede* whom only very few people knew.

In the *cem* Mehmet Ocak was seated on the stage of the auditorium.
In this particular *cem*, however, he was not to play the most significant
role. The lead role was taken by the Lütfi Kaleli, an elderly Alevi intellectual and writer from Istanbul who had been invited for a panel
discussion that was part of the series of events. In the *cem* Lütfi Kaleli
assumed the *hizmet* of the *rehber*, the assistant of the *dede*. But in fact it
was he as the *rehber* who directed the ritual. Lütfi Kaleli announced
the ritual as an *eğitim* (education, training) *cemi*. The explicit intention
of this *cem* was to teach the ritual's meaning and structure to the audience. In his introduction Lütfi Kaleli contrasted the *cem* to be performed
with a *görgü cemi*, that is, with a full ceremony in which only *musahip*s,
people fully initiated into Alevism, are allowed to take part. In order
to achieve the didactic purpose, the course of the performance was
frequently interrupted by Lütfi Kaleli, who then explained at length
what had happened so far and what was to come next. The *oniki hizmet*
were called to the stage one after the other and read the prayers from
their papers. The ritual sequence was changed. Most significantly, *halk
mahkemesi* was left out in the beginning. Yet when the *cem* was heading
towards the end, after the offerings (*lokma*) had been presented to the
dede, Lütfi Kaleli again interrupted the performance and announced:
"Now we will present a little example of the Alevi judicial system in the
cem ceremony. That is, we will have the so-called *halk mahkemesi*." He
then asked whether anybody had a complaint against anybody else in

the audience. A man rose and indeed voiced a complaint that was rather a fake issue, but which subsequently turned into a serious conflict. I will discuss this conflict in the next section. What concerns me here is to give an example of a *cem* that is "only" a performance. This *cem* was performed in an imaginary showcase and was commented upon from the outside. Although Lütfi Kaleli "played the role" of the *rehber*, he was not simply "acting" within the *cem* but interrupted the drama to assume a distanced position and to comment upon what was going on. Rather than simply being a *cem*, the performance was a presentation of what happens when a *cem* is performed. This distanced show of a *cem* was mirrored in the behavior of the audience. There was great unrest, and the people kept coming and going as they liked.

Later, this *cem* and similar performances were severely criticized by many members of the HAKM. I discussed the *cem* with Hasan Kılavuz. He too compared the ritual to drama:

> "*Cem* is a play, a theater. But all the persons who are part of it play together. One plays the *saz*, one performs *semah*, one cleans the place, the other brings *lokma*, all play together. Yet what we do here in Europe, this is only a symbolical show, it is not real."

I asked: "What is missing?"

> Hasan Kılavuz: "Many things are missing. Those who enter the *cem* do not know what they are doing! But one has to know that! When I play a drama I have to know the play by heart. Otherwise I cannot act. (…) It is the same in *cem*. Those who do not know anything, they should not attend the *cem*. It is a matter of concentration. It is a great mistake that *cem* is not really performed in Europe, that the people do not really experience it. They go in and out, this is not possible! There are rules! Imagine, you are at a theater, the actors play and then your mobile phone rings. What happens to your concentration? It is gone! You have to be very quiet at the theater, you are listening intensely, with concentration. It has to be like this in *cem*. The *dede* plays saz. He talks, prays, sings. And everybody joins. It has to be done as if everything is done by a single person."

Yet it is quite impossible to achieve this spiritual union in which the community becomes a single body in a *cem* like the one of October 1999. Many members of the association complained about the permanent disturbances. Some demanded that children must not be brought to a *cem*. The debate was summarized as follows by Musa Aksoy, a member of both the HAKM and HAAK BIR:

> *Cem* is a spiritual practice; it is not a cultural event. When somebody goes to church on Sundays this is also not a cultural event. (…) Religion is religion, faith is faith. We have to return from this folklorization to the fundament of *cem*, to what *cem* actually is. Unfortunately it has become a habit to dance *semah* like folklore at weddings. This is not good for *semah* and *cem*. Weddings and cultural shows are one thing but *cem* is something else.

Figure 6.1 *Dede* and *Zakir* at a *cem* of the HAKM, 2004 (photography by Martin Sökefeld).

Other members argued that normally *cem* takes too much time and that nobody could keep quiet for four or more hours. Some demanded that only people having faith should attend a *cem*. Interestingly, this idea was also voiced by some Alevis who considered themselves non-believers and who were of the opinion that they had no business to be in *cem*. It seems that this debate changed the ritual practice of the HAKM. After 1999 the association had no *cem* that took place in a location like an auditorium but convened in smaller places. The *cems* were performed in a Protestant church. By a rearrangement of the pews in a circular way in the church and by candlelight a more intimate atmosphere was created. Before the ritual, rules about the appropriate behavior in *cem* were mailed out together with the invitation. These rules explained not only that everybody was expected to bring something for *lokma*, that children below the age of eight should not come to the *cem*, and that it was not allowed to make noise and talk during the ritual or to leave the place before the end of *cem*. Rule number six said: "Those who do not accept the basic principles of Alevi faith and who do no honor the values of belief cannot participate in the *cem*."

Indeed, less people participated in these rituals, which lasted less than two hours. In order to shorten the *cem*, *halk mahkemesi* and *miraçlama* were left out. Further, the *oniki hizmet* performed their services silently, no papers were needed. These *cems* were directed by Hasan Kılavuz. He did not act as *dede* but as *rehber*, and he urged the *dede* to shorten the ritual. Before the *cem* started, the *rehber* instructed the participants again that they should not talk, make noise, or clap hands during the ritual. Yet this new, reduced way of having *cem* did not remain undisputed. Especially the prescription that only believers should attend the *cem* was criticized. Several people argued that this prescription violated the basic value of Alevism: its openness and tolerance.

Cem as a Site of Conflict

When *cem* ceases to be a closed ritual of an intimate community and becomes a public ritual of identity, relating to an imagined community, it can be expected that disputes about identity—disputes about what this imagined community *is*, how and by whom it should be represented—that is, politics of identity, become an issue in *cem*. One such issue concerned even the very first *cem* that was held in Hamburg in 1984, a time when the struggle of the PKK had become a significant problem in Turkey. *Dede* Şinasi Koç, who presided over this *cem*, was like many Alevis a staunch Kemalist for whom all political endeavors that might question the unity and cultural homogeneity of the Turkish nation were anathema. In fact, Kemalism has many supporters among Alevis, especially because Kemalism is understood as guarantee of laicism in Turkey. Some Alevis regard Atatürk almost as a kind of saint (see Dreßler 1999). Yet many of those Alevis that had been committed to the extreme left or to the Kurdish cause are quite critical of Kemalism, due to its repressive aspects and because it did not really implement a secularization of Turkish society.

At the time of the first *cem* in Hamburg, Hasan Kılavuz was the chairman of KOMKAR in the city, a nonmilitant Kurdish exile association related with the Kurdish Party PSK[15] in Turkey. Hasan Kılavuz wanted to make a short speech at the *cem* and to convey a message of greeting from KOMKAR. Yet *dede* Şinasi Koç was very suspicious about Kurds and insisted on reading the message himself before he allowed to be read publicly in the *cem*, to make sure that no separatist ideas were expressed. This issue produced considerable unrest and became quite a famous anecdote that is still frequently told by the veterans of the Alevi movement in Hamburg. Şinasi Koç was also involved in a conflict about the *cem* that was held during the Alevi Culture Week in October 1989. At that time Şinasi Koç was staying with some of his *talip*s in Hamburg. Many of the members of the Alevi Culture Group that organized the event were Kurds and Şinasi Koç was known, also from the earlier *cem*, as a strict Kemalist and Turkish nationalist. Şinasi Koç participated in a meeting of the Alevi Culture Group where the *cem* was discussed. The *dede* insisted that he was ready to preside over the *cem* only under the condition that a picture of Atatürk and the Turkish flag were displayed in the hall. A number of the activists were decidedly against displaying these symbols of the Turkish nation. Hasan Kılavuz explained:

> There are many Alevi symbols in *cem*. Why do we need the flag or Atatürk then? When I like [these symbols] I can put them up at home. But not in *cem*, in a place of prayer. I have nothing against the flag. OK, it is the symbol of a nation. But there is nothing like that in *cem*! In a mosque, a church, or a synagogue you will not find such national symbols. But, strangely, the Alevis are putting up Atatürk and the Turkish flag. There is no [Alevi] prayer that mentions the flag, Atatürk, or any general. Never! There is nothing like that in the prayer house.

Yet the majority of the group still supported the position of the *dede* and favored the national symbols in *cem*. The others played a little trick in order to avoid the display of the symbols. Şinasi Koç also wanted to videotape the *cem*. His opponents argued that these tapes might fall into the hands of the Turkish intelligence agencies and that this would create problems for the participants and for their families in Turkey. They insisted on taking a vote on the question of videotaping the *cem* and combined this issue with the question of the national symbols. Thus, both questions were put to a single vote and because many members feared the repression of the intelligence agencies, the majority voted against videotaping the *cem* and displaying the national symbols. A member of the group recalled that Şinasi Koç was shocked by the result of the vote—not only because the national symbols were disfavored but equally because the position and the authority of a *dede* had been rejected. Some days later he was asked again whether he was ready to conduct the *cem* but he insisted on the flag and Atatürk. Therefore the

---

[15] Partîya Sosyalîst Kurdistan (Socialist Party of Kurdistan).

Alevi Culture Group invited another *dede*, Ahmet Kömürcü, who was living in Munich, to direct the *cem*. The question of the national symbols continued to haunt the Alevi movement. I will discuss this matter more thoroughly in chapter eight. In the present context the issue serves as an example of how questions of identification—the identification of Alevism with a nation—invade the ritual sphere.

A conflict of different sorts emerged in the *halk mahkemesi* of the *cem* discussed above that was held by the HAKM in October 1999 on the occasion of its tenth anniversary. I have already described how this *cem* started without *halk mahkemesi*, but that towards the end of the ritual Lütfi Kaleli wanted to show how this element of *cem* worked and therefore asked whether anybody had a complaint against somebody present. A man came forward, one of the original founders of the Alevi Culture Group. He said that he had a complaint against the chairman of the AABF, Turgut Öker, who was also present and who was a founding member too. The man came to the stage and said that since his youth the chairman had been so much committed to the Alevi movement, investing all his time on the Alevi cause and never doing anything for himself, that he not even had found the time to marry. Therefore, he accused him of not being married. Obviously, this "complaint" was rather intended as a (somewhat garbled) praise of the chairman and his commitment to the movement. Because he had been accused Turgut Öker was also called to the stage by Lütfi Kaleli in order to make his statement on the issue. Yet Turgut Öker was quite reluctant to discuss the question of his marriage. He said he wanted to raise another matter:

> I am quite disappointed that after ten years of Alevi associations in Hamburg we still have to celebrate *cem* in a an improper place like a university auditorium. It is a pity that there are several Alevi associations now and still the HAKM, which was founded ten years ago, has no proper place of its own to celebrate *cem*.

He mentioned the case of Berlin, where a few weeks earlier several Alevi associations had jointly opened a *cemevi* in a former church, and expressed his desire that Hamburg should follow the example of Berlin. This was obviously a quite different complaint. The change in the course of the *halk mahkemesi* was explicitly acknowledged by Lütfi Kaleli, saying that the ceremony had started as a symbolical act, but that now it had touched upon something real and important. He recommended that the Alevi associations of Hamburg should increase their cooperation and asked the audience of the *cem* to support the leadership efforts for unity. With this statement Lütfi Kaleli wanted to end the *halk mahkemesi*. Many people in the audience expressed their agreement by clapping hands. Yet, another man rose and questioned the intentions of those apparently agreeing for more unity. He said:

Alevism is not a cheap thing. If you promise unity and cooperation here in prayer (*ibadet*), you are bound by your solemn promise. Many of you are not members of the HAKM, but your promise means that all of you have to become members of the association because is it is the first and most senior Alevi organization in Hamburg.

At that stage a member of the managing committee of HAAK BIR rose and said that it was a pity that the *cem* took place in the university. If the HAKM really wished greater cooperation, they could well have come to HAAK BIR and held this *cem* in the association's hall. Again Lütfi Kaleli tried to end the *halk mahkemesi* with some general remarks of recommendation, but again a man rose. This was Halis Tosun, another founding member of the Alevi Culture Group and the HAKM. In a very agitated voice he expressed that it was quite useless to talk about cooperation between HAAK BIR and the HAKM. He said:

> It was HAAK BIR that broke away from the HAKM and thereby ended the unity of Alevi associations in Hamburg. So, if you want cooperation you should come back! But there have been so many occasions to do so and you never did. Five years ago in a *cem* we debated the same and at that time you promised in *halk mahkemesi* that you will come back to the HAKM But you did not do so. You broke your *ikrar*! It is futile to talk about cooperation!

During the exchange of statements several people had been called to the stage: the author of the original complaint, the chairman of the AABF, the chairman of the HAKM as representative of the party accused by the second complaint, and the member of the managing committee of HAAK BIR. All the persons on the stage stood in a semicircle with their heads bowed in front of the *dede,* who remained seated on the *post.* The whole hearing was managed by Lütfi Kaleli, who now asked Ibrahim Renkliçay, the chairman of the HAKM, to comment upon the accusation. He explained that the different Alevi associations in Hamburg had ended their rivalry and entered a phase of serious cooperation. He mentioned the example of events organized jointly so far and added that he hoped that in future the cooperation would be even more intense. He expressed the wish that the Alevi associations of Hamburg could do something similar to what had been done in Berlin. After that no additional statements were heard. The *dede* issued his judgment, asking the associations to increase cooperation and to bury competition. He expressed his hope that one day the associations could indeed have a *cemevi* together.

This *cem* and the ensuing conflict exemplified that a strict separation between a "real" and a "symbolical," "as if" performance cannot be maintained. The symbolical performance touched a real conflict and became an arena for expressing this conflict. The symbolical performance of *halk mahkemesi* gravitated, apparently inexorably, towards the most serious split in the Alevi community in Hamburg. *Cem* has changed from a ritual of face-to-face community in the villages to a ritual of an imagined community. In *cem*, Alevis become visible as a community. It is no surprise then that *halk mahkemesi* in the new *cem* does not simply negotiate problems and conflicts between individuals, but also pretences for precedence among organized communities. Behind the dispute lies the question of which Alevi association in fact represents the Alevi community of the city. Is it the HAKM because it was the first and original association, whereas HAAK BIR originated as a split off faction? Or is it HAAK BIR because it possesses a proper place for the Alevi community to celebrate *cem*, thus offering a kind of home for the ceremony, a facility that the HAKM so far was unable to achieve? This dispute is certainly not only symbolical but has serious material aspects. HAAK BIR had taken on a considerable financial commitment in the acquisition of its building and had accrued substantial debt. It would be a great relief of this financial burden if the obligations could be shared and the building used by other associations too. However, a number of members of the HAKM expressed the sentiment: "Why should we solve their problem?" The issue of the building continued to be perceived as a matter of competition between the two associations.

Many more disputes refer to specific elements of the ritual practice in *cem*: Should verses from the Quran be read in *cem*? Should people be seated on chairs or on the floor? Should men and women sit separately? Such issues are debated with or among the *dede*s. Many of such matters finally refer to the question: Who has the ultimate authority in Alevism? Is it still the *dede*s? What is the place of *dede*s in the contemporary Alevi movement?

Dedes in the Alevi Movement

In "traditional," "village" Alevism, authority—not only religious but in many respects also mundane, political authority—was embodied by the *dede*s. Their authority was not conferred by humans but, because it was based on descent from the Imams, ultimately by God. *Dede*s were the central institution of Alevism. In a short paper on *dede*s, Ali Yaman who belongs himself to a family of *dede*s, writes: "The institution of the dede is the most important of all the institutions integral to the social and religious organization of Anatolian Alevis" (Yaman n.d.). This statement is certainly true for "traditional" Alevism but it applies much less to Alevism as it has been transformed by the Alevi movement. The most significant institution of contemporary Alevism is the Alevi association. Within the associations *dede*s may assume roles of variable importance. Although there were certainly *dede*s, or, better, *ocakzade*, i.e., members of *ocak*s, among the protagonists of the Alevi movement since the late 1980s, they did not play the central role. To the contrary, as many activists of the movement came from leftist organizations, they and the movement as a whole were regarded with thorough suspicion by many *dedes*. In the first instance, the Alevi movement meant a further loss of importance to the *dedes*. In Turkey, the movement was mainly a movement of intellectuals and authors who published a great number of books and articles on Alevism. Some of them were *ocakzade*, but most were not. Thus, the competence and authority to explain and interpret Alevism was appropriated by these intellectuals. These *araştırmacı-yazar* (researcher-writers) became the new authorities on Alevism. Their authority was not derived from genealogical descent, but from the act of writing and publishing texts about Alevism.[16] Many theories proposed by these writers were regarded with abhorrence by *dedes*—just remember *dede* Ismail Aslandoğan's rejection of Necat Birdoğan's thesis that Alevism is in part an offshoot of shamanism. The *dedes* had effectively lost the control of knowledge about Alevism.[17]

In some cases *dedes* were among the founding members of Alevi associations. In Germany *dedes* were mostly involved in the establishment of a specific kind of associations. Thus *dedes* like Derviş Tur of Rüsselsheim or Niyazi Bozdoğan of Cologne were central figures in the Hacı Bektaş Veli associations that combined in the first Alevi umbrella association, the Alevi Cemaatları Federasyonu. As I wrote in chapter three, these associations were rather opponents of the Alevi movement as it was proposed by the Alevi Culture Centers. The purpose of the *dede*-led Hacı Bektaş Veli associations was not to make Alevism an issue of public recognition, but to cater for the spiritual needs of the local Alevi community. *Dedes* were much less involved in the Alevi Culture Centers. After Sivas, both types of associations came together in the AABF that was dominated by the Culture Centers. Also the Alevi Culture Centers and the erstwhile leftists recognized *dedes* as an important element of Alevism. But they did not accept *dedes* as the first and final authority. Dede Şinasi Koç had this experience when against his will the Turkish flag and Atatürk were not displayed in *cem*. The relationship between Alevi associations on one hand and *dedes* on the other was frequently characterized by a contradiction of authority. The problem was based on the mutually exclusive sources for the legitimacy of authority. *Dedes* could claim the traditional legitimacy of genealogical descent whereas the associations, and their managing committees,

---

[16] Vorhoff (1995, 193–202) provides a very useful list with further information about these authors.

[17] The control of knowledge was further weakened by the increasing prominence of Alevi websites since the late 1990s. Here, ideas about Alevism are promulgated by young Alevis without the control of intellectuals and publishing houses. See Sökefeld 2002a.

claimed the legitimacy of democratic elections. The issue is also rooted in a fundamental contradiction of values *within* Alevism: democracy is considered a basic value of Alevism, just as is love for the *ehlibeyt* from whom the *dedes* claim descent. Although this conflict was not always openly visible, it surfaced in many instances. The AABF had to come to terms with the *dedes*. It tried to institutionalize the relationship with the *dedes* and asked them to form a *dedeler kurulu* (*dedes'* council) that was to act as an advisory body for the AABF. Yet several *dedes* left the council because the *dedes'* decisions were not heeded by the committee of the AABF. Hasan Kılavuz, who was asked several times to join the *dedeler kurulu* but preferred not to do so explained his refusal to me with the following words: "I asked the chairman [of the AABF]: 'When the *dedes* arrive at a decision that the committee does not like, would you then follow the *dedes'* decision? No, you wouldn't. Then what is the use of the *dedes'* making decisions?'" The issue is further complicated by the fact that there is no joint body or institutions of *dedes*[18] and that the *dedes* are very much divided among themselves. In fact, in many instances one *dede* does not even recognize the legitimacy of another one. Genealogical claims are not always accepted, and I have heard *dedes* saying about another *dede* things like "He is a *dede* only since yesterday!" or "Actually, he is not a *dede*, he is a butcher!"

This leads to the question: who is a *dede*? Most Alevis agree that first of all the *dede* has to be a member of an *ocak*, he has to be an *ocakzade*. But more criteria have to be fulfilled because not all *ocakzades* are *dedes*. One is the criterion of gender: *dedes* are male. Although women may acquire considerable spiritual charisma as we have seen in the case of Elif Ana of Pazarcık, this happens quite rarely and it never turns them into a *dede*.[19] Most Alevis would say that in order to be recognized as *dede* an *ocakzade* has to sit on the *post* and conduct *cem*, that is, a real *dede* is a *post dedesi*. Yet who among the male *ocakzade* is eligible as *post dedesi*? Generally it is said that a *post dedesi* requires considerable knowledge (in the first place knowledge about Alevism but also general knowledge) and unimpeachable moral conduct.[20]

---

[18] Some *ocaks* recognize the Çelebis, that is, the descendants of Hacı Bektaş Veli at the *tekke* of Hacıbektaş as the highest authority, but many, especially Kurdish, *ocaks* do not. In any case, this authority is not formalised and there is no hierarchical form of organization that could assure that the *dedes* heed this authority.

[19] Elif Ana belonged to a group of four dervishes in the area of Pazarcık and the other three members were men. It would be interesting to see whether Elif Ana's son Mehmet Ocak and his subsequent male descendants will indeed be recognized as *dedes* in future.

[20] Derviş Tur (2002, 351) lists the following criteria: descent, impeccable moral conduct as testified by a *pir* or *mürşit* (i.e. by a *dede* of whom the *dede* himself is *talip*), and knowledge. Derviş Tur also concedes that a man who is not *ocakzade*

But many Alevis express discontent especially with the knowledge of many *dedes*, and reprimand them for basing their claims mainly on genealogical descent and for sticking to a kind of knowledge that has become useless in modern times. It is debated what kind of knowledge is required by *dedes*, and this question is in many instances related with the debate about how *cem* should be conducted now. Should old traditions be kept or should the ritual be revised and be made fitting for the present? Such questions were discussed in the *dedeler kurulu*, but the members of the council were not able to arrive at a solution that was agreed upon by all. Rather, the *dedeler kurulu* became an arena of conflicts among *dedes*. Some *dedes* have acquired a reputation of being "reactionary" or even "fundamentalist" because they insist on certain things in *cem*. Ismail Aslandoğan *dede* is considered as "fundamentalist" by many Alevis in Hamburg because he had insisted on men and women sitting separately in *cem*. In his book Derviş Tur (2002, 344) also recommends this arrangement. For many Alevis this is an unforgivable violation of the Alevi value of not separating the sexes and treating them on equal terms. Also the question whether verses from the Quran should be recited in *cem* is part of the debate, and this is related to the general question whether Alevism is Islam or not. I have said already that some *dedes* insist on the Quran and on scriptural knowledge, and such *dedes* affirm the identity of Alevism and Islam also in *cem*, for instance with a prayer that contains the following lines:

Dinimiz Islam	Our faith is Islam
Kitabımız Ku'ran	Our book is the Quran
Dinimiz Islam	Our faith is Islam
Kaabemiz Insan	Our Kaaba is the human being

In the end, however, dedes and Alevi associations depend upon one another: The associations need the *dedes*, because having *cem* is counted among the required tasks of an association and there can be no *cem* without *dede*. But also the *dedes* depend on the associations, at least if they are interested in conducting *cem*, because there are generally no independently and privately organized *cems*. Yet it seems that the associations have the whip hand because they can freely choose among the *dedes*. Associations are not bound to a particular *dede* as the *talips* had been in the past, and most associations also do not have a *dede* of their own who regularly conducts *cem* for them.[21] Most associations call *dedes* from

---

may be conferred the right to conduct *cem* by a recognized *dede*. Such a *dede* is called a *dikme dede* ("planted *dede*"). A *dikme dede* cannot bequeath his authority to a successor, i.e., he does not possess a hereditary authority.

[21] More religiously oriented associations like the Hacı Bektaş Veli Association in Cologne have such "own" *dedes* who conduct a *cem* every week. Yet this is an exception.

outside. They may simply try one and call another one next time if the first *dede* did not suit their expectations. During the last few years a considerable market for ritual services was created by the Alevi movement. In the late 1980s and early 1990s there were few associations having *cem* as well as few *dedes* that offered this service. Dede Şinasi Koç died in the early 1990s while staying in Germany. Ahmet Kömürcü became the most frequently employed *dede* in these years. He had a reputation of being a liberal *dede* and he was one of the very few *dedes* living in Germany who were able to conduct *cem*. In fact, the *cem* he had directed during the Alevi Culture Week in Hamburg was only the second *cem* he had performed in his life, and his performance of *cem* during this event contributed considerably to his reputation. Subsequently not only the number of Alevi associations grew, but also more and more *dedes* living in Germany took to conducting *cem*. Some had done so already in Turkey, before they migrated to Germany. Others started to conduct *cem* only after they had come to Germany. Yet all of them had acquired the required ritual knowledge from their fathers or uncles in Turkey. That is, they had become *dede* in Turkey. Only since the late 1990s have some young *dedes* who had grown up in Germany and who had also acquired their ritual knowledge in this country started to conduct *cem*. The first of these was Zeynel Arslan, from a village on the German-Swiss border. He learned not only from accompanying other *dedes* as *zakir* in *cem* but also from books. He was the first to conduct *cem* in German, and he became also a kind of expert in interfaith ritual, officiating in a number of Alevi-Christian marriages. Other young *dedes* like Sedat Korkmaz from Mannheim and Cafer Kaplan from Hamm followed suit.

Both the demand and the supply of *dedes* have increased considerably. When an association calls a *dede* for *cem*, not only are his travel expenses covered but he also receives a certain fee. Some *dedes* like Ahmet Kömürcü and Zeynel Arslan are highly popular and frequently booked out. All German *dedes* are "part time *dedes*." They have regular jobs (some are also pensioners) and offer their ritual services only on weekends. In contrast with Turkey, where many *dedes* are employed by Alevi associations, there are up to now no such "professional" *dedes* in Germany. These associations in Turkey have *cem* almost every week, not only once or twice a year like most Alevi associations in Germany.

According to a survey on *cem* in Germany that I undertook among the membership associations of the AABF, there are at least thirty *post dedes* in Germany. Although there are now many *dedes* in Germany that conduct *cem*, it is generally feared that there will be a shortage of *dedes* in future when the old *dedes* die or become unable to perform the ritual. The problem is that there is no regular procedure for educating young *dedes*. The traditional method of religious formation in which a *dede* taught his son or nephew has become impracticable. To the best of my knowledge there is not a single son of a *post dedesi* in Germany that wants to become a *dede.* On the other hand, there are a few young *ocakzade* who want to become *dede* but whose fathers had not practised as *dedes.* Further, the traditional way of learning by accompanying the *dede* for years in his visits among his *talips* is not possible today. The younger *dedes* have mostly acquired their knowledge autodidactically.

In 2003 the Alevi Academy started a weekend course for educating future *dedes.* These courses are of academic character. Many of the lecturers teaching in the courses hold a Ph.D. in Islamic studies, Turkish studies, or anthropology. Not all of the lecturers are Alevis. Interestingly, only a very small part of the students are members of *ocakzade* and have the intention to act as *post dedesi* after the completion of the courses. Most students, among them also women, are simply interested in acquiring more knowledge about Alevism.

Hasan Kılavuz and a New Council of *Dedes*

In a previous article (Sökefeld 2002b) I presented biographical sketches of three men who exemplify three different ways of being *dede* in Germany: Ismail Aslandoğan is a very strict *dede,* giving great importance to scriptural knowledge; Ahmet Kömürcü is known for is liberal approach; and Zeynel Arslan tries to find a new approach in interfaith rituals, also conducting *cem* in German. Here I would like to introduce another *dede* in more detail, who has been elected the chairman of the reconstituted *dedeler kurulu* of the AABF in 2003, and who stands in the center of recent conflicts about Alevism in general and the role of *dedes* in particular. This is Hasan Kılavuz. In this work I have mentioned him already several times because he has been a central figure of the Alevi movement in Hamburg. He is different from the other *dedes* dealt with so far in that he does not act as *post dedesi.*

Hasan Kılavuz comes from the village Muhundu in the Mazgırt district, Tunceli province. He belongs to the *ocak* of Seyit Sabur. Among the *talips* of this *ocak* are the *dedes* of the *ocak* of Baba Mansur, one of the largest *ocaks.* He belongs to a family of Kurmancı-speaking Kurds. Kılavuz's father was *dede,* but he died in 1982. Since that time the responsibility has been taken over by Kılavuz's elder brother. Kılavuz studied engineering and came first to Hamburg in 1970, working with a German company while he still was a student. After four years he returned to Turkey intending to complete his studies, but because he was required to do his military service and because of the political conflicts between leftist and rightist students that paralyzed the universities, he could not do so. In 1978 he returned to Hamburg. Already as a student he had been involved with political parties of the left and with Kurdish politics. In Germany he joined KOMKAR, a Kurdish exile organization. In the mid 1980s he was the chairman of KOMKAR in Hamburg. He told me that during these years being a Kurd was more important for him than being Alevi. Yet he joined the Alevi Culture Group in early 1989 and became a founding member of the HAKM. He was always proud of being a member of a *dede* family, but he did not assume the role of a *dede* and was not addressed as such by the members of the association. Turgut Öker told how Hasan Kılavuz "became *dede*":

> Do you know how Hasan became *dede*? I made him a *dede*! Once we were sitting with friends in a restaurant. Hasan said jokingly: "You have to call me *dede*, you have to kiss my hands because I am the son of a *dede*!" But I said: "No, being the son of a *dede* is not sufficient for being a *dede*! You also have to know something. If you can tell me the names of the twelve Imams I will kiss your hand!" But he did not know the names of all the *imams*. A few days later we met again and he said: "Now ask me the names of the twelve Imams!" I said: "No, you have prepared yourself for this question. Now you have to answer some other questions too!" From this time he started to read much about Alevism and to acquire great knowledge. Now everybody calls him *dede*.

Hasan Kılavuz himself told about this time:

> When I had become a member of the Alevi association I talked much with Turgut and the others. Turgut said: "You are a *dede*, what do you know?" And I realized that I did not know much. Well, I have heard, seen, and experienced many things, but this is not enough. One has to take efforts to learn more, to read, to ask how it had been in earlier times. And then, when you go deep into this religion, when you read and learn, then you realize all this light, this brightness. It is beautiful. Otherwise there is darkness. If you do not know anything and if you are ignorant, there is darkness. When you learn, there is light. And therefore I am now interested in Alevism.

Yet although Kılavuz began to study Alevism seriously, he was not called *dede* until 1995, as a consequence of the conflict with Necati Turan about the chairmanship in the HAKM. At that time some of his supporters started to address him as *dede* in order to tease Necati Turan—who kept on to insist that Hasan was not *dede* (see chapter three). When he had become elected as chairman in the following year, Kılavuz was regularly addressed as *dede* by everybody in the association and he indeed gave much importance to religious topics. He started to give lectures on topics like *aşure* or sacrifice (*kurban*) in Alevism. He also published articles on religious questions in *Alevilerin Sesi*, the journal of the AABF. He also took on some ritual responsibilities. Sometimes he conducted marriages or funeral rites. Turgut Öker several times tried to get him involved in the *dedeler kurulu*, but Kılavuz refused to do so because he felt that the council was not sufficiently respected by the AABF, and also because he was of the opinion that the *dede*s in the council quarreled too much among themselves. Hasan Kılavuz is very critical of other *dedes* because most of them take Alevism as a part of Islam, whereas he himself is a very strict proponent of the idea that Alevism is different from Islam. He gives no importance to the Quran and is especially critical of reading from the Quran in *cem*. Referring to the great body of Alevi hymns and lyrics he says: "Our Quran is the *nefes* we sing!"

Yet, in spite of all this commitment to Alevism and in spite of his efforts to find a suitable form of having *cem*, Hasan Kılavuz does not conduct *cem* himself. There are several reasons for this: First, not he but his elder brother had taken the responsibility of the *dede* in his family. To conduct a *cem* himself would be an act of disrespect towards his brother. Second, he still feels that he needs to learn more about Alevism in order to be able to perform the ritual. And third, he is divorced and remarried. Alevism traditionally does not permit divorce, especially not among *dedes* who are required to be social and moral models for their *talips*. It is very probable that much gossip would start about a divorced *dede* sitting on the *post* if Hasan Kılavuz conducted a *cem*. Instead, he acts as *rehber* in *cem*, but at the same time requires that the *dedes* conducting the ritual for the HAKM follow his ideas of ritual practice.

The relationship between the AABF and its *dedeler kurulu* has been rather difficult. The committee of the AABF regarded the *dedes'* council as unproductive, and in fact there was no formalized, clear relationship between the AABF and the council. There were no statutes that specified the competences of the *dedeler kurulu*. In 2003, the AABF instituted a new *dedeler kurulu*, which had become necessary in the context of applications for Alevi religious instruction in schools. Among the legal preconditions for Alevi religious instruction under the aegis of the AABF was a clear self-positioning of the federation as a religious body, and this in turn required a clarified relationship between the association and the *dedes* that are considered the "clergymen" or "priests" (in German, *Geistliche*) of Alevism. I will discuss this in more detail in the next chapter. Yet beside this formal requirement the AABF also wanted to have a new *dedeler kurulu* because the *dedes'* council, and especially its long time chairman Derviş Tur, were considered as politically unreliable. The AABF intended to break the power of the elder and more traditional *dedes*.

New by-laws of the *dedeler kurulu* specified the procedure of how the members of the council are to be elected: Every local membership association of the AABF sends one *dede* as delegate to an assembly of *dedes* at the level of the German *Bundesländer* (i.e., the federal states). Each of these *Länder* assemblies elects a certain number of *dedes*, depending on the number of Alevi associations in the respective *Bundesland*, for an electoral council at the federal level that elects a *dedeler kurulu* of twelve members. Finally, the members of the *dedeler kurulu* elect a chairman among themselves. Thus the *dedes* were to be legitimized in the first place by the local Alevi associations; no *dede* who was not elected as delegate could become a member of the *dedeler kurulu*. The AABF tried to adopt a quite open stance on the question who could qualify as *dede*. Originally, it was not planned to restrict the eligible persons to *ocakzade*, but the *ocakzade* as descendants of the Imams had to be mentioned in the statues. However, also persons in the tradition of the Bektaşi *baba*s who are not *seyit* were explicitly named as eligible.[22]

Hasan Kılavuz was regarded as a "progressive" and "modern" *dede*, also due to his position on Islam. Therefore he was considered the best candidate for the chairmanship of the *dedeler kurulu*. However, he hesitated to declare his candidature—he feared that because of his position against Islam he was "too radical" and would create much unrest among the other *dede*s. He also was afraid of a defamation campaign from some other *dede*s.[23] Yet many people, not only in the AABF but also at the local level in Hamburg, encouraged him to take the challenge. In the months before the election the demand on Kılavuz became very high. Almost every weekend he was invited by one or two Alevi associations from throughout Germany to speak about Alevism. According to his own assessment most people responded quite positively to his positions, the rejection of Islam included.

Two weeks before the elections, half of the members of the old *dedeler kurulu* stepped down in order to register their protest against the new by-laws. In their view, being a *dede* was not a matter of election. Very shortly before the election, Hasan Kılavuz decided to stand for the position of the chairman of the *dedeler kurulu* and in mid–April 2003 he was elected. Besides him eleven other people were elected. These elections were quite revolutionary because a woman, Fatma Beyazit from Ludwigsburg, was elected to the council. She was an *ana* (mother), i.e., a female member of an *ocak*. The election of a female member of the *dedeler kurulu* had been very much hoped for by the committee of the AABF, in order to establish a further symbol of renewal and modernity. For the purpose of furthering the chances of a woman being elected, a female vicar of the Protestant Church had been invited to explain how the Church had come to accept women in the position of parish priests. On the occasion of the election a delegate of the *Almanya Alevi Kadınlar Birliği* (Union of Alevi Women in Germany) demanded that women should also be allowed to sit on the *post* and to conduct *cem*.[24]

---

[22] Cf. AABF Dedeler Kurulu İç Tüzüğü (internal by-laws of the *dede*s council of the AABF), section 3 2. *Baba*s are the spiritual leaders of the Bektaşi order who do not depend on genealogical legitimation but on personal commitment and spiritual achievement.

[23] At that time, however, he held no longer to the argument that the *dedeler kurulu* was not sufficiently respected by the AABF.

[24] Another *ana* from Berlin, Gülşen Erdoğan, has already sat several times on

On the following day the Turkish daily *Hürriyet* reported on the front page of its European section on the elections. The paper wrote about Hasan Kılavuz and quoted him saying that being divorced—especially if the divorce is not his own fault—should not necessarily prevent a *dede* from acting as *post dedesi*.[25] Subsequently there was much less talk about this issue than had been assumed before the elections.

Kılavuz started to write more regularly in the *Alevilerin Sesi*. His articles always appeared under the headline *Kiblesi insan olanlar*—those whose *kible* (Arabic *qibla*, the direction of Muslim prayer) is the human being. This title is both a reference to a well-know saying of Hacı Bektaş and an implicit rejection of Alevism being categorized as a form of Islam: Muslims orient their prayer toward the Kaaba in Mecca, while Alevis are oriented towards the fellow human being. In an article published in November 2003 he wrote that Alevism is a religion in its own right, arguing that the principles of Islam do not fit with Alevism.[26] In the same article he severely criticized the "zealous *dedes*" who equate Alevism with "true Islam." He demanded that women should be allowed to sit on the *post*. He repeated these ideas in a speech he made at a workshop of the European Confederation of Alevi Communities in early November. This speech was published in *Hürriyet*.[27] Kılavuz's ideas roused great interest—and strong criticism, especially on the part of other *dedes*. Most members of the *dedeler kurulu* rejected his arguments. In a meeting of the *dedes'* council the demand was raised to vote him out of office but this was rejected and prevented by his few supporters. In consequence of this dispute, the *dedeler kurulu* became virtually paralyzed. Subsequently, the dispute was fought publicly in the pages of *Hürriyet*, where Hasan Kılavuz was heavily attacked by Derviş Tur.[28] Kılavuz continued to tour the Alevi associations in Germany. According to his own view, most Alevis support his ideas—except the *dedes*.

For the *cem* held by the HAKM in February 2004, Kılavuz had intentionally brought a *dede* who was known for equating Alevism with real Islam and for quoting from the Quran in *cem*. He explained: "I wanted to see how he conducts *cem* and I wanted that the people experience such an 'Islamic' *cem*." The *dede* said some prayers in which he mentioned the Quran, and he reproached a woman because she wore trousers while performing the *hizmet* of the *süpürgeci*—according to the

---

the *post* at the side of the acting *post dedesi*. She had started to do this when, during a *cem* in 2001, Mehmet Yaman *dede* from Istanbul had invited her to sit on the *post*. Yet she did not conduct *cem* herself. See *Alevilerin Sesi* 51, January 2002, 18.

[25] Cf. *Hürriyet*, 14 April 2003.

[26] *Alevilerin Sesi* 69, November 2003: 18–19.

[27] *Hürriyet*, 17 and 18 November 2003.

[28] *Hürriyet*, April 18 and 19, 2004.

dede's opinion, women doing one of the duties in *cem* were not allowed to wear trousers. Yet he largely complied with the directive issued by Hasan Kılavuz that certain elements of the ritual should be left out in order to shorten the *cem*. After the *cem* some people indeed criticized the "Islamic style" of this *dede* and presumed that the *cem* would have been even "more Islamic" if Kılavuz had not intervened. But I am not sure whether this "Islamic style" of *cem* was rejected by the majority of the participants. The ritual had itself become an arena for the dispute about the suitable style of *cem* and also for competition about the power to determine how the ritual was carried out.

Ritual, Authority and the Construction of Community

"Rituals did not simply restore social equilibrium, they were part of the ongoing process by which the community was continually redefining and renewing itself" writes Catherine Bell (1997, 39). In the Alevi case, the ritual sphere is very far from the structural–functionalist paradigm of ritual as restoring social equilibrium within a community. The ritual's traditional function of renewing community notwithstanding, *cem*, as it has been revitalized within the Alevi movement, has become a focal site for disputing ideas about Alevism and the Alevi community. The ritual sphere is also the site where the competition for power and authority between the Alevi associations, as the central institutions of the new Alevi movement, and the *dede*s, as the traditional authorities of the community, is played out. The process by which the community "redefines and renews itself" is a highly disputed issue. The old order that was restored time and again by the traditional *cem* in the villages is gone, yet many of its central protagonists, the *dede*s, are still struggling with the emerging new order. The Alevi associations have not yet been able to integrate the *dede*s into the new order in a generally accepted way. *Cem* has been revitalized as a public ritual of an imagined community, and the representatives of this community are the associations with their activists, not the *dede*s. But many *dede*s are not ready to accept this subordination to the associations.

Eickelman and Anderson (1999) have emphasized the role of new media for the development of new religious public spheres among Muslims and for the emergence of new religious intellectuals that in many cases successfully compete with "traditional" authorities of Islam. In a recent study, Muhammad Qasim Zaman (2002) has shown that the "traditional" authorities of Sunni and Shia Islam, the *ulema*, have often been able to accommodate themselves to these new conditions and to withstand the challenges of new authorities. In contrast with the Muslim *ulema* who were frequently able to strategically exploit the new conditions, it seems that Alevi *dede*s in Germany have suffered much more generally a loss of importance. Two main points may explain this difference. First, the great inclination of Alevis towards secularism has made many of them generally highly critical of traditional religious authorities and their claims. Being established largely by erstwhile antireligious activists, Alevi associations as the principal institutions of contemporary Alevism can in many instances be regarded as the very embodiment of the secularist critique of religious authorities. Second, the new Alevi movement subverted the very sources of authority of the *dedes*. Traditional Alevism had been an oral culture in which religious knowledge was the monopoly of the *dedes*. This monopoly was very effectively cracked by the Alevi movement with its multiplication of sources of Alevi knowledge in new media (books, journals, websites). Whereas traditionally *dedes* had been distinguished by their descent as well as by their knowledge, only descent has remained as a distinction between *dedes* and *talips* in the present—and even the legitimacy of claims based on descent is currently challenged by many Alevis. Muslim *ulema* lost in many instances the monopoly of access to and interpretation of their religious sources as the ability to read and interpret the Quran has multiplied—but the significance of these sources has perhaps even increased in contemporary Islam. Yet Alevi *dedes* lost not only the monopoly but also their very sources of knowledge, because in the age of new media oral tradition lacks almost all significance.

It seems that the loss of significance of *dedes* is more pronounced in Germany than in Turkey because the break with tradition was more thorough in Germany: here, Alevism virtually had to be reinvented from scratch whereas in Turkey more lines of tradition had remained alive. In Turkey, there have recently been strong efforts to revive the role of the *dedes* and to inculcate a new self-consciousness in them. CEM Vakfı, one of the big Alevi associations in Turkey, has held large conventions with several hundreds of *dedes* from all over Anatolia. The official purpose of the conventions was "to find out what the pioneers of Alevi Islamic belief think," as the subtitle of a published volume on the first of these convention says (CEM Vakfı 2000). Yet the most significant effect of these meetings was to bring many *dedes* effectively under the influence of CEM Vakfı. The association presents itself as *the* representative organization of Alevis in Turkey. *Dedes*, especially many from the rural areas who had not been much involved with the Alevi movement in Turkey, felt appreciated by CEM Vakfı. The association made this appreciation visible by handing out commemorative certificates to all the *dedes* who took part in the convention. Because of this attitude towards the *dedes* and because of its unequivocal endorsement of the stance that Alevism is part of Islam, CEM Vakfı also has many followers among the more traditional *dedes* in Germany, especially among those who, like Ismail Aslandoğan or Niyazi Bozdoğan, refuse to cooperate with the AABF.

Like the *dedes*, also the ritual *cem* has not only changed its character but also lost much of its significance in diaspora. In the perception of many Alevis, *cem* lost a specific sacralized aura and became a kind of "as if performance." Having been reinvented as a public ritual of identity, *cem* became but one among many kinds of such public rituals that are performed in the context of the Alevi movement. Cultural festivals, for instance, draw many more participants and perhaps even accomplish the task of representing the (imagined) Alevi community more effectively. Responses to this development are diverse. On one hand, there are attempts to restore *cem* to a specific, sacralized sphere, which in the perception of religious–minded Alevis makes "real" *cem* possible in the first place. On the other hand, some special cultural festivals are perhaps becoming a new kind of *cem*. In May 2000, a very large festival was staged by the AABF in Cologne. Designed under the title *Bin Yılın Türküsü* (officially translated as "Saga of the Millennium") by Necati Şahin, a theater director and artist who from the start has been intimately involved with the Alevi movement, this festival was very different from previous events. Normally, Alevi culture festivals consist simply of a sequence of musical performances by different artists, without any intrinsic connection between the individual performances. *Bin Yılın Türküsü*, in contrast, was conceived as a dramatic representation of the history of Alevism from the earliest time to the present. Yet it was not simply conceived as a particularistic representation of Alevism. The scenario referred also to historical events outside of Alevism such as the French Revolution that was highlighted as a historical instantiation of central Alevi values like secularism, equality, and enlightenment. Alevism was equated with the universal values of modernity. As a token of the openness of Alevism musical performances of various non-Alevi traditions like a gospel choir and an African percussion group were part of the festival. Further, the festival included not only the usual row of famous singers and musicians, but also more than thousand young Alevis who played the *saz* and several hundred who danced *semah*. Especially for these young participants who had come from all over Germany and other European countries, the Alevi community became a tangible experience through this festival. Taking place in a large hall in Cologne, more than 15,000 people attended the event. *Bin Yılın Türküsü* was subsequently praised as an event in which the Alevi community in all its cultural wealth had become visibly manifest.

Two years later, in October 2002, *Bin Yılın Türküsü* was transferred to Turkey and staged in a hall in Istanbul. Now, the young *saz* players and *semah* dancers came from many different parts of Turkey, and they were joined by more than 500 people who had flown in, as participants or as spectators, from Western Europe. The festival was celebrated as an event in which Alevis from (almost) all over the world participated. In the introductory speeches it was announced time and again from what different countries the participants had come to Istanbul. And now several speakers also announced the event as a *cem*: "*Bin Yılın Türküsü cemimiz*" — "Our *cem*, the Saga of the Millennium." One speaker criticized the discrimination of Alevis by the Directorate for Religious Affairs and then exclaimed with determination: "*Cemimize devam edeceğiz!*" — "We will continue our *cem!*" Here the new meaning of *cem* as the site of the symbolic construction of the imagined community of Alevis became transferred to a new kind of cultural festival that was also perceived as a new kind of *cem*. While the ordinary *cem* perpetuates elements of the traditional village *cem* although its point of reference has changed from an intimate face-to-face village community to the (almost global) imagined Alevi community, *Bin Yılın Türküsü* employed only few elements of *cem*, in the first place *semah*. With the exception of Veliyettin Ulusoy, the present representative and descendant of Hacı Bektaş Veli, who said a prayer at the beginning, *dede*s played no role. *Bin Yılın Türküsü* can be interpreted symbolically as a largely secularized kind of *cem* that celebrated universal values and that through its very size and the mass of participants turned the imagined community to a certain extent into a real experience.

Yet *Bin Yılın Türküsü* — as it was realized and perceived in Germany — exemplified also the dilemma of the Alevis' public performances: although such performances are intended to address the general public, they remain largely limited to the *Alevi* public. Although the AABF took many efforts to publicize the event that was meant as a milestone toward the public recognition of Alevis in Germany, the participation of non–Alevi Germans and the coverage in the German media remained negligible. What does this failure of public recognition say about the Alevi politics of recognition and its larger political context? This question will be dealt with in the next chapter, in which I examine the Alevi efforts for recognition within the context of the German politics of migration.

7

RECOGNITION AND THE POLITICS OF MIGRATION IN GERMANY

Migration, Culture, and "Integration"

German studies of immigrants, and among them particularly studies on migrants from Turkey, have generally placed great emphasis on the "cultural baggage" that these immigrants brought to their new country of residence. Relating to Turks, cultural elements like a patriarchal family structure, a strict system of male honor, and Islam were pointed out as basic conditions that shaped their lives in Germany just as it was assumed that these conditions determined life back "home." This research perspective paralleled the dominant political approach to migration in Germany, which maintains that migrants have to "integrate" themselves and according to which the ability — or the lack of ability — of migrants to integrate is determined to a great extent by "their culture" (Sökefeld 2004c). These approaches conform with what Yasemin Soysal (1994, 5) calls "one of the driving suppositions of immigrant literature: the notion that guest workers' situations and cultures predict how they participate in and interact with host societies." In her book *Limits of Citizenship,* Soysal reverses this perspective and analyses instead "the institutional repertoire of host political systems which afford the model and rationale for both state and migrant action" (ibid.). Soysal distinguishes different "regimes of incorporating migrants" in different European countries. Incorporation refers to the processes by which a migrant population "becomes part of the polity of the host country" (30). Incorporation is a matter of political and societal discourse, as well as of policies and structures of institutions. According to Soysal's framework, the case of Germany is a combination of corporatist and statist patterns of integration. That is, there are certain avenues for migrants to organize collectively and to make their claims, but these processes are largely controlled by the state. Emphasizing similarly the importance of the state, Kaya (2001, 71) drives the argument to extremes and maintains in his study of Turkish migrant youth in Berlin that "the construction of ethnic-based political strategies is strictly dependent on the policies implemented by the government of the receiving society." Referring to the largest Alevi association in Berlin, the AAKM, he writes: "[the] Anatolian Alevis' Cultural Center (AAKM) can be interpreted as a client organization fulfilling the requirements of the hegemonic discourse of multiculturalism. As an obedient subject of the state, the AAKM, thus reaffirms the hegemony of the state" (Kaya 1998, 45). These statements completely ignore the agency of migrants expressed in the claims they make within the frameworks of the state, and again reduces them to a kind of victim determined now not by their culture but by the hegemonic state.

I agree with Soysal's idea that institutional and discursive frameworks set by state and society are indeed crucial for the form of the incorporation of migrants in a particular country—although I regard her specific model of patterns of incorporation debatable. A significant element of the German regime of incorporating migrants is what I have called elsewhere the "paradigm of cultural difference" (Sökefeld 2004b), i.e., the continuous attribution of cultural difference to migrants: migrants are incorporated as *cultural others*. Incorporation operates through a discourse of exclusion. "Integration" has become the hegemonic idea of the German discourse on migration, yet through the prevalent discourse on integration migrants are time and again reconstituted as cultural others. Migrants in Germany have to come to terms with the predicament that the discourse that demands that they should "integrate themselves" into German society obstructs this very integration because it perpetually construes migrants as largely nonintegrated others. Some migrants in Germany might indeed react to this predicament with a kind of "internal separatism" or withdrawal. Alevis, however, have tried a very different strategy: they argue that Alevis are not quite different and that Alevi culture is perfectly compatible with German culture. The claim that Alevis make is to be recognized as equal and "not so different"—or almost the same. In this chapter I will first analyze the paradigm of cultural difference in German policy of migration, and then turn to the strategies of integration employed Alevis and Alevi associations within this context.

The Paradigm of Cultural Difference in the German Discourse on Migration

In a widely acclaimed speech held on 12 May 2000, the then federal president of Germany, Johannes Rau, addressed Germans and migrants and called for "living together in Germany."[1] His speech was an appeal for mutual understanding. Rau warned against exclusion and the instrumentalization of racist images in political discourse. He demanded that prejudices be abandoned. However, Rau's efforts for mutual understanding of natives and immigrants, the explicit aim of "living together," were largely negated by the discursive means of his speech.

---

[1] Rau 2000.

The speech was marked by a continuous dichotomy of "we" and "the others," that is, of Germans and immigrants. The dichotomy of "us and them" confirms the difference. The boundary between *us*—the Germans—and *them*—the immigrants—remains intact. It is reconstructed in almost every single sentence of the speech. Immigrants remain excluded as others. The difference of migrants is taken as a matter of fact that is just as "natural" as is the presumed homogeneity of those who are designated as the "native population."

This speech of a Federal President is a typical example of the German discourse on migration.[2] Similarly, the much discussed report of an expert commission chaired by former president of parliament Rita Süßmut that gives high priority to integration mostly speaks of immigrants as *Ausländer* (foreigners) (Unabhängige Kommission Zuwanderung 2001, 227ff.). "Integration" is called for, but the same discourse that demands integration constructs immigrants as *foreigners* that remain different. Further, this discourse asserts that due to their nonintegration, migrants create all sorts of social problems.[3] Insufficient German–language skills and the formation of immigrant "ghettos" are regarded as prime indicators for the nonintegration of migrants. In almost every speech of a politician on issues of immigration, migrants are called for learning German. Thus, an image is conjured up according to which migrants in Germany generally do not speak the German language or even refuse to learn German. Although this image is proven wrong by daily encounters of Germans and migrants as well as by statistical surveys,[4] it seems to be immune against empirical refutation. The idea that migrants are radically different, that they are mostly not integrated and lack German language skills is not an outcome of empirical experience; it is a premise of discourse. In the same vein, it is frequently asserted that migrants in Germany are too much involved in "homeland politics" instead of committing themselves to integration in Germany. In their comparative study of migrant claims-making in Germany and Britain, Koopmans and Statham (1998: 37) find that migrants' claims that are related to what is considered their home country are ten times more frequent in Germany than in Britain. They conclude: "Germany sees immigrants as "foreigners," and that is exactly the way in which German minorities behave: they organize and identify themselves on

---

[2] For an analysis of the speech see Laviziano et al. 2001.

[3] On the discursive construction of migrants as a "problem" in Germany see Griese 2002.

[4] A recent survey that focussed on the media consumed by migrants from Turkey found that the number of migrants consuming only German media is larger than the number of those consuming exclusively Turkish media, and that among the younger migrants German–language competence outweighs Turkish language competence (Weiss and Trebbe 2001).

the basis of their national origin and are still, although many of them have been in Germany since decades, preoccupied with the politics of their homelands" (ibid., 45). In addition, even migrants that have naturalized as Germans largely experience rejection by the autochthonous population and therefore are often prevented from developing a sentiment of belonging in Germany (Begner 2000, 101).

The premise of the radical difference of migrants was strongly reflected in the until very recently politically dominant idea that Germany is *not* a country of immigration. Apparently, this denial of immigration was belied by the numbers of immigrants living in the country. Yet simply to speak about numbers of migrants is to miss the point. The issue is not about what was happening in the country, but about what *should* happen—or should *not* happen. The denial of immigration in Germany is a *normative* position. It is a question of national self-definition (Joppke 1999, 62f). The dominant concept of the German nation is based on the idea of the nation as a community of "blood" and common descent. Until the reform the German law of citizenship that was passed by the Social Democrat/Green coalition in 2000, citizenship was entirely conceived in terms of *ius sanguinis*. As a consequence of the prevalence of descent in the definition of "Germanness," ethnic Germans that had lived for generations in central Asia were considered as Germans and were entitled to full citizenship if they migrated to Germany, while second, or third, generation immigrants of non-German ethnic background living in Germany are considered foreigners and not citizens. Being German is in the first place a matter of ascription by birth: one has to be born German in order to be German, one cannot *become* German.

This particular concept of the German nation is mirrored in the negation of immigration. The negation of immigration is not a matter of the number of people actually entering German territory. Boundaries are conceptual and discursive rather than territorial. It is reflected in not considering those people that came to Germany and took up residence in the country as *immigrants* but as *foreigners.* An immigrant is a person who has crossed a threshold into another country, who has settled there for good, and who is on the way of becoming part of the (national) community of this country. In one way or another, an immigrant *belongs* to his country of residence. Immigrants might therefore even change the outlook of the national community. Foreigners, in contrast, do not belong, even if they stay for a very long time. They belong to some other nation. They are in some crucial regard essentially different.

In his study of the construction of German national identity, Jens Schneider (2001) confirms the significance of cultural boundaries for German self-definitions. He arrives at the conclusion that in spite of their different political perspectives, both leftists and conservatives share a definition of immigrants as culturally different that implies a notion of cultures as clearly delimited entities. The study reveals clearly that in this context difference is not a matter of experience but of construction. Cultural difference was emphasized especially by those respondents that lacked cross-cultural experience. The majority of his respondents—across the political spectrum—strictly rejected the idea of cultural mixing and hybridity (ibid., 223-33).[5]

Legally, the situation has changed since the new law that has introduced an element of *ius soli* into German citizenship: children of foreign parents now receive German citizenship under certain conditions by birth. Yet there was a very strong opposition against this law, which managed to change some of its original provisions. Also today there is much resistance to talk about immigration in Germany. A new word, *"Zuwanderung"* (literally "to-migration") has been invented in order to avoid the incriminated term *immigration* (*Einwanderung*). Further, being German is not entirely a matter of citizenship. Immigrants that have been naturalized continue in many cases to be considered as foreigners. Also, being "foreign" (*fremd*) is not a category of neutral difference. Foreigners not only constitute a "problem" but are in many instances considered as a potential or real "danger." In 1997, the leading political magazine in Germany, *Der Spiegel,* had a cover story which under the headline "Dangerously Foreign" (*Gefährlich fremd*) neatly summarized all these dangers: violence, crime, and political or religious extremism.[6] In the recent debate on terrorism and security, migrants—and in this context specifically Muslim migrants—are again framed as a potential danger.

To sum up, migrants have been discursively incorporated in Germany as others, as culturally different, as those who create social problems and pose a potential danger. The concept of culture that lingers in this discourse is the old idea of cultures as clearly bounded and delimited units which has recently been subjected to devastating critique in the social and cultural sciences. Yet new concepts of culture that highlight ideas of hybridity instead of clear-cut boundaries and that conceive of culture as a continuously changing outcome of human practice that is subject to power relationships have not yet trickled down to societal discourse in Germany.

This is not to say that discourse about migration in Germany is in all instances homogeneous. But the paradigm of cultural difference is a dominant and extraordinarily stable element of this discourse. It is shared by the exclusionary discourse of the political right that regards migrants quite unequivocally as a menace, and by multiculturalist discourse, situated more on the political left, which considers migrants, due to their cultural difference, as an "enrichment" and asset of society.

---

[5] On the difficulties on living and experiencing "hybrid" identities and multiple belonging in Germany see Mecheril 2003.

[6] *Der Spiegel* No. 16, 1997.

The discourse on migrants is a discourse that privileges past over present: origins and presumed "roots" are considered as more important than the continuous experience of living in Germany.

However, this discourse is not reflected in an institutionalized representation of cultural difference in the German context. There is no system of corporate representation of migrant "communities" in Germany. When Soysal (1994) speaks of a corporatist pattern of incorporation in Germany, she refers to semipublic German corporations like trade unions, churches and welfare organizations that have assumed or have been assigned the role of representing migrants in certain respects—she does not refer to forms of migrants' self-organizations. A formalized system of representation of migrants exists only at the municipal level: there are elected "foreigners' advisory councils" (*Ausländerbeiräte*) in some (but not all) cities, which enjoy only very limited competences.[7]

Alevis and the Discourse on Foreigners in Germany

The Alevi politics of recognition is framed by the discourse on foreigners in Germany and the paradigm of cultural difference. We have already seen in chapter two that the beginning of the Alevi movement in Hamburg was situated in a multiculturalist institutional and discursive context, and that the Alevis' claims for identity were in part a response to the multiculturalist idea that migrants should preserve their identity and cultural difference. As a consequence, the first significant document of the Alevi movement, the "Alevi Declaration," took up multiculturalist discourse and stated that "Alevism, like other cultural elements, is a source of wealth for this society."[8] Yet the particular difference/identity of Alevi culture is presented in a unique way: the difference from other Turkish (i.e., Sunni) migrants is asserted, not the difference of Alevi from German culture. The master Alevis/Sunnis difference is emphasized and translated into an assertion of similarity of Alevism and German culture. In the German-language brochure on Sivas that has already been quoted in chapter four it is underscored that Alevis do not differ from Germans with regard to fundamental rules and values. After pointing out the dangers of fundamentalist Islam and emphasizing that Alevis value democracy and the rule of law, the text criticizes that this value orientation of Alevis is not sufficiently recognized:

---

[7] For the ethnography of one such advisory council see Müller 2001.

[8] Cf. *Alevi Kültür Haftası* (program of the Alevi Culture Week), 3. An unpublished, photocopied German version of the declaration, which is not an exact translation of the Turkish original, says even more clearly: "The promotion [of Alevi culture] would be a significant contribution to multicultural life in Germany."

It is perplexing why the German public falls short in recognizing the democratic outlook of Alevis and thus fails to take them into account in discussions on Islam in Germany. In this way the German public over-looks a community of about 600,000 among the immigrants from Turkey who abide by German laws and introduce a great democratic potential into German society (AABF 1999, 4).

The Turkish verb *tanıtmak* became a prominent word in the dis-course of Alevi associations in Germany. *Tanıtmak* is the causative form of the verb *tanımak* which means "to know," "to recognize." The mean-ing of *tanıtmak*, then, is "to make known," "to cause to be recognized." The kind of recognition of and knowledge about Alevism that is in-tended by Alevis is not only knowledge about the particular practices and teachings of Alevism but also recognition of the compatibility of Alevi with German culture. A great part of Alevi efforts for recogni-tion in Germany is therefore invested in efforts to get Alevis recognized as different from Islam[9] and as not so different from German culture. The prevalent German discourse on Islam is closely mirrored in Alevi discourse. The public image of Islam in Germany is consistently nega-tive. According to a recent survey, ninety-three percent of Germans as-sociate Islam with the oppression of women, eighty–three percent with terror, eighty-two percent with fanaticism and radicalism, and seventy percent simply with danger.[10] The headscarf of Muslim women plays a particularly prominent role in this respect (Mandel 1989). For many Germans, the headscarf signifies not only repression of women and pa-triarchal family structures in Islam, but also general isolationism and intolerance of Islam. It has become the main symbol for all the negative stereotypes associated with this religion. The debate about the headscarf has become reinvigorated after a decision of the German constitutional court in 2003 about the question whether a female teacher in a public school should be allowed to wear the headscarf. In this debate, voices that favored permitting the headscarf in the name of religious freedom and tolerance were clearly outweighed by voices that considered the headscarf as a symbol of oppression.[11] Alevis share this perspective on the headscarf "problem" and are never tired of pointing out that Alevi

---

[9] These efforts are contextually separate from the intra-Alevi debate whether Alevism is part of Islam or not (cf. chapter four). The assertion that Alevism is different from Islam in the context of German debate on migrants is not seen as a contradiction with the theological position held by some Alevis that Alevism is "true Islam."

[10] *Frankfurter Allgemeine Zeitung*, 15 September 2004.

[11] In contrast with the parallel debate in France, there is consensus in Germany that female pupils should be allowed to wear the headscarf in school. On the significance of the headscarf for young Muslim women in Germany see the studies by Klinkhammer (2000) and Nökel (2002).

women do not wear the headscarf. I do not want to create the impression here that it is only Alevis who share this point of view. Migrants from Turkey that stand in the Republican and Kemalist tradition firmly oppose the headscarf.[12] Especially Lale Akgün, a Turkish migrant member of German parliament, has issued strong statements for the prohibition of the headscarf. Although she is not Alevi herself, she has become a close ally of the AABF in this issue. In the gross distinction put forward by the German discourse on foreigners which categorizes Muslims as "antimodern"[13] and the "most different" of migrants, Alevis position themselves firmly on the side of modernity, that is, on the German side of the divide. Alevi discourse parallels German discourse on Islam in regarding unequal gender relations, symbolized by the headscarf, an essential characteristic of Islam. The emphasis that Alevi women (like German women) do not wear headscarves is an effort to represent Alevis as nonforeign (or not so foreign) migrants. The headscarf issue is represented as a significant indication that Alevis have no problems with integrating themselves in German culture and society.

In chapter three I have pointed out that, the emphasis on gender equality in self–representations of Alevism notwithstanding, the structure and practice of Alevi associations is clearly gendered and that male predominance largely prevails. In private conversation, Alevi women often deplore the predominance of men, not only in the associations but also in many families, and point out the contradiction between the publicly expressed value of equality on one hand and unequal social practice on the other. Yet in public discourse such dissenting female voices most frequently remain silent and join in the collective affirmation of difference from (Sunni) Islam.

Alevism as the Embodiment of Universal Values

Yet Alevis are not content with pointing out that they are not really "foreign" in Germany and that Alevism is compatible with German

---

[12] In Kemalist Turkey the headscarf had been banned from the state-controlled public: neither in schools and universities nor in public offices the headscarf is permitted. Yet in the context of the recent success of Islamic politics in Turkey there have been strong efforts to undermine the ban of the headscarf. See among others Göle 1996 and Ewing 2000a.

[13] Many studies have pointed out that the Muslim headscarf is not quite an issue of tradition or "backwardness" of Islam, but rather a symbol of Islam's specific modernization and modernity (e.g., White 2002, 212ff.). Navaro-Yashin (2002, 78–113), for instance, analyses the commodification of Islamic fashion, including headscarves, in Turkey. Yet this more nuanced view is not reflected in public discourse about headscarves in Germany.

culture. Further, Alevism is represented as an embodiment of what are considered universal values of modernity: humanism, tolerance, and democracy. What Alevis seek to get recognized is not only Alevism as a distinct culture (or religion) but, significantly, the commitment of Alevism to such values. One of the aims of the AABF as laid down in its program is "to respect the universal principles of rights, of human rights and freedom, and to defend these principles under any circumstances" (AABF 1998, 6). The Alevi politics of recognition includes the emphasis that Alevis do not make derogatory distinctions among diverse cultures but accept the dignity and fundamental equality of all human beings. The sayings of Hacı Bektaş Veli are frequently quoted to illustrate the universalistic essence of Alevism. On of his most well–known sayings is "*Yetmiş iki millete bir nazarla bak.*" Literally, it means "view all seventy-two nations with the same regard," and is generally interpreted as an appeal to regard all people as equal.

It has been pointed out that more and more migrant communities relate to the discourse of citizenship and human rights and connect human rights with their politics of identity (Soysal 1994, 116). Islamic organizations "do not justify their demands by reaching back to religious teachings or traditions, but by recourse to the language of rights, and, thus, citizenship" (Soysal 1997, 519). Identity is framed as a human right and universal human rights (like freedom of religion) are referred to in order to make particularistic claims. Human rights are invoked by Muslims in Germany in order to demand, for instance, the right to slaughter animals in a religiously prescribed way. In this case, universal human rights, particularly the freedom of religion, have been invoked in order to demand the permission of a practice that is generally prohibited by German law. Yet the Alevis' reference to human rights differs from such a strategy because Alevi associations have up until now never relied on universal human rights for the purpose of making particularistic claims and securing exemption from law. There are also no Alevi ritual practices or religious prescriptions that contradict German law.

Institutional Integration

A second strategy for achieving recognition in Germany, besides discursive efforts to represent Alevis as "compatible," "not foreign" and "better integrated" migrants, is the endeavor towards institutional integration. By this term I refer to the establishment of cooperative relations between Alevi associations and various German civil and governmental institutions. Efforts towards institutional integration are undertaken on different levels. Sometimes such strategies target specific persons as representatives of public institutions. For instance, whenever an Alevi culture festival is organized anywhere in Germany, representatives of the local municipality or of other bodies are invited as special guests and asked to deliver messages of greeting. In Hamburg, on the occasion of cultural festivals the HAKM frequently invited the mayor (who never came), representatives of the city assembly, the chairman of the trade union, and the bishop of the Protestant church. On the occasion of *Bin Yılın Türküsü*, the large Alevi festival of the year 2000 in Cologne, the AABF was able to secure greeting messages of a number of high-ranking German politicians, including Chancellor Gerhard Schröder and the heads of government of the federal states of Bavaria and Hesse, and published them in the booklet of the festival (AABF 2000). Such messages are attributed great significance because they are seen as an evidence that Alevis are already recognized and given much importance by public representatives.

Local Alevi associations seek institutional cooperation with municipal institutions especially for the purpose of securing funds for their activities. Many German cities offer subsidies for programs that promote the integration of migrants at the local level. The Alevi Culture Center Stuttgart, for instance, receives financial support from the city of Stuttgart for German language courses, weekend seminars for young people, and tuition for pupils. Also the HAKM received funds from the city for groups of women and pensioners.

After a Social Democrat/Green coalition came to power in Germany in 1998, more federal funds became available for the purpose of "integrating" migrants and combating racism. The AABF benefited from several such programs. A campaign for promulgating information about the new citizenship law of 2000 was funded by the federal Ministry of Interior Affairs. Another federally funded project aimed at assisting disadvantaged youths, and more recently, the Ministry of the Interior sponsored an initiative of the AABF for enhancing dialogue among different religious communities. This project started with a large conference in December 2002. Asked in an interview why the ministry funded the conference of a religious community, a ministry representative replied: "We have no problems with the Alevis because they accept our political system. The Alevis are very open."[14] This statement clearly illustrates the success of the Alevi politics of recognition in Germany.

Additionally, there have been many official visits of delegations of the AABF to various offices of the federal government in Berlin. Before a visit to Berlin in summer 2001 which included encounters with representatives of the Ministry of the Interior and the Ministry of Foreign Affairs as well as with the Federal Commissioner for Foreigners and representatives of the Green Party, I asked Hasan Öğütcü, the then general secretary of the AABF, about his expectations for these meeting. He

---

[14] The interview was aired on the radio station NDR Info on 5 January 2003.

said: "First of all I want to learn what German politicians know about Alevis, I want to know whether they are informed to a certain degree. But or course we also have some demands. One demand is that we are not regarded as an association of foreigners."

Soysal (1994) argues that the institutional models and resources provided by the immigration country play an important role in shaping migrant organizations and the immigrants' incorporation into local society. In this sense, the institutional integration of Alevis in Germany is an outcome of the interaction of the efforts of Alevi associations with the German institutional environment that also feeds back onto the Alevi movement and has its effects on its specific form of institutionalization. The German institutional environment requires that migrant associations that intend to cooperate with that environment conform to certain rules. At the very basic level, the Alevi associations have to comply with the rules of German associational law (*Vereinsrecht*). By-laws have to be established that conform to a specific model in order to secure recognition as a non-profit association which enjoys exemption from taxes. In order to perpetuate this status, audits, supervised by the tax office, are required. The association has to be registered at the district court (*Amtsgericht*). Elections for the acting committee have to be held after a certain period of time and the members of the association have to be assembled at certain intervals. If any one of these rules is violated, the decisions of the association or its committee may be contested at the courts and ultimately the association may be dissolved. Further rules have to be heeded if public funds are applied for. The business of writing applications for support of specific projects and of putting together the subsequently required reports and statements is quite complex, requires much specific knowledge and consumes a lot of time.

Migrant associations have to adopt this model in order to qualify for institutional integration. Associations that do not conform with the formal rules will not receive public funds, and if their aims do not conform with the constitutional order of Germany they may even be declared illegal and closed down by the authorities.[15] In the framework of institutional integration, the model of organization provided by the migrants' country of residence is certainly more important for their self-organization than any "cultural baggage" brought from the country of origin. The institutionalization of the Alevi movement in the form of registered associations (*eingetragene Vereine*) in Germany requires compliance with this model.

---

[15] An Alevi association has never been outlawed in Germany, in contrast with other associations of Turkish migrants that were considered terrorist, like the Kurdish PKK and the leftist Dev Sol, or Islamists like the "state of caliphate" of Cemaleddin Kaplan (Schiffauer 2000). Others, like Milli Görüş, are put under strict surveillance of the state's agencies.

Yet, on the long run, the AABF aims at another form of institutionalization—and institutional recognition—that goes much beyond the model of registered associations. In 1995, the AABF applied for the legal status of a "corporation under public law" (*Körperschaft öffentlichen Rechts*). This legal status confers a number of rights and privileges and signifies the highest level of legal recognition that a nonstate institution can achieve in Germany. It is enjoyed by the Protestant and Catholic churches. The AABF submitted its application for this status with the government of North Rhine-Westphalia. Though the application has been pending since 1995 this is regarded already as a success by the Alevis, because similar applications by Islamic associations like the *Islamrat* (Council of Islam) and the *Zentralrat der Muslime in Deutschland* (Central Council of Muslims in Germany) have been almost immediately rejected (Erbektaş 1998b).

Institutional integration of Alevis takes place at all three levels of the German political system (municipalities, federal states, and federal government) and it is not limited to efforts of establishing cooperation with the state. Cooperation with civil organizations like trade unions and NGOs as well as with other religious communities, such as the Christian churches, is also sought for. Most local Alevi associations are involved in activities of interfaith dialogue. The sphere of religion is especially significant for Alevi institutional integration and recognition.

Efforts towards Alevi Religious Classes in School

The currently most significant project of recognition and institutional integration is the Alevi demand for Alevi religious classes in public schools. In Germany, the Catholic and Protestant churches enjoy the right to teach religious classes in schools. Religious instruction in school is even based on a specific article of the German constitution.[16] The debate about Islamic religious instruction in schools is a subfield of the discourse about migration in Germany. Although there are also some native German Muslims, Islamic instruction is exclusively discussed as an issue relating to migrants and foreigners (Özdil 1999, 97). Islam is clearly perceived as a "foreign" religion; it is perceived as the probably most foreign and, by implication, suspect, element of migrants' culture. The issue is quite complex, not only because the legal preconditions for religious classes differ among the federal states as they enjoy the legislative and administrative competences for the school system, but also because many different interests and positions are involved. A coalition of Muslim immigrant groups started in the late 1970s to demand Islamic classes

---

[16] Article 7.3. On the constitutional conditions of religious classes see von Campenhausen 1986.

in North Rhine-Westphalia. The administration responded favorably to this demand and pursued it as its own project although the coalition of Muslim associations, due to internal differences, quickly broke apart. One rationale behind the project was the idea that Islam had to be "integrated" into the school system if young Muslims were to be prevented from getting "trapped" in separate Muslim enclaves, beyond the reach and control of the state (cf. Schiffauer 1997; Özdil 1999, 78ff.). Yet while for the authorities Islamic classes were more an issue of integration and control, it was a question of equal rights and recognition for Muslim associations.

The Alevi efforts towards religious classes started much later, after the commencement of the Alevi movement and the formation of the associations. Alevi efforts were not simply a demand for recognition in Germany and a response to the German system of education but, at least equally important, a response to what was considered a Sunni Muslim encroachment. In 1982, the military junta in Turkey had made religious classes a compulsory subject in Turkish schools, as a step towards promulgating the "Turkish-Islamic synthesis" as national ideology. Because only Sunni Islam was taught in these classes, Alevis resented them as an instrument for assimilation. Protest against these compulsory religion classes is a constant element in the discourse of Alevi associations in Germany and Turkey. In Germany, Turkish pupils were offered Turkish language classes sponsored by the Turkish state that in the beginning were meant to facilitate the "reintegration" of migrants' children after their projected "return to the homeland."[17] The teachers for these classes were mostly graduates from Turkish universities. Alevis report that in many cases the language classes were mixed with religious instruction to the effect that Alevi children were taught Sunni Islam. In Hamburg, this practice was officially sanctioned by the educational authority, and here it was not regarded as a preparation for return but as an instrument of integration. A statement by the authority on the education of migrant children said:

> In order that Turkish pupils are not estranged from their faith, that they are able to preserve their cultural identity and for the purpose that their self-confidence is strengthened in the context of efforts towards integration, they may attend Turkish–Islamic classes in conjunction with Turkish language classes in primary school.[18]

What was framed here as an effort to "preserve" the "cultural identity" of Turkish children was in fact a measure against the "preservation

---

[17] Especially in Bavaria, even separate school classes for Turkish migrant children were created (Rist 1978, 206ff.).

[18] Behörde für Schule, Jugend und Bildung 1984, 32. In this quotation again the conjunction of integration and difference that is fundamental in German discourse on migration plays an important role.

of cultural identity" in the case of Alevi children. For some Alevi parents this was a sufficient reason that their children did not attend these classes and as a consequence also missed the language instruction, but those who sent their children to these classes also resented this practice. Sometimes also the children themselves refused to attend classes. In the context of the debate about Islamic religious classes, many Alevis feared that again they might be subsumed under the general rubric of "Islam" without regard to the specific difference of Alevi teachings. As a consequence even those Alevis who regard Alevism as a part of Islam favor separate Alevi classes instead of general Islamic instruction.

In 1991 the HAKM started a campaign to collect signatures in support of Alevi instruction in the schools of Hamburg. Yet the outcome of this campaign was not separate Alevi classes. Instead, the HAKM became involved in a project for interfaith religious instruction. From 1995 on, the association was a member of the "Round Table for Interfaith Religious Classes" (*Gesprächskreis interreligiöser Religionsunterricht*), sponsored by the Protestant Church. In this round table representatives from Jewish, Muslim, Buddhist, and Alevi communities and the Church cooperated in setting up a curriculum for interfaith religious classes in which pupils from all religious backgrounds participate and in which all the different religious traditions are jointly taught.[19] The aim of this "religious instruction for everybody" (*Religionsunterricht für alle*) was the promotion of mutual knowledge, understanding, and tolerance among children of different religious backgrounds. When the first interfaith curriculum for primary schools was adopted by the educational authorities of the city in 1998, this was celebrated as a great success by Alevis because for the first time elements of Alevism had become part of an official school curriculum.[20] In 2003 a similar curriculum was adopted for secondary schools. The HAKM favors this model of interfaith classes because it is seen as particularly fitting to the value of tolerance and openness that is emphasized by Alevis.[21] The other Alevi associations in Hamburg, however, were not involved in the round table.

---

[19] See Doedens and Weisse 1997. This model could be introduced in Hamburg only because, in contrast with the other *Bundesländer,* there are no denominationally separate classes for Protestant and Catholic pupils. After World War II the Catholic Church had opted out of the public school system and established private Catholic schools in the city, leaving religious education in the public schools entirely to the Protestant Church.

[20] This success was, however, mostly a matter of curricular theory because as a consequence of the still–insufficient interfaith training of the teachers and a lack of suitable teaching materials, the Alevi elements are rarely if ever actually taught in the classes. Religious instruction is still largely limited to Christian teachings seasoned with a little Islam, Buddhism, and Hinduism.

[21] See the statement of the HAKM in Doedens and Weisse 1997, 53f.

In Berlin, however, separate Alevi classes were established in autumn 2002.[22] Here, the legal situation is different. While in Hamburg and most other *Bundesländer* religious classes are organized by the state in cooperation with the religious community (that is, almost exclusively, with the Christian churches), religious classes in Berlin are organized by the religious communities themselves, although under the control of the authorities. In Berlin, religion is not a part of the regular school curriculum. As Berlin has a large Muslim migrant population, Muslim associations had applied for many years for the right to teach classes on Islam. The applications were rejected because the applying associations were not recognized as "religious communities." The recognition of Muslim associations as "religious communities" has also been a problem in other *Bundesländer*. The model for religious communities in Germany is constituted by the Christian churches, with their centralized and hierarchical form of organization. Muslim associations, in contrast, are simply registered associations. There are usually a considerable number of competing or cooperating Muslim associations in every city, and therefore no unified representation of Muslims. The authorities therefore have generally argued that a particular Muslim association in question is not a "religious community" in the sense of German law. Sometimes, however, it seemed that such arguments were only put forward as an excuse in order not to deal seriously with the question of Islamic religious classes. In Berlin, the education authorities had rejected the application of a Muslim association called "Islamic Federation Berlin" (*Islamische Föderation Berlin*), which is said to be closely related with Milli Görüş. In November 1998, however, the higher administrative court in Berlin ruled that the Islamic Federation had to be recognized as a religious community and therefore had to be granted the right to teach Islam in the city's primary schools. This decision was confirmed by the Federal Administrative Court in February 2000. Soon after, the Islamic Federation started its Islamic classes.

Due to the alleged relations between the Islamic Federation and Milli Görüş, other associations of Turkish migrants in Berlin were very alarmed by this development, as were the Alevis. Yet for the Alevis the recognition of the Islamic Federation as a religious community that was permitted to offer Islamic classes also offered a precedent for their own case. In May 2002, the *Anadolu Alevileri Kültür Merkezi* (AAKM, Culture Center of Anatolian Alevis) submitted an application for the right to teach Alevi classes in primary schools. A curriculum was prepared by local Alevi academics together with the AABF. In April 2002 the AAKM got the permission of the Berlin Senate to offer Alevi religion classes in primary schools. The permission was celebrated as a great success

---

[22] On the case of Alevi classes in Berlin see also Massicard 2003a.

of the Alevi associations.[23] According to a joint press statement of the AABF and the AAKM, by this decision Alevism was for the first time officially recognized as an original faith. No court procedure had been necessary. Beside the curriculum and the permission of the Senate, however, teachers were also required in order to start the classes. While the decision of the Senate was still pending, the AAKM had started to educate teachers in cooperation with the AABF. A study group was formed for this purpose in which Alevi academics with a background in pedagogic participated. In September 2002, five teachers started to teach Alevi classes in seven primary schools in which a total of sixty pupils participated. The parents of 200 pupils had submitted applications for the classes but due to organizational reasons the program had to start on a smaller scale. Yet the program grew and a year later Alevi classes could be offered in twenty schools.

Besides Hamburg and Berlin, there have also been efforts towards Alevi classes in other *Bundesländer*. In some of these, like Lower Saxony, the Alevi associations participated first in a "Round Table for Islamic Classes" that was commissioned with developing a curriculum for general Islamic classes, including Alevi teachings. After some meetings, however, it became clear that the Alevi point of view was only marginally taken into consideration and the Alevis left the round table.

The AABF applied for separate Alevi classes in the *Bundesländer* North Rhine–Westphalia, Hesse, Baden-Württemberg, and Bavaria. These applications have been combined and are dealt with under the overall charge of the administration of North Rhine-Westphalia. The administration commissioned two reports for the purpose of substantiating its decision. In the first case an expert in religious studies was asked whether Alevism is an original religion that should not subsumed under general Islam, and in the second an expert of law was asked to state whether the AABF is a religious organization. In order to present the AABF unambiguously as a religious community, the AABF adopted new by-laws in September 2002 in which the association is now explicitly designated as "religious community in the sense of the Basic Law of the Federal Republic of Germany"[24] (*Glaubensgemeinschaft*, i.e., literally "community of faith"). In the previous version, the AABF had been called a "democratic mass-organization" (*demokratik bir kitle örgütü*)—a clear remnant of leftist discourse. Simultaneously, the AABF was renamed in German as *Alevitische Gemeinde Deutschland* (Alevi community Germany instead of the previous *Föderation der Alevitengemeinden in Deutschland*). In German, the word *Gemeinde* (community) has a clear religious connotation. A Christian parish, for instance, is generally re-

---

[23] Cf. *Alevilerin Sesi* 55, May 2002.

[24] By-laws of the AABF, section 2,1, adopted 21 September 2002.

ferred to as *Gemeinde*. Also the efforts for a new regulation of the *dedeler kurulu* by the AABF that were discussed in the previous chapter have to be seen in the context of efforts for qualifying as religious community. A religious community also needs religious personnel and the relations to these personnel, that is, the *dedes*, in the Alevi case, have to be regulated.

In North Rhine-Westphalia two Islamic umbrella associations, the Central Council of Muslims and the Council of Islam, applied for Islamic classes. This application was rejected both by the Ministry of Education and subsequently by the administrative court, where the associations had filed a complaint against the Ministry's decision. The decisions were justified with the arguments that both associations were not religious communities as conceptualized by German law, and that they did not generally represent Muslims in the country but only small segments of the Muslim community (cf. Stock 2003, 70–74). Such an argument was hardly possible in the case of the Alevis. There was no Alevi umbrella association that could seriously compete with the AABF, which indeed represents the majority of local Alevi associations in North Rhine-Westphalia as well as in Germany in general. Both expert reports that had been commissioned turned out to be favorable for the Alevis, recognizing them as a separate religion and the AABF as a religious community in the sense of German law. In early December 2004, the two reports were published by the authorities of North Rhine-Westphalia[25] and at the same time the AABF was granted the right for religious classes in schools. With this decision, Alevism became for the first time a formal administrative category. When children are enrolled in schools, they are asked their religious affiliation. Up until now, only "Catholic," "Protestant," or "Jew" had been recorded as religious affiliations while all others were been categorized as "others." Since 2005, there is a fourth category for children in the schools of the four mentioned *Bundesländer*: "Alevi."

Religion as a Category of Recognition in Germany

In chapter four I have outlined the debate among Alevis whether Alevism is culture or religion. Although the general meeting of the AABF in 2002 decided unanimously to change its by-laws and to declare that the AABF is a "religious community," the debate on "religion or culture" is not finished. That is, the new by-laws are not simply the outcome of a new agreement among Alevis that Alevism is, in the first place, religion. There are still many Alevis in the associations who are of the opinion that Alevism is first of all culture. And there are still

---

[25] See Muckel 2004 and Spuler-Stegemann 2003.

many Alevi atheists. But they also agreed to the revision of the by-laws and to the struggle for Alevi classes in schools. The reason for this is that religion is a category of recognition in Germany. Culture, however, is no such category. There is no legal status of "cultural community" in Germany. Culture serves as an instrument for marking migrants as others yet cultural difference is not a category of recognition, except in the case of a few nonmigrant, autochthonous minorities in Germany.[26] German culture is imagined as homogeneous and this homogeneous culture, together with the idea of descent, forms the basis of the German nation. Culture as difference is a category of exclusion, not of integration. There is no way in which Alevis could struggle for the official recognition of Alevi *culture* in Germany. Religion, in contrast, offers an avenue of recognition.

Although Germany figures as a secular state, there are many institutionalized relationships between the state and religion. In this respect Germany differs radically from republican France where the separation between religion and the state is very strict. While in France cooperation between state and religion is regarded as a potential danger, a symbiosis of state and religion is regarded as an ideal state of affairs in Germany (Mannitz 2002, 137). We have seen that the German state is concerned in one way or another with providing religious education in schools. Churches are recognized as corporations under public law. The state collects their revenue. The churches provide manifold social services like kindergartens, schools, or hospitals and are therefore firmly bound to the state by institutionalized relationships. In contrast with culture, religion is a legally institutionalized category in Germany. Freedom of religion is guaranteed by the constitution, but not "freedom of culture." Further, while (German) culture is in the first instance imagined as singular and homogeneous—the cultures of migrants are taken as only a later and not essential addition—religion is from the outset conceptualized in the plural. Religion has originally been institutionalized as a duality because the state entertains relations with the Catholic as well as with the Protestant Church. This duality has been extended by the development of similar relationships with the Jewish community, and it is easily imaginable that it could be further expanded to a plurality with more components. Accordingly, decisions against Islamic classes in schools are not based on a general rejection of the possibility to offer another kind of religious classes in German schools, but only on organizational arguments. In my opinion, it is not surprising that the most stable associations—and those with the largest membership—of migrants in Germany are based on religious affiliation. Interestingly, the

---

[26] Danish, Sorbs, Sinti, and Friesians are recognised as *national* minorities in Germany. This status is restricted to autochthonous minorities that lived already before its establishment on the territory of the German nation-state.

cultural difference of migrants is also frequently framed in religious categories. Thus, the difference that is currently most hotly debated is not
cultural difference per se but specifically religious difference, as in the
case of the headscarf.

It is my thesis, then, that the refiguration of the Alevi associations and
especially of the AABF as a religious community is less an outcome of
a new religious orientation among Alevis in Germany than an effect
of the institutional and discursive requirements and strategies in the
course of efforts towards institutional integration and recognition. In republican France with its much stricter secularism, in contrast, the Alevi
federation does not figure as religious community. The statutes of the
Fédération de l'Union des Alevis en France (FUAF) do not refer to Alevism
as religion or a religious community, but only to Alevi philosophy and
culture.[27]

The importance of religion as a category of recognition in Germany
is not limited to institutional relations with organs of the state. Also in
the general public, religion is a significant category that is much more
concrete and tangible than the abstract category of culture. As a consequence, in explaining Alevism to Germans, even self-declared atheists
frequently introduce Alevis as a *religious* community. Alevi atheists also
approve Alevi classes in school although these classes are explicitly
conceptualized as *religious* classes and, without much reservation, take
part in interfaith dialogue.[28]

Citizenship and Naturalization

Besides debates on headscarves and Islamic classes citizenship law is
also a significant field of the German discourse on migration. Concepts
of citizenship occupy a central position in recent theory debates on migration and multiculturalism. It has been pointed out that in Europe
concepts of citizenship and the nation-state and, most importantly, the
relations between them, have been strongly affected by migration. Alternative concepts of belonging that reach beyond the traditional notion

---

[27] In the by-laws, the FUAF is defined as an *"Organization de masse démocra-
tique."* It aims at "protecting the philosophical and cultural values of the Alevi
community in France and Europe and at developing its cultures and customs"
(sections 2.1 and 2.6, by-laws adopted in Strasbourg, 24 December 1998).

[28] In order to complete the picture it has to be added that some Alevis still
disapprove of Alevi classes. These are not necessarily atheists, but people that
are of the opinion that Alevism cannot be taught in schools because such teaching requires a certain form of codification of Alevism (in the form of curricula,
for instance), which they regard as contradicting the antidogmatic character of
Alevism.

of citizenship based on the ideology of the homogeneous nation-state have been proposed—concepts such as "multicultural citizenship" (Kymlicka 1995) or "transnational citizenship" (Bauböck 1994). Indeed, many rights that earlier applied only to the citizens of a state—especially social benefits—have been extended to resident immigrants who retain citizenship in their country of origin. In Europe, progressing supranational integration into the European Union provides a further impetus in this direction. Yasemin Soysal (1994, 1996) has emphasized the emergence of a new "postnational" model of membership, which acknowledges fluid boundaries and multiple belonging and is based more on the idea of universal personhood than on the idea of a particular nationality. Yet Kostakopoulou (2001, 95–98) objects that the extension of citizenship rights onto noncitizens as well as a relaxation of naturalization procedures do not challenge the primacy of the nation-state. To the contrary, citizenship remains "wedded to the territorial nation–state" (ibid., 98). In fact, in Germany, as in other states, full participation and complete rights are still restricted to citizens. Until recently, citizenship had exclusively been framed in terms of (ethnic) nationality and *ius sanguinis:* a German citizen was a person of German descent, that is, a child of German parents. Citizenship transferred "by blood" served as an effective means to maintain congruent boundaries of the political nation and the ethnic nation. Avenues for naturalization were tightly restricted. Naturalization required long periods of legal residence in Germany as well as the fulfillment of a number of other restrictive conditions. Until a reform of the foreigners law that was put in force in 1991, naturalization was not considered as a natural option for non-Germans living in the country, but more as an act of favor granted by the state. Even if all legal conditions for naturalization were fulfilled by a migrant, he or she did not enjoy the *right* to naturalize. The reform of the German law of citizenship that largely dated from 1913 was an important point in the program in the Social Democrat/Green coalition that came to power in 1998.[29] The debate about this reform and its restriction allowed many insights into German conceptions of citizenship and the nation. An important rationale of the reform was the idea that the integration of migrants had largely failed because migrants were not accepted as full members of German society. Under the regime of the old law of citizenship, the rate of naturalizations per year calculated as the number of naturalizations relative to the total number of foreign residents remained very low, although it rose from 0.3 percent in 1986 to 1.2 percent in 1996 (Fücks 2002, 78). It was assumed that many migrants rejected the idea of naturalizing as Germans if at the same time they had to give up their original citizenship. As a consequence, the new law, as it was originally proposed in 1999, included a very liberal option

---

[29] On the history of German citizenship law see Gosewinkel 2002.

for dual citizenship. Yet this option for dual citizenship was strictly rejected by large segments of the German public and by the conservative Christian democratic parties CDU and CSU. While the legislation was under way, provincial elections were held in Hesse and the CDU made the rejection of the reform a major issue of its election campaign, arguing that dual citizenship undermined loyalty towards nation and state. Starting from Hesse, the CDU initiated a Germany-wide campaign to collected signatures for a petition endorsing the rejection of dual citizenship. This campaign was as much acclaimed by some sections of the public as it was criticized and rejected as racist by others. Many of those who signed the petition did not realize that it was against dual citizenship but simply wanted to sign "against foreigners." The CDU won the elections in Hesse, and it is generally agreed that the campaign against dual citizenship played a major role for this success. As a consequence of the elections in Hesse and the victory of the CDU, the Social-Democrat/ Green coalition had lost its majority in the *Bundesrat*, the council of the federal states (*Bundesländer*) that is the second legislative chamber at the federal level. Therefore the coalition lacked the power to pass the law single-handedly. If a reform of citizenship was to be achieved, a compromise with the CDU was required. The liberal option for dual citizenship fell victim of this compromise.[30] Still, the new law in force since 1 January 2000, brought a number of significant changes: conditions for naturalization are less restrictive, and naturalization is now an entitlement if these conditions are fulfilled. The most important point is that under certain conditions children born of foreign parents living in Germany receive German citizenship. With this provision, an elements of *ius soli* was for the first time introduced into German law of citizenship.[31]

Although certain restrictive aspects of the new citizenship law were criticized, the Alevi associations welcomed the reform. After the new law had been put into force, the AABF published a bilingual brochure that informed in detail about the new regulation of citizenship. 6,000 copies of the booklet were distributed. Yet the intention of the AABF was not only to inform about the opportunities of the new law, but also to encourage Alevis to make use of these opportunities. In the preface to the brochure, Turgut Öker, the chairman of the AABF, writes:

> During the last fifteen years we have increasingly started to settle down
> in the country in which we live. Our children were born here, grew up

---

[30] The new law is even more restrictive on dual citizenship than the old one has been: if a person, after being naturalised in Germany, reapplies for his or her previous citizenship the German citizenship may be withdrawn. Before, it had been a common practice of migrants from Turkey to reapply for Turkish citizenship after naturalizing in Germany.

[31] On the effects of the new law see Dornis 2002.

and received their education. The first generation has started to retire. As a consequence of this development migrants became a part of this country. In order to have a voice in this country and to achieve equal rights, we must not only learn the language, but must also fulfill the conditions of citizenship as envisaged by the laws (AABF 2000b, 4).

Coeval with the publication of the brochure the AABF initiated a program funded by the federal Ministry of Interior Affairs that promulgated information about the citizenship law and general information about the institutional structure of the German state. The title of the program was "Promotion of Naturalization" (*Förderung der Einbürgerung*). Seminars on these topics were held at the office of the AABF in Cologne. In these seminars multipliers from the local Alevi associations were trained who subsequently carried out such seminars in their cities. Almost fifty such seminars were held in various places.

I participated in one of the seminars for multipliers in Cologne. Interestingly, there was no debate about the question whether one should naturalize or not. It was taken for granted, both by the organizers and by the participants, that one should naturalize. Among the twenty participants in this seminar, fifteen had already naturalized and three more had submitted their applications for naturalization. I also conducted a seminar myself on citizenship in the HAKM, and in this seminar as well there was no debate whether one should naturalize or not. I got the impression that many Alevis had already acquired German citizenship before the reform of the law. In the survey conducted among the members of the Alevi associations in Hamburg in late 2002, I found that indeed 55.6 percent of the members had German citizenship, including 9.8 percent who possessed dual citizenship (n = 233).[32] Contrasted with the general rate of naturalization among people of Turkish background in Germany, this number is extraordinarily high. Setting the number of former Turkish citizens that have naturalized as Germans (by 2000 a total of 424,512) against the number of Turkish citizens living in Germany (1,998,534 in 2000),[33] we arrive at a total naturalization rate of 21.2 percent. Although both rates cannot be strictly compared, the fact remains that the naturalization rate among Alevis is much higher than among migrants from Turkey in general. Figure 7.1 shows that indeed most members naturalized before the reform of the law. Even most of those who acquired German citizenship in 2000 filed their applications earlier, because the procedure takes many months or even years. The HAKM called its members to naturalize already in the mid–1990s. In recent years, the rate of naturalization is even decreasing. This is a

---

[32] Four members or 1.7 percent were stateless.

[33] Figures are taken from Beauftragte der Bundesregierung für Ausländerfragen 2002, Tab. 6 and 16a.

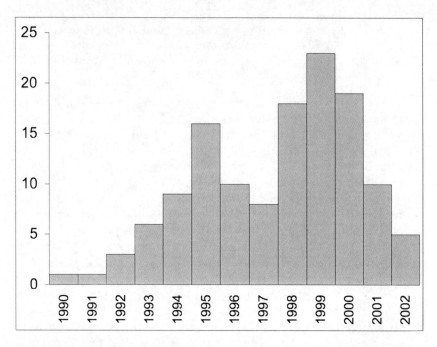

Figure 7.1 Naturalization of members of Alevi associations in Hamburg

consequence of the fact that most members who are legally entitled to naturalize did so already.[34]

34.6 percent of those members of the Alevi associations in Hamburg who had not acquired German citizenship responded that they would not apply for naturalization in future, while 20.2 percent said that they will soon apply for German citizenship. 29.8 percent remained undecided. The survey also included an open question about the reasons for naturalization. The answers were subsequently categorized and multiple categorization of answers was possible. Most persons responded that they had opted for German citizenship simply because they had settled down in Germany, but the wish for full political participation and for equal rights in general were also significant, as was the greater freedom to for travel (no visas required for German citizens within the EU). All categories of reasons for naturalization are stated in table 7.1. The reasons stated for naturalization are fairly pragmatic.[35] The met-

---

[34] About half of the members that have not acquired German citizenship are of the opinion that they fulfill the legal conditions for naturalization.

[35] In a forced-choice survey about reasons for naturalization among migrants from Turkey in general, the reasons that scored the highest results were "legal advantages/ secure residence status" and "I wanted to have political rights/ right to vote" with 76.5 percent respectively 72.6 percent of respondents (Sauer 2001, 205).

Table 7.1 Reasons for naturalization among members of Alevi associations in Hamburg

Life is settled in Germany	32.1%
Full political participation	28.6%
Generally equal rights	26.8%
Greater freedom to travel	20.5%
Economic reasons	14.3%
Children are settled in Germany	13.4%
More freedom in Germany as compared with Turkey	9.8%
Foreigners' specific problems related with authorities (e.g., periodically required renewal of residence permit)	6.3%
Military service in Turkey	5.4%
Enmity against foreigners in Germany	4.5%

aphysics of the nation that dominates much of German discourse on migrants, nationality, and citizenship ("Do you feel more intimately connected with Turkey or with Germany?" "Do you feel more like a Turk than like a German?") played no role.

The AABF responded positively to the new law of citizenship with its campaign that was supported by the government. Yet the Alevi practice of naturalization showed that Alevis did not need a campaign in order to apply for German citizenship. Most Alevis—at least among the members of the associations in Hamburg, but there is no indication that this cannot be generalized for Alevis in Germany—had naturalized already before the campaign and before the reform of the law. The positive attitude towards naturalization largely confirms Alevi discourse on integration. Asked their own opinion why Alevis decide more often for naturalization than Sunnis from Turkey do, Alevis frequently state that the most important reason is that Alevis are not nationalist. Quoting Hacı Bektaş Veli ("Regard all nations alike"), they emphasize that they can live and adjust anywhere. The idea of belonging to a specific nation is not particularly strong, at least among a significant part of Alevis.

Becoming Citizens—Remaining Foreigners

Yet naturalization and efforts toward "integration" on part of the migrants is not all that counts. Efforts have to be recognized in order to be effective. In some strands of official discourse migrants are recognized as citizens. In her preface to the brochure of the AABF on the new law of citizenship, the Undersecretary of the Ministry of the Interior writes:

Migrants have contributed much to our common home. They have also contributed in making Germany more international and open to the world. The new citizenship law recognizes this achievement. It acknowledges the fact that Germany has changed. For the first time, children of non-German parents ... will become German citizens by birth. From the first day of their life they will grow up as German citizens in Germany (AABF 2000b, 5).

These sentences capture the new law's rationale of welcoming new citizens and acknowledging that Germany is an immigration country. Significantly, the reform is presented as an acknowledgement of the contribution of immigrants. Thus, the familiar rhetoric of making demands on citizens (to learn German, to integrate themselves, etc.) has been discontinued here. However, the serious conflicts that preceded the law and that changed its content reveal that this new attitude has not yet become common sense in Germany. Although the new law has introduced an element of *ius soli*, popular conceptions still hold citizenship to be more a matter of "blood." Thus, citizens perceived as "non-Germans" due to their black hair, dark eyes, or other details of physical appearance are generally thought of as "foreigners" and not as German citizens. Alevis, like other migrants in Germany have the experience that German citizenship does not prevent them from being categorized as *Ausländer*. In many instances, public and everyday discourses time and again inscribe foreignness on migrants, irrespective of their citizenship, insisting that they have their "roots" and belong somewhere else. In the last instance, this is done by simply categorizing even those persons as *migrants* who never have migrated anywhere themselves but who happen to be descendants of migrants. This discourse is experienced as a practice of exclusion and discrimination. Nermin, a student in her mid-twenties who has grown up in Hamburg vividly described her experience:

I am really fed up with the constant necessity to justify myself, to justify that I am here at home! I always have to ask for tolerance! [Yet] I do not have to ask for tolerance, this is my country, I am a part of this country! This is not a question of tolerance. Why do I have to hope for tolerance, this is my country! Maybe I look a little different, but I have the same passport like everybody here, I speak the same language as everybody, perhaps even better than some others. I always feel disturbed that I have to justify myself for being here. And then the people do not accept when I say, well, that I feel German. But I am at home here. No, they want to make me believe that I *cannot* feel at home here. [...] I frequently have this experience, in discussions with Germans as well as with Turks. They try to persuade me that I am a Turk, that it cannot possibly be that I feel German. [They say] that I cannot feel German because I do not think German, but how do they know that? [In fact] I am dreaming German, I am thinking German, I know myself how I feel, I do not need other people who think about how I should feel. This is my business. One should feel at home at the place where one lives and I am living here in this country. Sometimes I go to Turkey for holidays but I am always happy when I return home, when I am back in my usual environment.

In this passage Nermin emphatically rejects the idea that she is a Turk and belongs to Turkey. In her own understanding, she belongs to the place where she is living and where she feels at home. Yet in the perception of others she belongs somewhere else and lives in Germany only by accident. According to this perspective, she *cannot* feel at home in Hamburg because she is *not* at home there. Nermin mentioned many instances in which she was made aware that she is categorized as "being foreign," belonging to some other place and country. When she made a phone call to an office at the university, her interlocutor took her without question as a foreign student after she had told her "Turkish" name. The Alevi youth organization of which she was a leading member was categorized as an association of foreigners by the police and therefore subjected to special requirements. Yet she insists on not being a foreigner. Significantly, Nermin said that not only Germans but also Turks define her as non-German and as out of place in Germany. The essentialist logic of deriving belonging from some "place of origin" is equally entrenched in Turkish national discourse as in German discourse. I will return to this issue in the next chapter. Indeed, with her strong insistence on being of Germany and not of Turkey, Nermin is not representative for Alevis in general. Age and generation matter in this respect. Especially many first–generation migrants support the idea that they belong to Turkey in the first place. Whenever first–generation Alevi migrants use the word *ülkemiz* (our country) in their discourses, they invariably refer to Turkey. According to their perspective Turkey is "their country" much more than Germany. Also elderly Alevis with German citizenship frequently say things like: "Here in Germany we can have Alevi classes in school. We cannot have that in *our* country." Yet I rarely encountered this way of talking among younger Alevis who have grown up in Germany.

The policy of the AABF is that Alevi migrants should not revoke their manifold relations with Turkey but that they should locate themselves firmly in the place in which they are living. It is said: "We cannot exist with our feet in Germany and our heads in Turkey. We have to keep feet and head together in the place where we are living." But this requires also that they are recognized as people that live in Germany and that they belong there. Hasan Öğütcü, the former general secretary of the AABF, explained:

We do not intend that the people give up their identity here. They come from Turkey, they should always be able to understand this country and its culture and they should maintain close contacts. Yet on the other hand they should also be ready to live here. In this country. They should not remain foreigners but they should be able to say: I live in this country, I am a German citizen, I have rights and duties.

Yet "national geographic" (Malkki 1997) that privileges roots over routes and that demands unequivocal classification and belonging in *one* and only one place is a pervasive idea in German migration discourse. Hasan Öğütcü described how an officer of the southern German town Ravensburg tried to fix Alevis onto a place somewhere else:

> Last year we prepared the tenth anniversary of our [local Alevi] association. For a number of reasons I had to speak with an officer of the municipal administration. I gave him a call and explained our plans. He asked me: "Well, where do you come from?" I said: "We come from Ravensburg, Friedrichshafen and Markdorf." He said: "I did not mean that." I asked him: "Then, what did you mean?" "Well, from which country [*Land*] do you come?" I said: "Baden-Württemberg." He again said: "I did not mean that!" And I again asked: "Well, *what did* you mean? Did you mean Germany?" He said: "I wanted to know…" I interrupted him: "I know very well what you wanted to know. But first of all you should understand that we are citizens of this country. After that we could talk about other places. I will not tell you where I come from. I am from Meersburg!" I explained all this also to the commissioner for foreigners (*Ausländerbeauftragter*) and to the vice mayor. I explained to them that the people have to give up these old thoughts [about origins] and that these people, like me, when they have lived here for twenty or thirty years, they are not foreigners. But you always remain a foreigner.

The officer wanted to know where Alevis, about whom he apparently had no idea, "originally," that is, "really," come from. And although Hasan Öğütcü pretended not to understand the question, he in fact understood very well because being asked one's origin and being located elsewhere is an everyday experience of migrants in Germany. In this instance he responded with an attitude of irony that intended to reveal the absurdity of the question.[36] It seems that the officer did not easily get the point. He kept on trying to get an answer to his question and appeared to be unable to reflect about the meaning of his question. Migrants are reconstituted as foreigners, as strangers marked by difference, by such apparently simple and innocent questions. Because migrants are continuously ascribed difference and foreignness and because especially scientific studies, including anthropological ones, play an important role in reconstituting this difference, I generally avoided in my research to ask questions like "Do you feel foreign in Germany?" "Do you feel more like a Turk or more like a German?" or "Where do you feel

---

[36] On strategies of irony employed by migrants in order to counter the German discourse of otherness see Köhl 2001.

at home: in Turkey or in Germany?" in order to avoid becoming an ac-
complice of this discourse.[37] Only when some time ago I was invited to
a conference that explicitly related to migrants as "strangers" (*Fremde*)
I tried to approach the topic of the supposed "strangeness" of migrants
more directly.[38] I asked Özlem about her feelings in relation to Hamburg, the city where she has lived since she came to Germany more
than twenty years ago, at the age of ten. She is a German citizen and
has a lively memory of her childhood in Turkey. Özlem said: "I am just
thinking … I wanted to say that Hamburg is my *Zuhause*, but I am not
sure whether it is my *Zuhause*. […] I mean, I am here since twenty years,
this is quite a long time. Yet, I believe, it is … well … maybe my *Zuhause*
is Turkey … or my *Heimat* is Turkey, but my *Zuhause* is Hamburg."

It is quite difficult to convey the semantic difference between *Zu-
hause* and *Heimat* in English because both words translate as "home."
In Özlem's sense, *Heimat* implies a more intense, emotional attachment.
She explained that she feels related with Turkey by a certain longing.
She can travel to Turkey every year without feeling bored. This is dif-
ferent for her younger niece, who was born in Hamburg and for whom
Turkey is just a country for holidays. Her niece does not like to go to
Turkey every year; she would prefer to also go to Spain, for example.
Özlem continued that she felt especially at home in Altona, in a district
of Hamburg with a large migrant population. She felt *zu Hause* in Al-
tona because she did not stand out there:

> I worked in Niendorf [another district of Hamburg] five or six years ago.
> And there, whenever I went out I got the impression that the people were
> staring at me. I said to myself, what happens, do I look unusual? Do I
> look like an alien? I was the only dark–haired person for miles around,
> also in the company where I was working. There were only Germans and
> elderly people, and all these people looked strangely at me as if they saw
> for the first time a dark-haired woman. This does not happen in Altona. If
> somebody looks at you, they look because you do not wear the headscarf.
> Otherwise, you do not stand out. There are so many migrants here.

When I asked her about her experiences of strangeness and foreignness (*Fremdheit*) she told me of an episode that she had experienced in
Turkey: Once she happened to be the only uncovered woman among
conservative, bearded Sunni men. There she felt as a stranger, not in
Hamburg. Yet she feels estranged in Hamburg by gazes that single her

---

[37] On the problem of reproducing excluding ascriptions in qualitative research
on migrants in Germany see Mecheril, Scherschel, and Schrödter 2003.

[38] The papers of this conference are published in Eder 2003. Several participants
criticized that migrants were referred to as "strangers" or "foreigners" (e.g.,
El-Tayeb 2003).

out as a dark-haired foreigner. These gazes mark her as a foreigner, a stranger, as *fremd*:

> "I do not feel *fremd* in Altona. But this is different elsewhere [in Hamburg]. I don't know, one stands out there. The gaze of the people and their behavior show somehow that one is not welcome there, that one is different. Perhaps they do not have bad intentions, but [they say] you are different. And I am like this! [...] One can see of course that I am a foreigner. And then ... one does not feel very well."
>
> I: "This feeling is produced by the glances of the people?"
>
> Özlem: "Yes, they make you feel that you do not belong here."

The experience of not being recognized as people who simply belong to the place where they live corresponds to the fact that many Alevis report the experience of racist discrimination. In the survey among the members of the associations in Hamburg, 53.6 percent of respondents stated that they had experienced racist discrimination at least once in their life. 41.6 percent had no such experience, and 4.8 percent did not respond to this question. Asked how they experienced racism, 69.9 percent of those who had suffered racism reported verbal aggression, while 22 percent reported bodily attacks. Highly significant is the experience of discrimination at the work place and in the job market (63.4 percent), in the housing market (60.2 percent) and in contacts with the government (57.7 percent).

Some Alevis, as many other migrants, reject the option of naturalization because according to their perception, German citizenship would not really alter their status in Germany: even with a German passport they would remain foreigners. Meral, a young woman who is strongly committed to HAAK BIR said, when I asked her about German citizenship: "I don't know, I don't have German citizenship and nobody in my family has it. What is the advantage of it except that you can cast your vote? Nothing! When I am out on the street I am simply a foreigner again. I will not apply for a German passport unless dual citizenship is possible. I do not want to be forced to give up my roots!" In her short statement, Meral mentions several reasons for not applying for German citizenship: it gives little advantage because one continues to be regarded as a foreigner, and naturalization is understood as giving up one's roots. The denial of dual citizenship furthers the idea that applying for German citizenship implies giving up one's roots. Similar ideas were stated by those respondents of my survey who rejected the idea of naturalization: they wanted to retain their identity and their Turkish citizenship, they did not expect a real change of status as a consequence of naturalization, and they did not see many advantages. Others stated that they were simply too old for such a step. Yet those who decidedly refuse to naturalize constitute a small minority of all respondents: 12.8 percent.

The Limits of Recognition

In this chapter I have discussed Alevi efforts toward "integration" in conjunction with the German discourse and policy of integration. Alevi associations have undertaken efforts toward institutional integration that aimed at the recognition of Alevism in Germany. We saw that in correspondence with Soysal's thesis, the form of organization that Alevis sought was predicated on the models of the German institutional and discursive environment. Alevis founded registered associations, they strove for the status of a corporation under public law, and redefined themselves as a religious community. At the same time Alevism is defined by Alevis as a nonforeign culture that endorses universal values and that is different from Islam. Individually, the majority of Alevis acquired the full status of legal and political integration, i.e., citizenship. Yet these efforts are only partially honored by public discourse and perception. Within the parameters of the German politics of migration and especially its paradigm of cultural difference, Alevis remain *others* and continue to be largely perceived and treated as *foreigners.*

In the national order of things migrants constitute a form of disorder, an anomaly. Migration contradicts the territorialized nation as a "powerful regime of classification, an apparently commonsensical system of ordering and sorting people into national kinds and types" (Malkki 1995, 6). Within the framework of the national order of things, two options are imaginable as a solution of this disorder: Migrants could be admitted to the (new) nation in a full sense that goes beyond legal citizenship and includes migrants also discursively within the nation. Or migrants could be excluded discursively and institutionally by fixing them to some place of origin, to their "roots." As the others of the nation, migrants play a significant role for the nation. National identity, like any identity, is defined by difference. In the history of the origins of nations, the role of the different other against which the nation was defined was mostly ascribed to external others and enemies. France played this role most prominently in the history of the German nation. Yet as a consequence of increasing supranational integration, external others have largely lost importance in this respect. The other has been internalized, in the form of migrants. It is not surprising, then, that a debate about German national identity and culture emerged in consequence of debates about new laws of citizenship and integration, which, from the national perspective, threatened to blur the boundary between the nation and its internal others. The status quo in Germany can be described as a tension between options one and two: the new law of citizenship constitutes an important step towards the full incorporation of migrants, yet it is countered by public discourse that continues to exclude migrants as foreigners.

There is, however, a third option that goes beyond the national order and that challenges the fundamental idea of the national framework and its hegemonic idea that a human being belongs to one and only one nation. The idea to introduce dual citizenship on a large scale was an attempt towards this option in Germany. Yet in the resistance against this nonexclusive model the national framework proved its power. The opponents of the new law of citizenship objected that dual citizenship would destroy the loyalty of the citizens, thereby framing loyalty as adherence to one and only one state and nation. In the national framework, multiple loyalty is inconceivable. Still, most migrants, forming an anomaly in the national order of things because they have moved across fixed boundaries and categories, do practice in one way or another multiple loyalties and relations across national boundaries. Most migrants are involved in transnational relations, although the degree and kind of this involvement may vary considerably. In the next chapter I will analyze transnational relations as they are practised and imagined by the Alevi movement in Germany. We will see that German Alevis are using transnational resources in the struggle towards recognition of Alevis in Turkey. The present chapter has shown how German discourse excludes migrants, including Alevis, as foreigners from the German nation. The next chapter will discuss also how the transnational commitment of Alevis is resented in the national discourse of Turkey, and how it is attempted to firmly enclose Alevis, including those living abroad, within the Turkish nation.

8

Transnational Connections and the Claims of the Nation

Questions of Loyalty and Belonging

Issues of national belonging are contested in Germany. For a long time, Germany was conceived as a "nonimmigration country," actual numbers of migrants notwithstanding. Boundaries of the nation were discursive and conceptual rather than simply territorial and physical. The ensuing situation of migrants is a paradox: originally, labor migrants had been conceptualized as temporal "guests" that were meant to return to their "home country." "Integration" of migrants was explicitly unwelcome. The maintenance of strong relationships with their "home country" was welcomed and taken for granted. Later, when migrants turned out to stay and to become permanent residents, the demand for "integration" was raised. Integration in the dominant German sense requires migrants to give up ties with their "homeland." As a consequence, migrants are suspiciously scrutinized regarding their relationships with the country from which they or their parents had come. "Dual commitments" and "dual loyalties" are regarded with alert. Dual citizenship is undesired, because it is perceived as weakening the commitment to the German state and nation. Migrant associations are categorized according to their "homeland orientation" (Diehl, Urbahn and Esser 1998). In the realm of media, the consumption of non-German language media is regarded as equally problematic. Turkish satellite TV and Turkish newspapers are considered as a general obstacle towards integration, not necessarily because "anti-integration" messages are disseminated through these media in every case, but simply because watching a daily soap on Turkish TV epitomizes that migrants look elsewhere. For the same reasons bilingualism of migrants is not generally welcomed but, in spite of contrary research findings, regarded as an obstacle to full proficiency in German. Integration in this sense aims at assimilation, as the German minister for interior affairs, Otto Schily, stated in an interview.[1] Integration then means the firm enclosure of migrants into one and only one nationalized space.[2]

---

[1] *Süddeutsche Zeitung,* 27 June 2002.

[2] Not only politicians but also researchers think in terms of exclusive affiliation and loyalty and thereby express the claims of nations and nationalised cultures.

A large and still growing body of recent research on migration shows, however, that migrants act very differently: they maintain relationships across borders. The recent prominence of concepts like transnationalism and diaspora signals a shift of perspective in research on migration that has largely given up traditional concerns such as the causes of migration and the issue of assimilation in the country of residence, and turned instead towards scrutinizing continuing cross-border relationships. Migration movements ceased to be considered "as primarily onetime, unidirectional, and permanent changing of location from one (national) 'society' to another" (Pries 1999, 27). The new concepts of research acknowledge that "migration does not simply mean a transition from one society to another: rather, migrants and their descendants often maintain long-term cultural, social, economic and political links with their society of origin as well as with co-ethnics all over the world" (Castles 2000, 25). Transnationalism is not simply about migration, then, but about postmigration, about relationships across state boundaries as enduring consequences of migration.

Alevis fit into this transnational pattern. Although it is acknowledged that circumstances and aspects of the community vary according to the national spaces that are inhabited by Alevis, the Alevi community is imagined as basically *one* community which, as a consequence of migration processes, spans several nationalized spaces. Besides this "transnational imagination," Alevis entertain a great diversity of transnational relationships. A great number of such transnational relationships are established by kinship and marriage. Brothers and sisters from the same village in southeastern Turkey have migrated, for instance, to Hamburg, Paris, and Strasbourg. Such a "fan-shaped" migration helps to establish lateral connections between differently situated local communities. Relations are maintained and renewed by mutual visits, in the first place on festive occasions like marriage or circumcision, as well as by more quotidian telecommunication. Yet relations with relatives living in Turkey are particularly significant. 91.8 percent of the respondents of my survey have relatives in Turkey that they visit at least once a year. 72.5 percent regularly support their relatives in Turkey materially. Almost half of the respondents (47.1 percent) can imagine living in Turkey again. On the other hand, the migrants' lives are quite firmly settled in Germany: only in 5.2 percent of cases was residence in Germany interrupted by a prolonged stay in Turkey.

Polat (2000, 21f) simply states that migrants are not able to be equally "loyal" to the culture of the country of residence and to the culture of the country of origin. Kağıtçıbaşı (1987, 197) criticises cultural alienation of Turkish migrants from Turkey and laments that Turkish parents in Germany are not able to "adequately transmit the cultural heritage of their home country."

Yet, my discussion of transnational relationships in this chapter will not refer to such "ordinary" transnational relationships, which are entertained by almost every migrant from Turkey and which do not distinguish Alevis from other migrants. I restrict my analysis to those transnational relationships that are part of the Alevi movement and particularly of its politics of recognition and identity. Further, I will discuss the contestation of this transnational politics of recognition by Turkish national discourse and show that transnational relationships of migrants are not necessarily considered problematic in the "receiving state" only, but also in and by the "sending state."

Concepts of Transnationalism

The phenomena that are researched and analyzed in the context of the new perspective on migration are framed with different but interrelated concepts. I suggest to employ *transnationalism* as generic concept that refers to the phenomena in general and includes the other concepts. Basch et al. have defined transnationalism "as the processes by which immigrants forge and sustain multistranded social relations that link together their societies of origin and settlement. We call these processes transnationalism to emphasize that many immigrants today build social fields that cross geographic, cultural, and political borders" (Basch, Glick Schiller, Szanton Blanc 1994, 8). The concept of transnationalism is related to the notion of globalization, yet both concepts, or rather the discourses and perspectives to which they relate, cannot be conflated. They remain distinct as regards their perspectives towards the nation-state: while globalization discourse prophecies a global world in which nation-states have lost most if not all of their importance, transnational-ism acknowledges the ongoing significance of states, boundaries, and localized identities. Nation-state and transnationalism are regarded as mutually constitutive rather than as antagonistic (Smith 2001, 3f; cf. Basch, Glick Schiller, Szanton-Blanc 1994; Bauböck 2003). Further, while globalization mainly works "from above" through governments and their international agreements about free trade or through transnational corporations, the transnationalism that is dealt with in the context of migration is "transnationalism from below" (Smith and Guarnizo 1998, cf. Portes 1996), the agents of which are largely ordinary people.

Basch et al. conceptualize transnationalism in terms of processes and links that result in the creation of social fields. Such fields are called *transnational social spaces* by Pries (1999) and Faist (1998, 1999). Faist (1999, 44) suggests a typology of transnational social spaces in which particular instances are distinguished by the intensity and by the dura-tion of their integration into networks of the (minimally) two involved nation-states. This typology ranges from short-lived transnational spaces of weak integration in both states that result in quick severing of ties with the sending country and assimilation in the society of the receiving country,[3] to spaces of long-lived and strong dual or multiple integration. For the purpose of the present study I am particularly interested in this last category of transnational social spaces, which is called *transnational communities* by Thomas Faist. He defines transnational communities as "dense networks of 'communities without propinquity' in both sending and receiving countries" (ibid., Figure 1). Faist writes: "Transnational social spaces are combinations of social and symbolic ties, positions in networks and organizations and networks of organizations that can be found in at least two geographically and internationally distinct places. These spaces denote dynamic social processes, not static notions of ties and positions" (ibid. 40).

Although I concur with the author that endurance and multiple integration are the significant characteristics of transnational communities, I would like to question his conflation of transnational communities with one kind of transnational social space. I prefer to keep both distinguished and regard transnational communities as inhabiting and partially creating transnational social space as well as using it as a social, cultural and political resource. Portes, Guarnizo, and Landolt (1999, 217) speak of transnational communities as "linking immigrant groups in the advanced countries with their respective sending nations and home-towns." According to their understanding, "back-and-forth movements" have resulted in an emergent social field composed of "a growing number of persons who live dual lives: speaking two languages, having homes in two countries, and making a living through continuous regular contact across national borders" (ibid.). Here we come close to the concept of *transmigrants* as suggested by Glick Schiller, Basch and Blanc-Szanton (1995, 48; cf. Glick Schiller, Basch, Blanc-Szanton 1992):

> Transmigrants are immigrants whose daily lives depend on multiple and constant interconnections across international borders and whose public identities are configured in relationship to more than one nation-state. They are not sojourners, because they settle and become incorporated in the economy and political institutions, localities, and patterns of daily life of the country in which they reside. However, at the same time, they are engaged elsewhere in the sense that they maintain connections, build institutions, conduct transactions, and influence local and national events in the countries from which they emigrated.

Portes et al. (1999, 219) warn against simply introducing a new term, transmigrant, to label phenomena that have adequately been dealt with

---

[3] Although Faist categorizes this form of "dispersion and assimilation" as a type of "transnational social space," it is rather not an instance of *transnational* space according to conventional understandings of transnationalism that are all based on the endurance of transnational ties.

under the concept of "immigrant." In order that the new term makes sense, differences between the old and the new concepts—and old and new phenomena—should be kept clear.[4] In order to highlight the distinction I propose to employ "migrant/immigrant" as the more inclusive concept, and to take as the specific difference between migrants and transmigrants a continuous and large-scale *social* commitment of the latter to the place/nation-state of origin and to the place/nation-state of settlement. In order to qualify as transmigrant, then, it is not sufficient to "maintain connections" across borders, because almost every migrant does so. In particular I exclude purely symbolical relationships from the relations that make a transmigrant: a sense of belonging, expressed, for instance, in the consumption of "homeland" media, is not sufficient to qualify as transmigrant. Further, I would like to exclude those migrants whose social relationships across borders are limited to occasional contacts like making holidays or visiting one's home village once a year. In my understanding it is useful to restrict the concept of transmigrants to those migrants that indeed "live dual lives," for whom travel is an almost quotidian experience and who in social, economic, or political respect are almost equally committed to two nationalized spaces.

Any definition of *transnational* community has to be built upon some notion of *community*. Benedict Anderson's concept of *imagined* communities (Anderson 1983) has moved the idea of community effectively away from small congregations that are constituted by face-to-face relationships to large groupings of people that are held together not by actual interaction but by symbolic ties and, simply, by the *idea* that they form a community. Étienne Balibar (1991, 346) emphasizes that not only "national communities" are built by "blocs of imagination" but also all kinds of communities that reach beyond immediate social relationships. Anthony Cohen (1985) similarly highlights the role of symbolic ties for the constitution of community. Although the social and the cultural can never be neatly distinguished because the social inevitably takes on cultural form and because the cultural is always socially constituted and reproduced, I would like to distinguish analytically social from cultural aspects of community formation. Social aspects of community relate to actual instances of interaction and communication among members, while cultural aspects comprise all elements of imagination and symbolical relationships, including the idea of a shared identity. Communities in any case depend on social as well as on cultural aspects, yet they may be distinguished according to the degree to which they are based on one or on the other. In a large-scale national community the social aspect is outweighed by the cultural aspect, while the reverse may be true in small-scale village communities.

---

[4] For a critical discussion see Kivisto 2001.

Transnational communities also have both social and cultural ("symbolic") aspects. Faist defines them accordingly: "Transnational communities characterize situations in which international movers and stayers are connected by dense and strong social and symbolic ties over time and across space to patterns of networks and circuits in two countries" (2000a, 207). Transnational communities may differ, then, according to the degree on which they are based upon social or cultural relationships. Further, not all members of a transnational community necessarily have to engage in transnational social relationships to the same extent. According to this understanding transmigrants and transnational communities have to be kept distinct: the members of transnational communities are not necessarily transmigrants, at least not all of them. Not all members of a transnational community live equally transnational lives. Differing degrees of transnationalism are easily imaginable and most probable. A transnational community may well be made up, on one hand, of individuals that entertain strong symbolic ties with some place of origin but that only rarely go there or get otherwise involved in social relationships across national borders, and on the other of transmigrants that continuously travel back and forth and that are equally embedded in social networks of both national spaces. In such a case it is probable that especially transmigrants contribute to the "glue" and the social and symbolic fabric that keeps the community together. Yet it may also be the case that symbolic ties with a place imagined as "home" are especially strong because people are prevented from going there and from maintaining actual social relationships. Conversely, we can imagine transmigrants that do not combine to a transnational community because the relationships they entertain remain largely individual and because an imagination of community is absent. Faist points to solidarity as another element of transnational communities that may be expressed in social relations as well as symbolically:

> For transnational communities to emerge, solidarity has to reach beyond narrow kinship systems. Such communities without propinquity do not necessarily require individual persons living in two worlds simultaneously or between cultures in a total "global village" of de-territorialized space. What is required, however, is that communities without propinquity link through exchange, reciprocity, and solidarity to achieve a high degree of social cohesion, and a common repertoire of symbolic and cultural representations (Faist 2002, 207–8).

Diaspora

Another concept that has recently gained great prominence in the discussion of transnational phenomena is *diaspora*. Steve Vertovec (1997) usefully distinguishes three meanings of diaspora in the current debate:

diaspora as a social form, as a kind of consciousness, and as a mode of cultural production. Generally, the understanding of diaspora has moved away from the classical case of the Jewish diaspora, although it continues to be regarded as the prototypical case by many authors. However, the concept has been greatly broadened so that now many different kinds of social forms are categorized as diasporas (e.g. Cohen 1997, van Hear 1998). Although diaspora certainly relates to transnationalism — Tölölyan (1991, 5) has called diasporas "the exemplary communities of the transnational moment" — the relationship between both concepts has not always been made explicit. Generally, it is loosely assumed that a diaspora is a kind of transnational community. Van Hear (1998, 6) largely equates transnational communities and diasporas, with the exception that he regards contiguous transborder communities as transnational communities but not as diasporas. Faist categorizes diasporas more specifically as a subtype of transnational community. For him, the specific difference between diasporas and other kinds of transnational communities consists in traumatic experience: "In diasporas, a group has suffered some kind of traumatic event which leads to the dispersal of its members, and there is a vision and remembrance of a lost homeland" (Faist 2000, 208). Faist's categorization is based upon a "classical" notion of diasporas that is derived from the prototypical Jewish case. He explicitly rejects the almost indiscriminate extension of the concept as it has been advocated by Cohen and even more so by Walker Connor or Richard Marienstras.[5] Faist's understanding is even more specific than the definition given by William Safran (1991: 83), which consists of a list of six definitional criteria omitting, however, the aspect of traumatic dispersal.[6]

---

[5] Connor (1986, 16) defines diaspora simply as "the segment of a people living outside the homeland," turning thereby any kind of migrant community into a diaspora. Similarly, Marienstras defines diaspora as "any community that has emigrated whose numbers make it visible in the host community" (1989, 125).

[6] According to this definition, "the concept of diaspora [can] be applied to expatriate minority communities whose members share several of the following characteristics: 1) they, or their ancestors, have been dispersed from a specific original 'center' to two or more 'peripheral,' or foreign, regions; 2) they retain a collective memory, vision, or myth about their original homeland — its physical location, history, and achievements; 3) they believe that they are not — and perhaps cannot be — fully accepted by their host society and therefore feel partly alienated and insulated from it; 4) they regard their ancestral homeland as their true, ideal home and as the place to which they or their descendants would (or should) eventually return — when conditions are appropriate; 5) they believe that they should collectively be committed to the maintenance or restoration of their original homeland and to its safety and prosperity; and 6) they continue to relate, personally or vicariously, to that homeland in one way or another, and their ethnocommunal consciousness and solidarity are importantly defined by the existence of such a relationship" (Safran, ibid.). Cohen (1997, 180ff.) com-

While these definitions regard diaspora as a type of community, other conceptualizations refer to diaspora as a kind of condition of consciousness or experience. According to Avtar Brah, the image of travel lies at the core of the concept of diaspora. But not every journey engenders diasporic experience: "Paradoxically, diasporic journeys are essentially about settling down, about putting roots 'elsewhere'" (Brah 1996, 182). Floya Anthias (1998, 565) sums up the experience of diaspora as "the experience of being from one place and of another." Similarly, I have written elsewhere that "diaspora is about *not being there*" (Sökefeld 2002a, 111), indicating that diaspora comprises an experience and consciousness of separation. It is the experience of living at a particular place but being nonetheless permanently related with some other place by imagination, memory, and symbols. In this context, Avtar Brah speaks about a "homing desire" that can be understood as the desire that the journey may return to its starting place, that the place where one presently lives may not be the final place. Paul Gilroy (1997, 318) refers to diasporic consciousness as an consciousness "in which identity is focused less on the equalizing, proto-democratic force of common territory and more on the social dynamics of remembrance and commemoration defined by a strong sense of the dangers involved in forgetting the location of origin and the process of dispersal."

A third strand of conceptualization regards diaspora as a "mode of cultural production" (Vertovec 1997) or a mode of aesthetics (Werbner 2000). Here, diaspora is celebrated as a creative space of mixing diverse cultural sensibilities, in which intellectuals and artists produce works of hybridity that transgress cultural boundaries and that in many cases become highly relevant for larger society and not only for a narrow diasporic community. Salman Rushdie is the epitomizing figure in this regard, and the story of his *Satanic Verses* proves that such diasporic creativity may even lead to rupture and estrangement between the artist and "his" diasporic community (Werbner 2002, 134–152).

As is the case with many concepts in the social and cultural sciences that rapidly gain prominence but at the same time lose much of their contours, also the concept of "diaspora" certainly lacks precision. Further, "diaspora" is not simply a scientific term but has gained equal prominence in literary discourses and in the arts. As usages in these contexts feed back into disciplinary discourse we are faced with the condition of dual hermeneutics (Giddens 1976), in which attempts to rigorously delimit a concept for scientific purposes seem almost futile. Nevertheless, I regard endeavors to arrive at a more precise concept for the purpose of social and cultural analysis necessary.

---

poses a similar list of criteria without giving an exact definition. According to him, these criteria constitute strands of meaning that make up a family resemblance of diasporas.

In the context of the Alevi case the meaning of diaspora as a social form, that is, as a type of community, and as a kind of consciousness is most significant.[7] Because any concept of diaspora is based on ideas of dispersal and dislocation, on being "elsewhere" and, perhaps, even "out of place," my conceptualization centers on the ties that make up a diaspora and link it with other places of reference. I chose this rather vague wording in order to escape the unequivocal privileging and essentializing of notions of "home" and "origin" in ideas of diaspora that Anthias (1998, 2000) has strongly criticized:

> Such continuing attachments to homeland, however, may not be an adequate reason for treating all these groupings with such an orientation as belonging to a single conceptual category. In fact, one is tempted to assume that the thing that most binds them together is an *attribution of origin*. If this is the case it already assumes that which it purports to investigate. The explanans becomes the explanandum (Anthias 1998, 565).

As with other types of communities, a problem of defining diasporas consists in that most probably not all its members share the same kind of consciousness. While some may indeed feel a strong "homing desire," regarding a place elsewhere unequivocally as their "home," others may have settled for good in the place in which they are living and have abandoned all imaginations of an "elsewhere." Accordingly, diaspora consciousness is not a self-explanatory given but rather an unstable condition that time and again has to be reconstituted and that needs specific agents and institutions in order to be reproduced (Sökefeld and Schwalgin 2000). A notion of diaspora as community or consciousness that is defined in the first place by an essentialized and privileged relation to some "home" or "origin" is also problematic, because it unequivocally attributes one particular kind of identity to diasporians and thereby neglects the multiplicity of identifications.

As a working concept I therefore suggest a more open notion that defines diaspora as a subtype of transnational communities, which is distinguished from other such communities in that the transnational relationships by which it is constituted are mainly of symbolic, i. e., cultural, kind and that these symbolic relationships are not necessarily based upon actual transnational social relationships constituted by interaction. In a way, my definition relates back to the paradigmatic case of the Jews, who maintained a strong diasporic imagination with-

---

[7] The meaning of diaspora as a mode of cultural and aesthetic production is less important in the Alevi context. One could speak of Turkish diasporic cultural production in Germany, which includes individual Alevi artists and which has produced works of literature, music, and, above all, highly acclaimed films, making significant contributions to German culture, but there is no comparable specific Alevi mode of diasporic cultural production.

out being able for centuries to live actual social relationships with their imagined "home." Similarly, Schwalgin (2004) has shown for the Armenian diaspora in Greece that Armenian imaginations of home were especially strong when the possibility of travel and actual social relationships with the homeland were severely limited.[8] This understanding also resembles Levitt's conceptualization that states the relationship between transnational community and diaspora as follows:

> Transnational communities are building blocs of potential diasporas that may or may not take shape. Diasporas form out of the transnational communities spanning sending and receiving countries and out of the real or imagined connections between migrants from a particular homeland who are scattered throughout the world. If a fiction of congregation takes hold, then a diaspora emerges (Levitt 2001, 15).

Diaspora can be defined then as a transnational imagined community that is based on an identity that is territorially related but not limited to the place in which the members of the diaspora are living. Linking diaspora in this way with identity means that diasporic experience may be an important aspect of self-identification, but also that it is neither necessarily the only nor even the principal form of self-identification. This definition neither implies a specific history of dispersal (for instance as a consequence of traumatic events) nor a specific content of consciousness (like a "homing desire" or the intention to "return"). Significant, however, is the idea of a shared identity[9] and a sentiment of solidarity that is implied in the imagination of community. That is, the members of the community take interest in the lives of those that are imagined as fellow members of the community elsewhere. Yet this interest and solidarity need not take the particular shape of a sentiment of home and origin that is projected on this "elsewhere".

This conceptualization accommodates the classical instances of diaspora as well as more recent cases like the Sikhs, but distinguishes diasporas from other kinds of categories of migrants that lack a strong sense of overall community, like Italian–Americans in the US (Tölölyan 1996, 16) or Turks in Germany (Østergaard-Nielsen 2003, 123).[10] Such

---

[8] Conversely, Setney Shami (1998) has emphasised that Circassian imaginations of home were severely shaken when long time residents of Jordan or Turkey "returned" to their "home" in the Caucasus.

[9] An idea of a shared identity does necessarily result in ideas about this particular identity being actually shared and agreed upon. They may well be utterly contested.

[10] The "diasporic status" of Turkish migrants in Germany is disputed. Based on definitions by Safran and Tölölyan, Chapin (1996) comes to the conclusion that they do form a diaspora community. As one indicator he emphasises is a strong "return orientation," maintaining that only five percent of Turkish migrants intend to remain permanently in Germany. Yet according to a recent survey,

a sense of community is very strong among Alevis in Germany. Most of them feel strongly related with Alevis in Turkey without, however, regarding Turkey necessarily as their home. We have seen in the last chapter that especially young Alevis clearly regard Germany as their home country and also most older, first–generation migrants have abandoned plans of return. But in spite of this lack of a general "homing desire," solidarity with Alevis in Turkey is strong and a determined politics of supporting Alevis in Turkey in their struggle for recognition is derived from this solidarity.

Transnational Communities, Diasporas, the Nation and the State

The Alevi movement in Germany is involved in transnational politics (Østergaard-Nielsen 2003). Supporting Alevis in Turkey in their struggle for recognition means that the German Alevi movement interferes in national politics in Turkey. The relationship between the nation-state and diasporas, respectively the nation-state and transnational communities has attracted great interest. Concepts of diaspora and transnational communities are deeply ingrained in images of nation and state—after all, we speak about trans*national* communities. Diasporas have been conceptualized as "the other of the nation-state" (Tölölyan 1991). While the nation-state is territorialized and firmly bounded, diasporas evade territorialization and boundedness.

Beside conceptualization, also actual, historical relationships between diasporas and nation-states have to be taken into consideration. Such relationships are ambivalent. On one hand, diasporas have been described as subverting the nation-state (Clifford 1994, 307) because their unboundedness and multiple attachments threaten the boundedness that is regarded as a defining principle of the nation-state. On the other hand, diasporas may actively be engaged in nation building and state formation. The most prominent case in this respect is Israel, the state that was made by diasporians coming "home." Diaspora and "long-distance nationalism" (Anderson 1998) frequently go hand in hand. According to Appadurai (1996, 161), "the nationalist genie, never perfectly contained in the bottle of the territorial state, is now itself diasporic."

The specific condition of diasporas and transnational communities in general consists in the fact that diasporas are related not to one but to at least two nation-states: to the "sending" and to one or more "receiving" states. The "sending" state is mostly conceptualized as the "home" of the diaspora while the "receiving" state is seen as the space and place of "displacement" and dispersal. Historically, however, relationships may

---

forty-six percent of migrants from Turkey definitely rule out a "return" (Şen, Sauer and Halm 2001, 95)

well be the opposite, as again the example of Israel shows. Here, the "sending" states were the spaces of dispersal where the Jewish diaspora communities lived while the "receiving" state that was created only in the moment of arrival was conceptualized as "home." The case of Israel exemplifies that, almost unavoidably, ideological constructions are involved in the conceptualization of relationships between states and diasporas.

In most cases, the subversive force of diasporas is projected upon the "receiving" state (Clifford 1994, Cohen 1996, Tölölyan 1996). The privileging of origin and home in notions of diaspora that Anthias has criticized is effective here. Lindholm Schulz (2003, 9) emphasizes that "there is often a strong sense of community with other members of that diaspora and an uneasy relationship with the host society." The diaspora's attachment elsewhere subverts the exclusive allegiance and loyalty demanded by the "receiving" state. Such ideas are effective in the German discourse on migrants, albeit the concept of diaspora is rarely used here.

The nation-building force of diasporas, in contrast, is mostly projected upon the "sending" states. As migrant workers that send remittances home, diasporians, for instance, significantly broaden the economic fundament of "their" nation-state, but they may also be directly involved in political processes of the state. When diasporians are seen as a disruptive and subverting power vis-à-vis the "sending" state, this is usually related to separatism, that is, to projected alternative nation-states, as in the case of the Sikh (Tatla 1999, Axel 2001), the Tamil (Fuglerud 1999), or the Kurdish (Wahlbeck 1999) diasporas.

The idea of the subversiveness of diasporas exemplifies, in the first place, the unbroken claims for precedence by nation-states, which in spite of repeated prophesies of its decline continues to be the globally dominant form of polity. Such claims also affect Alevis in Germany. Interestingly, relations of subversion are put upside down in the Alevi case: diasporic Alevis try their best not to appear as subversive in the "receiving" state, that is Germany, but they are in many instances regarded as subversive by the "sending" state, i.e., Turkey, although they do not entertain their own national project. The "subversion" in the case of Alevis consists simply in their rejection of Turkish claims for precedence. I will analyze this in three steps: first, transnational aspects of the Alevi movement in Germany are scrutinized, second, the Alevi transnational politics of recognition is considered, and then the claims of the Turkish nation vis-à-vis the transnational Alevi community are discussed.

Transnational Aspects of the Alevi Movement

The Alevi movement in Germany rose in a transnational context. I have shown that global ideas about the end of class struggle and a new politics of identity provided the intellectual environment in which the movement was conceived. More specifically, developments in Turkey, the growth of political Islam, and the struggle of the Kurds, gave an impulse to turn towards Alevi identity. Although the establishment of the Alevi Culture Group in Hamburg was a local event, it was related to global ideas and to events in Turkey, which at that time was probably regarded quite unequivocally as "home" by the Alevis in Hamburg. Yet beside ideas and events social relations also played an important role. One of the first meetings of the Alevi Culture Group in January 1989 was attended by the musician Arif Sağ, who was also a member of the Turkish parliament then and who happened to be in Hamburg for a campaign against anti-Kurdish politics in Iraq. This meeting can be regarded as the germ cell of transnational networking in the context of the Alevi movement. A significant extension into transnational space was achieved with the publication of the Alevi Declaration in summer 1989, as the declaration was distributed not only in Germany but also among Alevi intellectuals in Turkey.

The commitment to "homeland oriented" issues was not a new development but rather conventional practice among politically committed migrants from Turkey at that time (Østergaard-Nielsen 2003, 46f). Both precursors of the Alevi movement, the social democrats and the Marxists, had been firmly engaged in political relations that today could be termed "transnational." A more justified claim for novelty could be made by the Alevi Declaration, because by demanding recognition of Alevis in Turkey and in Germany it connected for the first time issues in the "sending" and "receiving" countries. Here, transnational, diasporic solidarity was expressed because Alevi migrants voiced their concern for the situation of fellow Alevis in Turkey.

The next decisive event, the Alevi Culture Week, had a significant transnational dimension too. As a result of transnational networking, two of the most important intellectuals of the early Alevi movement in Turkey, Nejat Birdoğan and Rıza Zelyut, participated in the event along with Arif Sağ. The Alevi Culture Week established one of the most important transnational practices of the Alevi movement, which consists in inviting intellectuals and artists from Turkey to give lectures and concerts in German cities. The possibility to perform in Europe offers considerable income opportunities to Alevi musicians from Turkey. Erdal Erzincanlı, one of the younger *saz* players, said in an interview that eighty percent of his concerts are performed in Europe.[11] Because the demand for musicians is high, prices have gone up. The AABF has tried to regulate the market by issuing a list that states what fees should be

---

[11] See *Dem* No. 26, May 2003. Also Greve (2003, 298f) emphasises the significance of Alevi associations in Germany for musicians from Turkey as well as from Germany.

222 ♦ *Struggling for Recognition*

paid to which musician by the local associations. Yet ideas and practices do not flow in one direction only. Thus, the idea of the Alevi Declaration was transferred to Turkey, and a declaration drafted by Rıza Zelyut was published there in 1990. Further, a book commissioned by the Alevi Culture Group was written by Nejat Birdoğan (1990). It was printed in Turkey but distributed in Turkey and Germany. One could speak of an initial transnational Alevi mediascape here. In the mid–1990s the AABF even opened an Alevi radio station in Turkey, *Radyo Mozaik*, but due to financial problems this endeavor had to be given up.

With the growth of the Alevi movement in Germany, such transnational relationships flourished. We have seen that the Alevi movement received a strong impulse from the Sivas massacre in 1993. Many more associations were established and many more Alevis joined the existing associations. Sivas, and Gazi two years later, can be regarded as transnational events: although both were local occurrences they were perceived and had significant consequences on a transnational scale. New practices of memory were established in consequence of Sivas. These practices were transnational not only in intent, as they aimed at remembering an event that happened in Turkey and at creating transnational solidarity, but also in practice because the commemorative ceremonies became another opportunity for inviting guests from Turkey. In 2003 the commemorative ceremonies were even organized on a transnational level by the Avrupa Alevi Birlikleri Konfederasyonu, which sent a kind of commemorative caravan of artists and politicians across Europe.

A further important consequence of Sivas was the reorganization of the Alevi federation as the Federation of Alevi Communities *in Europe* (*Avrupa* Alevi Birlikleri Federasyonu), that is, as a transnational association. Although the German associations were the most numerous and played the leading part, associations from other countries like England, France, Holland, and Austria were also involved. While the membership of the AABF was restricted to the diaspora, the association also engaged in several attempts to establish a transnational umbrella association that bridged the space from Turkey to Europe. The first attempt for a transnational Alevi-Bektaşi Temsilciler Meclisi was made in Istanbul in November 1994. Although this organization broke up in consequence of conflicts among the Turkish Alevi associations, similar attempts continued to be made. More important than the establishment of a formal transnational umbrella association was the dense networking between associations in Germany and associations in Turkey. While in the first years of the Alevi movement mainly Alevi musicians and authors were invited from Turkey, they were subsequently joined by the functionaries of Alevi associations in Turkey, like Ali Doğan from the Hacı Bektaş Veli Anadolu Kültür Vakfı, Attila Erdem from the Hacı Bektaş Veli Dernekleri, Ali Yıldırım from the Hüseyin Gazi Derneği, Ali Balkız from the Pir Sultan Abdal Kültür Dernekleri (all these associations are located in Ankara), and Izzettin Doğan of CEM Vakfı in Istanbul. All these and many other Alevi leaders from Turkey travel frequently to participate in panel discussions organized by Alevi associations in Germany or elsewhere in Europe. There is movement in the opposite direction too: in particular the chairmen of the AABF traveled very frequently to Turkey in order to participate in events, to give speeches, to reconfirm old and establish new relationships. Turgut Öker, the present chairman of the AABF, is also chairman of the European umbrella association AABK. He is constantly on the move, visiting Alevi associations and attending events in Germany, in other West European countries, and in Turkey.

It was also attempted to establish political ties between Turkey and the diaspora that went beyond the confines of Alevi associations. Activists from Germany were involved in the establishment of the Alevi *Barış Partisi* (BP), which was mainly funded by a Turkish Alevi businessman, Ali Haydar Veziroğlu. Veziroğlu decidedly sought support for his party among Alevis in Germany and chartered several planes that carried hundreds of Alevis from Germany to the founding congress of the party in Ankara. Beside this attempt to gain a foothold in the political institutions of Turkey, the German Alevi movement tried many other strategies to interfere in Turkish politics. Most of these will be dealt with in the next section. At this point I only want to mention the example of a delegation of the AABF that toured many Turkish cities in summer 1998 in order to voice protest against an initiative to reform the law against heterodox communities and practices in Turkey. It was intended to augment the fines that still sanctioned such practices, but the reform was subsequently abandoned.

To a much smaller extent, *dede*s also establish transnational relationships by visiting associations for the purpose of conducting *cem* or teaching Alevism. The first *cem*s in Germany were conducted by Dede Şinasi Koç from Ankara, who traveled in the 1980s to many different German cities. Some *dede*s from Turkey like Dertli Divani or Mehmet Yaman are still sometimes invited to Germany but most *cem*s in Germany are held now by *dede*s from the diaspora.[12] Many of the German *dede*s, however, travel across the diaspora for the purpose of conducting the ritual. All the three German *dede*s that I presented in more detail elsewhere (Sökefeld 2002b) traveled beyond the German boundaries. They had *cem*s in Switzerland, France, and Australia. When I visited the Alevi Culture Center in London in spring 2001, another *dede* from Germany stayed there for the purpose of *cem*. Conversely, the *cem*

---

[12] According to my survey data, almost ninety percent of *cem*s in Germany are conducted by *dede*s living in Germany, with less than ten percent being held by *dede*s from Turkey and the rest by *dede*s from other European countries.

organized by the HAKM in February 2002, was conducted by a *dede* from France.

Transnational networking and the invention of political strategies require a great amount of communication. The mobile phone has become an indispensable instrument of Alevi activists, still more than e-mail and the Internet. Yet, not all networking is done by telecommunication. Encounters in "real"—as different from "virtual"—spaces remain highly significant because they enable not only the exchange of verbal messages, but also the actual sharing of time and concerns. Talking through the night over glasses of *rakı* and a lavish meal or listening jointly to somebody playing the *saz* helps to establish more intimate, more reliable, and more lasting interpersonal relationships than short phone calls. Alevi activists from Turkey, from Germany, or from other countries meet at many places, during cultural events or at assemblies of the associations. Yet in particular one occasion has become a favorite opportunity for encounter. This is the festival in memory of Hacı Bektaş Veli that takes place every year from 16–18 August in the small town Hacıbektaş in central Anatolia, near Nevşehir.

The *tekke* of Hacı Bektaş Veli in the town had been closed down after the *Tekke ve zaviye yasası* ("law on dervish lodges") proscribing all activities of *tarikat* (Sufi orders) had been put into force in 1925. Yet, after the antireligious drive in Turkey had relaxed, restoration works were started in the *tekke* of Hacıbektaş in the 1950s (Norton 1992). In 1964 the *tekke* was reopened as a museum and the opening ceremony became the germcell of the annual festival. Especially in the 1970s the festival was turned into a highly politicized event. At present, the festival can best be understood as a symbol that is open to many different readings and practices, but that as a shared symbol nonetheless provides a focal point of reference for Alevis (Massicard 2003b). Religious ceremonies like visits of the *türbe* (tomb) of Hacı Bektaş Veli or rituals of sacrifice (*kurban*) are practised alongside an opening ceremony that has become a national political event, in which the president and high-level members of the administration participate and that is broadcast live by all major TV networks. Further, there are concerts in the evenings, as well as panel discussions on political topics and shows of *semah* during the day. During the festival, the whole town of Hacıbektaş is converted into a bazaar of Alevi devotional objects. Tens of thousands of Alevis both from all over Turkey and from other countries flood the town every year.[13]

In 1991 Derviş Tur, the chairman of the ACF, was invited by the Turkish ministry of culture, which at that time organized the festival, to give a speech there. He took the opportunity to establish further contacts with the activists of Alevi associations in Turkey. Since then a German

---

[13] On the festival see also Sinclair-Webb 1999.

Alevi delegation of considerable size has participated every year in the festival. In recent years, the AABF organized panel discussions during the event. The Hacı Bektaş Veli festival also provided the stage for formal meetings of the diverse Alevi associations in which various attempts for establishing transnational umbrella associations were made. Yet, beside these formal, official occasions, the festival also offers unofficial yet equally important opportunities to meet. As hotel facilities in Hacıbektaş itself are very limited, the invited musicians and speakers as well as the delegations of most Alevi associations are accommodated in two hotels in the nearby town of Avanos, which, due to its location in the touristic area of Cappadocia, is much better equipped. In the hotel lobby or in the garden all these people come together and share meals and drinks. Discussions last the whole night and deal not only with the festival itself but also with many issues concerning Alevis, including a considerable portion of gossip. It is a prime opportunity to consolidate friendships and to make new acquaintants.

The AABF has been engaged in some transnational projects that imply the transfer of money from Germany to Turkey. When a series of strong earthquakes shook the Marmara region in western Turkey in August 1999, the association started a relief project called *Umut Kent* (City of Hope) in Izmit, one of the most affected cities. A tent city was established that housed two hundred families. The AABF collected donations for this purpose among Alevis in Germany, and relief goods worth 250,000 DM were contributed by the German Ministry of Foreign Affairs. The AABF collaborated with Turkish Alevi associations in that project. The Hacı Bektaş Veli Anadolu Kültür Vakfı (Ankara) operated a medical center there.[14] The assistance offered by the project was not limited to Alevi victims of the earthquake. When the town of Pülümür, a district headquarter in Tunceli province, was affected by an earthquake in early 2003, the AABF and its membership associations again collected donations that amounted to 30,000 Euros. This money was distributed among affected families. In Hamburg, the HAKM collected contributions for Pülümür during a *cem*.

Another project consisted in assisting the construction of a *cemevi* in the city of Erzincan. The municipal administration of Erzincan had offered the local Alevi community a plot free of charge for the construction of a *cem* house. Yet because after some years construction work had still not begun due to a lack of funds, the municipal administration was about to reclaim the plot. In early 2003 the North Rhine–Westphalia section of the AABF whose chairman is from Erzincan himself decided

---

[14] See *Alevilerin Sesi* 34, October 1999. This relief project was also celebrated by the AABF as a instance of successful institutional integration. The contribution of the German government was regarded as a token of the recognition of the AABF as an organization of civil society (ibid., 5).

to assist the Erzincan Alevis. They organized a cultural festival in order to collect money for the construction of the *cem* house. The festival that took place in Duisburg was attended by about seven thousand people. 70,000 Euros were collected and in August 2003 the foundation stone of the *cemevi* in Erzincan was laid. Many representatives of the AABF, of local German Alevi associations, and of the Alevi federations of Denmark, Switzerland, and Austria participated in the ceremony.[15] In May 2004, the Alevi Culture Center in Kassel organized another festival for the purpose of raising further funds for Erzincan. Later, a similar project for the purpose of establishing a Pir Sultan Abdal culture center in Sivas was undertaken.

Since the commencement of the Alevi movement, a diverse transnational Alevi "landscape" has evolved that is made up of transnational actors (musicians, intellectuals, activists), transnational events (the Sivas massacre, but also culture festivals), transnational practices (travels, visits, communication), transnational locations (most importantly Hacıbektaş), transnational media (nowadays especially websites, see Sökefeld 2002a), and projects (Umut Kent, Erzincan) that are engaged in, support, enable, or are the result of a host of transnational relationships and connections. These relationships not only connect diasporic Alevis with Alevis in Turkey, but also Alevis living in various places of the diaspora. We find here the triadic pattern characteristic of diasporas that consists of links between the diasporic communities and the "homeland" as well as of connections among the diverse diasporic communities.

The Alevi movement has constituted a transnational social space that is created by transnational actors through their communication and interaction across national borders. Some of these transnational actors, activists like Turgut Öker or musicians like Arif Sağ, could, due to the large scale and intensity of their transnational activities, be regarded as transmigrants—although they remain settled by means of their households and families as well as by many quotidian commitments in one national space, that is, in Turkey in the case of Arif Sağ and in Germany in the case of Turgut Öker. In comparison to them, the transnational relations and activities of most diasporic Alevis are much more restricted. They might attend the Hacı Bektaş Veli Festival once or twice in their life, or visit another place of significance for Alevism during their holidays in Turkey.[16] They may invite musicians from Turkey if they happen to be members of the board of a local Alevi association, or they may simply attend the concerts of musicians that have come from Turkey.

---

[15] *Alevilerin Sesi* 68, October 2003.

[16] Regional places of pilgrimage like the *türbes* of Abdal Musa near Antalya or of Elif Ana near Gazi Antep draw a considerable number of visitors from the diaspora.

That is, they are not actively involved in the construction and maintenance of transnational social relations in the same manner as the transnational actors are. These diasporic Alevis could be regarded more as
"consumers" of the cultural phenomena that evolved in transnational
space than as their "producers." They are, however, firmly included
in the transnational imagined Alevi community, or Alevi diaspora, by
feeling and practising solidarity with Alevis elsewhere, by maintaining
concern about and interest in the affairs of Alevis in Turkey, and simply by imagining themselves as members of an Alevi community that
reaches beyond national boundaries. They read Alevi magazines or attend concerts and panel discussions because they entertain such solidarity and concern and because they imagine themselves as members
of the community. They relate to the symbols of the community like the
saz or *semah* because they consider them as their own symbols. Thus,
although such "ordinary" diasporic Alevis are not transnational actors
and do not, or only in a very limited manner, participate in the Alevi
transnational *social* space, they are firmly included in the Alevi transnational *cultural* space, which consists of such transnationally shared
symbols, concerns, sentiments, and imaginations.

One could say that the transnational social space constitutes the fundament of the transnational cultural space, because transnational social
relationships have to be established and interaction across boundaries
has to take place in order that all the phenomena that constitute the
transnational cultural sphere can be produced. Yet the relationship between social and cultural spaces, or between producers and consumers
of culture, is not one of unidirectional causality but rather one of mutual
constitution: the transnational social space of Alevis would be reduced
to a void if there were not Alevis who relate themselves to transnational
concerns in their imagination and practice. In spite of all networking by
transnational actors, no musician would come from Turkey to perform
in a German city if there were not large numbers of people who simply attend the performances. The consumers of transnational Alevi culture are not epiphenomenona in the context of Alevi transnationalism.
Drawing further on the economic metaphor, one could say that these
consumers play a quite active part because they constitute the demand
for the production of Alevi transnational culture.

Like any social movement, the Alevi transnational movement requires
mobilization that goes far beyond its core activists. The core activists
and leaders require people that can be mobilized on a lesser scale. The
Alevi movement needs chairmen who organize events as well as "ordinary" people who attend these events. It requires artists and authors
as well as people who consume their works. The mobilization for transnational concerns, the imagination of diaspora, and sentiments of community among "ordinary" Alevis cannot simply be taken for granted
but need permanent re-creation. Such sentiments and imaginations are

constantly invoked and reconstituted in the discourse produced by the agents of the movement. For instance, Alevis in Germany did not individually get the idea to make contributions for the construction of a *cemevi* in Erzincan. This idea was conceived and disseminated by the agents of the movement. In their discourses, Alevi leaders constructed the issue of an empty plot in the city of Erzincan that awaited the construction of a *cemevi* as an issue that concerned the whole Alevi community—and therefore every individual Alevi—and not only to those Alevis that live in Erzincan. In order that the idea could be conceived and disseminated in Germany, information about the plot and the imminence of its being reclaimed by the municipality first had to travel from Turkey to Germany. After the idea to support the construction of the *cemevi* had been adopted and disseminated by the Alevi activists in the AABF, it could be further exchanged among the Alevi public through the networks of the associations, with individual Alevis motivating and mobilizing each other to attend the cultural festival, ensuring thereby that sufficient contributions could be collected. This case exemplifies a network of communication channels that are quite effectively used and controlled by the Alevi umbrella association. Transnational communication is indeed mainly channeled by the AABF; there are very few direct transnational links between local Alevi associations in Turkey and in Germany. The example of the *cemevi* in Erzincan shows, however, that Alevis in the diaspora relate to transnational projects or can be mobilized for this purpose without being necessarily directly engaged in transnational relationships themselves. Although transnational social and cultural spaces are intricately interwoven, I regard it as useful to distinguish analytically between these two types of space because this distinction enables us to grasp the different modes of commitment of Alevis to the transnational Alevi community.

Bin Yılın Türküsü, the large festival representing Alevi history that was staged in Cologne in May 2000 and then again in Istanbul in October 2002, was another transnational event. I emphasized at the end of chapter five that due to the mass participation of hundreds of young saz players and semah dancers, *Bin Yılın Türküsü* turned the imagined community of Alevis to a certain degree into a real experience. I would like to add here that the festival enabled for many Alevis a direct experience of the Alevi *transnational* community. In the speeches that preceded the performance it was emphasized repeatedly that Alevis from many different countries beyond Turkey attended this event. The Alevi community was celebrated as a transnational and even almost global community. For the thousands of participants this was not merely a discursive construction, but an actual experience. On the spot in Istanbul, then, the transnational social and cultural spaces of Alevis became largely congruent.

Transnational Politics of Recognition

For Alevis in the diaspora, the question of recognizing Alevism in Turkey is the most pressing transnational concern. This concern can be framed as transnational politics of recognition. One of its most significant strategies is the engagement of the European Union in the context of Turkey's endeavor for accession to the EU. This will be dealt with in the subsequent section. Here, however, I will to give an overview of the perception and position of Alevis in Turkey, as regards recognition.

I use the word "recognition" as a cover term that includes all issues that indicate the lesser standing of Alevism as compared to Sunni Islam in official and public discourse and in institutional practice in Turkey. Alevis use the concept of recognition (*tanınması*) less frequently in relation to Turkey than in relation to Germany. Instead, in most cases they directly name the relevant issues. Matters that indicate the lesser standing of Alevism in Turkey are manifold, and no speech by an Alevi activist in Germany that relates to Turkey fails to address a number of them. Such issues include, in the first place, the instances of violence against Alevis, including the lack of impartial conduct of the administration, the security forces, and the judiciary in the context of the massacres, but also the mandatory religious classes in schools that fail to address Alevism on equal terms and force Alevi children to learn about Sunni Islam; the one-sidedness of the Directorate of Religious Affairs (DİB), which spends its huge budget on Sunni institutions only although it is financed also by Alevi taxes; the general prohibition to organize explicitly in the name of Alevism, the lack of constitutional guarantees for Alevism, and the nonrecognition of Alevis as a separate community in its own right beside the Sunni Muslims. Sometimes, the perception of such matters is different for diasporic Alevis and for Alevis in Turkey. During a discussion of the situation of Alevis in Turkey and Europe that was organized in Hacıbektaş by the AABF in 2001, a speaker of the organization lamented the lack of religious freedom for Alevis in Turkey. A man from the audience rose in response and raised objections. He said that he had learned for the first time at this occasion that he, as an Alevi living in Turkey, was lacking religious freedom. He saw things very differently and considered himself as enjoying freedom of religion. Alevis from Germany used to explain such discrepancies of perception by claiming that due to the continuous nonrecognition of Alevism in Turkey, Alevis in the country do not really know what religious freedom is. Similarly, after the speeches of politicians at the opening ceremony of the festival at Hacıbektaş, I have frequently heard comments of German Alevi visitors that these politicians "did not use the word 'Alevi'" (*Alevi kelimesi kullanmadılar*). Yet Turkish Alevis generally do not comment on this fact. Indeed, the only speakers who use the word at this occasion are representatives of Alevi associations. Twice I have listened to speeches of the Turkish president Sezer at Hacıbektaş in which he emphasized the necessity of religious freedom, but failed to mention Alevis explicitly although in the context of the festival he could only be understood as referring to Alevis. Generally, critical views about the position of Alevis in the country are voiced much more openly and explicitly in the statements delivered by diasporic Alevi activists in Hacıbektaş than in the speeches of Turkish Alevi activists.

The critical perspective of the AABF and of diasporic Alevis towards the situation of Alevis in Turkey translates into a generally critical view of government politics in Turkey. In many respects this critical perspective is also a continuation of the opposition attitude of the exiled radical leftists in the 1970s and 1980s. Most diasporic Alevi activists do not trust the Turkish government. It is frequently said that government officials made many promises for the improvement of the situation of Alevis but that generally these promises were not kept. The great mistrust towards the Turkish government became evident during another event that happened at the Hacibektaş Festival in 2003. On the second night of the festival the private TV network ATV broadcast a talkshow live from the open courtyard of the *tekke*. Artists, representatives of several Turkish Alevi associations, the chairman of the AABF, and delegates of most national Alevi federations in Europe participated. The host of the talkshow first asked Mustafa Özcivan, the Alevi mayor of the town, about the festival and about Alevis in Turkey in general. Özcivan responded with an exceptionally critical statement, taking the fact that the *tekke* as a place of central importance for Alevis was closed to *cem* as his point of departure. Shortly after his statement, all the TV spotlights suddenly went out while the normal lights of the *tekke* continued to be on. The program was interrupted. At once speculation rose among the participants from Europe that the Turkish government was censoring the show by cutting off electricity. Two of the Alevis from Germany had given notice about the program to their families at home because the program could also be received there via satellite. Immediately after the power failure they received messages from Germany on their mobile phones, which inquired about the interruption as no reason had been given by the TV network. In response, the speculation about censorship by the government was sent to Germany. The power failure, like the speculations, lasted for more than fifteen minutes. After the lights came back on and the program had been resumed, electricity failed again for a short time. Finally the program continued without disturbance. It turned out that the problem had not been censorship but local overloading due to the TV spotlights. Yet this episode vividly illustrates the distrust towards the Turkish government. Distrust increased after the AK Partisi, which had been developed out of the earlier Islamist Refah Party, assumed government in 2002.

The situation of Alevis in Turkey is ambivalent. On the one hand Alevis are acclaimed by the Kemalist elite as unequivocal supporters of secularism (Navaro-Yashin 2002, 145f.), but on the other hand Kemalism itself refuses the legal recognition of Alevis as a religious or cultural minority because such recognition is seen as a violation of the principle of a united and homogeneous Turkish nation. The equivocal situation of Alevis in Turkey is well symbolized by the *tekke* of Hacı Bektaş Veli: the place still operates as a museum controlled by the ministry of culture and not as a place of worship for Alevis. Because the *tekke* is a museum, visitors have to pay an entrance fee.[17] Many of the "visitors," especially during the festival, are however better termed as *pilgrims*. They queue up at the entrance in order to worship the *türbe* of the saint. They kiss the doorframe or the threshold to the burial chamber and circumambulate the tomb in a counterclockwise direction, sometimes on their knees. Some spread a scarf for a moment over the tombstone and take it home again as a token of blessing. These activities are tolerated by the museum administration, but other ritual practice is not allowed. Most importantly, it is not permitted to have a *cem* in the *tekke*. The *tekke* has a mosque that was built after it had been handed over to the Naqshbandiyya order when the Bektaşi order was disbanded by Sultan Mahmud II in 1826.[18] Although the *tekke* is officially not a religious place, the Muslim call for prayer (*ezan*) rings out five times a day from the minaret of this mosque—though Alevis in Turkey generally do not practice the *namaz*. Thus, although the *tekke* is not officially recognized as a religious place of Alevis, a certain kind of Alevi ritual practice is unofficially permitted, while the Sunni *ezan* is regularly sounded although the place has no particular significance to Sunnis and the *ezan* is of no importance for Alevis.

A similar equivocalness concerns the naming of Alevi associations. Although many Alevi associations have been established in Turkey especially since the 1990s, they have generally not been allowed to call themselves explicitly *Alevi* associations. The Kemalist ideology of a homogeneous nation is at stake here. Any affirmation of difference is perceived as a danger, as potential or actual separatism. Accordingly, Turkish associational law prohibits the establishment of associations that "endanger … the Turkish republic because they are supporting the separation according to language, race, class, religion or sect" or that "carry out activities on the basis or in the name of region, race, social class, religion or sect."[19] As a consequence, most Alevi associations do

---

[17] Since 2002, however, visitors that enter the *tekke* during the festival do not have to pay the fee.

[18] Ortayli 1999. For an overview over the Naqshbandiyya in Turkey see Mardin 1991 and Yavuz 1999b.

[19] Law no. 2908, sections 2 and 5.

not call themselves "Alevi" and do not refer explicitly to issues concerning Alevism in their statutes. The situation is quite a paradox because everybody, including the administration and the courts, knows that an association that is officially called "Pir Sultan Abdal Association" or "Hacı Bektaş Veli Association" is in fact an Alevi association. These names are not actually a disguise.[20] Yet the question is precisely one of *recognition:* Alevis are allowed to organize themselves and to carry out their activities, but they are not formally recognized. Alevism is tolerated, but this toleration does not translate into a legal right for Alevis.

Some associations went to the courts in order to claim the right to call themselves "Alevi." A first success was achieved by the Semah Vakfı in Istanbul that, after many years of litigation, was finally allowed by the Supreme Court to change its name to "Alevi–Bektaşi Eğitim Vakfı" (Alevi-Bektashi Education Foundation).[21] Yet this did not establish precedence. In January 2001, the registration of a newly established association in Ankara, the "Cem ve Kültür Evleri Yaptırma Derneği" (Association for the Construction of *Cem* and Culture Houses) was refused by the provincial administration because its by-laws give the construction of *cem* houses and the conduction of *cem* rituals as the aims of the association. In the same month also the registration of the Alevi-Bektaşi Kuruluşları Birliği (Union of Alevi-Bektashi Organizations, ABKB) was refused. The ABKB was a new transnational umbrella association that had been established in August 2000 on the occasion of the festival in Hacıbektaş. Most Turkish Alevi associations were involved as membership associations—with the exception of CEM Vakfı—as was the AABF. Turgut Öker was elected as a member of the ABKB's executive board. The provincial administration was not content with refusing the registration of the ABKB. Further, the members of its board were accused of separatist activities and had to appear in court. Because in the person of Turgut Öker also a German citizen was accused, the German embassy sent an observer to the court. In response to the administration's decision and the court procedure, the AABF not only started a protest campaign but also contacted officials in Berlin and Brussels on that matter. The aim was to turn the issue into an international affair that also touched Turkey's endeavor for EU membership. The court procedure was delayed several times, and then the accusation of separatism was dropped. But the ABKB appealed against the refusal to register the as-

---

[20] The most striking example of this masquerade of names is perhaps CEM Vakfı: the first part of its name seems to refer to the Alevi ritual (and would thus be prone to prohibition), but it is officially only an acronym of the full name which is "Cumhuriyetçi Eğitim ve Kültür Merkezi Vakfı" (Republican Education and Culture Center Foundation).

[21] One of the judges of the Supreme Court was Ahmet Necdet Sezer, who subsequently became president of Turkey.

sociation. In June 2002 the court of appeal referred the case back to the district court. In December 2002, the district court finally revoked its earlier decision and allowed the registration of the ABKB. This decision was made with only a very small majority: three of the five judges of the court voted for the admission of the ABKB, while two voted against.[22] Subsequently, the ABKB was legally registered. Yet again, this case did not establish a precedent for other associations.

Engaging the European Union

According to the assessment of the AABF, the court decision in favor of the ABKB was in the first place a result of the heightened international scrutiny that was placed on Turkey in the context of the country's intended accession to the European Union. It was clear that Turkey could hope for admission only if a number of problems in the field of human rights policy, including the issue of minorities, could be overcome. Turkey, like the other candidates for the EU, has to meet the Copenhagen criteria established in June 1993. The AABF was very aware of the significance of the accession process and tried to use it as a lever to work for changes in Turkey, attempting thereby a strategy of indirect political pressure (Østergaard-Nielsen 2003, 70). Together with most Alevis in Germany the association favors the admission of Turkey to the EU but insists at the same time that Turkey has to undertake significant reforms in order to meet the criteria of the EU. According to the AABF, legal recognition of the Alevis in Turkey has to be one of these mandatory reforms.

Already in the mid 1990s the AABF had started to establish relationships with members of the European Parliament and EU authorities. In June 1996, a German member of the European Parliament was invited to deliver a speech at the second Alevi Culture Festival at Cologne. These endeavors were subsequently assisted by Ozan Ceyhun, a German member of European Parliament from 1999 until 2004, first of the Green Party and later of the SPD, who is an Alevi himself and who shared with many Alevi activists a past commitment to Dev Yol. Ceyhun is a regular guest of the AABF in its meetings and events. In May 1999 the AABF held a symposium on Alevis in Europe and Turkey in Strasbourg that was meant to acquaint members of the European Parliament with Alevism. Since that time, delegations visit Brussels or Strasbourg regularly. In June 2002 the AABK was established as the umbrella association of the national Alevi federations in Europe. The founding meeting of the AABK took place in a conference hall of the

---

[22] See *Alevilerin Sesi* 60, December 2002. The legal documents relating to the case are given in Kaleli 2003, 87–102.

European Parliament in Brussels. A vice-president of the European Parliament and other members of parliament participated in the meeting.

A significant result of the efforts of the Alevi associations on the European level is that after 1999 the Alevis have been mentioned in the regular reports of the European Commission on Turkey's progress towards accession. The report of 2000 neatly summarized critical issues in a paragraph on freedom of religion:

> The official approach [of the Turkish government] towards the Alevis seems to remain unchanged. Alevi complaints notably concern compulsory religious instruction in schools and school books, which would not reflect the Alevi identity, as well as the fact that financial support is only available for the building of Sunni mosques and religious foundations (European Commission 2000, 18).

The following report stated that "no improvement in the situation of the non-Sunni Muslims hast taken place," criticized that "Alevi concerns have not been taken up by the Presidency of Religious Affairs," and reiterated the points addressed in the previous year (European Commission 2001, 27). The report of 2002 explicitly referred to the issue of the ABKB and summarized: "There has been no improvement on the status of the Alevis" (European Commission 2002, 38f.). In October 2003, the ABKB prepared a bilingual (German/English) brochure titled "Report about the Alevites in Turkey and in the Countries of the EU" (AABK 2003). This brochure presented Alevism in brief and explained the position of Alevis in Turkey and in the EU. Finally, demands are raised:

> The Alevitendom [sic] is to be legally recognized in Turkey and in Europe as an independent religious community and confession [sic] and to be protected against any kind of discrimination. The EU parliament in its negotiations with the Turkish government about the entrance of Turkey into the European Union should request equal rights for Alevites as a religious community in Turkey. This would include, e.g., the abolishment [sic] of compulsory religious education and Alevite instruction in the schools, no mosques in Alevite areas, equality of mosques and Cem houses. Any kind of religious discrimination is to be placed under punishment (AABK 2003, 11).

This brochure was distributed among members of the European Parliament and personally handed over to the officials who were responsible for the report on Turkey. The report of the commission, published in the same month, states:

> As far as the situation of non-Sunni Moslem communities is concerned, there has been a change as regards the Alevis. The previously banned Union of Alevi and Bektashi Associations [ABKB] was granted legal status in April 2003, which allowed it to pursue its activities. However, concerns persist with regard to representation in the Directorate of Religious Affairs (Diyanet) and related to compulsory religious instruction

in schools which fail to acknowledge the Alevi identity (European Commission 2003, 36).

Also the report of 2004, which was the basis for the decision of the EU to start formal negotiations with Turkey, refers to Alevis and criticizes that they "are not officially recognized as a religious community, they often experience difficulties in opening places of worship, and compulsory religious instruction in schools fails to acknowledge non-Sunni identities" (European Commission 2004, 44).

The Alevi associations have achieved a certain degree of institutional integration also at the EU level. This institutional integration provided new resources that could be utilized in order to exert pressure on Turkey. The AABF practised transnational politics of recognition directed at Turkey via the supranational European institutions. Yet at the same time, the politics of identity of Alevi associations also targets at the EU institutions themselves. On one hand, every meeting with EU officials is celebrated as another token of successful institutional integration. On the other hand, the European level is used just like the national framework in Germany to project Alevi identity. Thus, in all the statements made in Brussels or Strasbourg as well as in the publications targeting EU institutions, Alevism is presented as embodying modernity, tolerance, enlightenment, freedom, and as rejecting fanaticism, fundamentalism, the sharia, etc. A flyer by the AABK that was published in seven languages in May 2004 before the elections of the European Parliament stated "constitutionality, social justice, freedom of speech and religion, a mutual quest for peace, fight against racism, fundamentalism and terrorism" as the main goals of the association. Yet, in the European context even further claims for recognition of Alevis in Europe are voiced. The brochure of the AABK also demanded that

> The Alevitendom [sic] should be taught in the schools in Europe as religious education or in ethics classes. The EU states should provide for opportunities to study Alevite theory at universities in the European Union. The Alevite Union [of] Europe is to be represented in the parliamentary committees dealing with religious affairs and intercultural dialogue (AABK 2003, 11).

Efforts to employ EU institutions strategically for the purposes of achieving legal recognition of Alevis in Turkey are mixed with efforts towards the admission of Turkey to the EU. The Alevi associations actively try to support Turkey's accession—on the condition that the criteria for accession are met—and see themselves in a kind of bridging position. In his speech on the occasion of the inaugural meeting of the AABK, Turgut Öker said: "We Alevis are ready to assume our leading position in the relationships between Turkey and Europe." Shortly before the EU summit at Copenhagen in December 2002, the AABF actively coordinated a newly established political alliance called *Avrupalı Türkler*

Platformu (ATP, Platform of Turks from Europe), which intended to raise public support for Turkey's accession to the EU. The ATP campaign was a new experience for the AABF, because for the first time the Alevi federation became a leading actor in a larger platform of Turkish migrants' associations in Germany. Beside others like the *Türkische Gemeinde in Deutschland* (Turkish Community in Germany), even DİTİB, the foreign branch of the DİB, collaborated. Although there were a number of critical comments within the AABF especially about the collaboration with DİTİB, others interpreted this as a success: "The Sunnis realize now that we are not a marginal group!" said Hasan Öğütcü, who acted also as coordinator of the ATP. The local Alevi associations were mobilized to collect signatures in support of the accession and a press campaign was started. On 8 December 2002, Hasan Öğütcü handed over almost 100,000 signatures supporting the EU accession of Turkey to a representative of the government in Berlin.[23] Shortly after, conflicts with the other members of ATP developed. The AABF was the only association within the ATP that occupied a position of opposition towards the Turkish government. While the other members wanted to restrict the activities more to the national-conservative segment, the AABF attempted to involve also leftist media. When the AABF invited papers like *Özgür Politica* and *Evrensel* to the press conference of ATP, it was heavily attacked. "They wanted to drag us into the right corner," said a member of the board of the AABF. The AABF finally left ATP in November 2003 after the Turkish ambassador in Berlin had called on Milli Görüş to become a member of the platform.

The Claims of the Turkish Nation

The activities of the ATP were regarded with great favor by the Turkish national press and by the Turkish government, because they were perceived as being in line with Turkish interests. *Hürriyet*, the largest selling Turkish language newspaper in Germany and in Turkey, supported the campaign to collect signatures and the Turkish embassy paid for an advertisement of the ATP in the *Süddeutsche Zeitung*, the major liberal daily in Germany. Yet, the activities of the AABF were not always regarded as friendly. On the contrary, in 2000 and 2001 *Hürriyet* haunted the AABF with a campaign in which the association was stylized as a menace for and betrayer of the Turkish nation. This campaign can be interpreted as a response to the Alevi politics of recognition.

The campaign started on the occasion of the general meeting of the AABF in November 2000. I have referred to that meeting already in chapter three because the association was shaken by an opposition

---

[23] *Hürriyet*, 9 December 2002.

movement then. *Hürriyet* supported this opposition by publishing accusations against the committee of the AABF. The opposition was unable to take over the board of the AABF in the elections, but *Hürriyet* continued its accusations.[24] The committee of the AABF reacted by calling the paper an "enemy of Alevis" and by later taking *Hürriyet* to court for defamation and false assertions.[25]

Hürriyet continued to report on the AABF in this context from late November 2000 through mid February 2001. A second phase of campaign started in mid–May 2001 and lasted until the end of June. *Hürriyet*'s coverage was remarkable: the paper did not report on further events but issued quite harsh statements about the general politics of the AABF. For this purpose sometimes whole pages were devoted to the AABF. The German and European edition of *Hürriyet* that is printed in Frankfurt carries a special section of four to six pages on Germany, while the main body of the paper is the same as in Turkey. The texts on the AABF were published in the German section, that is, they were not published in Turkey. Several times the AABF found itself on the first page on *Hürriyet*'s German section. Coverage consisted of a mix of formats. Its backbone were the daily columns of Ertuğ Karakullukçu, the editor of *Hürriyet*'s European edition. Karakullukçu was based in Istanbul, not in Frankfurt. Within the three months of the first period of this campaign, Karakullukçu devoted 45 of his columns to the AABF. Besides, there were reports and, from mid–December 2000 on, letters to the editor, written by Alevis, expressing all kinds of criticism targeting the AABF. The tenor of this coverage was strictly anti-AABF. There was not a single positive news report or comment. After the initial allegations of illicit financial practices,[26] topics were quickly broadened. The subtext of all the issues that were subsequently addressed was that the

---

[24] In contrast with *Hürriyet,* other papers commented quite positively upon the meeting. Milliyet acclaimed that the newly elected committee had been "infused with youth." Also *Özgür Politika,* the Kurdish paper that supported the PKK, reported positively. See the issues of both papers of 27 November 2000.

[25] Litigation took almost three years. First the AABF secured an injunction against *Hürriyet* that prohibited the repetition of charges. Subsequently *Hürriyet* was sentenced to print a revocation of its earlier statements. Beside court proceedings, the AABF also organised a public campaign against *Hürriyet*'s attacks. *Hürriyet* was represented as an "enemy of Alevis" that attempted to divide the Alevi community. Thus, a central element of *Hürriyet*'s rhetoric against the AABF was replicated by the association. The attacks stopped after the owner of *Hürriyet,* Aydın Doğan, visited Germany in summer 2001 and met the German president Johannes Rau. Rau had been concerned about the many instances of campaign journalism in *Hürriyet* and he had put this concern also on the agenda of his meeting with Doğan (*Perşembe,* 19 July 2001).

[26] These allegations were subsequently proven wrong in court proceedings.

AABF embodied attitudes and practices directed against the Turkish state and the Turkish nation.

Available in the country since the early 1970s (Cryns et al. 1991, 22), *Hürriyet* has reached a circulation of more than one hundred thousand daily copies (Heinemann and Kamcili 2000, 121) and clearly dominates the Turkish press market in Germany (cf. Zentrum für Türkeistudien 1997, 7). According to a survey, *Hürriyet* is the preferred daily of thirty-eight percent of the immigrants from Turkey in Germany.[27] The paper has a strict nationalist and Kemalist outlook which is clearly expressed by the composition of its front page: in the masthead there is a Turkish flag waving over a portrait of Atatürk, with the sentence *"Türkiye Türklerindir"* ("Turkey belongs to the Turks"). According to Karacabey (1996, 26), *Hürriyet* intends to influence the public debate among immigrants from Turkey in Germany and to supply them with the topics to be discussed.[28] *Hürriyet's* selective coverage of events in Germany is strictly guided by the Turkish nationalist perspective. Only those events are reported that are regarded as directly concerning the migrants from Turkey. The paper is notorious in Germany for its campaign journalism that frequently targets persons who, by criticizing Turkey, fall out of line with the nationalist perspective. Generally, *Hürriyet* acclaims all activities that in one way or another "defend" a distinct identity of migrants from Turkey in Germany and is very critical of "integration" if it bears the danger of developing new, hybrid—or even German—identities (cf. Cryns et al. 1991, 56).

On 28 November 2000, Ertuğ Karakullukçu wrote his first column about the AABF in the present context. He accused the managing committee of the AABF and especially the chairman Turgut Öker of undemocratic, "Jacobinian behavior," arguing that with the charge of enmity against Alevis every voice of critique was silenced. He established a distinction between the AABF and the "Alevi community" by writing that the "enlightened Alevi community" did not deserve such an "undemocratic" leadership.[29] Thus a rhetorical strategy was launched that referred positively to the "Alevi community" but to the leadership of the AABF on entirely negative terms. Regarding its own role, *Hürriyet*

---

[27] Cf. *die tageszeitung*, 18 June 2001.

[28] According to Cryns the Turkish press in general is characterised by the intention not only to provide information but to "play an active role in the process of the development of society" (1991, 27). Cf. Heinemann and Kamcili 2000, 151; Heper and Demirel 1996.

[29] *"AABF ve eliştiri,"* (AABF and criticism) *Hürriyet*, 28 November 2000. A similar discourse distinguishing between the Alevi community and its leadership that attempts to lead the community astray can also be found in Turkey. Islamists argue that the Alevi leadership creates a rift among Muslims by dividing Alevis and Sunnis (see Massicard 2001).

rejected all charges of campaign journalism and emphasized that its coverage just intended to fulfill the paper's duty to inform the public.[30]

Hürriyet extended its accusations in the following days. In doing so the paper posed as spokesperson of those Alevis who are not represented by the AABF. Charges were not always voiced by *Hürriyet* itself but by (sometimes unidentified) Alevis. On 4 December 2000, anonymous informants were quoted alleging that members of the AABF committee had invested money with two Islamist enterprises. The report implicitly suspected that the money raised by the festival *Bin Yılın Türküsü* had been transferred to these companies. It was stated that these informants wanted to keep their names undisclosed because they feared repression by the AABF.[31] Given that the AABF had always followed a strict anti-Islamist policy, this was a very severe allegation. In his columns, Ertuğ Karakullukçu repeatedly quoted from AABF-critical letters to the editor. Letters from Alevi readers making various charges against the AABF were published. Not a single letter was published that sided with the AABF. Thereby, readers could get the impression that the whole "Alevi community" stood against the AABF.

In the subsequent paragraphs I want to focus on the charges of antinationalism and separatism or *"bölücülük"* that were raised by *Hürriyet* against the AABF. A good choice of such issues was addressed by Karakullukçu in his column on 1 December 2000. First he referred to the debate among Alevis in Germany whether Turkish national symbols like the flag or pictures of Atatürk should be displayed at the events of Alevi associations:

> For instance the dispute about Atatürk, the flag and the soil, which are put on the agenda of the Alevi community again and again. We know that there is no problem of flag and soil in the Alevi community. The flag with moon and star is the flag of all of us and Turkey is our common fatherland. But how should we interpret that during this congress [i.e., the general meeting of the AABF in November 2000] it was discussed as a negative attitude [of *Hürriyet*] that quite justified *Hürriyet* had some time ago directed attention toward the fact that the flag had not been present at an Alevi festival? We know that in the homes of our Alevi compatriots the Turkish flag and Atatürk's images are not missing. We know that there is no problem of flag and soil in the Alevi community. There are some problems that spring from the desire to practice their belief more peacefully. It is the responsibility of all of us to raise these questions.[32]

---

[30] This argument was made repeatedly. For the first time see *"AABF Yönetimi öfkesinde haklı mı?"* (Is the committee of the AABF right in its anger?) *Hürriyet,* 30 November 2000.

[31] *"Fadıl'a kaç para kaptırdınız?"* (How much money did you carry off to Fadıl?), *Hürriyet,* 4 December 2000.

[32] *"Alevi toplumu siyasal ve ekonomik getto olur mu?"* (Will the Alevi community be a political and economic ghetto?), *Hürriyet,* 1 December 2000.

The author then went on to say that Alevi children should not be forced to attend Sunni religious instruction in Turkish schools, but that they should be given their own religious classes. He also demanded that Alevis should be represented in the Directorate of Religious Issues (DİB). Karakullukçu here adopted old demands of Alevis and thereby intended to appear as an advocate of the Alevis. It is significant, however, that these lines were published only in the European section of *Hürriyet*, not in the edition for Turkey. Further, these demands were never repeated in any of the many articles subsequently published in *Hürriyet*. The function of the passage is obvious: it says that Alevis are good Turkish patriots—in contrast to the AABF—even if there are some problems for Alevis in Turkey. We have to keep in mind that this column was written about Alevis living in Germany, irrespective of whether they were Turkish or German citizens. German Alevis were referred to as *yurttaşlarımız*, "our compatriots," and also the synonymous term *vatandaşlarımız* was frequently employed. Thus Alevis were firmly included within the Turkish nation. This was the introduction for the separatist charges against the AABF.

In the next paragraph Karakullukçu referred to the term "Kurdistan," taking the Kurdish-Alevi federation and its (temporal) cooperation with the AABF in the context of demands for Alevi religious classes as point of departure: "What does 'Federation of Alevis from Kurdistan' mean? Is there a Kurdistan in Turkey? Does the committee of the AABF regard such an development as legal?"[33] The AABF was asked to answer these questions. In the following passage, Karakullukçu directly addressed the question of Alevi identity: "They behave as if there were a separate Alevism within the Turkish nation.[34] In this regard they are determined to insist on identity. They drive the concept 'Alevi identity' to extremes and speak from an endeavor to create a separate ethnic community."[35]

Charges of striving for an Alevi community that threatens the unity of the Turkish nation were specified in a subsequent section devoted to the *Mozaik* cooperative society, which had been established by Alevis initially under the aegis of the AABF. The chairman of Mozaik is quoted as having said: "We have started this business in order that Alevis become aware of their particular economic potential." Karakullukçu continued asking:

---

[33] Ibid. This passage refers implicitly to the speech held at the congress by Necati Şahin, at that time general secretary of the AABF, in which he asserted that he himself was of Kurdish descent and he had no problem with the term Kurdistan.

[34] In translation this passage loses much of its sharpness: the two terms employed are *Türklük* and *Alevilik*, that is, they appear as parallels—a parallel which in the eyes of Karakullukçu is absurd.

[35] *Hürriyet*, ibid.

In which manner are we to understand the concept of the "Alevi community's own economic potential"? Is this a potential outside of the Turkish community? Does not such an orientation give rise to colonization? And has the AABF—which we thought to be a religious institution or a social organization—turned into an economic organization? (...) Is it right to turn the Alevi community into an economic ghetto by politicizing it? We are always very much in need of unity. Are not our republic, Atatürk, and the flag the basic symbols of this unity? To stand up for these is for all of us of greater worth than anything else. We think that our Alevi compatriots sincerely share this view.[36]

A few days later, Karakullukçu turned toward a new topic, the Armenian genocide. The denial of the genocide is a central element in Turkish national discourse. According to the official Turkish version, Armenians were fought against in Anatolia between 1915 and 1921 because there was war, but there were no specific genocidal measures of the authorities to extinguish the Armenian presence in Anatolia. From the nationalist Turkish perspective, any recognition of the genocide is as serious an attack against the Turkish nation as is the recognition of Kurdistan. Here, the activities of another diaspora had their effects. The genocide became a pressing topic in *Hürriyet*'s pages in late 2000 because a resolution of the French Parliament recognizing the genocide was imminent. It was finally adopted on 18 January 2001.

On 8 December 2000, Karakullukçu wrote that an Alevi reader had referred him to the website of the AABF and that this website contained a text which was a blunt recognition of the genocide. The text, titled "Armenian massacre and Alevis" was quoted in full length. In this text, the Young Turks were held responsible for the genocide but Alevis were generally exempted from active participation in the atrocities against Armenians. The author of the text posed as Alevi and wrote in the final passage: "Because we Alevis have lived in this part of Armenia we know very well who were the real owners of this soil. The names of all our villages and towns are still Armenian names and if the majority of the names have officially been changed, they are still used by the people."[37] These were unacceptable sentences for any Turkish nationalist, especially because the area in question was referred to as a part of Armenia. The problem, however, was that this text was *not* published by the AABF on its website. It was included on a website by an undisclosed author or organization dealing with the Armenian question. Originally,

---

[36] Ibid. Later on, *Özgür Politika* (7 December 2000) commented on this passage, saying that all other religious organizations of Turkish immigrants have established their own businesses without being criticised by *Hürriyet*.

[37] *"Ermeni katliami ve Aleviler"* (Armenian massacre and Alevis); <http://www.geocities.com/ eurofrat/aleviler.html> (6/18/01). The text is quoted in *"AABF ve soykırımı"* (AABF and genocide), *Hürriyet*, 8 December 2000.

the site carried a link to the website of the AABF, and because of this link *Hürriyet* identified the text as authored by the AABF.

Karakullukçu took it as starting point for a new attack. After quoting the text in his column, he commented: "This is enmity against Turkey in an open and terrible form. Separatism. Turks and Alevis! Kurdistan! Are the Alevis a separate nation? Or our compatriots of Kurdish descent? There are some who do want this."[38] In January 2001, *Hürriyet* published in two parts an article written by a teacher who identified himself as Alevi, in which the assertions of the Internet text were refuted.[39] This article was written as an open letter to the managing committee of the AABF. The author used quite drastic language and wrote towards the end of the first part, referring to the passage quoted above: "If you call these cities 'Armenian cities' you can't even be entrusted with an ass, let alone with an Alevi federation. Because your brains have been washed and your consciousness blackened you are not different from a horde of cannibals."[40]

Only a very small selection of the attacks against the AABF can be quoted here. The organization was continually represented as collaborating with the enemies of Turkey, be they Armenians or advocates of Kurdistan. *Hürriyet* was very careful not to simply accuse "the Alevis" but to direct its charges specifically against the managing committee of the AABF. In contrast with them the "Alevi community" was always characterized as "enlightened," "tolerant," and as highly esteemed by *Hürriyet*. Thus *Hürriyet* made an effort to show that the committee and especially the chairman were not the true representatives of the Alevi community and that they tried to move the Alevi community into a wrong direction, alienating Alevis from Turkey's national values. The chairman Öker was repeatedly called "atheist," and he was said not to be a real Alevi but a *düşkün* (outcast).[41] This was made explicit in a column by Ertuğ Karakullukçu under the title: "Mr. Öker, you can't do this 'in the name of all Alevis!'":

> The chairman of the AABF ... and some of his friends may think that there is a region called Kurdistan in Turkey. They can separate Turks and Kurds from one another. They can search for an identity of Alevis outside of Turkish identity. They can claim that genocide was committed in

---

[38] "*AABF ve soykırımı*," *Hürriyet*, 8 December 2000.

[39] "*AABF'nın internet sayfasındaki soykırımı yazısına açık cevaptır*" (Open reply to the writing about the genocide on the internet site of the AABF), *Hürriyet*, 2 and 3 January 2001.

[40] *Hürriyet*, 2 January 2001.

[41] Eg. "*Söz, Alevi Vatandaşların*" (Word of Alevi compatriots), *Hürriyet*, 23 December 2000. To be declared *düşkün* was the most severe punishment within the Alevi legal system: in *cem* persons who have committed severe faults against the community could be expelled.

Turkey, that Armenians, Kurds, and Turks have been slaughtered cold–bloodedly (…) But they cannot do that in the name of the whole Alevi community! If they do that they cannot pose as if they were supported by the whole Alevi community! They cannot represent the Alevi community as supporters of the assertions of Kurdishness, Kurdistan, and the genocide, as opponents of Turkey! (…) The Alevi community cannot be represented by such an aggressive and libelous style. Eh, enlightened and bright Alevi compatriot, take up your conscience and tell us: aren't we right?[42]

Hürriyet took all efforts to depict the AABF as an "enemy" of the Turkish nation. *Hürriyet* assumes a strict nationalist perspective that presupposes a homogenous Turkish nation. In this perspective, neither minorities (Kurds, Alevis) nor emigration make a difference for the nation. All Turks are in the first place Turks, whether they are living in Turkey or somewhere abroad. The basic identity and the unity of the nation are not threatened by emigration as long as the emigrants retain their being Turkish as central point of reference: "Turkey wants its citizens abroad not to assimilate into their receiving countries, but to settle *as Turks*. Accordingly, a range of measures has been employed in order to strengthen the economic, political, and cultural ties between the Turkish citizen abroad and the homeland" (Østergaard-Nielsen 2003, 107, cf. Atilgan 2002, 136ff). Beside media like *Hürriyet* Turkish state institutions are also committed to preserve that orientation among emigrants. Turkey is engaged in what Bauböck (2003) calls "extra-territorial nation-building." The care of the state for the emigrants of the nation is even prescribed by the Turkish constitution: "The State shall take the necessary measures to ensure family unity, the education of the children, the cultural needs, and the social security of Turkish nationals abroad, and shall take the necessary measures to safeguard their ties with the motherland and help them on their return home" (Constitution of the Republic of Turkey, Section 62, quoted after Østergaard-Nielsen 203, 108). A report of the Directorate of Religious Affairs says, referring to its services for Turkish emigrants: "The number of our directorate's employees working in these [foreign] countries is growing every day (…) They are offering religious, social, and cultural services to our citizens and their children. In this way, our people living in these countries, preserving their true identities and culture, are assisted not to assimilate" (quoted in Shankland 1999, 31).

The continuing affiliation of migrants with the Turkish nation was also a premise of the Turkish language classes in Germany that were sponsored by the Turkish state. Turkish language was considered not only as an instrument of communication but also as a symbol of na-

---

[42] *"Bay Öker, bunları 'Bütün Aleviler adına' yapamazsınız!" Hürriyet,* 15 December 2000.

244 ◆ Struggling for Recognition

tional affiliation. Many Turkish teachers started classes with the Turkish national anthem or with Atatürk's phrase *"Ne mutlu Türküm diyene"* ("How happy is he who says I am a Turk").

The AABF did not play this nationalist game. The focus of its activities was Alevi, not Turkish identity. In Germany, Alevis were encouraged to take German citizenship. Although naturalization was not equated with cutting all ties with Turkey or ceasing to identify as Turk— after all, the AABF considered dual citizenship as the ideal option—the association certainly did not define Alevis as Turks in the first place. Instead, Alevism is considered a religious (or cultural) identity that is not necessarily bound to a particular national identity. Using my terminology on identity, I can say that the AABF endorses to a certain extent the intersecting plurality of identities. National affiliation is not considered as a form of membership that governs all other identifications. The idea of a homogeneous, unified, and clearly demarcated nation is thereby subverted. The Turkish nationalist view, however, does not allow for an intersecting plurality of identities: all other identities have to be subordinated to Turkish national identity. Everything that questions this order of precedence of identities is *bölücülük*, separatism—in Turkey the gravest political offence of all. As a consequence of migration, *bölücülük* threatens the Turkish state and nation not only from within—as in the assertion of Kurdish identity—but also from the outside, when migrants subvert the Turkish nation by emphasizing other modes of affiliation. In the view of *Hürriyet*, the AABF became an agent of separatism by encouraging Alevis to "integrate" in Germany, and by its transnational politics of recognition that sides with other states or with the EU to make claims in Turkey, against the Turkish state and government. *Hürriyet* depicted the AABF as subservient to the German government:

> They [the committee of the AABF] unite with the [German] government as if they had the whole Alevi potential behind them and create the impression as if this or that advantage could thereby be secured. But is it correct to make the Alevi community, without consulting it, the material of political and economic calculations in accordance with the wishes of Berlin, even at the cost of opposing Turkey?[43]

A reader, identified as Alevi, wrote that political circles in Germany and the German press run a campaign against Turkish values and invent a

> German Islam that fits the West. New identities like a German Alevism are invented. (...) They look for people who adopt a separatism promoted by the West. (...) The Anatolian mosaic shall be split up by promoting

---

[43] *"Alevi toplumuna yakışmayan bildiri"* (Communication not befitting the Alevi community), *Hürriyet*, 5 December 2000.

organizations on the basis of all kinds of ethnic, religious and cultural differences. The organizations that are created on this basis are used by the West to impede the path of development that was chosen by the nation-state of our native country and to divide it. In order to know the aim of this it is sufficient to look at the developments in the surroundings of our country: the plan to divide Yugoslavia stands before our eyes.[44]

He went on to accuse the AABF of taking money from the German state for its citizenship project in order to break the Alevis away from "their country" (i.e. Turkey) and organize a European identity for them. These accusations of alienating the Alevi community from the Turkish nation and making it an instrument of German or European interests against Turkey heightened the charges of endorsing separatism by collaborating with Kurdish or Armenian agents. Thus, the AABF is charged with supporting separatism in Turkey and assimilation in Germany. On the basis of the Turkish national ideology, both accusations are two sides of the same coin. Assimilation means that the central values of *mukluk* are given up. Thereby parts of the Turkish nation are lost. *Hürriyet* was not alone in its accusations. In Summer 2001 Abdulkadir Sezgin, a former high official of the Directorate of Religious Affairs, accused the transnational Alevi umbrella association ABKB, of which the AABF was a member, with planning to establish a separate state for Alevis.[45] He called the Alevis the "second most serious separatist menace after the PKK."[46]

The denial of difference and the affirmation of homogeneity in Turkish national discourse became also evident in an exchange between the AABF and the Turkish prime minister Tayyip Erdoğan during his visit in Berlin in September 2003. Part of the prime minister's program was a meeting with representatives of Turkish migrants' associations to which also the AABF had been invited. Hasan Öğütcü took the opportunity to claim equal rights for Alevis in Turkey. He referred to article ten of the Turkish constitution, which guarantees equality of religions, and demanded equal legal status for *cem* houses and mosques. The prime minister replied:

> You are referring to intra-Turkish questions. Whichever Alevi I meet says, we are Muslims. The prayer place of Muslims is the mosque. Alevism is not a religion [*din*]. Therefore one cannot compare [Islam and Alevism]. If we made this distinction, why should we divide Turkey. One is a house of prayer; the other is a culture house. *Cem* houses cannot receive the same

---

[44] *"AABF etrafında yürütülen tartışma ve bazı gerçekler"* (Debate about the AABF and some truths), *Hürriyet*, 16 January 2001.

[45] *Cumhuriyet*, 20. August 2001.

[46] *Milliyet*, 21 August 2001.

[financial] assistance that the mosques receive. If there is somebody who wants to support *cem* houses this cannot be hindered. Yet you are also a Muslim, you should go to the mosque.[47]

This statement was a clear rejection of claims for recognition and equality of Alevis in Turkey. According to the prime minister, Alevism cannot be treated on equal terms with Islam because Alevism is not a religion. Interestingly, Erdoğan's argument that Alevism is culture and not religion neatly replicates the position of many leftist Alevis. Yet, voiced by the prime minister, this designation of Alevism is not a neutral categorization but a denial of recognition. In this context, even atheists demanded the recognition of Alevism as religion. Alevis in Turkey and in Germany protested that Erdoğan "negated" Alevism.[48] Erdoğan also framed the affirmation of Alevism as dividing Turkey. The Turkish nation is defined by the joint affiliation with a religion, that is, Islam. The insistence on Alevis as a separate religion would endanger the unity of the nation.

We see that various agents of Turkish national discourse in the media and politics try to firmly include the Alevis within an undivided, homogeneous Turkish nation, and that these agents regard the assertion of a distinct Alevi identity and the idea that migrants are different from those Turks who stayed at home as a threat to the nation. In this perspective, the recognition of Alevism puts the Turkish nation into question. Accordingly, recognition is denied.

Yet, the relation with the Turkish nation is also disputed among Alevis themselves. While the AABF tried to leave a blank space in which national identity was not from the outset predicated upon Alevis, others, especially among first-generation migrant workers, demanded a more specific stance. In the first decade of the Alevi movement there were frequent disputes about the display of Turkish national symbols: the Turkish national flag with white crescent and star (*ay yıldız*) on red ground, and portraits of Atatürk. Both symbols are virtually omnipresent in Turkey, in official buildings as well as in private homes and in public space. These symbols are even frequently inscribed into the landscape: they are painted on rocks or displayed with colored stones that are arranged on hillsides. These symbols are almost sacralized and any disrespect in regard to them is considered a severe crime. When in 1996 a Turkish flag was thrown on the ground at a convention of a Kurdish party, the public was called for a "flag campaign" and almost the whole country was festooned with Turkish flags as a response to this

[47] Quoted after the website <www.aleviyol.com/cemevikultur.html> (4/9/2003). See also *Hürriyet* and *Milliyet*, 4 September 2003.
[48] Cf. press statement of the AABK, 6 September 2003. As a consequence, the AABF boycotted a similar meeting with Erdoğan during his next visit to Germany in April 2004.

"crime." The perpetrator of the incident was sentenced to twenty-two years in jail (Houston 2001, 7f.). Images or statues of Mustafa Kemal Atatürk, the epitomized "father of the nation," play the same role as the flag. Atatürk is of special importance for many Alevis because he is regarded also as the creator of Turkish secularism and thus as the one who has given Alevis civic rights.[49] Both symbols have been brought to Germany by migrant workers. They adorn the places of all non-leftist Turkish migrant associations. Many Alevi migrants considered Atatürk and the flag as natural symbols of their national belonging. They were displayed by the Yurtseverler Birliği as well as by the religiously oriented Hacı Bektaş Veli associations of the late 1980s. The flag and images of Atatürk even adorned the walls of the places where *cem* was held. Yet in leftist associations like Dev Yol, the national symbols were rejected as symbols of the state against which the leftists fought. As a consequence, many of the activists of the new Alevi movement who came from the leftist movement objected to displaying the flag and Atatürk. Besides the leftists also many Kurdish Alevis rejected the Turkish national symbols.

Due to the strong position of leftists and/or Kurds, many local associations never used the symbols although they were constantly haunted by this debate. The Alevi association in Hamburg-Harburg tried a special solution of the conflict: the German flag was displayed alongside the Turkish flag and Atatürk. The chairman of the association explained that for many members the flag was not a nationalist symbol, but rather a reminiscence of "home." In order to underline the non-nationalist character of the Turkish flag in this context, the German flag was added. Yet for many Alevis—especially of strong Kemalist association—to insist on the flag is also to insist on the Turkish national affiliation of Alevis. Further, the insistence on the flag is an implicit rejection of leftist ideology. Sometimes, Kemalist Alevis criticize the AABF and its association as not being Alevi but simply *political* associations. Such critics regard the AABF as a continuation of leftist politics under a new disguise. Interestingly, from this perspective the flag and Atatürk are not regarded as *political* symbols. Politics is identified exclusively as opposition towards Turkish state and government. The opponents of the flag frequently argue, quoting Hacı Bektaş Veli as having said "Regard all nations as equal," that Alevis should not make a distinction between different nations and privilege one by displaying its flag. There is an inversion of arguments in the debate about the flag and Atatürk: Kemalists, who often insist that Alevism is a religion, privilege the political over the religious while the former leftists, framing Alevism more frequently as a secular culture than not, take to religious arguments.

---

[49] In some strands of Alevi discourse, Atatürk is even literally sanctified and treated as an avatar of the Imam Ali and Hacı Bektaş Veli (Dreßler 1999).

In 1996, *Hürriyet* attacked the AABF heavily for not displaying the flag and Atatürk at a large Alevi festival in Cologne. Since then, the issue was taken up repeatedly by the paper, which time and again quoted Alevis who criticized the practice of the AABF. After many internal debates, the umbrella association finally fixed its position in its program:

> The Turkish flag is a symbol that represents Turkey and it is the official flag of Anatolian Alevis and other religious groups. As Turkish citizens we respect the flag. In the past the flag, which is a national symbol, had no place in *cem* ceremonies and in communal places of prayer. It should also not be placed there today. Atatürk is the leader of the Turkish republic. Atatürk is not a religious leader. Simply because of the struggle against sharia that took place in Atatürk's time and because of the gains of the Turkish Republic we cannot disregard his [i.e., Atatürk's] faults and mistakes (AABF 1998, 12).

The events and discourses discussed in this section can be read as the nation's claims of precedence over the transnational. Alevi transnational commitments take place in a space that is more trans*national* than *trans*national. The political space in which the Alevis' transnational politics of recognition operates is strictly structured into nationalized spaces. The transnational commitment is perceived as an encroachment into the jealously guarded space of the nation-state. Several authors have argued recently that globalization has resulted in the weakening of the nation-state because transnational migrants, associations, movements, corporations, etc. create their own spaces that transcend the narrow confines of the state. Arjun Appadurai (1996, 21f) diagnoses the "terminal crisis" of the nation-state and sees "diasporic public spheres" as the "crucibles of a postnational political order." Similarly, Yasemin Soysal (2000, 3) perceives the "national order of things" as being undermined by new forms of belonging, citizenship, and claims-making. On one hand, the Alevi case confirms this subversion of the nation-state and its political order. Alevis make their claims across national borders and strategically use the supranational body of the EU for their ends. Further, by invoking a (religious) community of Alevis that is not divided by national boundaries, they endorse a mode of belonging that is more nonnational than trans*national* and that relegates the national to a level of lesser significance. On the other hand, however, the Alevi case also exemplifies that the nation-state does not simply surrender to these nonnational forms of belonging. Instead, the nation-state continues to insist on its own primacy. This is quite obvious in the case of Turkey, but, less visible, it also applies in the German context with its discursive insistence on and essentialization of the difference of migrants. Also those Alevi migrants who insist on the significance of Turkish national symbols support the claims of the nation. Rather than witnessing the "terminal crisis" of the nation-state, we experience a continuing struggle between national and non-national forms of belonging. This struggle is not really new. Historically, religious formations that span considerable parts of the world predate the nation-state (Rudolph 1997). Religions, with the large-scale formations of the Muslim *umma* and the Catholic ("universal") church as the perhaps most obvious examples, have long offered modes of affiliation that transcended the narrow confines of the nation-state and that in many instances denied the claims of the national.

Opposition Diaspora and the Nation-state

In chapter five we have seen that Alevis give much importance to a historical perspective that represents Alevis as victims of violence and power. Alevi identity as it is projected from this perspective can be termed a "victim identity." This victim identity is an important source of transnational solidarity among Alevis. It seems almost self-suggesting to speak of the Alevi diaspora as a "victim diaspora." The category of a victim diaspora figures quite prominently in comparative perspectives on diaspora because it is exemplified by the prototypical cases of Jews and Armenians (Cohen 1997). Yet the Alevis do not fit into the category because the events that made Jews or Armenians victims were the events that caused the dispersal and produced the diaspora. In the case of Alevis, however, victimizing events were not the most important reasons for migration.

In the current chapter I have shown that the Alevi diaspora is perceived as subverting the nation-state. Yet Alevis do not subvert the "receiving" nation-state as would be suggested by much diaspora literature, but rather the "sending" nation-state although they do not entertain an alternative, competing, or separatist national project there, as is the case with many victim diasporas. The Alevi example fits into none of the patterns that are used to explicate the subversiveness of diasporas. The Alevi case receives its specific dynamics from two facts: first, the assertion and the claims for recognition of a distinctive Alevi identity subvert the idea of a homogeneous "sending" nation (although the inclusion of Alevis within the Turkish nation is not necessarily revoked thereby), and second, as a consequence of denied claims for recognition, the organized Alevi diaspora is in many respects positioned almost unanimously in opposition to the sending state and its policies.[50] Instead of identifying strongly with the nation-state of origin and thereby subverting the claims of the receiving nation-state (as is fre-

---

[50] To be more precise: what is opposed unanimously is the actual state and its policies, not the ideal state that is attributed to the ideas of Atatürk and that is held in high esteem by many (Kemalist) Alevis.

quently suspected by German discourse on migrants), the Alevis have looked for allies in diaspora for the purpose of articulating their claims *against* the nation-state of origin. The Alevi politics of institutional integration and the insistence on being much less different from Germans than from Sunni Turks cannot be understood without this dynamics of opposition against the Turkish state. By their commitment of opposition the Alevis remain firmly bound to the nation-state of origin. I therefore call the Alevi diaspora an *opposition diaspora* and suggest to add this notion to the row of "composite diasporas" that is suggested by Robin Cohen (1997).[51]

It is significant to understand that the opposition of Alevis is not so much directed towards a specific nation or state, but rather towards a particular conceptualization of the nation as a totalizing entity that claims exclusive and unequivocal loyalty and oppresses any other mode of identification. The subversiveness of Alevis as "opposition diaspora" is very different from the subversiveness of exile politics as practised for instance by the Kurdish PKK. The PKK's politics targets the territory of the Turkish nation-state and demands its partition or a considerable reorganization because it promotes the idea of *another* nation living within that territory. Hence, the ideas of nation, nation-state, and national territory are affirmed rather than subverted by the PKK's struggle. These ideas continue to provide the shared frame of reference for the conflicting perspectives. The conflict arises because the idea of the nation-state demands exclusivity. A territory, a population can belong to *one* nation and state only. Matters are very different for most Alevis. In the context of Alevi discourse, the concept of the nation and the nation-state are regarded as being of rather secondary importance. Instead of affirming the exclusiveness of the nation-state, the AABF encourages Alevis in Germany to develop multiple identifications. Alevis are not represented as belonging to the Turkish nation exclusively. The "conceptual absolutism" (Herzfeld 1986, 90) that governs the logic of the nation-state is thereby threatened. Michael Kearney (1991, 59) writes that "members of transnational communities … escape the power of the nation-state to inform their sense of collective identity." In some regard this is true in the Alevi case because *not* honoring Turkey's national symbols (Atatürk, the flag) is possible only outside of the immediate power realm of the Turkish nation-state.[52] Yet, many states and nations make efforts to keep transnational connections with their diasporas "alive." In the case of Turkey and the Alevis this effort has been undertaken most prominently by *Hürriyet*. The paper endeavored to define such connections as *national* affiliation. *Hür-*

---

[51] Cohen (1997) distinguishes between victim diasporas, labor diasporas, imperial diasporas, trade diasporas, and cultural diasporas.

[52] Alevi associations in Turkey invariably display all these symbols.

riyet here took the role of the "interpreter" for the dissemination of the national narrative (Bhabha 1990). In accordance with Benedict Anderson's (1983) ideas about the significance of media for the national imagination, the press is an important site for and instrument of the struggle of the hegemony of the nation. The agents of national hegemony take all efforts that the migrants *do not escape* their power of defining belonging and identification. *Hürriyet* forcefully attempted to extend the Turkish hegemony of national unity and homogeneity beyond territorial boundaries. It claimed every individual Alevi and the "Alevi community" as a whole for the Turkish nation and its state. It thereby took efforts to work against the "blurring ... of the binary cultural, social and epistemological distinctions of the modern period" (Kearney 1991, 55) that are implied by the national order of things. Interestingly, the Turkish nation is represented by *Hürriyet* as a trans-state nation that is not limited by the territorial boundaries of Turkey, but reaches beyond the frontiers of the state. Alevis (like other people of Turkish origin) living abroad are represented as no less Turkish than those who live within the boundaries of the Turkish state. *Hürriyet* represents the AABF as a most dangerous threat because it does not affirm the exclusiveness of national identification. In a limited sense, the perspective of the AABF could even be called "postnational" because it affirms multiple identifications and possibility of changing national affiliation.

Still, Turkey certainly continues to be an important focus of reference for Alevis in Germany and also for the AABF. On the one hand there is the opposition perspective, a critical and largely negative reference to the Turkish state because of its identification with Sunni Islam and with politics of nonrecognition towards Alevis. But on the other hand there is also much positive identification with Turkey as a *home country*, as the country where oneself or one's parents came from, where a great number of one's relatives live, and where the holy places of Alevism are situated. Here identification is not with the Turkish nation or its state, but with the "country," with particular regions, with images of landscape and memories of sentiment. It is this country and its cities or villages to which the dead bodies of most Alevis from the diaspora are still carried for burial. This positive identification with "Turkey as country" does necessarily engender a positive identification with "Turkey as nation-state" (at least among non-Kemalist Alevis), but rather increases the dissociation from this state because the state and its Sunni majority are held responsible for adverse living conditions of Alevis in that country.

Hence, by maintaining such identifications with Turkey, Alevis in Germany do not simply abide by the national order of things. Instead they exemplify the multivalence of concepts like nation, nation-state, and country that Clifford Geertz (2000, 231f.) has referred to. These terms are most frequently treated as synonyms (Malkki 1997), also in diaspora theory. *Hürriyet* too employed this "synonymization" of different terms that do not have quite the same meaning. According to Delaney (1995), Atatürk promulgated the idea of a Turkish nation by rhetorically establishing an intimate relation between "father *state*" and "mother*land*." By conflating these different meanings the idea of the nation receives its affective quality, which makes it almost impossible to negate or simply to disregard the nation. I suggest therefore that the different meanings attached to a particular nation should be taken apart. Examples like the Alevis show that this is a requirement of analytic precision, because for them the meanings of nation as imagined community, of the nation-state as a system of political institutions and policies, and of the country as prepolitical landscape of reference are indeed not congruous.

In the Alevi case, diaspora is indeed the "other of the nation-state." The Alevi diaspora negates the idea of homogeneity, which is the fundamental element of imagination that creates national communities. Instead, the Alevi diasporic associations endorse multiple identifications. Alevi politics of recognition is not limited to drawing ethnic or religious boundaries and constructing identities, but has entailed complex negotiations and strategies for participation in diverse political and public spheres across national boundaries. Diasporic subversion may not just replace one national imagination by another, but it may challenge the nation in a much more fundamental way by opening up spaces of identification that are precluded by the national imagination.

# Conclusion

A Social Movement towards Identity and Recognition

This work started from the idea that questions of identity are inextricably entangled with questions of politics, and that the concept of identity entails a dialogic relationship because identity calls for recognition. We have seen that the question of identity and recognition stands at the heart of the Alevi movement. The Alevi movement radically transformed Alevism by turning it into a public issue for which public recognition is demanded. Yet the claim for recognition is also voiced among Alevis themselves, demanding the recognition of Alevism by Alevis in specific manners, as, for instance, Islam or non-Islam, as religion or culture. Hence, self-recognition remains an important issue, which is also connected with questions of power because particular versions of Alevism are proposed by specific actors or organizations that claim to represent Alevis and Alevism.

Alevi conceptualizations of Alevi identity are mostly essentialist. Alevi identity is normally represented as being endowed with great historical depth, with almost timeless institutions like *cem* and the *dedes*, and with intrinsic values. Although many of its elements are hotly debated and contested, this contestation is only rarely included in self-representations of Alevi identity but rather silenced and glossed over, although, for an outsider, the related disputes are perhaps among the most outstanding features of Alevism. An antiessentialist analysis of Alevi identity can easily show that this identity has to be grasped in terms of difference, multiplicity, and intersectionality: Alevi identity is in the first place produced by the Alevi-Sunni master difference, but it is also shot through with other intersecting identities/differences like regional and national belonging, ethnic identity, political orientation, gender, identification as foreigner or Turk, etc. Claims for unity are contradicted by an organizational structure that in many cases reflects competition for power and positions, and that is also an embodiment of differing conceptualizations of Alevi identity. Yet in their efforts towards recognition Alevis have to represent themselves in a unified way, postulating the Alevi community as a collective subject that is, for instance, a religious community that is fundamentally different from (other) Muslims and that therefore is entitled to its own religious classes at school. Unified identity is the required condition for collective agency and for making legitimate claims.

Yet, identity and recognition are not only basic for the Alevi movement because they are the "subject matter" of this movement and define its aims. More fundamentally, my argument is that the discourse on identity, its institutionalization in multicultural centers in Hamburg, and the identity-related conflicts in Germany and Turkey provided the central framework that enabled the rise of the Alevi movement. To put it more precisely, the discourse on identity and the rise of identity politics as a central issue in society were the necessary conditions for the Alevi movement, because the very terms and claims of the movement could not have been conceived and articulated without this discourse. The activists of the Alevi movement, with their earlier commitment to class-based socialist politics and their subsequent shift to identity politics, provide a striking example for the paradigmatic shift from the politics of redistribution to the politics of recognition.

The theory of social movements conceives of social movements as contentious social action that emerges in and is enabled by a specific context of political opportunities and constraints, which together result in a specific political opportunity structure (Tarrow 1996b, 1998). The political opportunity approach focuses mainly on *structural* aspects of the context in which movements rise, like available resources, means for communication, social networks, political alliances, institutions, or instruments of repression. A "cost–benefit calculation" (Melucci 1996, 200) of the political opportunity structure by collective actors determines whether a movement promises possible success. For example, in his study of the Hamas movement in Palestine, Robinson (2004) identifies the search of the Israeli government for an alternative to the PLO, the rise of Islamist power especially in Iran, the Intifada, and the establishment of the Palestinian authority after the Oslo accords as the decisive changes in political opportunity structure that enabled the rise of Hamas. Yet I think that the focus on structural conditions is too narrow. Some social movements like the antislavery movement were started although their chances for success, according to a realistic cost-benefit calculation at the time of their rising, were utterly bleak (Keck and Sikkink 2000). What triggered the Alevi movement was in the first place not a shift in social or political structures, but a complex of ideas about identity and recognition that was spread in an almost contagious discourse. This complex of ideas enabled the conception of a specific Alevi identity that was employed as a frame by the Alevi movement. My concern is not to play another round of the old chicken-or-egg game and to insist on the primacy of ideas that are disseminated in discourse as against social structure. Rather, I would like to emphasize that discourses and ideas play a central role in the concert of political opportunities and that they provide the means that enable the articulation of an issue that is contended by a movement.

I employed the concept of social movement as a frame for my study in order to escape reifying notions of community and to enable a more precise analysis of the agent(s) of the Alevi politics of identity. The agent, the collective subject of Alevi claims for recognition is not the Alevi community. It is instead the network of Alevi associations, including, in Germany, most importantly the AABF, which, in their discourses and practices, claim to represent this community and thereby evoke and create it. These Alevi associations were created as new collective agents in the course of the development of the Alevi movement. Individual Alevis participate in the movement by taking up activities that are conceived by and through the associations. The Alevi associations embody the movement also in their often competitive and conflicting relationships, which in part point towards competing conceptions of Alevi identity.

To conceptualize Alevi politics of recognition as the politics of a social movement avoids the trap of a "communitarianism" that regards (and essentializes) the community as a pregiven entity of which every Alevi is "naturally" and in equal manner a member. Speaking of a movement enables us to distinguish different modes and degrees of commitment or noncommitment of individual actors, ranging from almost professional, full-time involvement to selective participation in particular activities, benign disinterest or even strict avoidance and opposition. To speak of a social movement that creates the Alevi community underlines the significance of mobilization. I do not want to say that the Alevi community is "only" a discursive construction of the movement (or that Alevi identity is "only" an imagination). The movement aims at substantiating its construction by mobilizing individuals who identify themselves as Alevis. Yet, we have become aware of a specific difficulty of identity-based movements: Melucci (1989) has emphasized the importance of a shared *collective identity* in a social movement that serves to orient individual action and helps to obtain solidarity within the movement. However, the conceptualization of identity has shown that identity is never without problems. In the Alevi movement, identity is a precarious frame. Identity may serve as a vehicle of solidarity in a social movement if particular conceptualizations of this identity are not too much taken into focus. If identity is not only a vehicle but also the very purpose of a movement, differences that intersect with this particular identity become obvious and may turn this identity into an object of contention instead of an instrument for solidarity. This has happened in the Alevi movement, where invocations of Alevi identity are meant to mobilize Alevis and where at the same time particular conceptions of Alevi identity have become disputed from a number of perspectives. Rather than simply enabling solidarity and unity within a movement, reference to identity may well breed contention and fission.

The Alevi movement has developed a number of practices that are employed for mobilizing people and committing them to the issue of Alevi identity and the struggle for recognition. The organization of *saz* courses can be considered the most basic form of mobilization because it enables the commitment of (especially young) Alevis to a focal symbol and medium of Alevism, that is, music and poetry. Yet diverse forms of conventions, cultural festivals, or demonstrations are equally invitations and appeals to join in the activities of the associations, to support their claims, and, perhaps, become their members. In large communal events like *Bin Yılın Türküsü*, the community becomes eventually tangible for those who participate. A central element of mobilization is the commemoration of the Sivas massacre. The commemoration of violence that members of the community have suffered at the hands of others allows the drawing of a clear-cut boundary around the community. The violence distinguished victims from perpetrators. Sivas is conceptualized as the exemplary instantiation of the Alevi-Sunni master difference. We have seen that the movement with its commemorative practices turns individual memory into communal memory, which creates the specific significance of the event. Discourses and ritualized practices of commemoration firmly inscribe the victims of Sivas into the texture of the discursive construction of community. They identify the victims with the community and conversely enable the identification of every individual Alevi with the victims: "It could have happened to all of us." Memory creates community.

The commemorative practices also point to the transnational character of the thus created community: Alevis in Germany commemorate victims of a massacre that took place in Turkey. However, the distinction of nationalized spaces is not taken up in the imagination of community: the Alevi community is imagined as basically one, above national boundaries. This is not to say that boundaries and nationalized spaces are denied and not taken into account. Forms of organization reflect the models provided by the institutional environment of the respective state and society. Claims for recognition are equally related to this specific environment. In the German context where migrants are most importantly framed as "foreigners" and where the dominant discourse on integration emphasizes the difference and foreignness of migrants, Alevis claim to be recognized as migrants who are not so different but who share basic value orientations, universal values in fact, with German society. In Alevi self-representations vis-à-vis the German public, the Alevi-Sunni master difference is employed as a template to show that Alevis differ from Muslims in almost the same way as the Germans do. Claims for recognition are also expressed in efforts toward institutional integration, in which the Alevi associations seek to be accepted as cooperating partners by German civil or governmental bodies. Religion plays a special role here because religion functions as a legal category of recognition in Germany: while cultural difference is not institutionally recognized, religious difference is. In this context Alevism is represented in the first instance as religion, although the debate among Alevis whether Alevism is primarily culture or religion remains to a

certain extent still unresolved. Yet as a religious community Alevi associations are able to pursue their currently most significant project of
recognition in Germany: the introduction of Alevi religious classes in
public schools. Further, citizenship is an important field, which, however, shows the limits of recognition. Most Alevis have naturalized in
Germany, expressing thereby that they do not reciprocate the exclusion
as foreigners that is the subtext of the German discourse on migration.
Recognition as full citizens with equal rights is demanded instead. But
Alevis, like other naturalized migrants, experience that the legal status
of citizenship is not sufficient to supersede the categorization as foreigners in discourse and in interaction with native Germans.

Efforts towards recognition and institutional integration in Germany
do not result in abandoning relationships with the larger segment of
the Alevi community that lives in what migration studies convention-
ally conceive as the "homeland." To the contrary, the Alevi associations
are actively involved in building and maintaining transnational connections with Alevis living in Turkey and in other countries of migration. Resources gained through institutional integration in Germany
and especially at the level of the European Union, are utilized in order
to engage in a transnational politics of recognition that intends to support the claims made by Alevis in Turkey.

However, not all Alevis in Germany are equally engaged in these
transnational connections. Grossly, those who mobilize can be distinguished from those who are mobilized. Transnational actors are engaged in the establishment of relationships that enable the transnational
flow of ideas, cultural production, practices, persons, news, and, to a
limited extent, money, in the context of the Alevi movement. Yet few
Alevis are transnational actors in this sense. Most Alevis are not or only
to a very limited degree actively involved in such transnational social
relationships. Nevertheless, they are included and imagine themselves
as being included in the Alevi transnational community. In order to
highlight this distinction of transnational commitment, I distinguished
analytically between transnational *social* space, constituted by social relationships and interaction, and transnational *cultural* space, made up
by shared symbols, concerns, and an imagination of community. While
the degree of participation of individual Alevis in the transnational social space differs widely, they are all equally included in a transnational
cultural space. Drawing on this distinction, I propose to define diaspora
as a transnational community in which the symbolic, cultural aspects
of community outweigh transnational social relationships constituted
by interaction.

Diasporas are frequently regarded as subverting the nation-state.
The diasporic subversion of the nation-state derives from the challenge
a diaspora poses to the homogeneity of the nation-state. Diasporic identity intersects with national identity. This applies on one hand to the

subversion of the "receiving" state, whose presumed cultural homogeneity is confronted with a diasporic community that is perceived as being of uncertain loyalty. On the other hand, subversion may also relate
to the "sending" state in cases of diasporic separatist movements that
project their own vision of a (separate) nation-state upon their "home
country." Diasporas are frequently regarded as the "other of the nation-
state," but conceptualizations of diasporas in many cases surprisingly
resemble notions of the nation-state: both are imagined as culturally
homogeneous and as territorially based—only that in the case of diaspora the territory is "somewhere else." Although particular nation-
states are subverted by particular diasporas, the mode of imagination
on which nation-states are based is affirmed and strengthened rather
than subverted by diasporas.

The Alevi case, however, is different in this respect. The Alevi diaspora does not entertain a kind of competing national imagination. In
contrast with Kurds there is no territory within Turkey that is claimed
as "Alevi territory" and also no project of a separate "Alevi state." Still,
especially the press campaign of *Hürriyet* shows that the diasporic Alevi movement is perceived as subverting and endangering the Turkish
nation. The Alevi movement is regarded as subversive because it regards national belonging as being of secondary importance, subverting
thereby the nation's claims for primacy and precedence. The agents of
the Turkish nation perceive the diasporic Alevi associations as working
against this nation, because they endorse naturalization in Germany
and deploy their transnational politics of recognition "against" the
Turkish state. They thereby render futile the efforts of the Turkish state
institutions to secure the fixed and enduring inclusion of emigrants
from Turkey within the Turkish nation, as well as their projection of a
homogeneous Turkish nation. The intimate connection of identity, power,
and recognition that I have spelled out in chapter one is in our present
world most clearly embodied in the nation-state. It is no surprise, then,
that the protagonists of the Turkish nation-state jealously attempt to
avert diasporic subversion.

Diaspora and Social Movements

In this study of Alevi politics of recognition, I began with conceptualizing Alevis as a social movement and ended with framing them as a
diaspora. This shift in conceptualization may seem to contain a certain
theoretical inconsistency, and it certainly begs the question of the relationship between both notions. In this section I will argue that the social
movement approach supplements rather than contradicts the diaspora
concept, and that it is able to level out some shortcomings of diaspora
theory.

While the question of mobilization figures prominently in social movement theory, it is virtually absent in the strand of diaspora theory that conceives diaspora as a type of social form (Vertovec 1997). Interestingly, most definitions of diaspora as a type of community refer less to structural features of the social formations in question than to elements of consciousness and imagination. Diaspora as a type of social form thereby comprises the second meaning of diaspora identified by Vertovec: diaspora as a type of consciousness. It is emphasized that diasporas maintain a collective identity embodied in highly valued symbols, a sense of solidarity with those "remaining at home," and a political orientation that implies "divided loyalties" (often simply called "homeland orientation"), and that they may even entertain a—however hypothetical—desire for return. Structural features that are included in such definitions, most importantly the maintenance of social relationships with those who "stayed at home" or who moved elsewhere, pose the question of consciousness and imagination, too: Why are such relationships maintained in the first place? Why do they engender the imagination of an overall community that far exceeds the actual range of such social relationships as they are practised by individual actors? Not all migrant congregations are diasporas—this is a consensus of the recent theoretical debate. Otherwise, efforts to specifically define diasporas would be superfluous. Because also other migrants that do not make up a diaspora community maintain, at least for some time, social relationships with people living elsewhere, the specific difference of diasporas has to be found in their particular kind of consciousness or mode of imagining community. This, however, poses a crucial question: where does this diasporic consciousness come from? To take diasporic consciousness, the imagination of a community that spans geographical distance and transcends boundaries of states, simply for granted gives rise to the critique of diaspora as a reifying, essentializing concept. Anthias (1998, 562), criticizes that in the conceptualization of diaspora "there is a natural and unproblematic 'organic' community of people without division or difference, dedicated to the same political project(s)." Similarly, Soysal (2000, 3) points out that by taking for granted "the perpetual longing for a then and there," diaspora theory "ignores the historical contingency of the nation-state, identity, and community, and reifies them as natural"—and also essentializes diaspora. Perhaps it could be taken for granted that people who move elsewhere take with them a "natural" sentiment of longing and belonging to the place where they came from and where they shared social relationships. Yet the perpetuation of such a sentiment over time, its transmission to subsequent generations, and, in the first place, its being turned into a sentiment and imagination of *community* require explanation. Alevis have maintained transnational relationships with their relatives in Turkey, with their hometowns, villages, and regions even before the formation

of an imagined transnational Alevi community. The formation of diaspora was not simply a "natural" consequence of such ties. Accordingly,
transnational relationships may be a necessary condition for the formation of diasporic consciousness, but they are not sufficient. To put it in
terms of the social movement approach, the question is how people
become mobilized and who mobilizes them for a diasporic communal
consciousness.

In the present study of Alevis living in Germany, I have shown that
the Alevi movement, embodied mainly in Alevi associations, discursively constituted the idea of the Alevi community—which I categorized
as a *diasporic* community because it is imagined across national boundaries—and also organized collective activities and events in which this
discursive construction could to some extent be turned into an experience. At such events, and through the media of the movement, the
discourse of community is disseminated and individual Alevis become
tuned to this discourse. The idea of solidarity with Alevis in Turkey
is emphasized, and the question of recognition of Alevism or the violence experienced by Alevis in Turkey are framed as issues that equally
concern Alevis in Germany because they form part of the same community. A transnational cultural space of Alevism is constituted, but
also transnational social relationships are established and maintained.
Thus, there is no a priori, "natural" Alevi diaspora community that was
established by the mere movements of migration. Rather, the community has been constituted *a posteriori* as a framework that gives meaning
to political and social developments in the "host" as well as the "home"
country. By imagining the community, predicated on a shared identity,
and establishing associations, Alevi migrants gained agency: they acquired the ability to act within these contexts and to pursue their claims
for recognition.

In case studies of diaspora "communities," various kinds of institutions like parties, churches, temples, or associations that create, disseminate, and sustain a discourse and consciousness or imagination of
diaspora and community often figure quite prominently. In an earlier
paper, Susanne Schwalgin and myself have compared the role of such
institutions in the Armenian and Alevi diasporas. Although Armenian
churches and parties are very different from Alevi associations, they
play comparable roles relating to the constitution of community (Sökefeld and Schwalgin 2000, on the Armenian diaspora in Greece see also
Schwalgin 2004). Similarly, in her study of the Palestinian diaspora,
Lindholm Schulz (2003) argues that the PLO was instrumental for the
perpetuation of a diasporic identity among Palestinians that essentially
comprised a sentiment of exile and the desire for return. The maintenance of a diasporic Palestinian identity was regarded as necessary
because it was assumed that if Palestinians simply settled down at the
places where they lived, a distinct Palestinian identity and the political

impetus derived therefrom would be lost. Analyzing the Sikh diaspora, Tatla shows that the destruction of the Golden Temple in Amritsar by the Indian army completely changed the consciousness of the Sikh diaspora: it "has turned a secure ethnic group's outlook towards a search for a homeland" (Tatla 1999, 193). Quickly, many competing diasporic Sikh associations were founded that embodied the call for an independent Sikh state. A sustained discourse of homeland disseminated by these organizations and their leaders became a central feature of the diaspora. Although Tatla frequently identifies simply "the Sikh diaspora" or "the Sikh community" as the (collective) subject of this new outlook, there is ample proof in his study for the decisive role of institutions like Sikh temples and political associations. He emphasizes the role of "community leaders" who are, first of all, the leaders of such associations and institutions. The example of the Tamil diaspora originating from Sri Lanka bears similar evidence: here, the militant Tamil nationalist organization LTTE played a significant role in creating a redefined imagination of a Tamil community, although only a minority of Tamils is related with the LTTE. Writing on Tamils in Norway, Fuglerud (1999) points to the importance of festivals organized by the LTTE for the transformation of "individual nostalgia" into a collective imagination:

> I wish to emphasize … that the majority of people present at this latter festival are normally not what I would call "LTTE-people" but people by whom the historical consciousness of this organization is sought in order to provide meaning to their own marginal existence in Norway. The grand narrative of revolutionary nationalism is adapted, by refugees who accept it, to provide a genesis of the diaspora (ibid. 179).

These examples show that various kinds of organizations and institutions with their personnel, activities, and media play a significant role in the discursive construction of diasporic (and community) consciousness. Yet this role of organizations is not sufficiently acknowledged in diaspora theory. Spelling out the contribution of such organizations and their discourses could, however, overcome the essentializing mysticism of community, of home and belonging, in diaspora literature. A diasporic consciousness, that is, the construction of a community that transcends boundaries of states and imagines people who have migrated together with people who have stayed as parts of one community, is not a natural consequence of migration. There have to be *efforts* to create such an imagination, often in response to particular events, and to disseminate it among the members of the presumed community. These efforts are undertaken by particular organizations that become the agents of this imagination. The empirical cases show that for this purpose it is not necessary that a great part of the targeted people or even the whole "community" becomes directly related with these organizations. However, the discourses they create and disseminate redefine the migrants' outlook and the terms in which they debate identity and make claims. Such discourses of community have to be appealing to the people that they attempt to include—they must offer a meaningful interpretation of their experiences. Further, such mobilization does not happen once and for all but remains a continuous task. Case studies show that the successful imagination of a community focuses on claims for recognition that the community, as a collective subject, makes: claims for the recognition of a separate identity that may include the demand for a separate, independent "homeland," but also claims for the recognition of a particular identity in the country of migration. It is well imaginable that once such issues of recognition are fulfilled and no longer contentious, that is, once the cause for mobilization is lost, the imagination of a particular diaspora fades away. A possible dynamic of increasing, decreasing, and shifting mobilization is exemplified by the Eritrean diaspora. Hepner (2003) describes how strong mobilization in the US diaspora for the Eritrean nation, which was strictly dominated by the Eritrean Peoples Liberation Front, gave way to subsiding interest in nationalism and a increasing reorientation towards more private religious identities once the EPLF's aim of an independent nation-state had been achieved. It surged again with the border war between Ethiopia and Eritrea (1998–2000), entailing this time, however, a strong questioning of the EPLF's hegemony over the nation.

Commenting on contemporary anthropological texts on ethnicity and identity, Eric Wolf (2001, 410) writes that there is "too little attention to how groups mobilize, shape, and reshape cultural repertoires and are shaped by them in turn; how groups shape and reshape their self-images to elicit participation and commitment and are themselves reshaped by these representations." In the realm of diaspora studies, an approach that frames the formation of diaspora as a social movement in which diasporic organizations play a central role can contribute significantly to overcoming such shortcomings. It has to devote primary attention to the mobilization of people as well as to the terms and agents of particular claims. It thereby avoids the pitfalls of much diaspora theory that fails to address precisely these issues by simply conceptualizing diaspora as "community."

 # APPENDIX 1

Organizations

AABK	Avrupa Alevi Birlikleri Konfederasyonu (European Confederation of Alevi Communities), umbrella association of Alevi federations in Europe.
AABF	Originally Avrupa Alevi Birlikleri Federasyonu (European Federation of Alevi Communities), later renamed as Almanya Alevi Birlikleri Federasyonu (German Federation of Alevi Communities), umbrella organization of Alevis in Germany.
AAKM	Anadolu Alevileri Kültür Merkezi (Culture Center of Anatolian Alevis), largest Alevi association in Berlin, member of the AABF.
ABTM	Alevi Bektaşi Temsilciler Meclisi (Council of Alevi-Bektashi Representatives), transnational Alevi umbrella organization, first established in 1994.
ACF	Alevi Cemaatları Federasyonu (Federation of Alevi Communities), first Alevi umbrella organization in Germany, later renamed as AABF.
CEM Vakfı	Cumhuriyet Eğetim ve Kültür Merkezi Vakfı (Republican Education and Culture Center Foundation), Alevi association founded in Turkey in 1995 by Izzettin Doğan, criticized by most other Alevi associations for its close relationship with the Turkish state.
CHP	Cumhuriyet Halk Partisi (Republican People's Party).
DİB	Diyanet Işleri Başkanlığı (Directorate for Religious Affairs), Turkish state authority for (Sunni) Islam.
HAAK BIR	Hamburg Anadolu Alevi Kültür Birliği (Hamburg Culture Union of Anatolian Alevis), the second Alevi organization in Hamburg, originated from a splitting of the HAKM.
HAKB	Harburg Alevi Kültür Birliği (Harburg Alevi Culture Union), Alevi association located in Hamburg-Harburg.

HAKM	Hamburg Alevi Kültür Merkezi (Alevi Culture Center Hamburg), the first formal local Alevi organization in Hamburg.
HDB	Halkçi Devrimci Birliği (Popular Revolutionary Union), the local organization of the HDF in Hamburg.
HDF	Halkçı Devrimci Federasyonu (Popular Revolutionary Federation), umbrella organization of Social Democrat immigrants from Turkey, closely related with the CHP in Turkey.
ÖCB	Öğrenci Canlar Birliği (Union of Student 'Canlar'), Alevi students' organization in Hamburg.
PKK	Partiye Karkaren Kurdistan (Kurdish Workers' Party), militant organization that fought for an independent Kurdish state.
PSAKD	Pir Sultan Abdal Kültür Derneği (Pir Sultan Abdal Culture Association), leftist Alevi association, organizer of the festival in Sivas in 1993.
RP	Refah Partisi (Welfare Party), Islamist Party led by Necmettin Erbakan. After a prohibition reestablished as Fazilet Partisi (Virtue Party). The present governing AK Partisi of Tayyıp Erdoğan is an offshoot of the Fazilet Partisi.
TBP	Türkiye Birlik Partisi (Turkey Unity Party), Alevi Party in Turkey founded in the late 1960s and closed after the military coup of 1980.
TGB	Türk Göçmen Birliği (Union of Turkish Migrants), umbrella association of Turkish migrant associations in Hamburg.
Wir-Zentrum	Multicultural center in Hamburg-Altona, meeting place for the Alevi Culture Group and later the HAKM.
YB	Yurtseverler Birliği (Union of Patriots), local association founded by Social-Democrat Alevis since 1979.
YBF	Yurtseverler Birlikleri Federasyonu (Federation of Unions of Patriots), umbrella association of YB.

 **APPENDIX 2**

Glossary of Alevi and Turkish Terms

Aşure	Day on which the martyrdom of Hüseyin, the third Imam is remembered. Alevis celebrate *aşure* on the twelfth day of the Islamic month *muharrem*. *Aşure* is also the name of a sweet dish that is distributed on this day.
Bağlama	Longneck lute.
Can	"Soul," "life," "friend," used as an address among Alevis.
Cem	Communal Alevi ritual.
Cemevi	Building in which *cem* is celebrated, community center of Alevis.
Dede	Alevi religious specialist, leader of the ritual, descendant of Ali and Fatima (sayyid).
Musahiplik	Alevi ritual kinship that was traditionally established between two married couples who assume mutual responsibility. Once a kind of final initiation to Alevism, *musahiplik* is hardly practiced today.
Namaz	Muslim prayer.
Rızalık	Consent. Important principle among Alevis. *Rızalık* is established in *cem*.
Saz	Generic word for musical instruments, especially for the longneck lute. Often synonymous with *bağlama*.
Semah	Ritual dance, important element of *cem*.
Şehit	Martyr, victim of violence.
Tekke	Derviş lodge.
Türbe	Tomb, venerated grave of a saint.

REFERENCES

AABF. 1998. *Avrupa Alevi Birlikleri Federasyonu Programı*. Cologne: AABF.

AABF. 1999. *Die Opfer des Massakers von Sivas*. Cologne: AABF.

AABF. 2000. *Bin Yılın Türküsü—Das Epos des Jahrtausends—Saga of the Millennium*. Cologne: AABF.

AABF. 2000b. *Das neue Staatsangehörigkeitsrecht—Yeni Vatandaşlık Yasası*. Cologne: AABF.

AABK. 2003. *Report about the Alevites in Turkey and in the Countries of the EU*. Cologne: AABK.

Alcoff, Linda Martín. 2000. Who's Afraid of Identity Politics? In Moya, Paula M. L., and Michael R. Hames-García, eds. *Reclaiming Identity: Realist Theory and the Predicament of Postmodernism*, 312–344. Berkeley: University of California Press.

Allouche, Adel. 1983. *The Origins and Development of the Ottoman-Safavid Conflict 906–962/1500–1555*. Berlin: Klaus Schwarz Verlag.

Amit, Vered, and Nigel Rapport. 2002. *The Trouble with Community: Anthropological Reflections on Movement, Identity and Collectivity*. London: Pluto Press.

Anderson, Benedict. 1983. *Imagined Communities*. London: Verso.

Anderson, Benedict. 1998. *The Spectre of Comparisons: Nationalism, South-East Asia and the World*. London: Verso.

Anthias, Floya. 1998. Evaluating "Diaspora": Beyond Ethnicity? *Sociology* 32: 557–580.

Anthias, Floya. 2001. "New Hybridities, Old Concepts: The Limits of "Culture". *Ethnic and Racial Studies* 24: 619–641.

Appadurai, Arjun. 1996. *Modernity at Large: Cultural Dimensions of Globalization*. Minneapolis: University of Minnesota Press.

Aronowitz, Stanley. 1992. *The Politics of Identity: Class, Culture, Social Movements*. New York: Routledge.

Asad, Talal. 1990. Ethnography, Literature and Politics. *Cultural Anthropology* 5: 239–269.

Assmann, Jan. 2002. *Das kulturelle Gedächtnis. Schrift, Erinnerung und politische Identität in frühen Hochkulturen*. München: Beck.

Atilgan, Canan. 2002. *Türkische Diaspora in Deutschland. Chance oder Risiko für die deutsch-türkischen Beziehungen*. Hamburg: Deutsches Orient-Institut.

Axel, Brian Keith. 2001. *The Nation's Tortured Body: Violence, Representation and the Formation of a Sikh "Diaspora."* Durham: Duke University Press.

Balibar, Étienne. 1991. "The Nation Form: History and Ideology". *Review* 13: 329–336.

Barrett, Michele. 1987. The Concept of "Difference". *Feminist Review* 26: 29–41.

Barth, Fredrik. 1969. Introduction to *Ethnic Groups and Boundaries: The Social Organization of Difference*. Bergen: Universitets Forlaget: 9–39.

Basch, Linda, Nina Glick Schiller and Cristina Szanton Blanc. 1994. *Nations Unbound: Transnational Projects, Postcolonial Predicaments, and Deterritorialized Nation-States*. Langhorne, PA: Gordon and Breach.

Bauböck, Rainer. 1994. *Transnational Citizenship: Membership and Rights in International Migration*. Aldershot: Edward Elgar.

Bauböck, Rainer. 2003. Towards a Political Theory of Migrant Transnationalism. *International Migration Review* 37: 700–723.

Baumann, Gerd. 1992. Ritual Implicates "Others": Rereading Durkheim in a Plural Society. In de Coppet, Daniel ed., *Understanding Rituals*. London: Routledge: 97–116.

Baumann, Gerd. 1996. *Contesting Culture: Discourses of Identity in Multi-Ethnic London*, Cambridge, Cambridge University Press.

Baumann, Gerd. 1999. *The Multicultural Riddle: Rethinking National, Ethnic, and Religious Identities*. London: Routledge.

Beauftragte der Bundesregierung für Ausländerfragen. 2002. *Daten und Fakten zur Ausländersituation*. Berlin.

Begner, Kai-Uwe. 2000. *Migranten und Integration. Eine Einführung in das Wanderungsgeschehen und die Integration der Zugewanderten in Deutschland*. Opladen: Leske und Budrich.

Behörde für Schule, Jugend und Bildung. 1984. *Richtlinien und Hinweise für die Erziehung und den Unterricht ausländischer Kinder und Jugendlicher in Hamburger Schulen*. Hamburg: BSJB.

Bell, Catherine. 1997. *Ritual: Perspectives and Dimensions*. New York: Oxford University Press.

Benhabib, Seyla. 1999. *Kulturelle Vielfalt und demokratische Gleichheit. Politische Partizipation im Zeitalter der Globalisierung*. Frankfurt: Fischer.

Berlin, Isaiah. 1976. *Vico and Herder: Two Studies in the History of Ideas*. London: The Hogarth Press.

Bhabha, Homi K. 1990. DisseminNation: Time, Narrative, and the Margins of the Modern Nation. In Bhabha, Homi, ed. *Nation and Narration*. London: Routledge: 291–322.

Birdoğan, Nejat. 1990. *Anadolu'nun Gizli Kültürü Alevilik*. Hamburg: Hamburg Alevi Kültür Merkezi.

Birge, John Kingsley. 1937. *The Bektashi Order of Dervishes*. London. Luzac.

Bozkurt, Mehmet F. 1988. *Das Gebot. Mystischer Weg mit einem Freund*. Hamburg: E.B.–Verlag Rissen.

Brah, Avtar. 1996. *Cartographies of Diaspora: Contesting Identities*. London: Routledge.

Brubaker, Rogers. 1992. *Citizenship and Nationhood in France and Germany*. Cambridge, MA: Harvard University Press.

Brubaker, Rogers and Frederick Cooper. 2000. Beyond "Identity". *Theory and Society* 29: 1–47.

Brunt, Rosalind. 1989. The Politics of Identity. In Hall, Stuart and M. Jacques, eds. *New Times: The Changing Face of Politics in the 1990s*, 150–159. London: Verso.

Bumke, Peter. 1979. Kızılbaş-Kurden in Dersim (Tunceli, Türkei). *Anthropos* 74: 530–548.

Burke, Peter. 1989. Geschichte als soziales Gedächtnis. In Assmann, Aleida and Dietrich Harth, eds. *Mnemosyne. Formen der kulturellen Erinnerung*, 289–304. Frankfurt: Fischer.

Calhoun, Craig. 1995. *Critical Social Theory*. Oxford: Blackwell.

Çamuroğlu, Reha. 1997. Some Notes on the Contemporary Process of Reconstructuring Alevilik in Turkey. In Kehl-Bodrogi, Krisztina, Barbara Kellner-Heinkele and Anke Otter–Beaujean, eds. *Syncretistic Religious Communities in the Near East*. Brill: Leiden.

Castles, Stephen. 2000. *Ethnicity and Globalization: From Migrant Worker to Transnational Citizen*. London: Sage.

CEM Vakfı. 2000. *Anadolu inanç önderleri birinci toplantIsı: Alevi İslam inancının öncüleri dedeler, babalar, ozanlar ne düşünüyor?* Istanbul: CEM Vakfı.

Cetinsaya, Gokhan. 1999. Rethinking Nationalism and Islam: Some Preliminary Notes on the Roots of "Turkish-Islamic Synthesis" in Modern Turkish Political Thought. *The Muslim World* 89: 350–376.

Chapin, Wesley D. 1996. The Turkish Diaspora in Germany. *Diaspora* 5: 275–301.

Clifford, James. 1994. Diasporas. *Cultural Anthropology* 9: 302–338.

Clifford, James. 2000. Taking Identity Politics Seriously: "The Contradictory, Stony Ground…". In Gilroy, Paul, Lawrence Grossberg and Angela McRobbie, eds. *Without Guarantees. In Honour of Stuart Hall*, 94–112. London: Verso.

Cohen, Anthony P. 1985. *The Symbolic Construction of Community*. London: Routledge.

Cohen, Robin. 1996. Diasporas and the Nation-State: From Victims to Challengers. *International Affairs* 72: 507–520.

Cohen, Robin. 1997. *Global Diasporas: An Introduction*. London: UCL Press.

Coleman, Dorothy Gabe. 1987. *Montaigne's Essais*. London: Allen and Unwin.

Connor, Walker. 1986. The Impact of Homelands upon Diasporas. In Scheffer, Gabriel ed. *Modern Diasporas in International Politics*, 16–46. New York: St. Martin's.

Conze, Werner. 1985. "Deutschland" und die "deutsche Nation" als historische Begriffe. In Büsch, Otto and James Sheehan, eds. *Die Rolle der Nation in der deutschen Geschichte und Gegenwart*, 21–38. Berlin: Colloquium Verlag.

Crosby, Christina. 1992. Dealing with Difference. In Butler, Judith and J. W. Scott, eds. *Feminists Theorize the Political*, 130–143. New York: Routledge.

Cryns, Manfred, Ayşe Özkan, Heidi Wedel, and Ferah Yarar-Zarif. 1991. *Zum Integrationspotential der türkischen Tagespresse in der Bundesrepublik Deutschland*. Opladen: Leske und Budrich.

Das, Veena. 1995. *Critical Events: An Anthropological Perspective on Contemporary India*. Delhi: Oxford University Press.

Delaney, Carol. 1991. *The Seed and the Soil: Gender and Cosmology in Turkish Village Society*. Berkeley: University of California Press.

Delaney, Carol. 1995. Father State, Motherland, and the Birth of Modern Turkey. In Yanagisako, Sylvia and Carol Delaney, eds. *Naturalizing Power: Essays in Feminist Cultural Analysis*, 177–199. New York: Routledge.

Della Porta, Donatella; Mario Diani. 1999. *Social Movements: An Introduction*. Oxford: Blackwell.

Diehl, Claudia, Julia Urbahn, and Hartmut Esser. 1999. *Die soziale und politische Partizipation von Zuwanderern in der Bundesrepublik Deutschland.* Bonn, Friedrich–Ebert-Stiftung.

Dodd, C. H. 1983. *The Crisis of Turkish Democracy.* Beverly: Eothen Press.

Doedens, Folkert and Wolfram Weisse. 1997. *Religionsunterricht für alle. Hamburger Perspektiven zur Religionsdidaktik.* Hamburg: Pädagogisch-Theologisches Institut.

Dornis, Christian. 2002. Zwei Jahre nach der Reform des Staatsangehörigkeitsrechts—Bilanz und Ausblick. In Bade, Klaus J. and Rainer Münz eds. *Migrationsreport 2002. Fakten—Analysen—Perspektiven,* 163–178. Frankfurt: Campus:

Dreßler, Markus. 1999. *Die civil religion der Türkei. Kemalistische und alevitische Atatürk-Rezeptionen im Vergleich.* Ergon: Würzburg.

Dreßler, Markus. 2002. *Die alevitische Religion. Traditionslinien und Neubestimmung.* Würzburg: Ergon.

Dural, Tamaşa F. 1995. *Aleviler… ve Gazi Olayları.* Istanbul: ANT Yayınları.

Durkheim, Émile. 1965 [1915]. *The Elementary Forms of the Religious Life.* New York: The Free Press.

Eder, Angelika, ed. 2003. *"Wir sind auch da!" Über das Leben von und mit Migranten in europäischen Großstädten.* Hamburg: Dölling und Galitz.

Eickelman, Dale F. and Jon W. Anderson. 1999. Redefining Muslim Publics. In Eickelman, Dale F. and Jon W. Anderson, eds. *New Media in the Muslim World: The Emerging Public Sphere* 1–18. Bloomington: Indiana University Press.

El-Tayeb, Fatima. 2003. Kanak Attak! HipHop und (Anti-)Identitätsmodelle der "Zweiten Generation". In Eder, Angelika, ed. *"Wir sind auch da!" Über das Leben von und mit Migranten in europäischen Großstädte*313–326. Hamburg: Dölling und Galitz.

Engin, Ismail. 1996. Thesen zur ethnischen und religiösen Standortbestimmung des Alevitentums. Türkischsprachige Publikationen der Jahre 1983–1995. *Orient* 37: 691–706.

Engin, Ismail. 1998. Izzettin Doğan, eine alevitische Führungspersönlichkeit in der Türkei. *Orient* 39: 541–547.

Eral, Sadık. 1995. *Çaldıran'dan Çorum'a Anadolu'da Alevi Katliamları.* Istanbul: ANT Yayınları.

Eral, Sadık. 1996. Sivas yangınının 3. yıldönümünde. *Alevilerin Sesi* 15, July 1996: 12–13.

Erbektaş, Sinan. 1998. Axiome und Organizationsformen der Aleviten. In Föderation der Alevitengemeinden in Deutschland, ed. *Renaissance des Alevismus.* Köln: AABF.

Erbektaş, Sinan. 1998b. Auf dem Weg zu einem Status der Körperschaft des öffentlichen Rechts. *Stimme der Aleviten* 26, June 1998: 28–39.

Erikson, Erik H. 1980 [1959]. *Identity and the Life Cycle.* New York: W. W. Norton.

Ewing, Katherine P. 2000a. The Violence of Non-Recognition: Becoming a "Conscious" Muslim Woman in Turkey. In Robben, Antonius C. G. M. and Marcelo M. Suárez-Orozco, eds. *Cultures under Siege: Collective Violence and Trauma,* 248–271. Cambridge: Cambridge University Press.

Ewing, Katherine P. 2003. Living Islam in the Diaspora: Between Turkey and Germany. *South Atlantic Quarterly* 102: 405–429.

European Commission. 2000. *2000 Regular Report from the Commission on Turkey's Progress towards Accession*. Brussels : European Commission.

European Commission. 2001. *2001 Regular Report on Turkey's Progress towards Accession*. Brussels: European Commission.

European Commission. 2002. *2002 Regular Report from the Commission on Turkey's Progress towards Accession*, Brussels, European Commission.

European Commission. 2003. *2003 Regular Report from the Commission on Turkey's Progress towards Accession*. Brussels : European Commission.

European Commission. 2004. *2004 Regular Report on Turkey's Progress towards Accession*. Brussels : European Commission.

Faist, Thomas. 1998. Transnational Social Spaces out of International Migration: Evolution, Significance and Future Prospects. *Archives Européenes de Sociologie* 33: 213–247.

Faist, Thomas. 1999. Developing Transnational Social Spaces: The Turkish-German Example. In: Pries, Ludger, ed. *Migration and Transnational Social Spaces*, 36–72. Aldershot: Ashgate.

Faist, Thomas. 2000. *The Volume and Dynamics of International Migration and Transnational Social Spaces*. Clarendon Press: Oxford.

Farooqhi, Suraya. 1981. *Der Bektaschi-Orden in Anatolien (vom späten fünfzehnten Jahrhundert bis 1826)*. Wien: Verlag des Instituts für Orientalistik der Universität Wien.

Fentress, James and Chris Wickham. 1992. *Social Memory: New Perspectives on the Past*. Oxford: Blackwell.

Fırat, Gülsün. 1997. *Sozio-ökonomischer Wandel und ethnische Identität in der kurdisch-alevitischen Region Dersim*. Saarbrücken: Verlag für Entwicklungspolitik.

Foucault, Michel. 1979. "Powers and Strategies," An Interview with Michel Foucault by the *Révoltes Logiques* collective. In Morris, Meghan and Paul Patton, eds. *Power, Truth, Strategy: Michel Foucault*, 49–58. Sydney: Feral Publications.

Foucault, Michel. 1982. Afterword: The Subject and Power. In Dreyfus, Hubert L. and Paul Rabinow, *Michel Foucault - Beyond Structuralism and Hermeneutics*, 208–226. Chicago: University of Chicago Press.

Foucault, Michel. 1991 [1975]. *Discipline and Punish: The Birth of the Prison*. London: Penguin.

Fraser, Nancy. 1997. *Justice Interruptus: Critical Reflections on the "Postsocialist" Condition*. London: Routledge.

Fraser, Nancy. 2001. Recognition without Ethics? *Theory, Culture & Society* 18: 21–42.

Frey, Frederick W. 1975. Patterns of Elite Politics in Turkey. In Lenczowski, George, ed. *Political Elites in the Middle East*, 41–80. Washington: American Enterprise Institute for Public Policy Research.

Friedman, Jonathan. 1996. The Politics of De-Authentification: Escaping from Identity, A Response to "Beyond Authenticity" by Mark Rogers. *Identities* 3: 127–136.

Fuchs, Martin. 1999. *Kampf um Differenz. Repräsentation, Subjektivität und soziale Bewegungen. Das Beispiel Indien*. Frankfurt: Suhrkamp.

Fücks, Ralf. 2002 . Reform of the Citizenship Law: The Debate over Dual Citizenship in Germany. In Levy, Daniel and Yfaat Weiss, eds. *Challenging Ethnic*

Citizenship: German and Israeli Perspectives on Immigration, 76–81. New York: Berghahn Books.

Fuglerud, Oeivind. 1999. *Life on the Outside: The Tamil Diaspora and Long-Distance Nationalism.* Pluto Press: London

Fuss, Diana. 1990. *Essentially Speaking: Feminism, Nature and Difference.* New York: Routledge.

Gedi, Noa and Yigal Elam. 1996. Collective Memory—What is it? *History and Memory* 8: 30–50.

Geertz, Clifford. 2000. *Available Light: Anthropological Reflections on Philosophical Topics.* Princeton: Princeton University Press.

Gellner, Ernest. 1964. *Thought and Change.* London: Weidenfeld and Nicholson.

Giddens, Anthony. 1976. *New Rules of Sociological Method.* London: Hutchinson.

Gilroy, Paul. 1997. Diaspora and the Detours of Identity. In Woodward, Kathryn, ed. *Identity and Difference,* 301–346. London: Sage.

Gleason, Philip. 1983. Identifying Identity: A Semantic History. *Journal of American History* 69: 910–931.

Glick Schiller, Nina, Linda Basch and Cristina Blanc-Szanton. 1992. Transnationalism: A New Analytic Framework for Understanding Migration. In *Towards a Transnational Perspective on Migration: Race, Ethnicity and Nationalism Reconsidered,* 1–24. New York: New York Academy of Sciences.

Glick Schiller, Nina; Linda Basch, Cristina Szanton-Blanc. 1995. From Immigrant to Transmigrant: Theorizing Transnational Migration. *Anthropological Quarterly* 68: 48–62.

Gluckman, Max. 1963. *Order and Rebellion in Tribal Africa.* New York: The Free Press.

Goffman, Erving. 1974. *Frame Analysis: An Essay on the Organization of Experience.* New York: Harper Colophon.

Gökalp, Altan 1980. *Tête rouges et bouches noires.* Paris: Societé d'Ethnographie.

Gölbaşı, Haydar. 1997. *Aleviler ve Sivas Olayları.* Istanbul: ANT Yayınları.

Göle, Nilüfer. 1996. *The Forbidden Modern: Civilization and Veiling.* Ann Arbor: University of Michigan Press.

Gosewinkel, Dieter. 2002. Citizenship and Naturalization Politics in Germany in the Nineteenth and Twentieth Centuries. In Levy, Daniel and Yfaat Weiss, eds. *Challenging Ethnic Citizenship: German and Israeli Perspectives on Immigration,* 59–75. New York: Berghahn Books.

Greve, Martin. 2003. *Die Musik der imaginären Türkei. Musik und Musikleben im Kontext der Migration aus der Türkei nach Deutschland.* Stuttgart: J.B. Metzler.

Griese, Hartmut M. 2002. Einleitung: Was ist eigentlich das Problem am "Ausländer-problem"? In Griese, Hartmut M., Elçin Kürşat-Ahlers, Rainer Schulte, Massoud Vahedi, and Hans-Peter Waldhoff, eds. *Was ist eigentlich das Problem am "Ausländerproblem"? Über die soziale Durchschlagkraft ideologischer Konstrukte,* 25–46. Frankfurt: IKO.

Groenhaug, R. 1974. *Tahtacilar: Macro-Factors in the Life of a Marginal Subpopulation. Micro-Macro Relations: Social Organization in Antalya, Southern Turkey.* Occasional Paper No 7. Bergen: Dept. of Social Anthropology.

Gümüş, Burak. 2001. *Türkische Aleviten vom osmanischen Reich bis zur heutigen Türkei.* Konstanz: Hartung-Gorre Verlag.

Habermas, Jürgen. 1997. Anerkennungskämpfe im demokratischen Rechtsstaat. In Taylor, Charles, *Multikulturalismus und die Politik der Anerkennung*, 147–196. Frankfurt. Fischer.

HAKM. 1999. *Onların Öyküsü. Hamburg Alevi Kültür Merkezi Tarihi*. Hamburg: HAKM.

Halbwachs, Maurice. 1985. *Das kollektive Gedächtnis*. Frankfurt: Fischer.

Hall, Stuart. 1991. "Old and New Identities, Old and New Ethnicities". In King, A. D., ed. *Culture, Globalization and the World System*, 41–68. London: Sage.

Hall, Stuart. 1996. Politics of Identity. In Ranger, Terence, Yunas Samad and Ossie Stuart, eds. *Culture, Identity, Politics*, 129–135. Avebury: Aldershot.

Handler, Richard. 1985. On Dialogue and Destructive Analysis: Problems in Narrating Nationalism and Ethnicity. *Journal of Anthropological Research* 41: 171–182.

Handler, Richard. 1988. *Nationalism and the Politics of Culture in Quebec*. Madison: University of Wisconsin Press.

Handler, Richard. 1994. Is "Identity" a Useful Cross-Cultural Concept? In Gillis, J., ed. *Commemorations: The Politics of National Identity*, 27–40. Princeton: Princeton University Press.

Harris, George. 1970. The Cause of the 1960 Revolution in Turkey. *Middle East Journal* 24: 438–454.

Hegel, Georg Wilhelm Friedrich. 1981 [1807]. *Phänomenologie des Geistes*. Frankfurt: Suhrkamp.

Heinemann, Lars; Fuat Kamcılı. 2000. Unterhaltung, Absatzmärkte und die Vermittlung von Heimat. Die Rolle der Massenmedien in deutsch-türkischen Räumen. In Faist, Thomas, ed. *Transstaatliche Räume: Politik, Wirtschaft und Kultur in und zwischen Deutschland und der Türkei*, 113–158. Bielefeld: Transcript.

Heper, Metin; Taner Demirel. 1996. The Press and the Consolidation of Democracy in Turkey. *Middle Eastern Studies* 32: 109–123.

Hepner, Tricia Redeker. 2003. Religion, Nationalism, and Transnational Civil Society in the Eritrean Diaspora. *Identities* 10: 269–293.

Herzfeld, Michael. 1986. Of Definitions and Boundaries: The Status of Culture in the Culture of the State. In Chock, Phyllis Pease and June R. Wyman, eds. *Discourse and the Social Life of Meaning*, 75–93. Washington: Smithsonian Institution Press.

Honneth, Axel. 2001. Recognition or Redistribution? Changing Perspectives on the Moral Order of Society. *Theory, Culture & Society* 18: 43–55.

Hony, H. C. 1947. *A Turkish-English Dictionary*. Clarendon Press: Oxford.

Houston, Christopher. 2001. *Islam, Kurds and the Turkish Nation State*. Oxford: Berg.

İlhan, Faysal. 1998. Semah: Ritual-Tanz. *Stimme der Aleviten* 26: 52–3.

Imber, Colin H. 1979. Persecution of the Ottoman Shiites According to the Muhimme Defteri, 1565-1585. *Der Islam* 56: 245–274.

Jansky, Herbert. 1964. Zeitgeschichtliches in den Liedern des Bektaşi-Dichters Pir Sultan Abdal. *Der Islam* 39: 130–142.

Joppke, Christian. 1999. *Immigration and the Nation-State: The United States, Germany and Great Britain*. Oxford: Oxford University Press.

Kağıtçıbaşı, C. 1987. Alienation of the Outsider: The Plight of Migrants. *International Migration* 25: 195–210.

Kaleli, Lütfi, 1997. *Kimliğini Haykıran Alevili.* Istanbul: Can Yayınları.

Kaleli, Lütfi. 2000. *Alevi Kimliği ve Alevi Örgütlenmeleri.* Istanbul: Can Yayınları.

Kaleli, Lütfi. 2003. *Bölücü Böö!* Istanbul: Can Yayınları.

Kaleli, Lütfi. n.d. *Sivas Katliamı ve Şeriat.* No place. Alev Yayınları.

Kaplan, Ismail. 2004. *Das Alevitentum. Eine Glaubens- und Lebensgemeinschaft in Deutschland.* Köln. AABF.

Karacabey, Makfi. 1996. *Türkische Tageszeitungen in der BRD: Rolle, Einfluß, Funktionen.* Ph.D. thesis, University of Frankfurt.

Karakaşoğlu-Aydın, Yasemin. 2001. "Unsere Leute sind nicht so" — Alevitische und sunnitische Studentinnen in Deutschland. In Pusch, Barbara, ed. *Die neue muslimische Frau,* 295–322. Würzburg, Ergon.

Karpat, Kemal. 1976. *The Gecekondu: Rural Migration and Urbanization.* Cambridge: Cambridge University Press.

Kaya, Ali. 1999. *Başlangıcından günümüze Dersim tarihi.* Istanbul: Can Yayınları.

Kaya, Ayhan. 1998. Multicultural Clientelism and Alevi Resurgence in the Turkish Diaspora: Berlin Alevis. *New Perspectives on Turkey* 18: 23–49.

Kaya, Ayhan. 2001. *Sicher in Kreuzberg.* Bielefeld: Transcript.

Kearney, Michael. 1991. Borders and Boundaries of State and Self at the End of Empire. *Journal of Historical Sociology* 4: 52–74.

Keck, Margaret; Kathryn Sikkink. 2000. Historical Precursors to Modern Transnational Social Movements and Networks. In: Guidry, Jouhn A., Michael D. Kennedy and Mayer N. Zald, eds. *Globalization and Social Movements: Culture, Power, and the Transnational Public Sphere,* 35–53. Ann Arbor: University of Michigan Press.

Kehl, Krisztina. 1999. Kurds, Turcs or a People in their Own Right? Competing Collective Identities Among the Zazas. *Muslim World* 89: 439–454.

Kehl, Krisztina. 2000. Prozesse ethnisch-sprachlicher Differenzierung am Beispiel der zazakisprachigen Alewiten aus Dersim. In Engin, Ismail; Erhard Franz, eds. *Aleviler/Alewiten. Vol. 1: Kimlik ve tarih/Identität und Geschichte,* 143–156. Hamburg: Deutsches Orient-Institut.

Kehl-Bodrogi, Krisztina. 1988a. *Die Kızılbaş/Aleviten. Untersuchungen über eine esoterische Glaubensgemeinschaft in Anatolien.* Berlin: Klaus Schwarz Verlag.

Kehl-Bodrogi, Krisztina. 1988b. *Die Tahtacı. Vorläufiger Bericht über eine ethnisch-religiöse Gruppe traditioneller Holzarbeiter in Anatolien.* Berlin: Verlag das Arabische Buch.

Kehl-Bodrogi, Krisztina. 1989. Beruf, Religion, Identität: Die traditionellen Waldarbeiter in der Türkei. In Waldmann, Peter and Georg Elwert, eds. *Ethnizität im Wandel,* 187–206. Saarbrücken: Breitenbach.

Kehl-Bodrogi, Krisztina, 1992. *Vom revolutionären Klassenkampf zum "wahren" Islam. Transformationsprozesse im Alevitentum der Türkei nach 1980.* Sozialanthropologische Arbeitspapiere 49. Berlin: Verlag Das Arabische Buch.

Kehl-Bodrogi, Krisztina. 1993. Die "Wiederfindung" des Alevitentums in der Türkei: Geschichtsmythos und kollektive Identität. *Orient* 34: 267–282.

Kehl-Bodrogi, Krisztina. 1996. Formen ritueller Verwandtschaft in der Türkei. In Elwert, Georg, Jürgen Jensen and Ivan R. Kortt, eds, *Kulturen und Innovationen.Festschrift für Wolfgang Rudolph,* 187–208. Berlin: Duncker und Humblot.

Kehl-Bodrogi, Krisztina. 1998. "Wir sind ein Volk!" Identitätspolitiken unter den Zaza (Türkei) in der europäischen Diaspora. *Sociologus* (NF) 48: 111–135.

Kieser, Hans Lukas. 1993. *Les Kurdes Alévis face au nationalisme Turc Kémaliste: L'Alévité dy Dersim et son rôle dans le premier soulévement Kurde contre Mustafa Kemal (Koçkiri, 1919–1921).* MERA Occasional Papers 18. Amsterdam.

Kieser, Hans Lukas. 1994. L'Alevisme Kurde. *Peuples Méditerranéens* 68/69: 57–76.

Kieser, Hans Lukas. 2003. Alevis, Armenians and the Kurdish Nationalis Movement. In White, Paul J. and Joost Jongerden, eds. *Turkey's Alevi Enigma: A Comprehensive Overview,* 177–196. Brill: Leiden.

Kılavuz, Hasan. 2003. Alevilerin inanç ve ibadeti çağdaş Dedeleri yol göstericidir. *Alevilerin Sesi* 69, October 2003: 18–19.

Kivisto, Peter. 2001. Theorizing Transnational Immigration: A Critical Review of Current Efforts. *Ethnic and Racial Studies* 24: 549–577.

Klinkhammer, Grit. 2000. *Moderne Formen islamischer Lebensführung. Eine qualitativ-empirische Untersuchung zur Religiosität sunnitisch geprägter Türkinnen der zweiten Generation in Deutschland.* Marburg: Diagonal.

Koç, Şinasi. 1989. *Gerçek Islâm Dini.* Ankara: Güven Matbaası.

Köhl, Christine. 2001. *Strategien interkultureller Kulturarbeit.* Frankfurt: IKO.

Koopmans, Ruud and Paul Statham. 1998. *Challenging the Liberal Nation-State? Postnationalism, Multiculturalism and the Collective Claims-Making of Migrants and Ethnic Minorities in Britain and Germany.* Berlin: Wissenschaftszentrum.

Korkmaz, Esat. 2003. *Alevilik-Bektaşilik Terimleri Sözlüğü:* Istanbul: Kaynak Yayınları.

Kostakopoulou, Theodora. 2001. *Citizenship, Identity and Immigration in the European Union: Between Past and Future.* Manchester: Manchester University Press.

Küçük, Hülya. 2002. *The Role of the Bektashis in Turkey's National Struggle.* Brill: Leiden.

Kymlicka, Will. 1995. *Multicultural Citizenship: A Liberal Theory of Minority Rights.* Oxford: Oxford University Press.

Lambek, Michael. 1996. The Past Imperfect: Remembering as a Moral Practice. In Antze, Paul and Michael Lambek, eds. *Tense Pasts: Cultural Essays in Trauma and Memory,* 235–254. New York: Routledge.

Lambek, Michael and Paul Antze. 1996. Introduction: Forecasting Memory. In Antze, Paul and Michael Lambek, eds. *Tense Pasts: Cultural Essays in Trauma and Memory,* xi–xxxviii. New York: Routledge.

Laviziano, Alex, Corinna Mein and Martin Sökefeld. 2001. To be German or not to be... Zur "Berliner Rede" des Bundespräsidenten Johannes Rau. *Ethnoscripts* 3, no. 1: 39–53.

Leach, Edmund. 1976. *Culture and Communication: The Logic by which Symbols are Connected.* Cambridge: Cambridge University Press.

Leezenberg, Michiel. 2003. Kurdish Alevis and the Kurdish National Movement in the 1990s. In: White, Paul J.; Joost Jongerden, eds. *Turkey's Alevi Enigma: A Comprehensive Overview,* 197–212. Leiden: Brill.

Levitt, Peggy. 2001. *The Transnational Villagers.* Berkeley: University of California Press.

Lindholm Schulz, Helena. 2003. *The Palestinian Diaspora: Formation of Identities and Politics of Homeland.* London: Routledge.

McAdam, Doug, Mohn D. McCarthy, and Mayer N. Zald. 1996. *Comparative Perspectives on Social Movements: Political Opportunities, Mobilizing Structures, and Cultural Framings.* Cambridge: Cambridge University Press.

Mahmood, Cynthia Keppley. 1996. *Fighting for Faith and Nation. Dialogues with Sikh Militants*. Philadelphia: University of Pennsylvania Press.

Malkki, Liisa. 1995. *Purity and Exile: Violence, Memory, and National Cosmology among Hutu Refugees in Tanzania*. Chicago: Chicago University Press.

Malkki, Liisa. 1997. National Geographic: The Rooting of Peoples and the Territorialization of National Identity among Scholars and Refugees. In Gupta, Akhil and James Ferguson, eds. *Culture Power Place: Explorations in Critical Anthropology*, 52–74. Durham: Duke University Press.

Mandel, Ruth. 1988. *"We Called Manpower, But People Came Instead." The Foreigner Problem and Turkish Guestworkers in West Germany*. Unpublished Ph.D. thesis, University of Chicago.

Mandel, Ruth. 1989. Turkish Headscarves and the "Foreigners Problem": Constructing Difference Through Emblems of Identity. *New German Critique* 46: 27–46.

Mandel, Ruth. 1990. Shifting Centers and Emergent Identities: Turkey and Germany in the Lives of Turkish Gastarbeiter. In: Eickelman, Dale and James Piscatori, eds. *Muslim Travellers*, Berkeley, University of California Press.

Mandel, Ruth. 1992. The Alevi-Bektahi Identity in a Foreign Context: The Example of Berlin. In: Popovic, Alexandre and Gilles Veinstein, eds. *Bektachiyya: Études sur l'ordre mystique des Bektachis et les groups relevant de Hadji Bektach*. Revue des Études Islamique 60: 419–426.

Mandel, Ruth. 1996. A Place of their Own: Contesting Spaces and Defining Places in Berlin's Migrant Community. In: Metcalf, Barbara D., ed. *Making Muslim Space in North America and Europe*, 147–167. Berkeley: University of California Press.

Mannitz, Sabine. 2002. Religion in vier politischen Kulturen. In: Schiffauer, Werner, Gerd Baumann, Riva Kastoryano, and Steve Vertovec, eds. *Staat—Schule—Ethnizität*, 101–138. Münster: Waxmann.

Maranhao, Tulio. 1985. The Hermeneutics of Participant Observation. *Dialectical Anthropology* 10: 291–309.

Marcus, Aliza. 1996. "Should I shoot you?" An Eyewitness Account of an Alevi Uprising in Gazi. *Middle East Report* 26, No. 199: 24–26.

Marcus, George E. 1995. Ethnography in/of the World System: The Emergence of Multisited Ethnography. *Annual Review of Anthropology* 24: 95–118.

Mardin, Şerif. 1966. Opposition and Control in Turkey. *Government and Opposition* 1: 375–387.

Mardin, Şerif. 1991. The Nakşibendi Order in Turkish History. In: Tapper, Richard, ed. *Islam in Modern Turkey: Religion, Politics and Literature in a Secular State*, 121–142. London: I.B. Tauris.

Marienstras, Richard. 1989. On the Notion of Diaspora. In: Chaliand, G., ed. *Minority People in the Age of Nation-States*, 119–125. London: Pluto.

Markoff, Irene Judyth. 1986a. *Musical Theory, Performance and the Contemporary Baglama Specialist in Turkey*. Unpublished Ph.D. thesis, University of Washington.

Markoff, Irene Judyth. 1986b. The Role of Expressive Culture in the Demystification of a Sect of Islam: The Case of the Alevis in Turkey. *The World of Music* 28: 42–56.

Markus, Gyorgy. 1993. Culture: The Making and the Make-Up of a Concept (an Essay in Historical Semantics). *Dialectical Anthropology* 18: 3–29.

Massicard, Elise. 2001. Alevismus in der Türkei: Kollektive Identität ohne starken Inhalt? In: Rammert, Werner, Gunther Knauthe, Klaus Buchenau and Forian Altenhöhner, eds. *Kollektive Identiäten und kulturelle Innovationen. Ethnologische, soziologische und historische Studien*, 155–173. Leipzig: Leipziger Universitätsverlag.

Massicard, Elise. 2003a. Alevist Movements at Home and Abroad: Mobilization Spaces and Disjunction. *New Perspectives on Turkey* 28-29: 163–188.

Massicard, Elise. 2003b. Alevism as a Productive Misunderstanding: The Hacıbektaş Festival. In: White, Paul J.; Joost Jongerden, eds. *Turkey's Alevi Enigma: A Comprehensive Overview*, 125–140. Leiden, Brill.

Mead, George Herbert. 1967 [1934]. *Mind, Self, and Society from the Standpoint of a Social Behaviorist*. Cicago: University of Chicago Press.

Mecheril, Paul. 2003. *Prekäre Verhältnisse. Über natio-ethno-kulturelle (Mehrfach-) Zugehörigkeit*. Münster: Waxmann.

Mecheril, Paul, Karin Scherschel, Mark Schrödter. 2003. "Ich möchte halt von dir wissen, wie es ist, du zu sein." Die Wiederholung der alienierenden Zuschreibung durch qualitative Forschung. In: Badawia, Tarek, Franz Hamburger and Merle Hummrich, eds. *Wider die Ethnisierung einer Generation. Beiträge zur qualitativen Migrationsforschung*, 93–110. Frankfurt: IKO.

Mélikoff, Iréne. 1992. *Sur les traces du Soufisme Turc*. Éditions Isis: Istanbul.

Mélikoff, Iréne. 1998. *Hadji Bektach. Un mythe et ses avatars. Genése et évolution du soufisme populaire en Turquie*. Brill : Leiden.

Mélikoff, Iréne; İlhan Başgöz; Nejat Birdoğan, Fuat Bozkurt, Esat Korkmaz and Ali Yıldırım. 1998. *Anadolu Aleviliği ve Pir Sultan Abdal*. Paris: Fransa Alevi Birlikleri Federasyonu.

Melucci, Alberto. 1989. *Nomads of the Present: Social Movements and Individual Needs in Contemporary Society*. London: Hutchinson Radius.

Melucci, Alberto. 1996. *Challenging Codes: Collective Action in the Information Age*. Cambridge: Cambridge University Press.

Mohanty, Satya P. 1997. *Literary Theory and the Claims of History: Postmodernism, Objectivity, Multicultural Politics*. Ithaca: Cornell University Press.

Muckel, Stefan. 2004. *Ist die Alevitische Gemeinde Deutschland e. V. eine Religionsgemeinschaft? Rechtsgutachten erstattet dem Ministerium für Schule, Jugend und Kinder des Landes Nordrhein-Westfalen*. Unpublished expert report. Cologne.

Müller, Ulrike. 2001. *Die Beteiligung von Migranten an der Lokalpolitik. Ethnographische Studien in einer südwestdeutschen Stadt*. Unpublished MA thesis, University of Tübingen.

Naess, Ragnar. 1988. Being an Alevi Muslim in South-Western Anatolia and in Norway: The Impact of Migration on a Heterodox Turkish Community. In: Gerholm, Tomas and Yngve G. Lithman, eds. *The New Islamic Presence in Western Europe*, 174–195. London: Mansell.

Navaro-Yashin, Yael. 2002. *Faces of the State: Secularism and Public Life in Turkey*. Princeton: Princeton University Press.

Nökel, Sigrid. 2002. *Die Töchter der Gastarbeiter und der Islam. Zur Soziologie alltagsweltlicher Annerkennungspolitiken*. Bielefeld: Transcript.

Norton, John David. 1992. The Development of the Annual Festival at Hacibektaş, 1964–1985. In: Popovic, Alexandre and Gilles Veinstein, eds. *Bektachiyya: Études sur l'ordere mystique des Bektachis et les groups relevant de Hadji Bektach*. Revue des Études Islamique 60: 187–196.

Oberoi, Harjot. 1994. *The Construction of Religious Boundaries.* Oxford: Oxford University Press.

Öker, Turgut. 1994. Yaşasın Halkları Kardeşliği: Mazlumun yanında, zalimin karşışındayız! *Alevilerin Sesi* 5, December 1994: 7–12.

Ortaylı, İlber. 1999. The Policy of the Sublime-Porte towards Naqshbandis and other *Tariqas* during the Tanzimat Period.. In Özdalga, Elisabeth, ed. *Naqshbandis in Western and Central Asia, 67–72.* Istanbul: Swedish Research Institute in Istanbul/Curzon.

Østergaard-Nielsen, Eva. 2003. *Transnational Politics: Turks and Kurds in Germany.* London: Routledge.

Özcan, Ertekin. 1992. *Türkische Immigrantenorganisationen in der Bundesrepblik Deutschland.* Berlin: Hitit.

Özdil, Ali-Özgür. 1999. *Aktuelle Debatten zum Islamunterricht in Deutschland.* Hamburg: E.B.-Verlag.

Pagden, Anthony. 1995. The Effacement of Difference: Colonialism and the Origins of Nationalism in Diderot and Herder. In: Prakash, Gyan, ed. *After Colonialism: Imperial Histories and Postcolonial Displacements, 129–152.* Princeton: Princeton University Press.

Pandey, Gyanendra. 2001. *Remembering Partition.* Cambridge: Cambridge University Press.

Polat, Ülger. 2000. Zwischen Integration und Desintegration. Positionen türkischstämmiger Jugendlicher in Deutschland. In: Attia, Iman and Helga Marburger, eds. *Alltag und Lebenswelten von Migrantenjugendlichen, 11–25.* Frankfurt: IKO.

Portes, Alejandro. 1996. Transnational Communities: Their Emergence and Significance in the Contemporary World System. In: Korzeniewicz, Roberto Patricio and William C. Smith, eds. *Latin America in the World Economy, 151–168.* Westport, Connecticut: Greenwood Press.

Portes, Alejandro; Luis E. Guarnizo; Patricia Landolt. 1999. 'The Study of Transnationalism: Pitfalls and Promise on an Emergent Research Field', *Ethnic and Racial Studies* 22: 217–237.

Poulton, Hugh. 1997. *Top Hat, Grey Wolf and Crescent: Turkish Nationalism and the Turkish Republic.* London: Hurst.

Pratt, Jeff. 2003. *Class, Nation and Identity: The Anthropology of Political Movements,* London: Pluto Press.

Pries, Ludger. 1999. New Migration in Transnational Spaces. In Pries, Ludger, ed. *Migration and Transnational Social Spaces, 1–35.* Alderhsot: Ashgate.

Rabinow, Paul. 1986. Representations are Social Facts: Modernity and Postmodernity in Anthropology. In: Clifford, James and George E. Marcus, eds. *Writing Culture. The Poetics and Politics of Ethnography, 234–261.* Berkeley, University of California Press.

Ransom, John S. 1997. *Foucault's Discipline: The Politics of Subjectivity.* Durham: Duke University Press.

Rau, Johannes. 2000. Gemeinsam in Deutschland leben (Berliner Rede). http: www.bundespraesident.de/reden/rau/de00_0512.htm. (5/18/2000)

Redhouse. 1990. *Redhouse Yeni Türkçe-İngilizce Sözlük.* Istanbul: Redhouse.

Reinhard, Ursula and Tiago de Oliveira Pinto. 1989. *Sänger und Poeten mit der Laute. Türkische Aşık und Ozan.* Berlin: Reimer.

Renan, Ernest. 1990 [1822]. What is a Nation? In: Bhabha, Homi, ed. *Nation and Narration*, 8–22. London: Routledge.

Rist, Ray C. 1978. *Guestworkers in Germany: The Prospects for Pluralism*. New York: Praeger.

Robinson, Glenn E. 2004. Hamas as Social Movement. In: Wiktorowicz, Quintan, ed. *Islamic Activism: A Social Movement Approach*, 112–139. Bloomington: Indiana University Press.

Rudolph, Susanne Hoeber. 1997. Introduction: Religion, States, and Transnational Civil Society. In: Rudolph, Susanne Hoeber and James Piscatori, ed. *Transnational Religion and Fading States*, 1–24. Boulder: Westview Press:.

Safran, William. 1991. Diasporas in Modern Societies: Myths of Homeland and Return. *Diaspora* 1: 83–99.

Said, Edward. 1978. *Orientalism: Western Conceptions of the Orient*. London: Routledge and Kegan Paul.

Şahin, Necati. 1998. Cemalı Avrupa... *Alevilerin Sesi* 30, December 1998: 10–11.

Şahin, Sehriban. 2001. *The Alevi Movement: Transformation from Secret Oral to Public Written Culture in National and Transnational Social Spaces*. Unpublished Ph.D. thesis, New School for Social Research, New York.

Sauer, Martina. 2001. Die Einbürgerung türkischer Migranten in Deutschland. Befragung zu Einbürgerungsabsichten und dem Für und Wider der Einbürgerung. In: Goldberg, Andreas, Dirk Halm and Martina Sauer, eds. *Migrationsbericht des Zentrums für Türkeistudien*, 165–228. Münster: Lit.

Schechner, Richard. 2002. Ritual and Performance. In: Ingold, Tim, ed. *Companion Encyclopedia of Anthropology*, 613–647. London: Routledge.

Schieffelin, Edward L. 1998. Problematizing Performance. In: Hughes-Freeland, Felicia, ed. *Ritual, Performance, Media*, 194–207. London: Routledge.

Schiffauer, Werner. 1997. Islam as a Civil Religion: Political Culture and the Organization of Diversity in Germany. In: Modood, Tariq and Pnina Werbner, eds. *The Politics of Multiculturalism in the New Europe: Racism, Identity and Community*, 147–166. London: Zed.

Schiffauer, Werner. 2000. *Die Gottesmänner. Türkische Islamisten in Deutschland*. Frankfurt: Suhrkamp.

Schneider, Jens. 2001. *Deutsch sein. Das Eigene, das Fremde und die Vergangenheit im Selbstbild des vereinten Deutschland*. Frankfurt: Campus.

Schüler, Harald. 1998. *Die türkischen Parteien und ihre Mitglieder*. Hamburg: Deutsches Orient-Institut.

Schüler, Harald. 2000. Secularism and Ethnicity: Alevis and Social Democrats in Search of an Alliance. In: Yerasimos, Stefanos, Günter Seufert and Karin Vorhoff, eds. *Civil Society in the Grip of Nationalism*, Orient Institut, 197–250. Istanbul and Würzburg: Ergon.

Schulze, Hagen. 1999. *Staat und Nation in der europäischen Geschichte*. München: Beck.

Schwalgin, Susanne. 2004. *"Wir werden niemals vergessen!" Trauma, Erinnerung und Identität in der armenischen Diaspora Griechenlands*. Bielefeld: transcript.

Şen, Faruk, Martina Sauer and Dieter Halm. 2001. Intergeneratives Verhalten und (Selbst-)Ethnisierung von türkischen Zuwanderern. Gutachten des ZfT für die Unabhängige Kommission "Zuwanderung". In: Goldberg, Andreas, Dirk Halm and Martina Sauer, eds. *Migrationsbericht des Zentrums für Türkeistudien*, 11–164. Münster: Lit.

Seufert, Günter. 1997a. Between Religion and Ethnicity: A Kurdish Alevi Tribe in Globalizing Istanbul. In: Öncü, Ayşe and Petra Weiland, eds. *Space, Culture and Power: New Identities in Globalizing Cities*, 157–176. London: Zed.

Seufert, Günter. 1997b. *Politischer Islam in der Türkei. Islamismus als symbolische Repräsentation einer sich modernisierenden muslimischen Gesellschaft*. Istanbul: Steiner.

Seufert, Günter. 1998. Das Gewaltpotential im türkischen Kulturkampf. In: Bielefeld, Heiner and Wilhelm Heitmeyer, eds. *Politisierte Religion. Ursachen und Erscheinungsformen des modernen Fundamentalismus*, 360–392. Frankfurt: Suhrkamp.

Seufert, Günter. 1999. Die Millî-Görüş-Bewegung (AMGT/IGMG): Zwischen Integration und Isolation. In: Seufert, Günter and Jacques Waardenburg, eds. *Turkish Islam and Europe*, 295–322. Istanbul: Franz-Steiner-Verlag.

Shami, Seteney. 1998. Circassian Encounters: The Self as Other and the production of the Homeland in the North Caucasus. *Development and Change* 29: 617–646.

Shankland, David. 1999. *Islam and Society in Turkey*. Huntingdon: The Eothen Press.

Shankland, David. 2003. *The Alevis in Turkey: The Emergence of a Secular Islamic Tradition*. London: Routledge.

Sieyes, Emmanuel. 1970 [1789]. *Qu'est-ce que le Tiers état?* Geneva: Droz.

Sinclair-Webb, Emma. 1999. Pilgrimage, Politics and Folklore: The Making of Alevi Community. *Les Annales de l'Autre Islam* 6: 259–274.

Sinclair-Webb, Emma. 2003. Sectarian Violence, the Alevi Minority and the Left, Kahramanmaraş 1978. In: White, Paul J. and Joost Jongerden, eds. *Turkey's Alevi Enigma: A Comprehensive Overview*, 215–236. Leiden: Brill.

Smith, Michael Peter. 2001. *Transnational Urbanism: Locating Globalization*. Oxford: Blackwell.

Smith, Michael Peter; L. E. Guarnizo, eds. 1998. *Transnationalism from below*. New Brunswick: Transaction Publishers.

Snow, David A.; Robert D. Benford. 1992. Master Frames and Cycles of Protest. In: Morris, Aldon D. and Carol McClurg Mueller, eds. *Frontiers in Social Movement Theory*, 133–155. New Haven: Yale University Press.

Sökefeld, Martin. 1997. *Ein Labyrinth von Identitäten in Nordpakistan. Zwischen Landbesitz, Religion und Kaschmir-Konflikt*. Cologne: Köppe.

Sökefeld, Martin. 1998. "The People Who Really Belong to Gilgit": Theoretical and Ethnographical Perspectives on Identity and Conflict. In: Stellrecht, Irmtraud and Hans-Georg Bohle, eds. *Transformation of Social and Economic Relationships in Northern Pakistan*, 93–224. Cologne: Köppe.

Sökefeld, Martin. 1999. Debating Self, Identity and Culture in Anthropology. *Current Anthropology* 40: 417–477.

Sökefeld, Martin. 2001. Reconsidering Identity. *Anthropos* 96: 527–544.

Sökefeld, Martin. 2002a. Alevism Online: Re-Imagining a Community in Virtual Space. *Diaspora* 11: 85–123.

Sökefeld, Martin. 2002b. Alevi Dedes in the German Diaspora: The Transformation of a Religious Institution. *Zeitschrift für Ethnologie* 127: 163–186.

Sökefeld, Martin. 2003a. Alevis in Germany and the Politics of Recognition. *New Perspectives on Turkey* 28-29: 133–161.

Sökefeld, Martin. 2003b. Statistisch betrachtet: Die Mitglieder der alevitischen Vereine in Hamburg und Umgebung. *Alevilerin Sesi* 68: 92–96.

Sökefeld, Martin, 2004a. Religion or Culture? Concepts of Identity in the Alevi Diaspora. in: Kokot, Waltraud, Khachig Tölölyan and Carolin Alfonso, eds. *Diaspora, Identity and Religion, New Directions in Theory and Research*, 143–165. London: Routledge.

Sökefeld, Martin, ed. 2004b. *Jenseits des Paradigmas kultureller Differenz. Neue Perspektiven auf Einwanderer aus der Türkei*. Bielefeld: transcript.

Sökefeld, Martin. 2004c. Das Paradigma kultureller Differenz: Zur Forschung und Diskussion über Migranten aus der Türkei in Deutschland. In Sökefeld, Martin, ed. *Jenseits des Paradigmas kultureller Differenz. Neue Perspektiven auf Einwanderer aus der Türkei*, 9–34. Bielefeld: transcript.

Sökefeld, Martin and Susanne Schwalgin. 2000. Institutions and their Agents in Diaspora, *Transnational Communities Working Papers Series*, WPTC-2K-11, Oxford. http://www.transcomm.ox.ac.uk/wwwroot/frames1.htm.

Soysal, Yasemin Nuhoğlu. 1994. *Limits of Citizenship: Migrants and Postnational Membership in Europe*. Chicago: University of Chicago Press.

Soysal, Yasemin Nuhoğlu. 1997. Changing Parameters of Citizenship and Claims-Making: Organized Islam in European Public Spheres. *Theory and Society* 26: 509–527.

Soysal, Yasemin Nuhoğlu. 2000. Citizenship and Identity: Living in Diasporas in Post-War Europe? *Ethnic and Racial Studies* 23: 1–15.

Spivak, Gayatri Chakravorty. 1988. Subaltern Studies: Deconstructing Historiography. In Ranajit Guha, and Gayatri Chakravorty Spivak, eds. *Selected Subaltern Studies*, 3–32. Oxford: Oxford University Press.

Spuler-Stegemann, Ursula. 2003. *Ist die Alevitische Gemeinde Deutschland e. V. eine Religionsgemeinschaft? Religionswissenschaftliches Gutachten erstattet dem Ministerium für Schule, Jugend und Kinder des Landes Nordrhein-Westfalen*. Unpublished expert report. Marburg.

Steuerwald, Karl. 1972. *Türkisch-Deutsches Wörterbuch*. Wiesbaden: Harrassowitz.

Steuerwald, Karl. 1988. *Türkisch-Deutsches Wörterbuch*. Second improved and extended edition. Wiesbaden: Harrassowitz.

Steuerwald, Karl. 1998 [1974]. *Deutsch-Türkisches Wörterbuch/Almanca Türkçe Sözlük*. Istanbul: ABC Kitabevi.

Stirling, Paul. 1960. A Death and a Youth Club: Feuding in a Turkish Village. *Anthropological Quarterly* 33: 51–75.

Stock, Martin. 2003. *Islamunterricht: Religionskunde, Bekenntnisunterricht oder was sonst?* Münster: Lit.

Stokes, Martin. 1996. Ritual, Identity and the State: An Alevi (Shi'a) *Cem* Ceremony. In Schulze, Kirsten E., Martin Stokes and Colm Campbell, eds. *Nationalism, Minorities and Diasporas: Identities and Rights in the Middle East*, 188–202. London: I. B. Tauris.

Strothmann, R. 2002. Takiyya. In: *Encyclopaedia of Islam* (CD-Rom). Brill: Leiden.

Tachau, Frank. 1984. 'The Political Culture of Kemalist Turkey', in: Landau, Jakob, ed. *Atatürk and the Modernization of Turkey*, Boulder, Col., Westview Press: 59–76.

Tarrow, Sidney. 1988. National Politics and Collective Action: Recent Theory and Research in Western Europa and the United States. *Annual Review of Sociology* 14: 421–440.

Tarrow, Sidney. 1996a. Social Movements. In Kuper, Adam, Jessica Kuper, eds. *The Social Science Encyclopedia*, 792–794. London: Routledge.

Tarrow, Sidney. 1996b. States and Opportunities: The Political Structuring of Social Movements. In McAdam, Doug, John D. McCarthy and Mayer N. Zald, eds. *Comparative Perspectives on Social Movements: Political Opportunities, Mobilizing Structures and Cultural Framings*, 41–61. Cambridge: Cambridge University Press.

Tarrow, Sidney. 1998. *Power in Movement: Social Movements and Contentious Politics*. Cambridge: Cambridge University Press.

Tatla, Darshan Singh. 1999. *The Sikh Diaspora: The Search for Statehood*. Seattle: University of Washington Press.

Taylor, Charles. 1989. *Sources of the Self*. Cambridge: Cambridge University Press.

Taylor, Charles. 1992. *Multiculturalism and the "Politics of Recognition."* Princeton: Princeton University Press.

Thornton, Robert. 1988. The Rhetoric of Ethnographic Holism. *Cultural Anthropology* 3: 285–303.

Tölölyan, Khachig. 1991. The Nation-State and its Others: In Lieu of a Preface. *Diaspora* 1: 3–7.

Tölölyan, Khachig. 1996. Rethinking *Diaspora*(s): Stateless Power in the Transnational Movement. *Diaspora* 5: 3–36.

Torpey, John. 2000. *The Invention of the Passport: Surveillance, Citizenship and the State*. Cambridge: Cambridge University Press.

Tosun, Halis. 2002. *Alevi Kimliğiyle Yaşamak*. Istanbul: Can Yayınları.

Touraine, Alain. 1981. *The Voice and the Eye: An Analysis of Social Movements*. Cambridge: Cambridge University Press.

Touraine, Alain. 1985. An Introduction to the Study of Social Movements. *Social Research* 52: 749–787.

Touraine, Alain. 1988. *Return of the Actor: Social Theory in Postindustrial Society*. Minneapolis: University of Minnesota Press.

Touraine, Alain. 2000. *Can We Live Together? Equality and Difference*. Cambridge: Polity Press.

Tur, Derviş. 2002. *Erkânname. Aleviliğin Islam'da Yeri ve Alevi Erkânları*. Rüsselsheim: Erenler Yayın.

Turner, Victor. 1957. *Schism and continuity in an African Society*. Manchester: Manchester University Press.

Turner, Victor. 1974. *Dramas, Fields, and Metaphors. Symbolic Action in Human Society*. Ithaca: Cornell University Press.

Turner, Victor. 1995 [1969]. *The Ritual Process: Structure and Anti-Structure*. New York: Aldine de Gruyter.

Unabhängige Kommission "Zuwanderung." 2001. *Zuwanderung gestalten — Integration fördern*. Bericht der Unabhängigen Kommission "Zuwanderung." Berlin.

Van Beek, Martijn. 2000. Dissimulations: Representing Ladakhi Identity. In Driessen, Henk and Ton Otto, eds. *Perplexities of Identification: Anthropological Studies in Cultural Differentiation and the Use of Resources*, 164–188. Aarhus: Aarhus University Press.

Van Bruinessen, Martin. 1994. Genocide in Kurdistan? The Suppression of the Dersim Rebellion in Turkey (1937-38) and the Chemical War against the Iraqi Kurds (1988). In Andreopoulos, George J. ed. *Genocide: Conceptual and Historical Dimensions*, 141–170. Philadelphia: University of Pennsylvania Press.

Van Bruinessen, Martin. 1997. "Aslını inkar eden haramzadedir:" The Debate on the Ethnic Identity of Kurdish Alevis. In Kehl-Bodrogi, Barbara Kellner-Heinkele and Anke Otter-Beaujean, eds. *Synchretistic Religious Communities in the Middle East*, 1–23. Leiden: Brill.

Van Dülmen, Richard. 1997. *Die Entdeckung des Individuums 1500–1800*. Frankfurt: Fischer.

Van Hear, Nicholas. 1998. *New Diasporas: The Mass Exodus, Dispersal and Regrouping of Migrant Communities*. London: UCL Press.

Vertovec, Steven. 1997. Three Meanings of "Diaspora," Exemplified among South Asian Religions. *Diaspora* 6: 277–299.

Von Campenhausen, Axel. 1986. Staats- und kirchenrechtliche Aspekte der Einführung des islamischen Religionsunterrichts an deutschen Schulen. In Kiesel, Doron, Klaus Philipp Seif and Ulrich O. Sievering, eds. *Islamunterricht an deutschen Schulen?* 1–19. Frankfurt: Haag und Herrchen.

Von Dirke, Sabine. 1994. Multikulti: The German Debate on Multiculturalism. *German Studies Review* 17: 513–536.

Vorhoff, Karin. 1995. *Zwischen Glaube, Nation und neuer Gemeinschaft: Alevitische Identität in der Türkei*. Berlin: Klaus Schwarz Verlag.

Vorhoff, Karin. 1998. "Let's Reclaim Our History and Culture!" Imagining Alevi Community in Contemporary Turkey. *Die Welt des Islams* 38: 220–252.

Vorhoff, Karin. 1999. Alevism, or Can Islam Be Secular? *Les Annales de l'Autre Islam* 6: 135–151.

Wahlbeck, Östen. 1999. *Kurdish Diasporas: A Comparative Study of Kurdish Refugees Communities*. London: Macmillan.

Weber, Eugen. 1976. *Peasants into Frenchmen: The Modernization of Rural France 1870–1914*. Stanford: Stanford University Press.

Wedel, Heidi. 1999. *Lokale Politik und Geschlechterrollen. Stadtmigrantinnen in türkischen Metropolen*. Hamburg: Deutsches Orient-Institut.

Weiss, Hans-Jürgen; Joachim Trebbe. 2001. *Mediennutzung und Integration der türkischen Bevölkerung in Deutschland. Ergebnisse einer Umfrage des Presse- und Informationsamtes der Bundesregierung*. Potsdam: GöfaK Medienforschung.

Werbner, Pnina. 2000. Introduction: The Materiality of Diaspora—Between Aesthetic and "Real" Politics. *Diaspora* 9: 5–20.

Werbner, Pnina. 2002. *Imagined Diasporas among Manchester Muslims*. Oxford: James Currey.

White, Jenny B. 2002. *Islamist Mobilization in Turkey: A Study in Vernacular Politics*. Seattle: University of Washington Press.

Wilmsen, Edwin N. 1996. Introduction: Premises of Power in Ethnic Politics. In Wilmsen, Edwin N. and Patrick MacAllister, eds. *The Politics of Difference: Ethnic Premises in a World of Power*, 1–23. Chicago: University of Chicago Press.

Wilpert, Czarina. 1988. Religion and Ethnicity: Orientations, Perceptions and Strategies among Turkish Alevi and Sunni Migrants in Berlin. In Gerholm, Tomas and Yngve Lithman, eds. *The New Islamic Presence in Western Europe*, 88–106. London: Mansell.

Wimmer, Andreas. 2002. *Nationalist Exclusion and Ethnic Conflict: Shadows of Modernity*. Cambridge: Cambridge University Press.

Wimmer, Andreas and Nina Glick Schiller. 2002. Methodological Nationalism and Beyond: Nation-State Building, Migration and the Social Sciences. *Global Networks* 2: 301–334.

Wolf, Eric. 2001. *Pathways of Power: Building an Anthropology of the Modern World.* Berkeley: University of California Press.

Yalman, Nur. 1969. Islamic Reform and the Mystic Tradition in Eastern Turkey. *Archives Européennes de Sociologie* 10: 41–60.

Yaman, Ali. no date. *Anadolu Aleviliği'nde Ocak Sistemi ve Dedelik Kurumu.* http://www.alevibektasi.com/dedelik.htm (7/9/2001).

Yaman, Mehmet. 1998. *Alevilikte Cem.* Istanbul. Ufuk Matbaacılık.

Yavuz, M. Hakan. 1999a. Media Identities for Alevis and Kurds in Turkey. In Eickelman, Dale F. and Jon W. Anderson, eds. *New Media in the Muslim World: The Emerging Public Sphere,* 180–199. Bloomington: Indiana University Press.

Yavuz, M. Hakan. 1999b. The Matrix of Modern Turkish Islamic Movements: The Naqshbandi Sufi Order. In Özdalga, Elisabeth, ed. *Naqshbandis in Western and Central Asia,* 129–146. Istanbul: Swedish Research Institute in Turkey/Curzon Press.

Yıldız, Celal, Veli Aydın and Mehmet Gülmez. No date. *AABF' de yeni dönem için hedeflenen iki yıllık çalışma programı.* Privately printed brochure, Duisburg.

Yürür, Ahmet Engin. 1989. Miraçlama in the Liturgy of the Alevis of Turkey. A Structural and Gnostic Analysis. Unpublished Ph.D. thesis, University of Maryland, Baltimore.

Zaman, Muhammad Qasim. 2002. *The Ulama in Contemporary Islam: Custodians of Change.* Princeton: Princeton University Press.

Zelyut, Rıza. 1990. *Öz kaynaklarına göre Alevilik.* Istanbul: Anadolu Kültürü Yayınları.

Zentrum für Türkeistudien. 1997. *Medienkonsum der türkischen Bevölkerung in Deutschland und Deutschlandbild im türkischen Fernsehen.* Essen: Zentrum für Türkeistudien.

Quoted newspapers and magazines:
Cumhuriyet
Cumhuriyet Hafta
Der Spiegel
die tageszeitung
Frankfurter Allgemeine Zeitung
Hürriyet
Milliyet
Özgür Politika
Perşembe
Süddeutsche Zeitung

INDEX